introduction to
FILM
READER
third edition

Drew Casper

with
Richard L. Edwards

School of Cinema-Television

University of Southern California

McGraw Hill **Custom Publishing**

Boston Burr Ridge, IL Dubuque, IA Madison, WI New York
San Francisco St. Louis Bangkok Bogotá Caracas Kuala Lumpur
Lisbon London Madrid Mexico City Milan Montreal New Delhi
Santiago Seoul Singapore Sydney Taipei Toronto

Introduction to FILM *Reader*

McGraw-Hill's Primis Custom Publishing consists of products that are produced from camera-ready copy. Peer review, class testing, and accuracy are primarily the responsibility of the author(s).

Page 356 constitutes a continuation of the copyright page.

1 2 3 4 5 6 7 8 9 0 QSR QSR 0 9 8 7 6 5 4

ISBN 0-07-296085-X

Editor: Julie Kehrwald
Production Editor: Nina Meyer
Page Layout and Design:
Cover Design: Maggie Lytle
Printer/Binder: Quebecor World

ACKNOWLEDGEMENTS

We would like to thank all the Teaching Assistants, both past and present, who have contributed their time and effort to CTCS 190, Introduction to Film. We especially wish to thank Paul N. Reinsch and Robert Buerkle for their incredible help on the third edition. Thanks also to Chris Cooling for his valuable suggestions, contributions and help. We also wish to thank all the teaching assistants who contributed critical film analyses to this edition: Peter Britos, Robert Buerkle, Heidi Cooley, Chris Cooling, Brody Fox, Mary Kearney, Philantha Kon, Shannon Mader, Christie Milliken, Jaime Nasser, Paul N. Reinsch, Bobby Simmons, Andrew Syder, Dan Walkup, William Whittington, Chia-chi Wu, and Harmony Wu. Finally, we would like to thank our editor and designer at McGraw-Hill: Julie Kehrwald and Maggie Lytle.

ABOUT THE AUTHORS

Dr. Drew Casper is the Alma and Alfred Hitchcock Professor of American Film in the Division of Critical Studies, University of Southern California's School of Cinema-Television.

Dr. Richard L. Edwards is a former CTCS 190 Lead TA and he received his Ph.D. in Critical Studies from the University of Southern California's School of Cinema-Television.

TABLE OF CONTENTS

1

FILM AS TECHNOLOGY, BUSINESS, ART/ENTERTAINMENT AND CULTURAL PRODUCT

Making a film means, first of all, to tell a story. That story can be an improbable one, but it should never be banal. It must be dramatic and human. What is drama, after all, but life with the dull bits cut out. The next factor is the technique of film-making, and in this connection, I am against virtuosity for its own sake. Technique should enrich the action. One doesn't set the camera at a certain angle just because the cameraman happens to be enthusiastic about that spot. The only thing that matters is whether the installation of the camera at a given angle is going to give the scene its maximum impact. The beauty of the image and movement, the rhythm and effect—everything must be subordinated to the purpose.

—*Alfred Hitchcock*

CTCS 190 LECTURE OUTLINE – WEEK I   **LECTURE 1**

A. **Introduction**
    1. Format of course
    2. Importance of the film image in our culture
          Visual Analysis: *Precious Images* (Chuck Workman, USA, 1986)
B. **Technology**
    1. The 19th century's scientific spirit and the "recreation of life in motion"
       a. The "many-locations/same-time" syndrome
       b. The six major developments necessary to produce the "recreation of life in motion"
          1. the persistence of vision
          2. still photography
          3. the motion picture camera
          4. film stock
          5. the printer
          6. the motion picture projector
             Visual Analysis: *The Arrival of a Train at the Station* (Lumiere Brothers, France, 1895)
    2. The development and refinement of various technological realities that influence the production, aesthetics, and the experience of film as well as the business
    3. The power of film technology
C. **Business**
    1. Film and popularity
          Visual Analysis: *The Great Train Robbery* (Edwin S. Porter, USA, 1903)
    2. Business Triumvirate: Producer, Distributor, Exhibitor/Exhibition
    3. The influence of business upon technology and entertainment/art
D. **Entertainment/Art**
    1. The difference between entertainment and art
    2. Film as art: a paradox
    3. Film and the other arts
    4. The influence of entertainment/art upon technology and business
E. **Cultural Product**
F. **Introduction and Screening**

Notes

Notes

A SURVEY HISTORY OF FILM TECHNOLOGY

Compiled by Mary Kearney

The six major developments necessary to produce the "recreation of life in motion":

1) The Persistence of Vision
   - 130 AD – discovered by Ptolemy of Alexandria
   - 1765 – first scientific studies by Chevalier d'Arcy
   - 1824 – first described scientifically by Peter Mark Roget → gave rise to future studies
   - 1912 – "phi phenomenon" / apparent motion → by Gestalt psychologist Max Wertheimer

   Toys based on these two principles:
   - 1826 – Thaumatrope (Gk. "magical / miracle turning")
     – first introduced to the public by Dr. John Ayrton Paris
     – coin / disk spun by thread / chain
   - 1833 – Phenakistoscope (Gk. "deceitful view") – two spinning disks
     – created by Joseph Plateau (using ideas from Michael Faraday)
   - 1832-1833 – Stroboscope invented by Simon Stampfer – similar to the Phenakistoscope
   - 1834 – Daedalum (after ancient artist's drawings) by George Horner
     – strip of paper in cylinder
     – not patented until 1860s
   - 1867 – Zoetrope (Gk. "live turning) by William E. Lincoln
   - 1868 – flip or flicker book patented in 1868

2) Still Photography
   - camera obscura ("dark room")
     – 10th century – Al Hazen, Arabic astronomer
     – Leonardo da Vinci
   - shadow plays originate in India or Java several thousand years ago
     – spread to Europe by the late Middle Ages – very successful in late 1700s
   - magic lantern – projects images onto a screen
     – either 1664 by Thomas Rasmussen Walgenstein
       or 1694 by Christianen Huygens
   - 1826 – Joseph Nicéphore Niépce develops first photographs with camera obscura
     – fixed images on a pewter plate covered with chemical emulsion
     – exposure time took eight hours
   - 1839 – Louis Mandé Daguerre invents Daguerreotype
     – introduced silvered copper plates sensitized with iodine vapor
     – reduced the exposure time to thirty minutes
     – prints were positive and not reproducible

■ 1840 – William Henry Fox Talbot invents Talbottype / Calotype
  – imprinted images on negative paper stock coated with silver chloride salts
  – infinite number of reproductions possible
  – exposure time was three minutes

3) The Motion Picture Camera
  ■ series photography ("chronophotography"):
    – 1874 – Pierre Jules César Janssen invents "photographic revolver"
      – 48 instantaneous exposures on light-sensitive plate
      – used Maltese cross for intermittent movement of plate
    – 1877 – Eadweard Muybridge wins former Gov. Leland Stanford's racing bet
      – 12 (later 24) electrically-operated cameras used
      – placed through Zoetrope to reproduce movement
    – 1879 – Muybridge demonstrates his results on Zoopraxiscope projector
      – ("magic lantern"-like device that projected images from glass disk)
    – 1882 Etienne-Jules Marey invents chronographic gun
      – 12 images on glass plate – based on design by Pierre-Jules-César Janssen

  ■ 1888 – Augustin Le Prince patents camera / projector used to project moving pictures; he disappeared in 1890
  ■ 1889 – William Friese-Greene and Mortimer Evans patent camera for making rapidly successive series of photographs (300) on unperforated celluloid
  ■ 1891 – William Kennedy Laurie Dickson (Thomas Edison's assistant) invents Kinetograph
    – developed so that motion pictures could illustrate sounds made by phonograph
    – stop-motion device – insures intermittent but regular flow of film strip
  ■ 1895 – Auguste and Louis Lumière patent camera / projector – Cinématographe
    – first camera / projector with reversible motion
    – first camera / projector to move the film intermittently by a claw mechanism

4) Film Stock
  ■ 1800-30s – photographers use metal (pewter or copper) or glassplates
  ■ 1847 – Louis Ménard and Flores Domonte invent collodion
  ■ 1851 – Frederick Scott Archer proposes practical use of collodion for photography
    – wet collodion film plates (pyroxylin) reduced exposure time to 10 seconds
  ■ 1856 – Parkes patents celluloid as film base – unable to use photographically
  ■ 1869 – John Wesley Hyatt produces negatives on semirigid celluloid sheets
  ■ 1874 – Peter Mawdsley introduces possibility of utilizing gelatin silver bromide papers for photographic printing
  ■ 1880 – silver bromide paper generally adapted by photographers
  ■ 1887 – Hannibal Goodwin first used celluloid roll film with light-sensitive emulsions
    – patent not granted until 1898 following legal disputes with Eastman
  ■ 1889 – George Eastman and Henry N. Reichenback produce transparent celluloid film
    – widely preferred for making negatives in motion picture production
  ■ 1891 – Edison / Dickson use four perforations per frame for film movement through camera
    – their measurements become standard for motion picture film
  ■ 1894/5 – Parker B. Cady of Blair Camera Company invents thicker celluloid film used for the positive prints of motion pictures
  ■ 1908/9 – cellulose acetate (acetic acid, anhydride of acetic acid, sulfuric acid) film developed

- 1896 – Eastman Kodak Company mass produces positive and negative films for motion picture production
- 1909 – standard dimensions for film stock (35 mm with 4 perforations per frame) agreed upon as professional standard for international exchange
- 1948 – Eastman Kodak Company introduces cellulose triacetate "safety film"
- 1949 – Eastman ceases to manufacture flammable nitrate film

5) The Printer (see also "Still Photography" and "Film Stock" above)
- 1840 – William Henry Fox Talbot patents his calotype (negative/positive) printing process which is necessary for the reproduction of motion picture films
- 1866 – Carey Lea observes possibility of mechanical printing of photographic images
- 1883 – Scholotterhoss first to construct a printing automat for mass reproduction using light-sensitive silver chloride paper (400-500 prints per hour)
- 1892 – Arthur Schwartz (with Benjamin Falk) takes over Urie's patent for an automatic printing machine with silver bromide papers in rolls
- 1896 – Eastman Kodak Company developing both positive and negative film stock for motion pictures

6) The Motion Picture Projector
- 1866 – L. S. Beale – Choreutoscope (slide system for magic lantern)
  – uses modified Maltese cross / Geneva stop mechanism already used by many watchmakers
- 1887 – Ottomar Anshutz invents electrotachyscope for presentation of sequence photos
  – apparent motion produces as transparencies from photographs
  – rotated in front of Geissler tube producing flash of light
- 1888 – Augustin Le Prince patents camera / projector used to project moving pictures; he disappeared later that year
- 1889 – William Friese-Greene (with Mortimer Evans) patents first camera / projector
- 1891 – Thomas Edison receives patents (U. S. only) on Kinetoscopes to project film
  – first use of perforated films
- 1/12/1894 – C. Francis Jenkins patents a motion picture projector "phatascope"
  – intermittent motion accomplished by perforated film
- 4/14/1894 – Andrew Holland opens first Kinetoscope parlor in converted shoe store at 1155 Broadway in New York City (25 cents a peep)
- 11/1/1895 – Max and Emile Skladänowsky demonstrate Bioskop publicly
  – required 2 strips running simultaneously; considered impractical
- 3/22/1895 – Auguste and Louis Lumière first demonstrate their Cinématographe
  – built to run at 16 fps (established the standard for silent film)
  – *La Sortie des ouvriers de L'usine Lumière (Workers Leaving the Lumière Factory)*
- 12/28/1895 – first paying / public demonstration of Cinématographe featured:
  – *L'Arrivéê d'un train en gare (Arrival of a Train at a Station)*
  – *Le Repas de bébé (Baby's Lunch)*
  – *L'Arroseur arrosé (The Sprinkler Sprinkled)*
- 1896 – Edison buys out C. Francis Jenkins and Thomas Armat's design featuring the "Latham loop" (which redistributes the stress of winding film that often led to film breakage)
  – Edison renames his invention the Vitascope
- 4/23/1896 – first public demonstration of Vitascope at Koster and Bial's Music Hall, NYC

BIBLIOGRAPHY

Coe, Brian. *The History of Movie Photography.* Westfield, NJ: Eastview Editions, 1981.

Eder, Josef Maria. *History of Photography.* Trans. Edward Epstean. New York: Dover Publications, 1978 (originally published in 1945).

Happé, L. Bernard. *Basic Motion Picture Technology.* New York: Hastings House, 1975 (2nd edition).

Hecht, Hermann. *Pre-Cinema History: An Encyclopaedia and Annotated Bibliography of the Moving Image Before 1896.* London: Bowker-Saur, 1993.

Neale, Steve. *Cinema and Technology: Image, Sound, Color.* Bloomington: Indiana University Press, 1985.

Salt, Barry. *Film Style and Technology.* London: Starward, 1983.

THE INVENTION AND EARLY YEARS OF THE CINEMA, 1880s–1904

from *Film History: An Introduction* (1994) by Kristin Thompson and David Bordwell

The nineteenth century saw a vast proliferation of visual forms of popular culture. The industrial era offered ways of easily duplicating large numbers of lantern slides, books of photographs, and cheap illustrated fiction. The middle and working classes of many countries could visit elaborate dioramas—painted backdrops with three-dimensional figures depicting famous historical events. Circuses, "freak" shows, amusement parks, and music halls provided other forms of inexpensive entertainment. In the United States, numerous dramatic troupes toured, performing in the theaters and opera houses which at that time existed even in small towns.

Hauling entire theater productions from town to town, however, was expensive. Similarly, most people had to travel long distances to visit major dioramas or amusement parks. In the days before airplane travel, few could hope to see for themselves the exotic lands they glimpsed in static view in their stereopticon viewers or in books of travel photographs.

The cinema was to offer a cheaper way of providing visual sorts of entertainment to the masses. Actors would be able to record performances which then could easily be shown to audiences around the world. Travelogues would bring the sights of far-flung places, with movement, directly to spectators' hometowns. Movies would become the popular visual art form of the late Victorian ace.

The cinema was invented during the 1890s. It appeared in the wake of the industrial revolution, as did the telephone (invented in 1876), the phonograph (1877), and the automobile (developed during the 1880s and 1890s). Like them, it was a technological device that became the basis of a large industry. It was also a new form of entertainment and a new artistic medium. During the first decade of the cinema's existence, inventors were working to improve the machines for making and showing films. Filmmakers also had to explore what sorts of images they could record, and exhibitors had to figure out how to present those images to audiences.

The Invention of the Cinema

The cinema is a complicated medium, and before it could be invented, several technological requirements had to be met.

Preconditions for Motion Pictures

First, scientists had to realize that the human eye will perceive motion if a series of slightly different images is placed before it in rapid succession—minimally around sixteen per second. During the nineteenth century, scientists explored this property of vision. A number of optical toys were marketed that gave an illusion of movement by using a small number of drawings, each altered somewhat. In 1832, Belgian physicist Joseph Plateau and Austrian geometry professor Simon Stampfer independently created the device that came to be called the Phenakistoscope (Fig. 1.1). The Zoetrope, invented in 1833, contained a series of drawings on a narrow strip of paper inside a revolving drum (Fig. 1.2). The Zoetrope was widely sold after 1867, along with other optical toys. Similar principles were later used in films, but in these toys, the same motion was simply repeated over and over.

A second technological requirement for the cinema was the capacity to project a rapid series of images on a surface. Since the seventeenth century, entertainers and educators had been using "magic lanterns" to project glass lantern slides, but there had been no way to flash large numbers of images fast enough to create the illusion of motion.

A third prerequisite for the invention of the cinema was the ability to use photography to make successive pictures on a clear surface. The exposure time would have to be short enough to take sixteen or more frames in a single second. Such techniques came about slowly. The first still photograph was made on a glass plate in 1826 by Claude Niepee, but it required an exposure time of eight hours. For years photography was done on glass or metal, without the use of negatives, so only one copy of each image was possible; exposures took several minutes each. In 1839, Henry Fox Talbot introduced negatives made on paper. At about this same time, it became possible to print photographic images on glass lantern slides and project them. Not until 1878, however, did split-second exposure times become feasible.

Fourth, the cinema would require that photographs be printed on a base flexible enough to be passed through a camera rapidly. Strips or discs of glass could be used, but only a short series of images could be registered on them. In 1888, George Eastman devised a still camera that made photographs on rolls of sensitized paper. This camera, which he named the Kodak, simplified photography so that unskilled amateurs could take pictures. The next year Eastman introduced transparent celluloid roll film, creating a breakthrough in the move toward cinema. The film was intended for still cameras, but inventors could use the same flexible material in designing machines to take and project motion

Fig. 1.1 A Phenakistoscope, with a spinning disc of figures which the user views through a slot to perceive the illusion of movement.

Fig. 1.2 Looking through the slots in a revolving Zoetrope, the viewer receives an impression of movement.

pictures (though it was apparently about a year before the stock was improved enough to be practical).

Fifth, and finally, experimenters needed to find a suitable intermittent mechanism for their cameras and projectors. A strip of film sliding continuously past the gate would create a blur unless the light source was quite dim. The film had to be repeatedly stopped for a split-second exposure and then covered with a shutter as the next frame moved into place. Fortunately, other inventions of the century also needed intermittent mechanisms to stop their movement many times per second. For example, the sewing machine (invented in 1846) held cloth still several times per second while a needle pierced it.

By the 1890s, all the technical conditions necessary for the cinema existed. The question was, who would bring the necessary elements together in a way that could be successfully exploited on a wide basis?

Major Precursors of Motion Pictures

Some inventors made important contributions without themselves achieving moving photographic images. Among these men were several interested in analyzing motion. In 1878, photographer Eadweard Muybridge was asked by ex-governor of California Leland Stanford to find a way of photographing running horses so as to facilitate the study of their gaits. Muybridge set up a row of twelve cameras, each making an exposure in one-thousandth of a second. The photos recorded one-half-second intervals of movement (Fig. 1.3). Muybridge later made a lantern to project moving images of horses, but these were drawings copied from his photographs onto a revolving disc. Muybridge did not go on to invent motion pictures, but he made a major contribution to anatomical science through the thousands of motion studies in still photographs that he made using his multiple-camera setup.

In 1882, inspired by Muybridge's work, French physiologist Etienne Jules Marey studied the flight of birds and other rapid animal movements by means of a photographic gun. Shaped like a rifle, it exposed twelve images around the edge of a circular glass plate that made a single revolution in one second. In 1888, Marey built a box-type camera that used an intermittent mechanism to expose a series of photographs on a strip of paper film, at speeds of up to 120

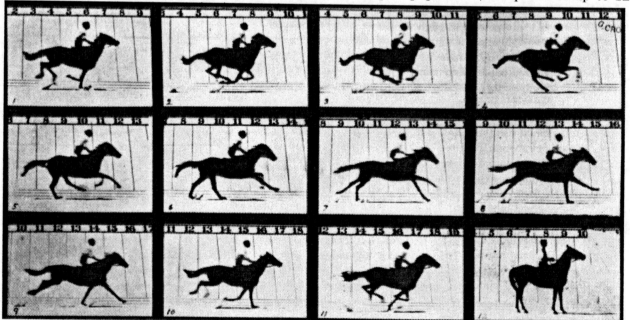

Fig. 1.3 One of Muybridge's earliest motion studies, photographed on June 19, 1878.

frames per second. Marey was the first to combine flexible film stock and an intermittent mechanism in photographing motion. He was interested in analyzing movements rather than in reproducing them on a screen, but his work inspired other inventors. During this same period, many other scientists used various devices to record and analyze movement.

A fascinating and isolated figure in the history of the invention of the cinema was Frenchman Emile Reynaud. In 1877, he had built an optical toy, the Projecting Praxinoscope. This was a spinning drum, rather like the Zoetrope, but one in which viewers saw the moving images in a series of mirrors rather than through slots. Around 1882, he devised a way of using mirrors and a lantern to project a brief series of drawings on a screen. In 1889, Reynaud exhibited a much larger version of the Praxinoscope. From 1892 on, he regularly gave public

performances using long, broad strips of hand-painted frames (Fig. 1.4). These were the first public exhibitions of moving images, though the effect on the screen was jerky and slow. The labor involved in the making of the bands meant that Reynaud's films could not easily be reproduced. Strips of photographs were more practical, and in 1895 Reynaud started using a camera to make his Praxinoscope films. By 1900 he was out of business, however, due to competition from other, simpler motion-picture projection systems. In despair, he destroyed his machines, though copies have recently been reconstructed.

Fig. 1.4 Using long flexible bands of drawings, Reynaud's Praxinoscope rear-projected cartoon figures onto a screen upon which the scenery was painted.

Another Frenchman came close to inventing the cinema as early as 1888—six years before the first commercial showings of moving photographs. That year, Augustin Le Prince, working in England, was able to make some brief films, shot at about sixteen frames per second, using Kodak's recently introduced paper roll film. To be projected, however, the frames needed to be printed on a transparent strip; lacking flexible celluloid, Le Prince apparently was unable to devise a satisfactory projector. In 1890, while traveling in France, he disappeared, along with his valise of patent applications, creating a mystery that has never been solved. Thus his camera was never exploited commercially and had virtually no impact on the subsequent invention of the cinema.

An International Process of Invention

It is difficult to attribute the invention of the cinema to a single source. There was no one moment when the cinema emerged. Rather, the technology of the motion picture came about through an accumulation of contributions. These came primarily from the United States, Germany, England, and France.

In 1888, Thomas Edison, already the successful inventor of the phonograph and the electric light bulb, decided to design machines for making and showing moving photographs. Much of the work was done by his assistant, W. K. L. Dickson. Since Edison's phonograph worked by recording sound on cylinders, the pair tried fruitlessly to make rows of tiny photographs around similar cylinders. In 1889, Edison went to Paris and saw Marey's camera, which used strips of flexible film. Dickson then obtained some Eastman Kodak film stock and began working on a new type of machine. By 1891, the Kinetograph camera and Kinetoscope viewing box (Fig. 1.5)

Fig. 1.5 The Kinetoscope was a peephole device that ran the film around a series of rollers. Viewers activated it by putting a coin in a slot.

Fig. 1.6 Edison's studio was named after the police paddy wagons, or "Black Marias," that it resembled. The slanted portion of the roof opened to admit sunlight for filming, and the whole building revolved on a track to catch the optimal sunlight.

were ready to be patented and demonstrated. Dickson cut the Eastman film into 1-inchwide strips (roughly 35 millimeters) and punched four holes on either side of each frame so that toothed gears could pull the film through the camera and Kinetoscope. These early decisions influenced the entire history of the cinema, for 35mm film stock with four perforations per frame has remained the norm. (Amazingly, an original Kinetoscope film can be shown on a modern projector.) Initially, however, the film was exposed at about forty-six frames per second—much faster than the average speed later adopted for silent filmmaking.

Edison and Dickson needed films for their machines before they could exploit them commercially. They built a small studio, called the "Black Maria," on the grounds of Edison's New Jersey laboratory and were ready for production by January 1893 (Fig. 1.6). The films lasted only twenty seconds or so—the longest run of film that the Kinetoscope could hold. Most films were brief excerpts from the acts of noted vaudeville and sports figures. Dancers and acrobats performed (Fig. 1.7). Annie Oakley displayed her shooting ability, and a bodybuilder flexed his muscles. A few Kinetoscope shorts were knockabout comic skits, forerunners of the story film.

Fig. 1.7 Amy Muller danced in the Black Maria on March 24, 1896. The black background and path of sunlight from the opening in the roof were standard traits of Kinetoscope films.

Edison had exploited his phonograph by leasing it to special phonograph parlors, where the public paid a nickel to hear records through earphones. (Only in 1895 did phonographs become available for home use.) He did the same with the Kinetoscope. On April 14, 1894, the first Kinetoscope parlor opened in New York. Soon other parlors, both in the United States and abroad, exhibited the machines (Fig. 1.8). For about two years the Kinetoscope was highly profitable, but it was eclipsed when other inventors, inspired by Edison's new device, found

Fig. 1.8 A typical entertainment parlor, with phonographs (note the dangling earphones) at left and center, and a row of Kinetoscopes at the right.

Fig. 1.9 Unlike many other early cameras, the Lumière Cinématographe was small and portable. This 1930 photo shows Francis Doublier, one of the firm's representatives who toured the world showing and making films during the 1890s, posing with his Cinématographe.

ways to project films on a screen.

Another early system for taking and projecting films was invented by Max and Emil Skladanowsky. Their Bioscop held two strips of film, each 3_ inches wide, running side by side; frames of each were projected alternately. The Skladanowsky brothers showed a fifteen-minute program at a large vaudeville theater in Berlin on November 1, 1895—nearly two months before the famous Lumière screening at the Grand Café. The Bioscop system was too cumbersome, however, and the Skladanowskys eventually adopted the standard 35mm, single-strip film used by more influential inventors. The brothers toured Europe through 1897, but they did not establish a stable production company.

The Lumière brothers, Louis and Auguste, invented a projection system that helped make the cinema a commercially viable enterprise internationally. Their family was the biggest European manufacturer of photographic plates. In 1894, a local Kinetoscope exhibitor asked them to make films that would be cheaper than the ones sold by Edison. Soon they had designed an elegant little camera, the Cinematographe, which used 35mm film and an intermittent mechanism modeled on that of the sewing machine (Fig. 1.9). The camera could serve as a printer when the positive copies were made. Then, mounted in front of a magic lantern, it formed part of the projector as well. One important decision that the Lumières made was to shoot their films at sixteen frames per second (rather than the forty-six frames per second used by Edison); this rate became the standard international average film speed for about twenty-five years. The first film made with this system was *Workers Leaving the Factory,* apparently shot in March 1895 (Fig. 1.10). It was shown in public at a meeting of the Societe d'Encouragement a l'Industrie Rationale in Paris on March 22. Six further showings to scientific and commercial groups followed, including additional films shot by Louis.

On December 28, 1895, one of the most famous film screenings in history took place. The location was a room in the Grand Cafe in Paris. In those days, cafes were gathering spots where people sipped coffee, read newspapers, and were entertained by singers and other performers. That evening, fashionable patrons paid a franc to see a twenty-five minute program of ten films, about a minute each. Among the films shown were a close view of Auguste Lumière and his wife

Fig. 1.10 The Lumière brothers' first film, *Workers Leaving the Factory*, was a single shot made outside their photographic factory. It embodied the essential appeal of the first films; realistic movement of actual people.

Fig. 1.11 Birt Acres's *Rough Sea at Dover*, one of the first films projected on a screen in both England and the United States. It showed large waves crashing against a seawall.

feeding their baby, a staged comic scene of a boy stepping on a hose to cause a puzzled gardener to squirt himself (later named *Arroseur arrosé,* or "The Waterer Watered"), and a view of the sea.

Although the first shows did moderate business, within weeks the Lumières were offering twenty shows a day, with long lines of spectators waiting to get in. They moved quickly to exploit this success, sending representatives all over the world to show and make more short films.

At the same time that the Lumière brothers were developing their system, a parallel process of invention was going on in England. The Edison Kinetoscope had premiered in London in October 1894, and the parlor that displayed the machines did so well that it asked R. W. Paul, a maker of photographic equipment, to make some extra machines for it. For reasons that are still not clear, Edison had not patented the Kinetoscope outside the United States, so Paul was free to sell copies to anyone who wanted them. Since Edison would supply films only to exhibitors who had leased his own machines, Paul also had to invent a camera and make films to go with his duplicate Kinetoscopes.

By March 1895, Paul and his partner, Birt Acres, had a functional camera, which they based partly on the one Marey had made seven years earlier for analyzing motion. Acres shot thirteen films during the first half of the year, but the partnership broke up. Paul went on improving the camera, aiming to serve the Kinetoscope market, while Acres concentrated on creating a projector. On January 14, 1896, Acres showed some of his films to the Royal Photographic Society. Among these was *Rough Sea at Dover* (Fig. 1.11), which would become one of the most popular very early films. Seeing such one-shot films of simple actions or landscapes today, we can hardly grasp how impressive they were to audiences who had never seen moving photographic images. A contemporary review of Acres's Royal Photographic Society program hints, however, at their appeal:

> The most successful effect, and one which called forth rounds of applause from the usually placid members of the "Royal," was a reproduction of a number of breaking waves, which may be seen to roll in from the sea, curl over against a jetty, and break into clouds of snowy spray that seemed to start from the screen.[1]

Acres presented other demonstrations, but he did not attempt to exploit his projector and films systematically.

Projected films were soon shown regularly in England, however. The Lumière brothers sent a representative who opened a successful run of the Cinématographe in London on February 20, 1896, about a month after Acres's first screening. Paul went on improving his camera and

---

[1] From *The Photogram,* quoted in John Barnes, *The Beginnings of the Cinema in England* (New York: Barnes & Noble, 1976), p. 64.

invented a projector, which he used in several theaters to show copies of the films Acres had shot the year before. Unlike other inventors, Paul sold his machines rather than leasing them. By doing so, he not only speeded up the spread of the film industry in Great Britain but also supplied filmmakers and exhibitors abroad who were unable to get other machines. These included one of the most important early directors, Georges Méliès.

During this period, projection systems and cameras were also being devised in the United States. Three important rival groups competed to introduce a commercially successful system.

Woodville Latham and his sons Otway and Gray began work on a camera and projector during 1894 and were able to show one film to reporters on April 21, 1895. They even opened a small storefront theater in May, where their program ran for years. The projector did not attract much attention, because it cast only a dim image. The Latham group did make one considerable contribution to film technology, however. Most cameras and projectors could use only a short stretch of film, lasting less than three minutes, since the tension created by a longer, heavier roll would break the film. The Lathams added a simple, but effective, loop to relieve the tension, allowing much longer films to be made. The Latham loop has been used in most cameras and projectors ever since. Indeed, so important was the technique that a patent involving it was to shake up the entire American film industry in 1912. An improved Latham projector was used by some exhibitors, but other systems able to cast brighter images gained greater success.

A second group of entrepreneurs, the partnership of C. Francis Jenkins and Thomas Armat, first exhibited their Phantoscope projector at a commercial exposition in Atlanta in October 1895, showing Kinetoscope films. Partly due to competition from the Latham group and a Kinetoscope exhibitor, who also showed films at the exposition, and partly due to dim, unsteady projection, the Phantoscope attracted skimpy audiences. Later that year, Jenkins and Armat split up. Armat improved the projector, renamed it the Vitascope, and obtained backing from the entrepreneurial team of Norman Raff and Frank Gammon. Raft and Gammon were nervous about offending Edison, so in February they displayed the machine for him. Since the Kinetoscope's big initial popularity was fading, Edison agreed to manufacture Armat's projector and supply films for it. For publicity purposes, it was marketed as "Edison's Vitascope," even though he had had no hand in devising it.

The Vitascope's public premiere was at Koster and Bial's Music Hall on April 23, 1896. Six films were shown, five of them originally shot for the Kinetoscope; the sixth was Acres's *Rough Sea at Dover*, which again was singled out for praise. The showing was a triumph, and although it was not the first time films had been projected commercially in the United States, it marked the beginning of projected movies as a viable industry there.

The third major early invention in the United States began as another peepshow device. In late 1894, Herman Caster patented the Mutoscope, a

Fig. 1.12 A Mutoscope, a penny-in-the-slot machine with a crank that the viewer turned in order to turn a drum containing a series of photographs. The stand at the left shows the circular arrangement of the cards, each of which flipped down and was briefly held still to create the illusion of movement.

flip-card device (Fig. 1.12). He needed a camera, however, and turned to his friend W. K. L. Dickson for advice; the latter, unhappy with his situation at Edison, cooperated. With other partners, they formed the American Mutoscope Company. By early 1896, Caster and Dickson (who left Edison) had their camera, but the market for peepshow movies had declined, and they decided to concentrate on projection. Using several films made during that year, the American Mutoscope Company soon had programs playing theaters around the country and touring with vaudeville shows.

The camera and projector were unusual, employing 70mm film that yielded larger, clearer images. By 1897, American Mutoscope was the most popular film company in the country. That year the firm also begin showing its films in penny arcades and other entertainment spots, using the Mutoscope. The simple card holder of the Mutoscope was less likely to break down than was the Kinetoscope, and American Mutoscope soon dominated the peepshow side of film exhibition as well. (Some Mutoscopes remained in use for decades.)

By 1897, the invention of the cinema was largely completed. There were two principal means of exhibition: peepshow devices for individual viewers and projection systems for audiences. Typically, projectors used 35mm film with sprocket holes of similar shape and placement, so most films could be shown on different brands of projector. But what kinds of films were being made? Who was making them? How and where were people seeing them?

SINGIN' IN THE RAIN (1952)

from *Stanley Donen* (1983) by Dr. Drew Casper

[Gene Kelly's *An American in Paris*] wrapped on January 8, 1951; [Stanley Donen's *Love Is Better Than Ever*] exactly two weeks later. Now (Arthur) Freed's court jesters could give their undivided attention to their next collaboration with (Betty) Comden and (Adolph) Green.

> *Betty, Adolph, Gene, and I knew we wanted to make a movie about the transition from silents to talkies. The Arthur Freed-Nacio Herb Brown catalogue was going to be the music. We had decided what those songs would fit into was quite obviously a movie about this changeover. We looked at a lot of movies based on early talkies. One was* Bombshell *(Victor Fleming, 1933) with Jean Harlow. We even considered that for a while. Comden and Green felt they could write a plot that would work better. Gene and I loved it. Whatever thoughts we had for additions or deletions were incorporated into the script. The published* Rain *script is the script taken off the screen after all our changes before and even during the production ... not the script Betty and Adolph gave us. Adolph's forward in the book is incorrect.[2]*

The script possesses an astute knowledge and an intense affection for what it ribs—Hollywood and the movies—and is brilliant in its use of film's thematic and technical vocabulary as its own raw material. And since the collaborators' memory of this naively giddy time and its equally giddy artifacts are happy ones, it is idealized and tinged with the yearning to return, relive, and be a part of it—thus the pathos so characteristic of Comden and Green's writing.

The movies' archetypical romantic motif is deliciously spoofed: boy meets girl, boy loses girl, boy finds girl. Also parodied is the on-screen fire but off-screen ice of star teams; the industry's collaborative friendships, where recognition and appreciation vary directly with one's proximity to the front of the lens (the Lockwood-Brown combo has much in common with the Kelly-Donen one), and the stars' egotism, gall, and insecurity.

These motifs are set against the farcical turmoil that resulted when the hoydenish movies learned to talk and act like a lady: the weird sound demo pics, the excruciating diction lessons for the players, the thorny business of recording sound, the previewing of those embarrassing 100-percent squawkies, the insertion of numbers in dramatic films solely to exploit the soundtrack, the haphazard birth of the musical film, and the demise of the star who could not speak. The film's first three shots deftly set the scene with their emphasis on the so-called miracle of sound: the tinny voice of the woman at the microphone heard even as far back as the last rows of the audience watching the premiere, the three children straddling a huge amplifier in the treetops that makes the sound possible, and the portly commentator dwarfed by the mike.

Embroidering this rich tapestry are a thousand and one loving lampoons. Honky tonks are seen to be the training ground of a screen god. The movies' thrilling feats are performed by stuntmen, the screen's real heroes. Classic slapstick routines, such as the kick in the pants, the

---

[2] Betty Comden and Adolph Green. *Singin' in the Rain* (New York: Viking, 1972).

tux caught in the jalopy door, the pie in the kisser (even acknowledged by Kathy as she takes the object in hand, "Here's one thing I've learned from the movies!"), and the cop at the end, are winked at. Also, razzed are the silent swashbuckler, the studios' assembly-line production of college pics, westerns, Jungle adventures; the MacDonald-Eddy operetta; the use of title cards to provide narrative continuity; and the Hollywood montage, always visually arresting and enlivening a movie's pace. But the roast does not stop here. The razzle-dazzle premieres at which the new royalty tread a scarlet carpet to the picture palace, the rainy (good luck) preview at the nabe where the stars hide behind dark glasses and slouch hats worn very low, and filmdom's fabulous parties also come in for their fair share of knocks.

Yet the creators, no matter how clinical the dissection of Hollywood, never dispel the enchantment. As a matter of fact, the magic of movies and movieland is so pervasive—the premiere's beautiful people, the flickering silent images, a jalopy catching a falling star, a pull of a few switches turning an empty sound stage into a rose trellised bower, Kathy's voice coming from Lina's mouth—that it emerges as a definite motif. Of course, *Rain*'s homage to the most popular of all the arts was practically lost in the pre-Bogdanovich days of the film's release.

The characters, as written, bear just a trace of caricature so as not to eclipse their humanity, which the performers in their enactment, never lose sight of either. We connect with these people. Dora Bailey (Madge Blake) is the gushing Louella Parsonsish gossip columnist who watches like a mother hen over her brood of stars. These include the flaming flapper of the Clara Bow variety, Zelda Zanders (Rita Moreno), femme fatale Olga Mara (Judy Landon) in the Nita Naldi mold, Lina Lamont (Jean Hagen), a Pickford copy, Don Lockwood (Gene Kelly), Fairbanks through and through, and eventually Kathy Selden (Debbie Reynolds), Gaynor crossed with Keeler.

As portrayed by Hagen, who received an Academy Award nomination for Best Supporting Actress, Lina is at once childish and shrewdly adult. The laughter she elicits never dispels our sympathy for the character, as in her mad exit-right frame, presumably never to be heard from again. And her voice, entirely her invention, is a marvelous instrument. Most surely, *Born Yesterday*'s dumb-smart blonde, which Hagen essayed on the road, influenced her performance.

As Don, Kelly transposes *The Pirate*'s Serafin from the nineteenth to the twentieth century, insisting upon the narcissism and insecurity of an actor as well as the prankishness at the heart of every man. In doing so, he both draws from and spoofs his own personality.

Donen gives Kelly a marvelous entrance when he has the camera cut a path through a throng of encircling fans and then stop to gaze upon him. The director will continue to give his leads marvelous debuts and departures (as Hagen's, above). Being a lover of movies, he is aware of the power of entrances and exits, how they linger in the corners of the mind because of our anticipation of the star at the beginning and regret at his or her leave-taking at the end.

In her first major role Reynolds is allowed to give the obliging ingenue a streak of mimicry. And as for O'Connor, a Universal-International expatriate, he turns the sidekick Cosmo into a hilarious clown, full of droll asides, grimaces that occur always behind a person's back, puns, shtick as well as ideas. The directors' insistence on a dancer in the part eventually prevailed over Freed's choice of piano *raconteur* Oscar Levant.

Director Roscoe Dexter (Douglas Fowley) is a blend of Josef von Sternberg and Charlie Chase. R. F. Simpson (Millard Mitchell), the vastly imposing but easily intimidated head of Monumental Pictures, understands only one thing about movies, box office, as did most of the founding fathers. Rod (King Donovan) is the typical overzealous press agent. And the diction coaches (Kathleen Freeman and Bobby Watson), imported from the New York stage, are a termagant and an epicene, eccentrics really, in keeping with the way Hollywood considered and portrayed New Yorkers at the time.

Art directors Gibbons and Randall Duell relied on production stills and twenty-five-year-old photos of the studio. Decorators Willis and Jacques Napes recreated old Cooper-Hewitt stage lights, early recording and dubbing equipment, even an old glass sound stage. The actual process of silent and early sound picture-making in a studio was a unique playing area for the musical in 1952.[3]

The decor, Walter Plunkett's hideously right costumes, Sydney Guilaroff's hairstyles, and William Tuttle's makeup are at once satiric and nostalgic, playing out the film's tone in another key. Plunkett, who entered the business at the height of the flappers' era, was an on-the-spot research library as far as what people looked liked then.

> *Freed* hated *the idea of '20s costumes. He thought it was going to alienate audiences. He wanted the characters to look in '50s vogue.*

Donen, along with Kelly and photographer Rosson, who replaced the unsympathetic John Alton, here takes his first bold steps in color experimentation. The pop of flashbulbs, the roving spotlight that, when it passes the camera's lens, momentarily blanches the frame, Don's white polo coat, white fedora, and mouth full of capped ivories, Lina's silver lamé cape trimmed in white fox fur, and her platinum hair and powdered face render the premiere dazzlingly ethereal in the midst of the drab groundlings.

The three black-and-white movies within the Technicolor one counterpoint yesterday with today. The pink, lavender, and apricot rainbow of "You Were Meant for Me" inside the sound stage assails the flat noon light on the tan wall outside. The ballet's yellow pinspot, in which the hoofer stands engulfed by blackness, is suddenly slashed by the garish colors from more than fifty full-size electric Times Square signs hanging at various angles and heights, which, in turn, are supplanted by washed-out pastels. In having these colors move, along with the actors, camera, and cutting, to the music's beat, Donen and Kelly push their experiment with choreographed film even farther.

This choreographing of the straight passages, which makes the transitions between them and the numbers practically seamless, contributes to the film's unfaltering pace as do the three extended montages, each devilishly satiric, each illustrative of the magic-of-movies motif. This vivacious tempo allows us to feel the Jazz Age's frenzy and Tinsel Town's tumult in our bones.

The first montage highlights Don's progress from shoeshine boy in a disreputable pool hall to superstar at Grauman's Chinese by matching objects between shots and dissolves. The chronicling of three decades within a few minutes is not the only extraordinary thing going on, for while Don's voice-over insists upon the "dignity" of his background, the images depict the very opposite. This Eisensteinian montage of image contradicting sound, which incidentally happens to summarize the film's central issue, puts us in the godlike position of seeing two sides of the same coin at once.

The second montage is a historical kaleidoscope of musical-picture styles at the advent of sound. Featuring very little, if any, dancing, the montage is achieved by a series of direct cuts climaxing with the intercutting of all the pieces in an accelerated fashion, mirroring the barrage of musicals at the time.

The last montage details the process of dubbing Kathy's voice for Lina's. Its cohesion is ensured by Kathy's singing "Would You?" uninterruptedly in spite of temporal and spatial changes and by slow dissolves, melting one situation into another.

The Musical Sequences

Excepting "Moses," with Comden and Green's words and Edens's music, the tuneful and zingy score was culled from the movie repertoire of lyricist Freed and composer Nacio Herb Brown[4]

---

[3] Before *Rain, Showgirl in Hollywood* (Robert Lord, 1930) sported scenes detailing how early sound films were made. Since, *Rain, Goldilocks* (1958), *Fade-Out Fade-In* (1964) and *Mack and Mabel* (1974) have used a similar backdrop.

(Al Goodhart and Al Hoffman contributed "Fiddle's" melody). That zing also derives from the numbers' satirical mounting and their perfect integration with the text.

Don's reprise of "All I Do Is Dream of You" to a bedside photograph of Kathy and her "You Are My Lucky Star" to a billboard of Don were shot but excised before the film's release to make the film play faster.

"Singin' in the Rain" (precredit sequence): In this first of Donen's half dozen precredits, the camera dollies toward yellow-suckered Don, Kathy, and Cosmo singing and tramping in a sea of blue rain: a pleasant irony, since most people grumble and hurry in the rain.

"Fit as a Fiddle": This extended part of the first montage's concert tour finds Don and Cosmo in an antic routine in Kansas City. We are the audience, viewing the act from the other side of the proscenium arch and panning with our eyes as the duo cavorts onstage in the knock-'em-dead but cloying style of novices. Their squeaky violins, which they play in the most preposterous positions, are as spastic as their limbs, even sprouting flowers on the last strike of the bow. Their large-checked emerald suits resemble horse blankets; their inflexible wide grins seem painted on.

"All I Do Is Dream of You": The flapper, with beestung lips and frenetic limbs, is joshed at R. F.'s bash, where a double line of pink-and-gold Coconut Grovers, including Kathy, squeal and Charleston while hurling confetti everywhere.

"Make 'Em Laugh": Cosmo lightens Don's gloom by proclaiming, illustrating, and especially ribbing the "show must go on" philosophy of entertainers and of the genre as well (every musical dispenses these amphetamines freely). He transforms the adversities he encounters on several dismantled sets into comic gags in spite of a good deal of self-brutalization.

The number works on several levels. It furthers the plot, crystallizes the tone by simultaneously revering and reviling the fabled tradition, and enriches the film's setting by suggesting that it is commonplace for show people to entertain on the set and by featuring a compendium of silent-movie slapstick turns and conflicts. The number delineates character as well, being another instance of the "idea man" slighted, this time by the workers and cleaning help who, despite his humorous entertainment and attendant pain, pay him no mind.

The toned-down color scheme and tight shooting enable us to focus on O'Connor's brilliant but bruising ballet. Unfortunately, the song's close similarity to Porter's "Be a Clown" from *The Pirate* mars the number's luster.

"Beautiful Girl": The tableau, a type of number Busby Berkeley perfected at Warners,[5] and the fashion show, which inevitably found its gratuitous way into the early musicals, are on the block here.

After crooning among a bevy of ice-blue-chiffoned cuties, the straw-hatted and caned Dick Powell type individually introduces, by means of doggerel couplets, a dozen showgirls, each exemplifying in a separate panel the attire proper to a month of the year. A Berkeleyesque overhead shot, which reduces the ensemble to two concentric pinwheels revolving around the clean-cut lead, wraps up the sequence.

---

[4] "Broadway Melody," "You Were Meant for Me," and "The Wedding of the Painted Doll," were lifted from *The Broadway Melody* (Harry Beaumont, 1929); "Should I?" from *Lord Byron on Broadway* (William Nigh and Harry Beaumont, 1929); "Singin' in the Rain" from *Hollywood Revue of 1929* (Charles Reisner, 1929); "Beautiful Girl" from *Going Hollywood* (Raoul Walsh, 1933) and *Stage Mother* (Charles Brabin, 1933); "Fit as a Fiddle" from *College Coach* (William Wellman, 1933); "Temptation" from *Going Hollywood*; "All I Do is Dream of You" from *Sadie McKee* (Clarence Brown, 1934); "I Got a Feelin' You're Foolin'" and "You are My Lucky Star" from *Broadway Melody of 1936* (Roy del Ruth, 1935); "Would You?" from *San Francisco* (W.S. Van Dyke, 1936); and "Good Mornin'" from *Babes in Arms* (Busby Berkeley, 1939). Freed and Brown wrote "Make 'Em Laugh" for *Rain*.

[5] Not strictly a dance, the tableau is an expression of an object, idea, emotion, or event in terms of décor, costumes, a male and/or female chorus, their movement and positioning, accompanied by instrumental and/or vocal music. Florenz Zeigfeld crystallized this type of number in his series revues on Broadway during the 1910s and 1920s; Berkeley made the tableau cinematic.

"You Were Meant for Me": This courtly love pas de deux by Don and Kathy on a transformed sound stage defines a relationship and demonstrates the movies-as-magic motif, while gently kidding the shamelessly romantic passages in movies.

The camerawork and choreography make no false moves. As the romantics' ardor mounts, for example, the camera opens up the space more and more while the movement becomes more tactile and animated: their static stance on opposite sides of a ladder passes on to their descent, with each, still unsure of the other, clinging to the ladder's sides, then her following his nonchalant steps, and finally his taking her in his arms for a spirited whirl. Whereas the space in "The Bandit Chief Ballet" was used to emphasize the rococo and exotic, here it conveys simplicity and purity.

"Moses Supposes": In true Marx Brothers fashion, Don and Cosmo pummel the diction coach's pomposity, pedantry, and smugness by throwing his tongue twisters back in his face and by vigorously tapping around him while dismantling his sanctum. At the end the wags seat the startled teacher on the desk and cover him with just about everything that's movable in the room, including the "vowel A" wall sign. The frame suddenly resembles Magritte's "Le Thérapeute."

In the salad days of sound the studios had to raid theater for playwrights, actors, dialogue directors, and coaches—though somewhat resentfully, for they were aware that the stage fairly contemned the upstart medium. The number sends up this love-hate relationship.

"Good Mornin'": Don's self-pity over the disastrous preview, the untouched sandwiches on the plate, the gray-and-beige color pattern, and especially the insistent patter of rain outside the dining room window set the melancholy tone.

Cosmo's idea to turn *The Dueling Cavalier* into a musical, a swipe at the industry's coping with sound, disperses the gloom in a flash. Kathy rips off the calendar page on the kitchen wall—it is 1:30 A.M.–heralding the celebration that travels all over the star's Spanish-mission-style home. The camera even passes through a wall to pre-serve the dance's energy. In the movie industry an idea—good, bad, or indifferent—is regarded as being no less than the Second Coming.

A collapse onto the sofa, which they tilt back to the floor with their feet (a variation of the "Open Your Eyes" finale), and thoughts of Lina plunge them into the dumps once again. Thus, the number also teases the genre's mercurial temperament.

"Singin' in the Rain": The movie musical's most celebrated sequence is an affecting mood piece that also smiles at those untrammeled bursts of joy synonymous with the genre. It is, further, a profound psychological portrait.

The joy of being in love and of saving the movie releases the child that lurks within Don. Despite the rain, he discards the trappings of the adult world: his waiting limousine, his umbrella, hat, and the opinion of passersby. He begins to sing, dance, and play in and with the rain. Setting the expression of joy on a deserted city sidewalk in a black, soggy night is a highly ironic and dramatically effective conception, turning a musical cliché inside out.

Children are always tilting at gravity: Don jumps onto the base of a street lamp. To the child, the animate and inanimate are inseparable: Don sings to the 'bathing belle" advertisement in the pharmacy window. In a child's imagination an object or activity can trigger an association with something else: Don's umbrella becomes his waltzing amour and then a jolly old stick blithely passed along a grating and twirled in the air. Children come up with surprising reversals: Don places an open umbrella on the ground to catch water. He next stands under a broken drainpipe, allowing the torrent to drench his conservative tweeds. Only the pure in heart are capable of such defiance. He spins around in circles and then hopscotches along the curb like Chaplin's barber in *The Great Dictator* (1940). No belt on the head from a frying pan induces Don's action, though. His playfulness is intrinsic and natural.

In the middle of the street he splashes in puddles, creating his own little hurricane. He becomes momentarily self-conscious as he catches the gaze of an incredulous cop. Despite the appearance of the ultimate parent in black slicker and cap and brandishing a stick, the child wins out. Don shakes the water off his feet, shrugs his soaked shoulders, and matter-of-factly proffers an explanation: "I'm dancin' and singin' in the rain." He takes to the sidewalk while glancing humorously back at the policeman. An umbrella-less passerby approaches, and Don, with a childlike gesture full of spontaneous largesse, hands the adult his bumbershoot.

The number's structure is solid. The beginning states the premise and carefully bridges the transition from talk to song, walk to dance. On Kathy's stoop Don's last words, "From where I stand, the sun is shining all over the place," give way to humming underlined by soft instrumental music, then to the famous "doodedoo-doo-doodedoodedoo-doo," and finally to the lyrics recalling Don's words. After reposing in the doorway a moment, he walks down the steps, waves the chauffeur away, and saunters along the sidewalk.

In the middle section the child's ecstatic mood builds with the melody. It climaxes with his splashing around in the street puddles.

The end, marked by the policeman's appearance, contains the falling action, the smooth transitions out: Don's *recitativo* explanation and return to the pavement and an exquisite final flourish—Don's charity—that flavors the entire sequence.

The artless lyrics and lively melody, the ambling, jumping, and tapping and their interaction with the environment, which Kelly's rust-colored shoes never let us lose sight of, define the state of joyful childhood.

Camera movement and angling enhance meaning: it stays at rest with Don on the stoop, saunters beside him, tightens on his transfigured countenance, "Come on with the rain/I've a smile on my face," and rises and pulls out to behold him cutting moving circles all over the place as he twirls around with outstretched hands grabbing an open umbrella. The camera skips a beat when the officer enters.

Who could have danced in the rain onstage or captured it on canvas or on the page? The number's fluidity is the signature of film itself, resulting in a poetry that can hold its own beside the graced moments in Renoir, Ford, Bergman, or Fellini.[6]

"Broadway Melody-Broadway Rhythm": This sequence takes a jab at the Brobdingnagian production number that Berkeley was so fond of and its hackneyed motifs. Country verses city: young-hick hoofer (Don) arrives in Times Square with his suitcase; after setbacks he auditions at a speakeasy, where he confronts a curvaceous femme fatale (Cyd Charisse), who opts for a gangster's diamond bracelet. The rags-to-riches climb: the kid performs in scratch burlesque on the Columbia Wheel, in vaudeville at the Palace, and in Ziegfeld's Follies—the robustness and entertainment level of the same act vary inversely with the respectability of its surroundings. The coincidental meeting of the former love: in a swank casino after his triumph he sees the siren again. The dream: he fantasizes being with the girl. Unrequited love: the girl flips a coin in his face and walks away. The work ethic: he will find happiness in singing and dancing. The phantasmagoric finale: a cutout of the tuxedoed star advances toward us while the throng of Broadwayites recedes in the background. The gangster film is put on the burner with the coin-tossing George Raftish leader, his moll in her Louise Brooks hairdo and makeup, exhaling a plume of smoke from cigarette holder, and the gambling milieu. Also on the block is the

---

[6] Stanley Kubrick obliquely pays tribute to the passage's lyricism in his chilling futuristic foray *A Clockwork Orange* (1971), when he used the "Singin' in the Rain" track against a scene of excessive violence. Paul Mazursky in his comedy *Next Stop, Greenwich Village* (1975) also honors the number by duplicating its situation, content, and, most particularly, its denouement. Late at night protagonist Larry Lepinski (Lenny Baker) has just seen his girl home and walks to the Brooklyn El. On the platform he creates his own little world in which he pretends at being Brando and other famous actors and even thanks the Academy for his Oscar, for which an empty beer can substitutes. An incredulous cop on the beat eventually interrupts and ends the fantasy. Moishe Mizrahi in *Madame Rosa*, the Academy's Best Foreign Film for 1977 from France, also pays tribute in the scene in which the fourteen-year-old male protagonist goes to the park with his puppet creation to perform and is enthralled by a large string puppet manipulated to sing and dance to the original cast recording of Kelly's vocal. So, too, Masuto Harada in *Goodbye, Flickmania* (1979) and Alan Parker in *Fame* (1980) who have their protagonists mimic Kelly's antics in the rain.

mindless, and therefore, disruptive, insertion of a number within a story line: the modern tale is totally incongruous with The *Dancing Cavalier*'s universe.

Among the amazing things in the dream sequence is the mellow pas de deux on a pink-and-gray plane, with an eerie clarity of perspective that counterpoints reality's ferocious tap and arm-waving in an expressionistic setting of hard colors. Also noteworthy is Charisse's Grecian-type outfit, with its streamer of China silk, about twenty-five feet long, attached to her shoulders. It undulates in rhythm with her movements, indicating that even the wind machines were choreographed.

Donen, Kelly, and musical director Lennie Hayton, who was nominated for an Oscar for Musical Scoring, combined the thirty-two bars of both songs, "Broadway Melody" and "Broadway Rhythm" into one piece. The seventeen-minute ballet took a month to rehearse and was shot in two weeks.

"You Are My Lucky Star": In this takeoff on the happy ending every camera move discloses triumph. After tightening on the embracing lovers' duet onstage at the premiere, we dissolve to Don's Arrow-collar profile vis-à-vis Kathy's marcelled one on a billboard advertisement of their first Monumental Picture and then pull back to the stars themselves hugging on a green hillside bathed in sunshine before their famous profiles.

Virtually all the critics loved the movie, as did the public.

> *It's great fun, with an ingenious script and some of the most wonderful performances in a musical. It was the most expensive film I did at Metro ... in the neighborhood of $2.5 million. But then, we only built one wall of Grauman's. If Vincente directed, he would have been allowed to build the whole damn moviehouse.*

Only in our age of enlightened film consciousness has *Singin' in the Rain* received the kudos it deserves. With a successful reopening at Radio City Music Hall in 1975, the film has made the Best Ten List in a startling number of film publications and is studied in schools for its accurate account of the transition from silents to talkies, its technical virtuosity, and its perfection of form.

Since so much of film is expendable, we cannot help wondering what our descendants will still be viewing in the next hundred years or so: Chaplin and Keaton, no doubt; Astaire and Kelly's routines; some of Bergman and Fellini. Perhaps *Rain* will also prove indestructible.

> *The danger to each person who happens to be connected with something which later in life turns into something of memorable quality is that you might let that inflate you into believing you are some sort of historical figure yourself. Another danger is that everybody pays attention to that work alone and measures everything else beside it.*

CRITICAL FILM ANALYSES

SUNSET BOULEVARD (1950)

Mary Kearney

Paramount Pictures, 1950. Producer - Charles Brackett. Director - Billy Wilder. Screenplay - Charles Brackett, D. M. Marshman, Jr., & Billy Wilder. Director of Photography - John F. Seitz. Special Photographic Effects - Gordon Jennings. Editor - Arthur Schmidt. Assistant Director - C.C. Coleman, Jr. Art Direction - Hans Dreier & John Meehan. Set Design - Sam Comer & Ray Moyer. Music - Franz Waxman. Sound Design - John Cope & Harry Lindgren. 111 minutes.

CAST: Gloria Swanson (Norma Desmond); William Holden (Joe Gillis); Erich von Stroheim (Max von Mayerling); Nancy Olson (Betty Shaefer); Fred Clark (Sheldrake); Jack Webb (Artie Green); Lloyd Gough (Morino); Cecil B. DeMille (himself); Hedda Hopper (herself); Ray Evans (himself); Jay Livingston (himself); Buster Keaton, Anna Q. Nilsson, and H. B. Warner ("The Waxworks"); Franklyn Farnum (undertaker); Larry Blake and Charles Dayton (finance men).

I'm still big. It's the pictures that got small.

—Norma Desmond in Sunset Boulevard

In their last collaboration as a producer-director team, Charles Brackett and Billy Wilder brought to the silver screen a story no other filmmakers had risked making. Coming out of an industry (and a country) obsessed with youth and glamour, *Sunset Boulevard* was the first Hollywood film to make the aging process its primary concern, focusing specifically on the relationship which develops between a fading silent movie queen and a much younger, down-on-his-luck screenwriter. Using the *noir* style employed to such phenomenal effect in *Double Indemnity* (1944) and *The Lost Weekend* (1945) to emphasize the codependent impotency of this couple, Wilder's *Sunset Boulevard* remains significant in portraying the new mood of disillusionment that was emerging in a post-war society no longer convinced that achieving the American Dream was possible.

With a keen understanding of how women in Hollywood have typically lacked the option of a full career since their contribution to film is determined more by their youthful appearance than by their acting aptitude, Wilder and Brackett's story remains to this day one of the best commentaries about Hollywood as a factory where talent is consumed in a "binge and purge" manner—exploiting the best and brightest stars, while leaving the "has beens" to fade away without the respect they deserve. Like her decrepit mansion on Sunset Boulevard, Norma Desmond, the film's female protagonist (played by Gloria Swanson), is an anachronism; with her old-fashioned acting techniques of exaggerated facial expressions and bodily gestures, she has become, not a glamorous older star, but an unsightly leftover of a previous era. Reversing the typical "May and December" relationship of a younger woman and an older man, Norma's mutually exploitative relationship with the young screenwriter-turned-gigolo, Joe Gillis (William Holden), works effectively as a metaphor for not only the crisis of traditional gender roles happening in post-war America, but, perhaps more importantly, for the vampirism inherent in the film business which attempts to defy the aging process by feeding off the talent of its younger employees, who, in turn, exploit their older colleagues in order to get a lucky break.

At the time of its release, *Sunset Boulevard* was considered by many to be Wilder's inappropriate "settling of accounts" with the film industry. For example, after the premiere of the film in Los Angeles, M-G-M studio mogul Louis B. Mayer cursed Paramount Pictures for allowing Wilder to make such a film. Shaking his fist at the director, Mayer screamed, "You bastard. You have disgraced the industry that made you and fed you. You should be tarred and feathered and run out of Hollywood."[7]

In spite of such criticism, however, the formal and thematic sophistication of *Sunset Boulevard* has never been challenged, especially in being one of the first films to self-reflexively portray the various stages of the filmmaking process, bringing to light both the glamour of cinema and its less-appealing underside. Not only do we see the pre-production stage develop via Joe's various attempts at screenwriting, we are also exposed to the actual production of a film when Norma visits Cecil B. DeMille at the Paramount studio. In turn, the act of spectatorship can be seen when Max, Norma's butler (Erich von Stroheim), projects one of her old films for the fading star and her gigolo boyfriend. (Wilder's black humor is perhaps most evident in the inclusion of excerpts from this film—*Queen Kelly*—which proved to be a professional disaster for von Stroheim when he was fired as its director by Swanson, the film's producer and star.) Finally, we witness the star system at work when newsmen, photographers, and gossip columnists descend upon Norma's house to catch glimpses of her "last scene" and the dead body which floats in her pool.

Sunset Boulevard also demonstrates the incredible transformative effect the introduction of sound had on the film industry. While conversion to the new sound system almost bankrupt the studios, it also cost many actors their jobs, for the arrival of sound required not only new technology and equipment, but new actors who could perform in "talkies." Making a subtle but effective comment on the ruthless expunction of silent screen talent, *Sunset Boulevard* is populated with celebrities from the "old days" of silent cinema. For example, the film's main star, Gloria Swanson, was one of Hollywood's most glamorous silent movie queens, and Erich von Stroheim, who plays her butler, Max, was a notorious silent film director. Other Hollywood celebrities who make appearances in *Sunset Boulevard* include Cecil B. DeMille (who directed Swanson in several of her earlier films and became one of Hollywood's first celebrity directors), Hedda Hopper (the Hollywood gossip columnist), and several other early film stars—Buster Keaton, H. B. Warner, and Anna Q. Nilsson—whose blazing days of glory on the silent screen had faded to a dim glow during the rise of sound cinema.

---

[7] Quoted in Maurice Zolotow's *Billy Wilder in Hollywood* (NY: G. P. Putnam's Sons, 1977) 168.

Although some critics have debated the sincerity of a film which passed judgment on Hollywood's treatment of old stars while it too exploited their position as victims, these critics obviously failed to consider how *Sunset Boulevard* affected the lives of the actors who appeared in it. For, despite Swanson's earlier success as a silent film actress, she is best remembered for her own "comeback" performance as Norma, a role which, in foregrounding the effects of age, ironically rejuvenated Swanson's career on screen.[8] Indeed, her performance earned her a nomination for Best Actress that year, and von Stroheim, an aging actor as well as a "has been" director, was nominated for his chilling and sympathetic performance of Max. Similarly, William Holden, who had spent several years as a contract player at both Columbia and Paramount studios, suddenly rose to star stature with his Best Actor nomination for the portrayal of Joe Gillis.

Although clearly not a blockbuster at the box office (the film earned only a little more than $2 million), *Sunset Boulevard* was nominated for six Academy Awards, including Best Picture and Best Director. Unfortunately, because of fierce competition from other great films that year (especially All About Eve which dominated the Oscars), *Sunset Boulevard* won only for Best Original Story and Screenplay. With time Sunset Boulevard has become a classic in Hollywood cinema, a monument to a unique cultural medium that crosses the boundaries of art and entertainment, technology and business. Perhaps there is no finer tribute to this extraordinary film than its contemporary musical adaptation for the stage by Andrew Lloyd Webber (with film star Glenn Close playing Norma) almost fifty years after Wilder, Brackett, and Marshman inked their original story.

---

[8] The part of Norma Desmond was originally offered to silent screen star Mae West who, like Pola Negri after her, was insulted that she could be considered a "has been" and turned down the part immediately. The role was also considered for Mary Pickford, another silent screen wonder; however, Wilder felt that her demands on the set would far exceed his own. After consulting with director George Cukor, Wilder offered the part to Swanson who had left her acting career in Hollywood over ten years before after *Music in the Air*, the film for which Wilder was first credited as writer.

SINGIN' IN THE RAIN (1952)
Dan Walkup

A Metro-Goldwyn-Mayer (MGM) production. Produced by Arthur Freed. Directed by Gene Kelly and Stanley Donen. Story and screenplay by Adolph Green and Betty Comden; suggested by the song 'Singin' in the Rain.' Lyrics by Arthur Freed. Music by Nacio Herb Brown. Musical director, Lennie Hayton. Musical numbers staged and directed by Gene Kelly and Stanley Donen. Director of photography, Harold Rosson. Art directors, Cedric Gibbons and Randall Duell. Film editor, Adrienne Fazan. Recording supervisor, Douglas Shearer. Orchestration by Conrad Salinger, Wally Heglin and Skip Martin. Vocal arrangements by Jeff Alexander. Set decorators, Edwin B. Willis and Jacques Mapes. Special effects, Warren Newcombe and Irving G. Ries. Costumes designed by Walter Plunkett. Hairstyles designed by Sydney Guilaroff. Make-up created by William Tuttle. Color by Technicolor. Technicolor color consultants, Henri Jaffa and James Gooch.

CAST: Gene Kelly (Don Lockwood), Donald O'Conner (Cosmo Brown), Debbie Reynolds (Kathy Seldon), Jean Hagen (Lina Lamont), Millard Mitchell (R. F. Simpson), Cyd Charisse ('Broadway Melody' Dancer), Douglas Fowley (Roscoe Dexter), and Rita Moreno (Zelda Zanders). Running time 103 minutes. Released March 1952.

Throughout *Singin' in the Rain*, the artifice behind the magic of the moving image is exposed. This reflexive musical, which follows the transition of the fictional Monumental Pictures from silence to sound, satirically explores the foibles of the studios' players as they struggle to stay current with the new technology. Through its self-conscious account, audiences since the fifties have been encouraged to laugh with the on-screen personae. Even those who have never seen *Singin' in the Rain* are able to recall the tune of the title number and Gene Kelly's signature dance style as he hangs lithely on a lamp post, singin' and dancin' in the rain. This movie has become an important part of our cultural unconscious, epitomizing the Arthur Freed/MGM/Gene Kelly musical. However, the movie's reflexivity is not limited to the representation of the coming of sound to Monumental pictures; and perhaps it is its sophisticated self-reflexive relationship to the history of musical pictures which has sustained *Singin' in the Rain* over the decades.

On the level of representation, we see the comedy of errors as Monumental attempts to compete with Warner Brothers' all-time smash, *The Jazz Singer*. With its 1927 release, *The Jazz Singer*, Warner Brothers introduced the "talkie" to American audiences. Monumental's first attempt at the talkie is a romantic-melodrama, *The Dueling Cavalier*, featuring the fictional stars of the silent screen, Don Lockwood and Lina Lamont. Lina's inability to talk into the microphone as well as her grating, whiny Brooklynese destroys whatever aura of sophistication she held as a purely visual figure. Further, at the films preview, the audience bursts into laughter when they hear Don's ad-libbed "I love you, I love you, I love you…." While he had done this in the silent pictures, sound made the crescendo-ing repetition of his adorations inappropriately comical. Problems with the synchronization of the sound further disrupt *The Dueling Cavalier*'s preview. In an attempt to save the film, and relying on Don's past in burlesque and vaudeville, *The Dueling Cavalier* becomes the musical, *The Dancing Cavalier*.

The origins of the musical are shown in the biographical sketch provided by Don at the opening of *The Royal Rascal*. Don's recollections do not match the images—we hear Don stressing the dignity of his past, while we see his past in burlesque and vaudeville. To appear respectable, Don and the movies deny their past in popular "entertainment" mediums, aspiring instead to the status of art. At another point, Kathy argues with Don, suggesting the mundane popularity of the movies could never stand up to the respectability of the artful stage. However, in *The Dancing Cavalier*, Don's past in burlesque and vaudeville are fictionalized for the screen culminating in the "Broadway Melody" number where an unknown hoofer goes to New York to make it big.[9] It is not merely coincidental that Don's life story and that of the fictional hoofer parallel each other. With the acceptance of their "populist" past, both *The Dancing Cavalier* and Don and Kathy's relationship are guaranteed success.

The lives on-screen parallel those off-screen. *Singin' in the Rain* features Gene Kelly; and like Don's story to the Louella Parsons-like Madge Blake at the Mann Chinese Theater, the movie suggests a tell-us-your-story for Gene Kelly, the boy from Pittsburgh who played vaudeville before making it in the MGM musicals. It was Kelly's idea as director/choreographer/performer to add to the title song to include dancin' in "singin' and dancin' in the rain." In this playful number, Kelly indelibly etches his mark on the film with his athletic combination of tap, ballet, and modern jazz dance. It is only after he, Kathy and Cosmo come up with a scheme to save *The Dueling Cavalier* and he acknowledges his feelings for Kathy with a goodnight kiss that this song—and dance—of euphoric abandon may be performed. As Professor Casper has pointed out,

The artless lyrics and lively melody, the ambling, jumping, and tapping and their interaction with the environment, which Kelly's rust-colored shoes never lose sight of, define the state of joyful childhood.[10]

This is not to say that Kelly is the only one allowed to exhibit his talents. In his role as Cosmo, for which he received a Golden Globe for Best Actor in a Musical or Comedy, Donald O'Conner continues the self-reflexivity of the film with "Make 'Em Laugh." In this slapstick number where Cosmo tries to cheer-up Don, the audience is let in on one of the goals of entertainment—from Shakespeare to vaudeville—"Make 'Em Laugh." Cosmo dances with the studio props on the Monumental lot including false façades, painted perspectives, and paper-thin walls. Don uses the studio props again when he tries to profess his love for Kathy. The techniques for staging a romantic scene are laid out one by one, from the mountain mist to the stars in the night sky.

Another moment of comic self-reflexivity occurs when R. F. Simpson, the producer, responds to Don's "pitch" of the "Broadway Melody" scene with "I can't quite visualize it. I'll have to see it on film first." Ironically, the audience of *Singin' in the Rain* has just finished watching the scene as Don describes it to R. F. The "Broadway Melody" also highlights the talents—and the legs that won't quit—of dancer Cyd Charisse in her only on-screen appearance. Charisse would later go on to star in a number of MGM musicals, including *The Band Wagon* and *Silk Stockings*, both with Fred Astaire.

While the film seems to completely reveal the artifice of filmic production, there are also moments when the magic of movie-making is allowed to remain concealed. While Kathy is hired

---

[9] "Broadway Melody" is an interesting example of intertextuality in that the first Arthur Freed/MGM musical released in 1929 was *Broadway Melody*.
[10] Joseph Andrew Casper, *Stanley Donen* (Metuchen, NJ: The Scarecrow Press, 1983) 54.

to dub over Lina's voice for *The Dancing Cavalier*, it is actually Jean Hagen's own voice—without the Brooklyn whine—dubbed over Kathy as she speaks and sings for Lina.

More than a film about the coming-of-sound in 1927, *Singin' in the Rain* is also about the contemporary turn-of-events in the post-war film industry. In 1948, the U. S. Supreme Court handed down its decision in the Paramount case beginning the breakdown of the studio system which until then could produce, distribute and exhibit their own movies. *Singin' in the Rain* provides an almost nostalgic look at the history of the monumental studio, MGM. In one scene we see the making of various silent features, including an African epic, a football game in a snowstorm, and a Western. Likewise, the history of the MGM musical is shown in a montage of musical sequences highlighting crooning through a megaphone and Busby Berkeley-like dance numbers.

Another change that encouraged the downfall of the studios was the post-war suburbanization of America and the rise in popularity of television. With the competition of the television and the loss of the urban audience, cinema had to re-invent itself and provide the public something it could not get on television. Stars, widescreen formats, Technicolor productions, "3-D," and lavish productions—such as all-star musicals—helped to revitalize the publics love for the movies. It was at this time that *Singin' in the Rain* was made.

The French play-write Molière encouraged the separation of art and entertainment, valuing the popular over the elite. In *The Critique of 'The School for Wives'*, he includes a discussion of art and entertainment,

> Uranie:When I go to a show, I just consider the things that move me, and if I've enjoyed myself, I don't start worrying about whether I ought to have or whether Aristotle's rules forbid me to laugh.
>
> Dorante: Surely the rule of all rules is to please?[11]

I wonder what Molière would say about *Singin' in the Rain*. The people spoke clearly enough: it made $4,220,605 at the box office. But as to art or entertainment, the question is left to you. Is it art? or is it entertainment? or perhaps—arguing with Molière—is it both?

---

[11] Quoted in Richard Dyer, "The Notion of Entertainment," *Only Entertainment* (London: Routledge, 1992), 11.

2
LITERARY DESIGN

In a sense, a screenplay, whether a romance or a detective story, is a series of surprises. We detonate these as we go along. But for a surprise to be valid, we must first set the ground rules, indicate expectations.

—William Goldman, from Adventures in the Screen Trade (1983)

CTCS 190 LECTURE OUTLINE – WEEK II   **LECTURE 2**

A. **The Script**
   1. Original; Adaptations
   2. Types of Scripts
       a. The writer's script
       b. The shooting script/director's script/tech script; the text or the film itself; the published script
   3. The authorship dilemma
   4. The functions of the film writer
B. **Literary Determinations**
   1. Title
   2. Subject and theme
   3. Life; Story; Plot; Narrative
       a. Elements of plot:
           1. Causality
           2. Spatial contiguity and temporal continuity
           3. Goal-oriented protagonist
           4. Actions in a setting
           4. Antagonist
           4. Unity/coherence
           4. Suspense
           4. Ending/closure
       b. The concept of character
       c. Types of setting
       d. Relationship of plot and character
   4. Dramatic structure and the "arrangement" of actions
       a. Classical/Linear/Traditional
       b. Episodic
       c. Thematic/Contextual
   5. Narrative
       a. Chronological
       b. Achronological
       c. Parallel or contrasting actions
       d. Objectivity and subjectivity
   6. Point-of-view (POV)
       a. Omniscient
       b. First person (inside and outside the story)
       c. Third person
       d. Multiple
       e. Authorial
   Visual Analysis
   7. Motif; symbol; allusion
C. **Introduction and Screening**

Notes

Notes

POETICS

Aristotle, 350 BC
Translated by S. H. Butcher

I

I propose to treat of Poetry in itself and of its various kinds, noting the essential quality of each, to inquire into the structure of the plot as requisite to a good poem; into the number and nature of the parts of which a poem is composed; and similarly into whatever else falls within the same inquiry. Following, then, the order of nature, let us begin with the principles which come first.

Epic poetry and Tragedy, Comedy also and Dithyrambic poetry, and the music of the flute and of the lyre in most of their forms, are all in their general conception modes of imitation. They differ, however, from one another in three respects—the medium, the objects, the manner or mode of imitation, being in each case distinct.

For as there are persons who, by conscious art or mere habit, imitate and represent various objects through the medium of color and form, or again by the voice; so in the arts above mentioned, taken as a whole, the imitation is produced by rhythm, language, or 'harmony,' either singly or combined.

Thus in the music of the flute and of the lyre, 'harmony' and rhythm alone are employed; also in other arts, such as that of the shepherd's pipe, which are essentially similar to these. In dancing, rhythm alone is used without 'harmony'; for even dancing imitates character, emotion, and action, by rhythmical movement.

There is another art which imitates by means of language alone, and that either in prose or verse—which verse, again, may either combine different meters or consist of but one kind—but this has hitherto been without a name. For there is no common term we could apply to the mimes of Sophron and Xenarchus and the Socratic dialogues on the one hand; and, on the other, to poetic imitations in iambic, elegiac, or any similar meter. People do, indeed, add the word 'maker' or 'poet' to the name of the meter, and speak of elegiac poets, or epic (that is, hexameter) poets, as if it were not the imitation that makes the poet, but the verse that entitles them all to the name. Even when a treatise on medicine or natural science is brought out in verse, the name of poet is by custom given to the author; and yet Homer and Empedocles have nothing in common but the meter, so that it would be right to call the one poet, the other physicist rather than poet. On the same principle, even if a writer in his poetic imitation were to combine all meters, as Chaeremon did in his Centaur, which is a medley composed of meters of all kinds, we should bring him too under the general term poet.

So much then for these distinctions.

There are, again, some arts which employ all the means above mentioned—namely, rhythm, tune, and meter. Such are Dithyrambic and Nomic poetry, and also Tragedy and Comedy; but between them originally the difference is, that in the first two cases these means are all employed in combination, in the latter, now one means is employed, now another.

Such, then, are the differences of the arts with respect to the medium of imitation.

II

Since the objects of imitation are men in action, and these men must be either of a higher or a lower type (for moral character mainly answers to these divisions, goodness and badness being the distinguishing marks of moral differences), it follows that we must represent men either as better than in real life, or as worse, or as they are. It is the same in painting. Polygnotus depicted men as nobler than they are, Pauson as less noble, Dionysius drew them true to life. Now it is evident that each of the modes of imitation above mentioned will exhibit these differences, and become a distinct kind in imitating objects that are thus distinct. Such diversities may be found even in dancing, flute-playing, and lyre-playing. So again in language, whether prose or verse unaccompanied by music. Homer, for example, makes men better than they are; Cleophon as they are; Hegemon the Thasian, the inventor of parodies, and Nicochares, the author of the Deiliad, worse than they are. The same thing holds good of Dithyrambs and Nomes; here too one may portray different types, as Timotheus and Philoxenus differed in representing their Cyclopes. The same distinction marks off Tragedy from Comedy; for Comedy aims at representing men as worse, Tragedy as better than in actual life.

III

There is still a third difference—the manner in which each of these objects may be imitated. For the medium being the same, and the objects the same, the poet may imitate by narration—in which case he can either take another personality as Homer does, or speak in his own person, unchanged—or he may present all his characters as living and moving before us.

These, then, as we said at the beginning, are the three differences which distinguish artistic imitation—the medium, the objects, and the manner. So that from one point of view, Sophocles is an imitator of the same kind as Homer—for both imitate higher types of character; from another point of view, of the same kind as Aristophanes—for both imitate persons acting and doing. Hence, some say, the name of 'drama' is given to such poems, as representing action. For the same reason the Dorians claim the invention both of Tragedy and Comedy. The claim to Comedy is put forward by the Megarians—not only by those of Greece proper, who allege that it originated under their democracy, but also by the Megarians of Sicily, for the poet Epicharmus, who is much earlier than Chionides and Magnes, belonged to that country. Tragedy too is claimed by certain Dorians of the Peloponnese. In each case they appeal to the evidence of language. The outlying villages, they say, are by them called komai, by the Athenians demoi: and they assume that comedians were so named not from komazein, 'to revel,' but because they wandered from village to village (kata komas), being excluded contemptuously from the city. They add also that the Dorian word for 'doing' is dran, and the Athenian, prattein.

This may suffice as to the number and nature of the various modes of imitation.

IV

Poetry in general seems to have sprung from two causes, each of them lying deep in our nature. First, the instinct of imitation is implanted in man from childhood, one difference between him and other animals being that he is the most imitative of living creatures, and through imitation learns his earliest lessons; and no less universal is the pleasure felt in things imitated. We have evidence of this in the facts of experience. Objects which in themselves we view with pain, we delight to contemplate when reproduced with minute fidelity: such as the forms of the most ignoble animals and of dead bodies. The cause of this again is, that to learn gives the liveliest pleasure, not only to philosophers but to men in general; whose capacity, however, of learning is more limited. Thus the reason why men enjoy seeing a likeness is, that in contemplating it they find themselves learning or inferring, and saying perhaps, 'Ah, that is he.' For if you happen not to have seen the original, the pleasure will be due not to the imitation as such, but to the execution, the coloring, or some such other cause.

Imitation, then, is one instinct of our nature. Next, there is the instinct for 'harmony' and rhythm, meters being manifestly sections of rhythm. Persons, therefore, starting with this natural gift developed by degrees their special aptitudes, till their rude improvisations gave birth to Poetry.

Poetry now diverged in two directions, according to the individual character of the writers. The graver spirits imitated noble actions, and the actions of good men. The more trivial sort imitated the actions of meaner persons, at first composing satires, as the former did hymns to the gods and the praises of famous men. A poem of the satirical kind cannot indeed be put down to any author earlier than Homer; though many such writers probably there were. But from Homer onward, instances can be cited—his own Margites, for example, and other similar compositions. The appropriate meter was also here introduced; hence the measure is still called the iambic or lampooning measure, being that in which people lampooned one another. Thus the older poets were distinguished as writers of heroic or of lampooning verse.

As, in the serious style, Homer is pre-eminent among poets, for he alone combined dramatic form with excellence of imitation so he too first laid down the main lines of comedy, by dramatizing the ludicrous instead of writing personal satire. His Margites bears the same relation to comedy that the Iliad and Odyssey do to tragedy. But when Tragedy and Comedy came to light, the two classes of poets still followed their natural bent: the lampooners became writers of Comedy, and the Epic poets were succeeded by Tragedians, since the drama was a larger and higher form of art.

Whether Tragedy has as yet perfected its proper types or not; and whether it is to be judged in itself, or in relation also to the audience—this raises another question. Be that as it may, Tragedy—as also Comedy—was at first mere improvisation. The one originated with the authors of the Dithyramb, the other with those of the phallic songs, which are still in use in many of our cities. Tragedy advanced by slow degrees; each new element that showed itself was in turn developed. Having passed through many changes, it found its natural form, and there it stopped.

Aeschylus first introduced a second actor; he diminished the importance of the Chorus, and assigned the leading part to the dialogue. Sophocles raised the number of actors to three, and added scene-painting. Moreover, it was not till late that the short plot was discarded for one of greater compass, and the grotesque diction of the earlier satyric form for the stately manner of Tragedy. The iambic measure then replaced the trochaic tetrameter, which was originally employed when the poetry was of the satyric order, and had greater with dancing. Once dialogue had come in, Nature herself discovered the appropriate measure. For the iambic is, of all measures, the most colloquial we see it in the fact that conversational speech runs into iambic lines more frequently than into any other kind of verse; rarely into hexameters, and only when we drop the colloquial intonation. The additions to the number of 'episodes' or acts, and the other accessories of which tradition tells, must be taken as already described; for to discuss them in detail would, doubtless, be a large undertaking.

V

Comedy is, as we have said, an imitation of characters of a lower type—not, however, in the full sense of the word bad, the ludicrous being merely a subdivision of the ugly. It consists in some defect or ugliness which is not painful or destructive. To take an obvious example, the comic mask is ugly and distorted, but does not imply pain.

The successive changes through which Tragedy passed, and the authors of these changes, are well known, whereas Comedy has had no history, because it was not at first treated seriously. It was late before the Archon granted a comic chorus to a poet; the performers were till then voluntary. Comedy had already taken definite shape when comic poets, distinctively so called, are heard of. Who furnished it with masks, or prologues, or increased the number of actors—these and other similar details remain unknown. As for the plot, it came originally from Sicily; but of Athenian writers Crates was the first who abandoning the 'iambic' or lampooning form, generalized his themes and plots.

Epic poetry agrees with Tragedy in so far as it is an imitation in verse of characters of a higher type. They differ in that Epic poetry admits but one kind of meter and is narrative in form. They differ, again, in their length: for Tragedy endeavors, as far as possible, to confine itself to a single revolution of the sun, or but slightly to exceed this limit, whereas the Epic action has no limits of time. This, then, is a second point of difference; though at first the same freedom was admitted in Tragedy as in Epic poetry.

Of their constituent parts some are common to both, some peculiar to Tragedy: whoever, therefore knows what is good or bad Tragedy, knows also about Epic poetry. All the elements of an Epic poem are found in Tragedy, but the elements of a Tragedy are not all found in the Epic poem.

VI

Of the poetry which imitates in hexameter verse, and of Comedy, we will speak hereafter. Let us now discuss Tragedy, resuming its formal definition, as resulting from what has been already said.

Tragedy, then, is an imitation of an action that is serious, complete, and of a certain magnitude; in language embellished with each kind of artistic ornament, the several kinds being found in separate parts of the play; in the form of action, not of narrative; through pity and fear effecting the proper purgation of these emotions. By 'language embellished,' I mean language into which rhythm, 'harmony' and song enter. By 'the several kinds in separate parts,' I mean, that some parts are rendered through the medium of verse alone, others again with the aid of song.

Now as tragic imitation implies persons acting, it necessarily follows in the first place, that Spectacular equipment will be a part of Tragedy. Next, Song and Diction, for these are the media of imitation. By 'Diction' I mean the mere metrical arrangement of the words: as for 'Song,' it is a term whose sense every one understands.

Again, Tragedy is the imitation of an action; and an action implies personal agents, who necessarily possess certain distinctive qualities both of character and thought; for it is by these that we qualify actions themselves, and these—thought and character—are the two natural causes from which actions spring, and on actions again all success or failure depends. Hence, the Plot is the imitation of the action—for by plot I here mean the arrangement of the incidents. By Character I mean that in virtue of which we ascribe certain qualities to the agents. Thought is required wherever a statement is proved, or, it may be, a general truth enunciated. Every Tragedy, therefore, must have six parts, which parts determine its quality—namely, Plot,

Character, Diction, Thought, Spectacle, Song. Two of the parts constitute the medium of imitation, one the manner, and three the objects of imitation. And these complete the fist. These elements have been employed, we may say, by the poets to a man; in fact, every play contains Spectacular elements as well as Character, Plot, Diction, Song, and Thought.

But most important of all is the structure of the incidents. For Tragedy is an imitation, not of men, but of an action and of life, and life consists in action, and its end is a mode of action, not a quality. Now character determines men's qualities, but it is by their actions that they are happy or the reverse. Dramatic action, therefore, is not with a view to the representation of character: character comes in as subsidiary to the actions. Hence the incidents and the plot are the end of a tragedy; and the end is the chief thing of all. Again, without action there cannot be a tragedy; there may be without character. The tragedies of most of our modern poets fail in the rendering of character; and of poets in general this is often true. It is the same in painting; and here lies the difference between Zeuxis and Polygnotus. Polygnotus delineates character well; the style of Zeuxis is devoid of ethical quality. Again, if you string together a set of speeches expressive of character, and well finished in point of diction and thought, you will not produce the essential tragic effect nearly so well as with a play which, however deficient in these respects, yet has a plot and artistically constructed incidents. Besides which, the most powerful elements of emotional interest in Tragedy—Peripeteia or Reversal of the Situation, and Recognition scenes—are parts of the plot. A further proof is, that novices in the art attain to finish of diction and precision of portraiture before they can construct the plot. It is the same with almost all the early poets.

The plot, then, is the first principle, and, as it were, the soul of a tragedy; Character holds the second place. A similar fact is seen in painting. The most beautiful colors, laid on confusedly, will not give as much pleasure as the chalk outline of a portrait. Thus Tragedy is the imitation of an action, and of the agents mainly with a view to the action.

Third in order is Thought—that is, the faculty of saying what is possible and pertinent in given circumstances. In the case of oratory, this is the function of the political art and of the art of rhetoric: and so indeed the older poets make their characters speak the language of civic life; the poets of our time, the language of the rhetoricians. Character is that which reveals moral purpose, showing what kind of things a man chooses or avoids. Speeches, therefore, which do not make this manifest, or in which the speaker does not choose or avoid anything whatever, are not expressive of character. Thought, on the other hand, is found where something is proved to be or not to be, or a general maxim is enunciated.

Fourth among the elements enumerated comes Diction; by which I mean, as has been already said, the expression of the meaning in words; and its essence is the same both in verse and prose.

Of the remaining elements Song holds the chief place among the embellishments.

The Spectacle has, indeed, an emotional attraction of its own, but, of all the parts, it is the least artistic, and connected least with the art of poetry. For the power of Tragedy, we may be sure, is felt even apart from representation and actors. Besides, the production of spectacular effects depends more on the art of the stage machinist than on that of the poet.

VII

These principles being established, let us now discuss the proper structure of the Plot, since this is the first and most important thing in Tragedy.

Now, according to our definition Tragedy is an imitation of an action that is complete, and whole, and of a certain magnitude; for there may be a whole that is wanting in magnitude. A whole is that which has a beginning, a middle, and an end. A beginning is that which does not itself follow anything by causal necessity, but after which something naturally is or comes to be.

An end, on the contrary, is that which itself naturally follows some other thing, either by necessity, or as a rule, but has nothing following it. A middle is that which follows something as some other thing follows it. A well constructed plot, therefore, must neither begin nor end at haphazard, but conform to these principles.

Again, a beautiful object, whether it be a living organism or any whole composed of parts, must not only have an orderly arrangement of parts, but must also be of a certain magnitude; for beauty depends on magnitude and order. Hence a very small animal organism cannot be beautiful; for the view of it is confused, the object being seen in an almost imperceptible moment of time. Nor, again, can one of vast size be beautiful; for as the eye cannot take it all in at once, the unity and sense of the whole is lost for the spectator; as for instance if there were one a thousand miles long. As, therefore, in the case of animate bodies and organisms a certain magnitude is necessary, and a magnitude which may be easily embraced in one view; so in the plot, a certain length is necessary, and a length which can be easily embraced by the memory. The limit of length in relation to dramatic competition and sensuous presentment is no part of artistic theory. For had it been the rule for a hundred tragedies to compete together, the performance would have been regulated by the water-clock—as indeed we are told was formerly done. But the limit as fixed by the nature of the drama itself is this: the greater the length, the more beautiful will the piece be by reason of its size, provided that the whole be perspicuous. And to define the matter roughly, we may say that the proper magnitude is comprised within such limits, that the sequence of events, according to the law of probability or necessity, will admit of a change from bad fortune to good, or from good fortune to bad.

VIII

Unity of plot does not, as some persons think, consist in the unity of the hero. For infinitely various are the incidents in one man's life which cannot be reduced to unity; and so, too, there are many actions of one man out of which we cannot make one action. Hence the error, as it appears, of all poets who have composed a Heracleid, a Theseid, or other poems of the kind. They imagine that as Heracles was one man, the story of Heracles must also be a unity. But Homer, as in all else he is of surpassing merit, here too—whether from art or natural genius—seems to have happily discerned the truth. In composing the Odyssey he did not include all the adventures of Odysseus—such as his wound on Parnassus, or his feigned madness at the mustering of the host—incidents between which there was no necessary or probable connection: but he made the Odyssey, and likewise the Iliad, to center round an action that in our sense of the word is one. As therefore, in the other imitative arts, the imitation is one when the object imitated is one, so the plot, being an imitation of an action, must imitate one action and that a whole, the structural union of the parts being such that, if any one of them is displaced or removed, the whole will be disjointed and disturbed. For a thing whose presence or absence makes no visible difference, is not an organic part of the whole.

IX

It is, moreover, evident from what has been said, that it is not the function of the poet to relate what has happened, but what may happen—what is possible according to the law of probability or necessity. The poet and the historian differ not by writing in verse or in prose. The work of Herodotus might be put into verse, and it would still be a species of history, with meter no less than without it. The true difference is that one relates what has happened, the other what may happen. Poetry, therefore, is a more philosophical and a higher thing than history: for poetry tends to express the universal, history the particular. By the universal I mean how a person of a certain type on occasion speak or act, according to the law of probability or necessity; and it is this universality at which poetry aims in the names she attaches to the personages. The particular is—for example—what Alcibiades did or suffered. In Comedy this is already apparent: for here the poet first constructs the plot on the lines of probability, and then inserts characteristic names—unlike the lampooners who write about particular individuals. But tragedians still keep to real names, the reason being that what is possible is credible: what has not happened we do not at once feel sure to be possible; but what has happened is manifestly possible: otherwise it would not have happened. Still there are even some tragedies in which there are only one or two well-known names, the rest being fictitious. In others, none are well known—as in Agathon's Antheus, where incidents and names alike are fictitious, and yet they give none the less pleasure. We must not, therefore, at all costs keep to the received legends, which are the usual subjects of Tragedy. Indeed, it would be absurd to attempt it; for even subjects that are known are known only to a few, and yet give pleasure to all. It clearly follows that the poet or 'maker' should be the maker of plots rather than of verses; since he is a poet because he imitates, and what he imitates are actions. And even if he chances to take a historical subject, he is none the less a poet; for there is no reason why some events that have actually happened should not conform to the law of the probable and possible, and in virtue of that quality in them he is their poet or maker.

Of all plots and actions the episodic are the worst. I call a plot 'episodic' in which the episodes or acts succeed one another without probable or necessary sequence. Bad poets compose such pieces by their own fault, good poets, to please the players; for, as they write show pieces for competition, they stretch the plot beyond its capacity, and are often forced to break the natural continuity.

But again, Tragedy is an imitation not only of a complete action, but of events inspiring fear or pity. Such an effect is best produced when the events come on us by surprise; and the effect is heightened when, at the same time, they follows as cause and effect. The tragic wonder will then be greater than if they happened of themselves or by accident; for even coincidences are most striking when they have an air of design. We may instance the statue of Mitys at Argos, which fell upon his murderer while he was a spectator at a festival, and killed him. Such events seem not to be due to mere chance. Plots, therefore, constructed on these principles are necessarily the best.

X

Plots are either Simple or Complex, for the actions in real life, of which the plots are an imitation, obviously show a similar distinction. An action which is one and continuous in the sense above defined, I call Simple, when the change of fortune takes place without Reversal of the Situation and without Recognition.

A Complex action is one in which the change is accompanied by such Reversal, or by Recognition, or by both. These last should arise from the internal structure of the plot, so that what follows should be the necessary or probable result of the preceding action. It makes all the difference whether any given event is a case of propter hoc or post hoc.

XI

Reversal of the Situation is a change by which the action veers round to its opposite, subject always to our rule of probability or necessity. Thus in the Oedipus, the messenger comes to cheer Oedipus and free him from his alarms about his mother, but by revealing who he is, he produces the opposite effect. Again in the Lynceus, Lynceus is being led away to his death, and

Danaus goes with him, meaning to slay him; but the outcome of the preceding incidents is that Danaus is killed and Lynceus saved.

Recognition, as the name indicates, is a change from ignorance to knowledge, producing love or hate between the persons destined by the poet for good or bad fortune. The best form of recognition is coincident with a Reversal of the Situation, as in the Oedipus. There are indeed other forms. Even inanimate things of the most trivial kind may in a sense be objects of recognition. Again, we may recognize or discover whether a person has done a thing or not. But the recognition which is most intimately connected with the plot and action is, as we have said, the recognition of persons. This recognition, combined with Reversal, will produce either pity or fear; and actions producing these effects are those which, by our definition, Tragedy represents. Moreover, it is upon such situations that the issues of good or bad fortune will depend. Recognition, then, being between persons, it may happen that one person only is recognized by the other—when the latter is already known—or it may be necessary that the recognition should be on both sides. Thus Iphigenia is revealed to Orestes by the sending of the letter; but another act of recognition is required to make Orestes known to Iphigenia.

Two parts, then, of the Plot—Reversal of the Situation and Recognition—turn upon surprises. A third part is the Scene of Suffering. The Scene of Suffering is a destructive or painful action, such as death on the stage, bodily agony, wounds, and the like.

XII

The parts of Tragedy which must be treated as elements of the whole have been already mentioned. We now come to the quantitative parts—the separate parts into which Tragedy is divided—namely, Prologue, Episode, Exode, Choric song; this last being divided into Parode and Stasimon. These are common to all plays: peculiar to some are the songs of actors from the stage and the Commoi.

The Prologue is that entire part of a tragedy which precedes the Parode of the Chorus. The Episode is that entire part of a tragedy which is between complete choric songs. The Exode is that entire part of a tragedy which has no choric song after it. Of the Choric part the Parode is the first undivided utterance of the Chorus: the Stasimon is a Choric ode without anapaests or trochaic tetrameters: the Commos is a joint lamentation of Chorus and actors. The parts of Tragedy which must be treated as elements of the whole have been already mentioned. The quantitative parts—the separate parts into which it is divided—are here enumerated.

XIII

As the sequel to what has already been said, we must proceed to consider what the poet should aim at, and what he should avoid, in constructing his plots; and by what means the specific effect of Tragedy will be produced.

A perfect tragedy should, as we have seen, be arranged not on the simple but on the complex plan. It should, moreover, imitate actions which excite pity and fear, this being the distinctive mark of tragic imitation. It follows plainly, in the first place, that the change of fortune presented must not be the spectacle of a virtuous man brought from prosperity to adversity: for this moves neither pity nor fear; it merely shocks us. Nor, again, that of a bad man passing from adversity to prosperity: for nothing can be more alien to the spirit of Tragedy; it possesses no single tragic quality; it neither satisfies the moral sense nor calls forth pity or fear. Nor, again, should the downfall of the utter villain be exhibited. A plot of this kind would, doubtless, satisfy the moral sense, but it would inspire neither pity nor fear; for pity is aroused by unmerited misfortune, fear by the misfortune of a man like ourselves. Such an event, therefore, will be neither pitiful nor terrible. There remains, then, the character between these two extremes—that of a man who is not eminently good and just, yet whose misfortune is brought about not by vice or depravity, but by some error or frailty. He must be one who is highly renowned and prosperous—a personage like Oedipus, Thyestes, or other illustrious men of such families.

A well-constructed plot should, therefore, be single in its issue, rather than double as some maintain. The change of fortune should be not from bad to good, but, reversely, from good to bad. It should come about as the result not of vice, but of some great error or frailty, in a character either such as we have described, or better rather than worse. The practice of the stage bears out our view. At first the poets recounted any legend that came in their way. Now, the best tragedies are founded on the story of a few houses—on the fortunes of Alcmaeon, Oedipus, Orestes, Meleager, Thyestes, Telephus, and those others who have done or suffered something terrible. A tragedy, then, to be perfect according to the rules of art should be of this construction. Hence they are in error who censure Euripides just because he follows this principle in his plays, many of which end unhappily. It is, as we have said, the right ending. The best proof is that on the stage and in dramatic competition, such plays, if well worked out, are the most tragic in effect; and Euripides, faulty though he may be in the general management of his subject, yet is felt to be the most tragic of the poets.

In the second rank comes the kind of tragedy which some place first. Like the Odyssey, it has a double thread of plot, and also an opposite catastrophe for the good and for the bad. It is accounted the best because of the weakness of the spectators; for the poet is guided in what he writes by the wishes of his audience. The pleasure, however, thence derived is not the true tragic pleasure. It is proper rather to Comedy, where those who, in the piece, are the deadliest enemies—like Orestes and Aegisthus—quit the stage as friends at the close, and no one slays or is slain.

XIV

Fear and pity may be aroused by spectacular means; but they may also result from the inner structure of the piece, which is the better way, and indicates a superior poet. For the plot ought to be so constructed that, even without the aid of the eye, he who hears the tale told will thrill with horror and melt to pity at what takes Place. This is the impression we should receive from hearing the story of the Oedipus. But to produce this effect by the mere spectacle is a less artistic method, and dependent on extraneous aids. Those who employ spectacular means to create a sense not of the terrible but only of the monstrous, are strangers to the purpose of Tragedy; for we must not demand of Tragedy any and every kind of pleasure, but only that which is proper to it. And since the pleasure which the poet should afford is that which comes from pity and fear through imitation, it is evident that this quality must be impressed upon the incidents.

Let us then determine what are the circumstances which strike us as terrible or pitiful.

Actions capable of this effect must happen between persons who are either friends or enemies or indifferent to one another. If an enemy kills an enemy, there is nothing to excite pity either in the act or the intention—except so far as the suffering in itself is pitiful. So again with indifferent persons. But when the tragic incident occurs between those who are near or dear to one another—if, for example, a brother kills, or intends to kill, a brother, a son his father, a mother her son, a son his mother, or any other deed of the kind is done—these are the situations to be looked for by the poet. He may not indeed destroy the framework of the received legends—the fact, for instance, that Clytemnestra was slain by Orestes and Eriphyle by Alcmaeon—but he ought to show of his own, and skillfully handle the traditional material. Let us explain more clearly what is meant by skilful handling.

The action may be done consciously and with knowledge of the persons, in the manner of the older poets. It is thus too that Euripides makes Medea slay her children. Or, again, the deed of horror may be done, but done in ignorance, and the tie of kinship or friendship be discovered afterwards. The Oedipus of Sophocles is an example. Here, indeed, the incident is outside the drama proper; but cases occur where it falls within the action of the play: one may cite the Alcmaeon of Astydamas, or Telegonus in the Wounded Odysseus. Again, there is a third case—[to be about to act with knowledge of the persons and then not to act. The fourth case] is when some one is about to do an irreparable deed through ignorance, and makes the discovery before it is done. These are the only possible ways. For the deed must either be done or not done—and that wittingly or unwittingly. But of all these ways, to be about to act knowing the persons, and then not to act, is the worst. It is shocking without being tragic, for no disaster follows It is, therefore, never, or very rarely, found in poetry. One instance, however, is in the Antigone, where Haemon threatens to kill Creon. The next and better way is that the deed should be perpetrated. Still better, that it should be perpetrated in ignorance, and the discovery made afterwards. There is then nothing to shock us, while the discovery produces a startling effect. The last case is the best, as when in the Cresphontes Merope is about to slay her son, but, recognizing who he is, spares his life. So in the Iphigenia, the sister recognizes the brother just in time. Again in the Helle, the son recognizes the mother when on the point of giving her up. This, then, is why a few families only, as has been already observed, furnish the subjects of tragedy. It was not art, but happy chance, that led the poets in search of subjects to impress the tragic quality upon their plots. They are compelled, therefore, to have recourse to those houses whose history contains moving incidents like these.

Enough has now been said concerning the structure of the incidents, and the right kind of plot.

XV

In respect of Character there are four things to be aimed at. First, and most important, it must be good. Now any speech or action that manifests moral purpose of any kind will be expressive of character: the character will be good if the purpose is good. This rule is relative to each class. Even a woman may be good, and also a slave; though the woman may be said to be an inferior being, and the slave quite worthless. The second thing to aim at is propriety. There is a type of manly valor; but valor in a woman, or unscrupulous cleverness is inappropriate. Thirdly, character must be true to life: for this is a distinct thing from goodness and propriety, as here described. The fourth point is consistency: for though the subject of the imitation, who suggested the type, be inconsistent, still he must be consistently inconsistent. As an example of motiveless degradation of character, we have Menelaus in the Orestes; of character indecorous and inappropriate, the lament of Odysseus in the Scylla, and the speech of Melanippe; of inconsistency, the Iphigenia at Aulis—for Iphigenia the suppliant in no way resembles her later self.

As in the structure of the plot, so too in the portraiture of character, the poet should always aim either at the necessary or the probable. Thus a person of a given character should speak or act in a given way, by the rule either of necessity or of probability; just as this event should follow that by necessary or probable sequence. It is therefore evident that the unraveling of the plot, no less than the complication, must arise out of the plot itself, it must not be brought about by the Deus ex Machina—as in the Medea, or in the return of the Greeks in the Iliad. The Deus ex Machina should be employed only for events external to the drama—for antecedent or subsequent events, which lie beyond the range of human knowledge, and which require to be reported or foretold; for to the gods we ascribe the power of seeing all things. Within the action there must be nothing irrational. If the irrational cannot be excluded, it should be outside the scope of the tragedy. Such is the irrational element the Oedipus of Sophocles.

Again, since Tragedy is an imitation of persons who are above the common level, the example of good portrait painters should be followed. They, while reproducing the distinctive form of the original, make a likeness which is true to life and yet more beautiful. So too the poet, in representing men who are irascible or indolent, or have other defects of character, should preserve the type and yet ennoble it. In this way Achilles is portrayed by Agathon and Homer.

These then are rules the poet should observe. Nor should he neglect those appeals to the senses, which, though not among the essentials, are the concomitants of poetry; for here too there is much room for error. But of this enough has been said in our published treatises.

XVI

What Recognition is has been already explained. We will now enumerate its kinds.

First, the least artistic form, which, from poverty of wit, is most commonly employed—recognition by signs. Of these some are congenital—such as 'the spear which the earth-born race bear on their bodies,' or the stars introduced by Carcinus in his Thyestes. Others are acquired after birth; and of these some are bodily marks, as scars; some external tokens, as necklaces, or the little ark in the Tyro by which the discovery is effected. Even these admit of more or less skilful treatment. Thus in the recognition of Odysseus by his scar, the discovery is made in one way by the nurse, in another by the swineherds. The use of tokens for the express purpose of proof—and, indeed, any formal proof with or without tokens—is a less artistic mode of recognition. A better kind is that which comes about by a turn of incident, as in the Bath Scene in the Odyssey.

Next come the recognitions invented at will by the poet, and on that account wanting in art. For example, Orestes in the Iphigenia reveals the fact that he is Orestes. She, indeed, makes herself known by the letter; but he, by speaking himself, and saying what the poet, not what the plot requires. This, therefore, is nearly allied to the fault above mentioned—for Orestes might as well have brought tokens with him. Another similar instance is the 'voice of the shuttle' in the Tereus of Sophocles.

The third kind depends on memory when the sight of some object awakens a feeling: as in the Cyprians of Dicaeogenes, where the hero breaks into tears on seeing the picture; or again in the Lay of Alcinous, where Odysseus, hearing the minstrel play the lyre, recalls the past and weeps; and hence the recognition.

The fourth kind is by process of reasoning. Thus in the Choephori: 'Some one resembling me has come: no one resembles me but Orestes: therefore Orestes has come.' Such too is the discovery made by Iphigenia in the play of Polyidus the Sophist. It was a natural reflection for Orestes to make, 'So I too must die at the altar like my sister.' So, again, in the Tydeus of Theodectes, the father says, 'I came to find my son, and I lose my own life.' So too in the Phineidae: the women, on seeing the place, inferred their fate—'Here we are doomed to die, for here we were cast forth.' Again, there is a composite kind of recognition involving false inference on the part of one of the characters, as in the Odysseus Disguised as a Messenger. A said [that no one else was able to bend the bow; ... hence B (the disguised Odysseus) imagined that A would] recognize the bow which, in fact, he had not seen; and to bring about a recognition by this means—the expectation that A would recognize the bow—is false inference.

But, of all recognitions, the best is that which arises from the incidents themselves, where the startling discovery is made by natural means. Such is that in the Oedipus of Sophocles, and in the Iphigenia; for it was natural that Iphigenia should wish to dispatch a letter. These recognitions alone dispense with the artificial aid of tokens or amulets. Next come the recognitions by process of reasoning.

XVII

In constructing the plot and working it out with the proper diction, the poet should place the scene, as far as possible, before his eyes. In this way, seeing everything with the utmost vividness, as if he were a spectator of the action, he will discover what is in keeping with it, and be most unlikely to overlook inconsistencies. The need of such a rule is shown by the fault found in Carcinus. Amphiaraus was on his way from the temple. This fact escaped the observation of one who did not see the situation. On the stage, however, the Piece failed, the audience being offended at the oversight.

Again, the poet should work out his play, to the best of his power, with appropriate gestures; for those who feel emotion are most convincing through natural sympathy with the characters they represent; and one who is agitated storms, one who is angry rages, with the most lifelike reality. Hence poetry implies either a happy gift of nature or a strain of madness. In the one case a man can take the mould of any character; in the other, he is lifted out of his proper self.

As for the story, whether the poet takes it ready made or constructs it for himself, he should first sketch its general outline, and then fill in the episodes and amplify in detail. The general plan may be illustrated by the Iphigenia. A young girl is sacrificed; she disappears mysteriously from the eyes of those who sacrificed her; she is transported to another country, where the custom is to offer up an strangers to the goddess. To this ministry she is appointed. Some time later her own brother chances to arrive. The fact that the oracle for some reason ordered him to go there, is outside the general plan of the play. The purpose, again, of his coming is outside the action proper. However, he comes, he is seized, and, when on the point of being sacrificed, reveals who he is. The mode of recognition may be either that of Euripides or of Polyidus, in whose play he exclaims very naturally: 'So it was not my sister only, but I too, who was doomed to be sacrificed'; and by that remark he is saved.

After this, the names being once given, it remains to fill in the episodes. We must see that they are relevant to the action. In the case of Orestes, for example, there is the madness which led to his capture, and his deliverance by means of the purificatory rite. In the drama, the episodes are short, but it is these that give extension to Epic poetry. Thus the story of the Odyssey can be stated briefly. A certain man is absent from home for many years; he is jealously watched by Poseidon, and left desolate. Meanwhile his home is in a wretched plight—suitors are wasting his substance and plotting against his son. At length, tempest-tost, he himself arrives; he makes certain persons acquainted with him; he attacks the suitors with his own hand, and is himself preserved while he destroys them. This is the essence of the plot; the rest is episode.

XVIII

Every tragedy falls into two parts—Complication and Unraveling or Denouement. Incidents extraneous to the action are frequently combined with a portion of the action proper, to form the Complication; the rest is the Unraveling. By the Complication I mean all that extends from the beginning of the action to the part which marks the turning-point to good or bad fortune. The Unraveling is that which extends from the beginning of the change to the end. Thus, in the Lynceus of Theodectes, the Complication consists of the incidents presupposed in the drama, the seizure of the child, and then again ... [the Unraveling] extends from the accusation of murder to the end.

There are four kinds of Tragedy: the Complex, depending entirely on Reversal of the Situation and Recognition; the Pathetic (where the motive is passion)—such as the tragedies on

Ajax and Ixion; the Ethical (where the motives are ethical)—such as the Phthiotides and the Peleus. The fourth kind is the Simple. [We here exclude the purely spectacular element], exemplified by the Phorcides, the Prometheus, and scenes laid in Hades. The poet should endeavor, if possible, to combine all poetic elements; or failing that, the greatest number and those the most important; the more so, in face of the caviling criticism of the day. For whereas there have hitherto been good poets, each in his own branch, the critics now expect one man to surpass all others in their several lines of excellence.

In speaking of a tragedy as the same or different, the best test to take is the plot. Identity exists where the Complication and Unraveling are the same. Many poets tie the knot well, but unravel it. Both arts, however, should always be mastered.

Again, the poet should remember what has been often said, and not make an Epic structure into a tragedy—by an Epic structure I mean one with a multiplicity of plots—as if, for instance, you were to make a tragedy out of the entire story of the Iliad. In the Epic poem, owing to its length, each part assumes its proper magnitude. In the drama the result is far from answering to the poet-'s expectation. The proof is that the poets who have dramatized the whole story of the Fall of Troy, instead of selecting portions, like Euripides; or who have taken the whole tale of Niobe, and not a part of her story, like Aeschylus, either fail utterly or meet with poor success on the stage. Even Agathon has been known to fail from this one defect. In his Reversals of the Situation, however, he shows a marvelous skill in the effort to hit the popular taste—to produce a tragic effect that satisfies the moral sense. This effect is produced when the clever rogue, like Sisyphus, is outwitted, or the brave villain defeated. Such an event is probable in Agathon's sense of the word: 'is probable,' he says, 'that many things should happen contrary to probability.'

The Chorus too should be regarded as one of the actors; it should be an integral part of the whole, and share in the action, in the manner not of Euripides but of Sophocles. As for the later poets, their choral songs pertain as little to the subject of the piece as to that of any other tragedy. They are, therefore, sung as mere interludes—a practice first begun by Agathon. Yet what difference is there between introducing such choral interludes, and transferring a speech, or even a whole act, from one play to another.

XIX

It remains to speak of Diction and Thought, the other parts of Tragedy having been already discussed. Concerning Thought, we may assume what is said in the Rhetoric, to which inquiry the subject more strictly belongs. Under Thought is included every effect which has to be produced by speech, the subdivisions being: proof and refutation; the excitation of the feelings, such as pity, fear, anger, and the like; the suggestion of importance or its opposite. Now, it is evident that the dramatic incidents must be treated from the same points of view as the dramatic speeches, when the object is to evoke the sense of pity, fear, importance, or probability. The only difference is that the incidents should speak for themselves without verbal exposition; while effects aimed at in speech should be produced by the speaker, and as a result of the speech. For what were the business of a speaker, if the Thought were revealed quite apart from what he says?

Next, as regards Diction. One branch of the inquiry treats of the Modes of Utterance. But this province of knowledge belongs to the art of Delivery and to the masters of that science. It includes, for instance—what is a command, a prayer, a statement, a threat, a question, an answer, and so forth. To know or not to know these things involves no serious censure upon the poet's art. For who can admit the fault imputed to Homer by Protagoras—that in the words, 'Sing, goddess, of the wrath, he gives a command under the idea that he utters a prayer? For to tell some one to do a thing or not to do it is, he says, a command. We may, therefore, pass this over as an inquiry that belongs to another art, not to poetry.

XX

Language in general includes the following parts: Letter, Syllable, Connecting Word, Noun, Verb, Inflection or Case, Sentence or Phrase.

A Letter is an indivisible sound, yet not every such sound, but only one which can form part of a group of sounds. For even brutes utter indivisible sounds, none of which I call a letter. The sound I mean may be either a vowel, a semivowel, or a mute.

A vowel is that which without impact of tongue or lip has an audible sound. A semivowel that which with such impact has an audible sound, as S and R. A mute, that which with such impact has by itself no sound, but joined to a vowel sound becomes audible, as G and D. These are distinguished according to the form assumed by the mouth and the place where they are produced; according as they are aspirated or smooth, long or short; as they are acute, grave, or of an intermediate tone; which inquiry belongs in detail to the writers on meter.

A Syllable is a nonsignificant sound, composed of a mute and a vowel: for GR without A is a syllable, as also with A—GRA. But the investigation of these differences belongs also to metrical science.

A Connecting Word is a nonsignificant sound, which neither causes nor hinders the union of many sounds into one significant sound; it may be placed at either end or in the middle of a sentence. Or, a nonsignificant sound, which out of several sounds, each of them significant, is capable of forming one significant sound—as amphi, peri, and the like. Or, a nonsignificant sound, which marks the beginning, end, or division of a sentence; such, however, that it cannot correctly stand by itself at the beginning of a sentence—as men, etoi, de.

A Noun is a composite significant sound, not marking time, of which no part is in itself significant: for in double or compound words we do not employ the separate parts as if each were in itself significant. Thus in Theodorus, 'god-given,' the doron or 'gift' is not in itself significant.

A Verb is a composite significant sound, marking time, in which, as in the noun, no part is in itself significant. For 'man' or 'white' does not express the idea of 'when'; but 'he walks' or 'he has walked' does connote time, present or past.

Inflection belongs both to the noun and verb, and expresses either the relation 'of,' 'to,' or the like; or that of number, whether one or many, as 'man' or 'men'; or the modes or tones in actual delivery, e.g., a question or a command. 'Did he go?' and 'go' are verbal inflections of this kind.

A Sentence or Phrase is a composite significant sound, some at least of whose parts are in themselves significant; for not every such group of words consists of verbs and nouns—'the definition of man,' for example—but it may dispense even with the verb. Still it will always have some significant part, as 'in walking,' or 'Cleon son of Cleon.' A sentence or phrase may form a unity in two ways—either as signifying one thing, or as consisting of several parts linked together. Thus the Iliad is one by the linking together of parts, the definition of man by the unity of the thing signified.

XXI

Words are of two kinds, simple and double. By simple I mean those composed of nonsignificant elements, such as ge, 'earth.' By double or compound, those composed either of a significant and nonsignificant element (though within the whole word no element is significant), or of elements that are both significant. A word may likewise be triple, quadruple, or multiple in form, like so many Massilian expressions, e.g., 'Hermo-caico-xanthus [who prayed to Father Zeus].'

Every word is either current, or strange, or metaphorical, or ornamental, or newly-coined, or lengthened, or contracted, or altered.

By a current or proper word I mean one which is in general use among a people; by a strange word, one which is in use in another country. Plainly, therefore, the same word may be at once strange and current, but not in relation to the same people. The word sigynon, 'lance,' is to the Cyprians a current term but to us a strange one.

Metaphor is the application of an alien name by transference either from genus to species, or from species to genus, or from species to species, or by analogy, that is, proportion. Thus from genus to species, as: 'There lies my ship'; for lying at anchor is a species of lying. From species to genus, as: 'Verily ten thousand noble deeds hath Odysseus wrought'; for ten thousand is a species of large number, and is here used for a large number generally. From species to species, as: 'With blade of bronze drew away the life,' and 'Cleft the water with the vessel of unyielding bronze.' Here arusai, 'to draw away' is used for tamein, 'to cleave,' and tamein, again for arusai—each being a species of taking away. Analogy or proportion is when the second term is to the first as the fourth to the third. We may then use the fourth for the second, or the second for the fourth. Sometimes too we qualify the metaphor by adding the term to which the proper word is relative. Thus the cup is to Dionysus as the shield to Ares. The cup may, therefore, be called 'the shield of Dionysus,' and the shield 'the cup of Ares.' Or, again, as old age is to life, so is evening to day. Evening may therefore be called, 'the old age of the day,' and old age, 'the evening of life,' or, in the phrase of Empedocles, 'life's setting sun.' For some of the terms of the proportion there is at times no word in existence; still the metaphor may be used. For instance, to scatter seed is called sowing: but the action of the sun in scattering his rays is nameless. Still this process bears to the sun the same relation as sowing to the seed. Hence the expression of the poet 'sowing the god-created light.' There is another way in which this kind of metaphor may be employed. We may apply an alien term, and then deny of that term one of its proper attributes; as if we were to call the shield, not 'the cup of Ares,' but 'the wineless cup'.

A newly-coined word is one which has never been even in local use, but is adopted by the poet himself. Some such words there appear to be: as ernyges, 'sprouters,' for kerata, 'horns'; and areter, 'supplicator', for hiereus, 'priest.'

A word is lengthened when its own vowel is exchanged for a longer one, or when a syllable is inserted. A word is contracted when some part of it is removed. Instances of lengthening are: poleos for poleos, Peleiadeo for Peleidou; of contraction: kri, do, and ops, as in mia ginetai amphoteron ops, 'the appearance of both is one.'

An altered word is one in which part of the ordinary form is left unchanged, and part is recast: as in dexiteron kata mazon, 'on the right breast,' dexiteron is for dexion.

Nouns in themselves are either masculine, feminine, or neuter. Masculine are such as end in N, R, S, or in some letter compounded with S—these being two, PS and X. Feminine, such as end in vowels that are always long, namely E and O, and—of vowels that admit of lengthening—those in A. Thus the number of letters in which nouns masculine and feminine end is the same; for PS and X are equivalent to endings in S. No noun ends in a mute or a vowel short by nature. Three only end in I—meli, 'honey'; kommi, 'gum'; peperi, 'pepper'; five end in U. Neuter nouns end in these two latter vowels; also in N and S.

XXII

The perfection of style is to be clear without being mean. The clearest style is that which uses only current or proper words; at the same time it is mean—witness the poetry of Cleophon and of Sthenelus. That diction, on the other hand, is lofty and raised above the commonplace which employs unusual words. By unusual, I mean strange (or rare) words, metaphorical, lengthened—anything, in short, that differs from the normal idiom. Yet a style wholly composed of such words is either a riddle or a jargon; a riddle, if it consists of metaphors; a jargon, if it consists of strange (or rare) words. For the essence of a riddle is to express true facts under impossible combinations. Now this cannot be done by any arrangement of ordinary words, but by the use of metaphor it can. Such is the riddle: 'A man I saw who on another man had glued the bronze by aid of fire,' and others of the same kind. A diction that is made up of strange (or rare) terms is a jargon. A certain infusion, therefore, of these elements is necessary to style; for the strange (or rare) word, the metaphorical, the ornamental, and the other kinds above mentioned, will raise it above the commonplace and mean, while the use of proper words will make it perspicuous. But nothing contributes more to produce a cleanness of diction that is remote from commonness than the lengthening, contraction, and alteration of words. For by deviating in exceptional cases from the normal idiom, the language will gain distinction; while, at the same time, the partial conformity with usage will give perspicuity. The critics, therefore, are in error who censure these licenses of speech, and hold the author up to ridicule. Thus Eucleides, the elder, declared that it would be an easy matter to be a poet if you might lengthen syllables at will. He caricatured the practice in the very form of his diction, as in the verse:

Epicharen eidon Marathonade badizonta,
I saw Epichares walking to Marathon,

or,

ouk an g'eramenos ton ekeinou elleboron.
Not if you desire his hellebore.

To employ such license at all obtrusively is, no doubt, grotesque; but in any mode of poetic diction there must be moderation. Even metaphors, strange (or rare) words, or any similar forms of speech, would produce the like effect if used without propriety and with the express purpose of being ludicrous. How great a difference is made by the appropriate use of lengthening, may be seen in Epic poetry by the insertion of ordinary forms in the verse. So, again, if we take a strange (or rare) word, a metaphor, or any similar mode of expression, and replace it by the current or proper term, the truth of our observation will be manifest. For example, Aeschylus and Euripides each composed the same iambic line. But the alteration of a single word by Euripides, who employed the rarer term instead of the ordinary one, makes one verse appear beautiful and the other trivial. Aeschylus in his Philoctetes says:

phagedaina d'he mou sarkas esthiei podos.
The tumor which is eating the flesh of my foot.

Euripides substitutes thoinatai, 'feasts on,' for esthiei, 'feeds on.' Again, in the line, nun de m'eon oligos te kai outidanos kai aeikes, Yet a small man, worthless and unseemly, the difference will be felt if we substitute the common words,

nun de m'eon mikros te kai asthenikos kai aeides.
Yet a little fellow, weak and ugly.

Or, if for the line,

diphron aeikelion katatheis oligen te trapezan,
Setting an unseemly couch and a meager table,
we read,

diphron mochtheron katatheis mikran te trapezan.
Setting a wretched couch and a puny table.

Or, for eiones booosin, 'the sea shores roar,' eiones krazousin, 'the sea shores screech.'

Again, Ariphrades ridiculed the tragedians for using phrases which no one would employ in ordinary speech: for example, domaton apo, 'from the house away,' instead of apo domaton, 'away from the house;' sethen, ego de nin, 'to thee, and I to him;' Achilleos peri, 'Achilles about,' instead of peri Achilleos, 'about Achilles;' and the like. It is precisely because such phrases are not part of the current idiom that they give distinction to the style. This, however, he failed to see.

It is a great matter to observe propriety in these several modes of expression, as also in compound words, strange (or rare) words, and so forth. But the greatest thing by far is to have a command of metaphor. This alone cannot be imparted by another; it is the mark of genius, for to make good metaphors implies an eye for resemblances.

Of the various kinds of words, the compound are best adapted to dithyrambs, rare words to heroic poetry, metaphors to iambic. In heroic poetry, indeed, all these varieties are serviceable. But in iambic verse, which reproduces, as far as may be, familiar speech, the most appropriate words are those which are found even in prose. These are the current or proper, the metaphorical, the ornamental.

Concerning Tragedy and imitation by means of action this may suffice.

XXIII

As to that poetic imitation which is narrative in form and employs a single meter, the plot manifestly ought, as in a tragedy, to be constructed on dramatic principles. It should have for its subject a single action, whole and complete, with a beginning, a middle, and an end. It will thus resemble a living organism in all its unity, and produce the pleasure proper to it. It will differ in structure from historical compositions, which of necessity present not a single action, but a single period, and all that happened within that period to one person or to many, little connected together as the events may be. For as the sea-fight at Salamis and the battle with the Carthaginians in Sicily took place at the same time, but did not tend to any one result, so in the sequence of events, one thing sometimes follows another, and yet no single result is thereby produced. Such is the practice, we may say, of most poets. Here again, then, as has been already observed, the transcendent excellence of Homer is manifest. He never attempts to make the whole war of Troy the subject of his poem, though that war had a beginning and an end. It would have been too vast a theme, and not easily embraced in a single view. If, again, he had kept it within moderate limits, it must have been over-complicated by the variety of the incidents. As it is, he detaches a single portion, and admits as episodes many events from the general story of the war—such as the Catalogue of the ships and others—thus diversifying the poem. All other poets take a single hero, a single period, or an action single indeed, but with a multiplicity of parts. Thus did the author of the Cypria and of the Little Iliad. For this reason the Iliad and the Odyssey each furnish the subject of one tragedy, or, at most, of two; while the Cypria supplies materials for many, and the Little Iliad for eight—the Award of the Arms, the Philoctetes, the Neoptolemus, the Eurypylus, the Mendicant Odysseus, the Laconian Women, the Fall of Ilium, the Departure of the Fleet.

XXIV

Again, Epic poetry must have as many kinds as Tragedy: it must be simple, or complex, or 'ethical,' or 'pathetic.' The parts also, with the exception of song and spectacle, are the same; for it requires Reversals of the Situation, Recognitions, and Scenes of Suffering. Moreover, the thoughts and the diction must be artistic. In all these respects Homer is our earliest and sufficient model. Indeed each of his poems has a twofold character. The Iliad is at once simple and 'pathetic,' and the Odyssey complex (for Recognition scenes run through it), and at the same time 'ethical.' Moreover, in diction and thought they are supreme.

Epic poetry differs from Tragedy in the scale on which it is constructed, and in its meter. As regards scale or length, we have already laid down an adequate limit: the beginning and the end must be capable of being brought within a single view. This condition will be satisfied by poems on a smaller scale than the old epics, and answering in length to the group of tragedies presented at a single sitting.

Epic poetry has, however, a great—a special—capacity for enlarging its dimensions, and we can see the reason. In Tragedy we cannot imitate several lines of actions carried on at one and the same time; we must confine ourselves to the action on the stage and the part taken by the players. But in Epic poetry, owing to the narrative form, many events simultaneously transacted can be presented; and these, if relevant to the subject, add mass and dignity to the poem. The Epic has here an advantage, and one that conduces to grandeur of effect, to diverting the mind of the hearer, and relieving the story with varying episodes. For sameness of incident soon produces satiety, and makes tragedies fail on the stage.

As for the meter, the heroic measure has proved its fitness by hexameter test of experience. If a narrative poem in any other meter or in many meters were now composed, it would be found incongruous. For of all measures the heroic is the stateliest and the most massive; and hence it most readily admits rare words and metaphors, which is another point in which the narrative form of imitation stands alone. On the other hand, the iambic and the trochaic tetrameter are stirring measures, the latter being akin to dancing, the former expressive of action. Still more absurd would it be to mix together different meters, as was done by Chaeremon. Hence no one has ever composed a poem on a great scale in any other than heroic verse. Nature herself, as we have said, teaches the choice of the proper measure.

Homer, admirable in all respects, has the special merit of being the only poet who rightly appreciates the part he should take himself. The poet should speak as little as possible in his own person, for it is not this that makes him an imitator. Other poets appear themselves upon the scene throughout, and imitate but little and rarely. Homer, after a few prefatory words, at once brings in a man, or woman, or other personage; none of them wanting in characteristic qualities, but each with a character of his own.

The element of the wonderful is required in Tragedy. The irrational, on which the wonderful depends for its chief effects, has wider scope in Epic poetry, because there the person acting is not seen. Thus, the pursuit of Hector would be ludicrous if placed upon the stage—the Greeks standing still and not joining in the pursuit, and Achilles waving them back. But in the Epic poem the absurdity passes unnoticed. Now the wonderful is pleasing, as may be inferred from the fact that every one tells a story with some addition of his knowing that his hearers like it. It is Homer who has chiefly taught other poets the art of telling lies skillfully. The secret of it lies in a fallacy. For, assuming that if one thing is or becomes, a second is or becomes, men imagine that, if the second is, the first likewise is or becomes. But this is a false inference. Hence, where the first thing is untrue, it is quite unnecessary, provided the second be true, to add that the first is or has become. For the mind, knowing the second to be true, falsely infers the truth of the first. There is an example of this in the Bath Scene of the Odyssey.

Accordingly, the poet should prefer probable impossibilities to improbable possibilities. The tragic plot must not be composed of irrational parts. Everything irrational should, if possible, be excluded; or, at all events, it should lie outside the action of the play (as, in the Oedipus, the hero's ignorance as to the manner of Laius' death); not within the drama—as in the Electra, the messenger's account of the Pythian games; or, as in the Mysians, the man who has come from Tegea to Mysia and is still speechless. The plea that otherwise the plot would have been ruined, is ridiculous; such a plot should not in the first instance be constructed. But once the irrational has been introduced and an air of likelihood imparted to it, we must accept it in spite of the absurdity. Take even the irrational incidents in the Odyssey, where Odysseus is left upon the shore of Ithaca. How intolerable even these might have been would be apparent if an inferior poet were to treat the subject. As it is, the absurdity is veiled by the poetic charm with which the poet invests it.

The diction should be elaborated in the pauses of the action, where there is no expression of character or thought. For, conversely, character and thought are merely obscured by a diction that is over-brilliant.

XXV

With respect to critical difficulties and their solutions, the number and nature of the sources from which they may be drawn may be thus exhibited.

The poet being an imitator, like a painter or any other artist, must of necessity imitate one of three objects—things as they were or are, things as they are said or thought to be, or things as they ought to be. The vehicle of expression is language—either current terms or, it may be, rare words or metaphors. There are also many modifications of language, which we concede to the poets. Add to this, that the standard of correctness is not the same in poetry and politics, any more than in poetry and any other art. Within the art of poetry itself there are two kinds of faults—those which touch its essence, and those which are accidental. If a poet has chosen to imitate something, [but has imitated it incorrectly] through want of capacity, the error is inherent in the poetry. But if the failure is due to a wrong choice—if he has represented a horse as throwing out both his off legs at once, or introduced technical inaccuracies in medicine, for example, or in any other art—the error is not essential to the poetry. These are the points of view from which we should consider and answer the objections raised by the critics.

First as to matters which concern the poet's own art. If he describes the impossible, he is guilty of an error; but the error may be justified, if the end of the art be thereby attained (the end being that already mentioned)—if, that is, the effect of this or any other part of the poem is thus rendered more striking. A case in point is the pursuit of Hector. if, however, the end might have been as well, or better, attained without violating the special rules of the poetic art, the error is not justified: for every kind of error should, if possible, be avoided.

Again, does the error touch the essentials of the poetic art, or some accident of it? For example, not to know that a hind has no horns is a less serious matter than to paint it inartistically.

Further, if it be objected that the description is not true to fact, the poet may perhaps reply, 'But the objects are as they ought to be'; just as Sophocles said that he drew men as they ought to be; Euripides, as they are. In this way the objection may be met. If, however, the representation be of neither kind, the poet may answer, 'This is how men say the thing is.'

applies to tales about the gods. It may well be that these stories are not higher than fact nor yet true to fact: they are, very possibly, what Xenophanes says of them. But anyhow, 'this is what is said.' Again, a description may be no better than the fact: 'Still, it was the fact'; as in the passage about the arms: 'Upright upon their butt-ends stood the spears.' This was the custom then, as it now is among the Illyrians.

Again, in examining whether what has been said or done by some one is poetically right or not, we must not look merely to the particular act or saying, and ask whether it is poetically good or bad. We must also consider by whom it is said or done, to whom, when, by what means, or for what end; whether, for instance, it be to secure a greater good, or avert a greater evil.

Other difficulties may be resolved by due regard to the usage of language. We may note a rare word, as in oureas men proton, 'the mules first [he killed],' where the poet perhaps employs oureas not in the sense of mules, but of sentinels. So, again, of Dolon: 'ill-favored indeed he was to look upon.' It is not meant that his body was ill-shaped but that his face was ugly; for the Cretans use the word eueides, 'well-flavored' to denote a fair face. Again, zoroteron de keraie, 'mix the drink livelier' does not mean 'mix it stronger' as for hard drinkers, but 'mix it quicker.'

Sometimes an expression is metaphorical, as 'Now all gods and men were sleeping through the night,' while at the same time the poet says: 'Often indeed as he turned his gaze to the Trojan plain, he marveled at the sound of flutes and pipes.' 'All' is here used metaphorically for 'many,' all being a species of many. So in the verse, 'alone she hath no part... , oie, 'alone' is metaphorical; for the best known may be called the only one.

Again, the solution may depend upon accent or breathing. Thus Hippias of Thasos solved the difficulties in the lines, didomen (didomen) de hoi, and to men hou (ou) kataputhetai ombro.

Or again, the question may be solved by punctuation, as in Empedocles: 'Of a sudden things became mortal that before had learnt to be immortal, and things unmixed before mixed.'

Or again, by ambiguity of meaning, as parocheken de pleo nux, where the word pleo is ambiguous.

Or by the usage of language. Thus any mixed drink is called oinos, 'wine'. Hence Ganymede is said 'to pour the wine to Zeus,' though the gods do not drink wine. So too workers in iron are called chalkeas, or 'workers in bronze.' This, however, may also be taken as a metaphor.

Again, when a word seems to involve some inconsistency of meaning, we should consider how many senses it may bear in the particular passage. For example: 'there was stayed the spear of bronze'—we should ask in how many ways we may take 'being checked there.' The true mode of interpretation is the precise opposite of what Glaucon mentions. Critics, he says, jump at certain groundless conclusions; they pass adverse judgement and then proceed to reason on it; and, assuming that the poet has said whatever they happen to think, find fault if a thing is inconsistent with their own fancy.

The question about Icarius has been treated in this fashion. The critics imagine he was a Lacedaemonian. They think it strange, therefore, that Telemachus should not have met him when he went to Lacedaemon. But the Cephallenian story may perhaps be the true one. They allege that Odysseus took a wife from among themselves, and that her father was Icadius, not Icarius. It is merely a mistake, then, that gives plausibility to the objection.

In general, the impossible must be justified by reference to artistic requirements, or to the higher reality, or to received opinion. With respect to the requirements of art, a probable impossibility is to be preferred to a thing improbable and yet possible. Again, it may be impossible that there should be men such as Zeuxis painted. 'Yes,' we say, 'but the impossible is the higher thing; for the ideal type must surpass the realty.' To justify the irrational, we appeal to what is commonly said to be. In addition to which, we urge that the irrational sometimes does not violate reason; just as 'it is probable that a thing may happen contrary to probability.'

Things that sound contradictory should be examined by the same rules as in dialectical refutation—whether the same thing is meant, in the same relation, and in the same sense. We should therefore solve the question by reference to what the poet says himself, or to what is tacitly assumed by a person of intelligence.

The element of the irrational, and, similarly, depravity of character, are justly censured when there is no inner necessity for introducing them. Such is the irrational element in the introduction of Aegeus by Euripides and the badness of Menelaus in the Orestes.

Thus, there are five sources from which critical objections are drawn. Things are censured either as impossible, or irrational, or morally hurtful, or contradictory, or contrary to artistic correctness. The answers should be sought under the twelve heads above mentioned.

XXVI

The question may be raised whether the Epic or Tragic mode of imitation is the higher. If the more refined art is the higher, and the more refined in every case is that which appeals to the better sort of audience, the art which imitates anything and everything is manifestly most unrefined. The audience is supposed to be too dull to comprehend unless something of their own is thrown by the performers, who therefore indulge in restless movements. Bad flute-players twist and twirl, if they have to represent 'the quoit-throw,' or hustle the coryphaeus when they perform the Scylla. Tragedy, it is said, has this same defect. We may compare the opinion that the older actors entertained of their successors. Mynniscus used to call Callippides 'ape' on account of the extravagance of his action, and the same view was held of Pindarus. Tragic art, then, as a whole, stands to Epic in the same relation as the younger to the elder actors. So we are told that Epic poetry is addressed to a cultivated audience, who do not need gesture; Tragedy, to an inferior public. Being then unrefined, it is evidently the lower of the two.

Now, in the first place, this censure attaches not to the poetic but to the histrionic art; for gesticulation may be equally overdone in epic recitation, as by Sosistratus, or in lyrical competition, as by Mnasitheus the Opuntian. Next, all action is not to be condemned—any more than all dancing—but only that of bad performers. Such was the fault found in Callippides, as also in others of our own day, who are censured for representing degraded women. Again, Tragedy like Epic poetry produces its effect even without action; it reveals its power by mere reading. If, then, in all other respects it is superior, this fault, we say, is not inherent in it.

And superior it is, because it has an the epic elements—it may even use the epic meter—with the music and spectacular effects as important accessories; and these produce the most vivid of pleasures. Further, it has vividness of impression in reading as well as in representation. Moreover, the art attains its end within narrower limits for the concentrated effect is more pleasurable than one which is spread over a long time and so diluted. What, for example, would be the effect of the Oedipus of Sophocles, if it were cast into a form as long as the Iliad? Once more, the Epic imitation has less unity; as is shown by this, that any Epic poem will furnish subjects for several tragedies. Thus if the story adopted by the poet has a strict unity, it must either be concisely told and appear truncated; or, if it conforms to the Epic canon of length, it must seem weak and watery. [Such length implies some loss of unity,] if, I mean, the poem is constructed out of several actions, like the Iliad and the Odyssey, which have many such parts, each with a certain magnitude of its own. Yet these poems are as perfect as possible in structure; each is, in the highest degree attainable, an imitation of a single action.

If, then, tragedy is superior to epic poetry in all these respects, and, moreover, fulfills its specific function better as an art—for each art ought to produce, not any chance pleasure, but the pleasure proper to it, as already stated—it plainly follows that tragedy is the higher art, as attaining its end more perfectly.

Thus much may suffice concerning Tragic and Epic poetry in general; their several kinds and parts, with the number of each and their differences; the causes that make a poem good or bad; the objections of the critics and the answers to these objections....

CRITICAL FILM ANALYSES

Mildred Pierce (1945)

Paul N. Reinsch

CREDITS. Director: Michael Curtiz. Producer: Jerry Wald. Executive Producer: Jack L. Warner. Screenplay: Ranald MacDougall. Based on the novel by James M. Cain. Cinematography: Ernest Haller. Editing: David Weisbart. Art Direction: Anton Grot. Set Decoration: George James Hopkins. Costume Design: Milo Anderson. Original Music: Max Steiner. Makeup: Perc Westmore. Warner Bros. 109 minutes.

CAST. Joan Crawford (Mildred Pierce) Jack Carson (Wally Fay) Zachary Scott (Monte Beragon) Ann Blyth (Veda Pierce) Eve Arden (Ida Corwin) Bruce Bennett (Bert Pierce) Lee Patrick (Mrs. Maggie Biederhof) Moroni Olsen (Inspector Peterson) Jo Ann Marlowe (Kay Pierce) Butterfly McQueen (Lottie)

"I was doing all right. I was doing fine. I was able to afford an expensive singing teacher for Veda and a good dancing school for Kay. Only one thing worried me - that someday Veda would find out that I was a waitress." -- Mildred

"You think just because you've made a little money you can get a new hairdo and some expensive clothes and turn yourself into a lady. But you can't, because you'll never be anything but a common frump, whose father lived over a grocery store and whose mother took in washing. With this money, I can get away from every rotten, stinking thing that makes me think of this place or you!" -- Veda (to Mildred)

Last week you saw the titular character of today's film, *Mildred Pierce*, in Chuck Workman's *Precious Images*.[12] Do not be alarmed; Workman's film is packed full of iconic images from the history of cinema. But after today, you will not be able to miss the image of Joan Crawford in

---

[12] For good measure, Workman also uses Crawford from the horror film *Whatever Happened to Baby Jane?* where she and Bette Davis finally get to go at each other and a clip from the film *Mommie Dearest*, based on her daughter's hateful memoir, where Faye Dunaway caricatures Crawford and forever negatively shaped our perception of Crawford as a woman and actress.

Workman's film. Crawford's portrayal of Mildred won her her only Academy Award and further etched her place in screen history. The fictional Mildred and real life Crawford are unique, driven, unforgettable and "precious" only in the sense that each is irreplaceable. Based on the book of the same name by James M. Cain, and worked on by several writers including William Faulkner, Warner Bros.' film was a financial and critical success. For her performance, Crawford won not only the Academy Award but also the National Board of Review's award for best actress. The film was nominated for several Academy Awards, including Best Picture, Best Screenplay, best cinematography and best supporting actress: both Eve Arden and Ann Blyth. *Mildred Pierce* remains a favorite of critics and audiences today, in no small part because of Crawford's performance.

Yet it is Blyth's character – Veda, Mildred's favorite daughter – which propels the story. This is even truer of Cain's novel. Mildred's inexhaustible drive to please Veda transforms her life in ways she can not foresee but embraces in order to achieve her goal. The pair of quotations listed at the top state plainly the core of the film and novel: Mildred's attempts, successful we must add, to provide for her daughter after separating from her possibly philandering husband Bert. There is tension in the marriage in part because Bert feels Mildred spoils the children. And it soon becomes evident that Bert is correct. The other quote above indicates Veda's intense attachment to the class into which she was born and her disgust for everything "common." Money and goods are not enough for Veda and in her eyes Mildred will never have class. Mildred tries desperately to gain her daughter's approval, including marrying the shady Monte Beragon. She may even resort to murdering Monte.

The film is structured in part as a series of first person narratives by Mildred. Three times her voice takes the police and the audience back in time to search for the identity of Monte's killer. Mildred's descriptions reach back in an attempt to understand the present and possibly improve the future. Time is more traversable in the film than in the novel, possibility suggesting less determinism than the novel offers. When the confession appears in Cain's novels it frequently takes place as the speaker is about to die and the chance of any future has long since been destroyed. The look back is an attempt to sort why things are the way they are, but the conclusion is that this is how things had to be.[13] The protagonist's actions have foreclosed all possibilities and only death remains. Cain's other work, including *Double Indemnity and The Postman Always Rings Twice*, uses this form it is pointedly not the form of Mildred Pierce (it is one of his few third person narratives). For Cain's novel is not a story of crime but a study of America over the course of nearly an entire decade told chronologically and objectively in order to best present changes to the culture. As Cain meticulously notes the passing of each year and dollar which Mildred earns, spends, or saves, the novel presses forward to the conclusion of the destructive relationship between mother and daughter. Of course the novel accomplishes much more than this goal. Cain's focus is the nation, southern California (a subject which few writers before or since have captured so well) and the position of women in society. His dissection of bourgeois life and its attendant aspirations is sordid and without pity.

Like many writers responding to the call of talking pictures, Cain left his journalism career in New York City for Hollywood and the money it offered. Cain was suited for both professions since they allowed him to turn his keen eye on all of his surroundings. He also lived in turbulent times, serving in the First World War, and experiencing the widely different decades which followed. As William Marling puts it: "To sharpen his senses initially, he had the contrast of New York and California, of the Roaring Twenties and the Depression thirties."[14] These pairings inform Cain's view of the world and his work. He addressed not only Hollywood

---

[13] Note that Mildred uses this very line when talking to Bert's parents about her separation from him.
[14] William Marling. *The American Roman Noir: Hammett, Cain, and Chandler.* Athens: University of Georgia Press, 1995. p. 161.

but the sprawl of Los Angeles and the culture of Southern California. His characters, including Mildred, undergo great change and respond in extreme, often violent, ways to these changes. Cain's America is populated with those for whom a little is seldom enough. An America where money is the problem and is always also mistaken for the solution. A land where there is contempt for work since money is something one is either born with or steals. The restless energy of the characters, especially the women, is misspent and wasted. Sexual gratification is possible, but it too is fleeting, base and unromantic.

Director Michael Curtiz, an underappreciated artist whose career spans Hollywood's Golden Age and beyond, created a film true to this view of the world. The film also necessarily alters Cain's work for the medium of cinema. *Mildred Pierce* participates in the style which historians call "film noir," a trans-generic style which crystallized in American in 1940. What the film loses in documenting the years which the novel covers and analyzing southern California, it makes up for in screen acting and Curtiz's ability, along with the cream of Warner Bros. staff, to fashion a remarkable play of light and shadow. Hollywood in the early 40s was responding to fiction of the day (Hardboiled authors like Cain, Hammett, and Chandler), theater, the war, a more permissive culture and other changes.[15] As a result of these determinants, noir films frequently focus on unstable protagonists negotiating an altered landscape typically expressed through strong shadows and deep space. Cinematographer Ernest Haller's use of low key lighting, most noticeable in moments of crisis, perfectly embraces the work of art director Anton Grot and set decorator George James Hopkins to depict a treacherous world of shifting alliances. Mildred's position is insecure both within the film frame and in relation to other characters despite her achievements as an entrepreneur. Her relations with men are unsatisfying and of course her family is fractured. It is not typical for noir to feature a female protagonist but not impossible, as this film proves. Additionally, Veda's actions are often those befitting a femme fatale as she uses her charms to lure men into danger and willfully deceives a number of others, most notably her mother.

Ultimately, *Mildred Pierce* is more than a fine film adapted from a respected work of literature, and more than a female melodrama or film noir. About the film, author and screenwriter Barry Gifford says, "This is a fierce movie, better than the book, which is unwieldy and clunky and uneven."[16] Cain's work is more expansive than the film, as we have noted above and also focuses more on emotional rather than physical violence. But we do not have to agree with Gifford's sentiments about Cain's novel; we need only agree that *Mildred Pierce*, the character and film, is "fierce." It is a film that only Hollywood in the 40s could (and thankfully did) bring into the world.

---

[15] The filmmakers encountered resistance to their efforts to turn Cain's novel into a film. Veda, for example, is more despicable in the film in part to conform to the edicts of the Production Code.

[16] Barry Gifford. *Out of the Past: Adventures in Film Noir*. Jackson, Miss.: U of Mississippi Press, 2001. p. 113.

L.A. CONFIDENTIAL (1997)

Christie Milliken

New Regency release of an Arnon Milchan, Curtis Hanson and Michael Nathanson production. Directed by Curtis Hanson. Based on the novel by James Ellroy. Screenplay by Brian Helgeland and Curtis Hanson. Director of Photography: Dante Spinotti. Editor: Peter Honess. Costume Designer: Ruth Meyers. Production Design: Jeannine Oppewall. Original Score: Jerry Goldsmith. Distributed by Warner Bros. A Time Warner Entertainment Company. Running time: 136 minutes.

CAST: Russell Crowe (Bud White), Kevin Spacey (Jack Vincennes), Guy Pearce (Ed Exley), James Cromwell (Dudley Smith), Kim Basinger (Lynn Bracken), Danny De Vito (Sid Hudgens), Pierce Pratchett (David Straithairn), D.A. Ellis Loew (Ellis Rifkin).

> What I want in a story is psychological gravity, plot density. I want deeply ambiguous, darkly driven, deeply committed, passionate men, riding the wave of history on a huge canvas. And I hate the noble loner myth.
>
> —James Ellroy

In the mid 1950s, the French journal *Cahiers du Cinema* revolutionized film criticism when one of its critics, Francois Truffaut (later to become an influential French New Wave director), published an essay entitled "A Certain Tendency in the French Cinema." In this polemical piece, Truffaut proposed a concept described as "*la politique des auteurs*" (translated to "auteur theory") which came to dominate lively debates in film journals throughout France, Great Britain and the United States in the 50s and 60s. Auteur theory is predicated on the basic assumption that the best films are generally the result of the controlling vision of a single author/auteur. This concept was imported into the US primarily through the writing of critic Andrew Sarris, to access and rank a whole pantheon of Hollywood directors according to their unique artistic signature and style. Sarris and others would examine the work of various directors vis a vis recurring themes, motifs and obsessions which could be found throughout the body of films (oeuvre) created by an individual director.

While the notion of authorship hardly seems like a novel way of thinking about cinema, it is important to bear in mind that this view is not without its problems. If the best films are interpreted as the work of an auteur, it is also true that filmmaking is a highly collaborative (and industrial-based) venture, demanding a range of talent from the technical skills and creative contributions of actors, musicians, composers, set and costume designers, cinematographers, editors, special effects technicians, electricians and so on. Perhaps the authorship dilemma is nowhere more apparent than when we consider the notion of adaptation. In the case of *L.A. Confidential*, for example, the task of adapting best-selling crime novelist James Ellroy's 500 page novel, set between 1950 and 1958, with close to 100 characters and 8 plot lines into a two hour motion picture would indeed seem monumental. The film's director and co-scripter (along with Brian Helgeland) talks about the difficulties of such a process, and the labor of generating seven drafts of the screenplay, condensing the time span, plot lines and drastically reducing the number of characters in the transformation of the novel into a screenplay form. In an interview about the film and Ellroy's work, Hanson muses about his desire to remain faithful to the novel: "The task of adapting this epic, labyrinthine novel was enormous. The challenge was to consolidate the plot, tell it in movie terms, yet try to preserve Ellroy's unique voice, and be true to the characters." Critical praise (and Ellroy's endorsement) of the film indicate that Hanson achieved this task,

Set in 1950s L.A., both the film and the novel weave together a complex series of events against a backdrop involving multiple murders, scandal sheet journalism, heroin heists, extra-legal police intrigue, and an elaborate, high end prostitution ring that trades on the cosmetic manufacture of Hollywood glamour and dream factory desires. The intertwining stories coalesce around the investigations (and obsessions) of three morally tainted rogue cops—Jack Vincennes (Kevin Spacey), Bud White (Russell Crowe) and Ed Exley (Guy Pearce). While all three are very different, they are united in their preoccupation with a closed case that the media and the L.A.P.D. have dubbed the "Nite Owl Massacre," a coffee shop killing spree attributed to three black youths who are murdered by Exley before they are properly tried for that crime. The Nite Owl massacre provides an archetypal "road to Damascus" experience through which all three protagonists come to understand that they are employed for something other than punishing predators, protecting innocents and finding "absolute justice."

Retaining the centrality of the Nite Owl massacre is one of the ways in which Helgeland and Curtis were able to reconceive the novel in cinematic terms. The other decision the co-writers made was to remove every scene from the book that didn't have the three main cops in it and to work from those scenes out into a narrative that is more linear than the episodic structure of the novel. Moving from 8 plot fines to 3, and hence removing elements of the novel including a child-murdering serial killer named "Dr. Frankenstein" (a crime investigated and "solved" by Edmund's father-former police officer, Preston Exley), the Walt-Disney-esque animation king Raymond Dieterling, and the sordid creation of his movie-driven theme park Dream-a-Dreamland, as well as love interests for Vincennes and Exley, enabled the screenwriters to concentrate on the dramatic force which propels the novel: the conflict and turmoil of three men working out their destiny.

Although *L.A. Confidential* has, to some extent, the hard-boiled the veneer of old noir films, many of the colorful characteristics of L.A. in the 1950s that it portrays—a police department in turmoil, a runaway population explosion (including the rapid development of freeways and suburbia), the glorification of Hollywood, tabloid culture, theme parks and the pleasure-seeking California lifestyle espoused in television and movies—are still emblematic of the city today. The seeds for L.A.'s present status as a late twentieth century megalopolis were being directly planted during the post-World War II era. In fact, it could be argued that the biggest star in *L.A. Confidential* is the city itself L.A. has always been a metaphor for the American Dream. In this respect, both Ellroy (in the novel) and Hanson (in the film) show the extent to which the American ethos has always been engineered in the Hollywood's Dream Factory.

While the film garnered rave reviews from critics virtually across the board, *L.A. Confidential* was not a box office smash. Made for $35 million (modest by studio standards where films routinely cost between $60 to $80 million), from the time the film opened in Sept. 1997 to the most recent box office count in June 1998, earnings for the film were $64.6 Million domestically, with foreign revenues to that date being $50 Million (totaling $114.6 Million). It was nominated for nine Oscars, including Best Picture, Best Cinematography, Original Dramatic Score, Art Direction, Editing and others, but won only two: Best Supporting Actress for Kim Basinger and Best Adapted Screenplay for Brian Helgeland and Curtis Hanson. *L.A. Confidential* won Best Picture of 1997 from five of the country's most notable film societies: The Boston Society of Film Critics, the L.A. Film Critics Association, the New York Film Critics Circle and the National Board of Review, an honor no picture has ever achieved. *L.A.*

Confidential also won USC's Scripter Award, the only accolade that recognizes achievement in two media—an original book and its translation to the screen.

The Hours (2002)

Heidi Cooley

Paramount Pictures and Miramax Films. Producers: Robert Fox and Scott Rudin; Mark Huffman (Executive); Michael Alden, Ian MacNeil and Marieke Spencer (Associate). Director: Stephen Daldry. Screenplay: David Hare, based on the novel by Michael Cunningham. Cinematography: Seamus McGarvey. Editor: Peter Boyle. Music: Philip Glass. Production Design: Maria Djurkovic. Art Direction: Nick Palmer, Mark Raggett and Judy Rhee. Set Decoration: Philippa Hart, Barbara Peterson and Harriet Zucker. Costume Design: Ann Roth. 114 minutes.

CAST: Nicole Kidman (Virginia Woolf). Julianne Moore (Laura Brown). Meryl Streep (Clarissa Vaughn). Stephen Dillane (Leonard Woolf). Miranda Richardson (Vanessa Bell). John C. Reilly (Dan Brown). Jack Rovello (Richie Brown). Toni Collette (Kitty Barlowe). Ed Harris (Richard Brown). Allison Janney (Sally Lester). Claire Danes (Julia Vaughn). Jeff Daniels (Louis Waters).

> But I still have to face the hours, don't I? And then the hours after the party, and the hours after that.
> —Richard Brown (Ed Harris) in *The Hours*

> Leonard, always the years between us, always the years; always the love; always the hours..."
> —Virginia Woolf (Nicole Kidman) in *The Hours*

To speak in terms of "the hours" in which we find ourselves is to acknowledge our particular relation to time, a relation that is dichotomous. On the one hand, it is an indication of our implication in a system of time that is organized according to hours, minutes, days, years, etc. In which case, we think of time as structure, segmentation, progress and history; this is the time of charting the past, managing the present, and planning the future. It is the time of narrative, the time of sequence, of beginning-middle-end. As such, it allows us to take account of ourselves in the world from a pretended position of objectivity, rationality and wished-for mastery, a position that exists just beyond the ever-progressing line of time. On the other hand, there are singular moments when we engage time as an organic, embodied unfolding. Within these moments, the time of the clock no longer governs with its heavy hand and, instead, dissolves into the vitality and intensity of experience. This time cannot be calculated or plotted; it can only be lived bodily, in the moment. We might understand this time as the temporality of dreams (experienced not narrated) and surprise, which is perhaps irrational and knows no limits. Both forms of time happen for us: we function socially according to the dictates of the first but we always have the possibility of the second.

The Hours (2002), carefully adapted from Michael Cunningham's Pultzer-Prize winning novel of the same name, which itself is a theme-and-variations on Virginia Woolf's *Mrs. Dalloway*, initially titled "The Hours," explores the double character of time. Like Cunningham's novel, the film is the site of an intersection of three women's lives: that of Laura Brown in Los Angeles, on a day in 1951; Virginia Woolf in Richmond, England, on a day in 1923; and Clarissa "Mrs. Dalloway" Vaughn in New York, on a day in 2001. For all three women, time is a matter of social obligation, whether it be duty to home and family (Laura Brown), sanity (Virginia Woolf), the day's schedule of tasks and deadlines (Clarissa Vaughn). But also, all three women experience a single moment of vitality, in which the dictates of duty-bound time dissipate in a "stolen" kiss. It is the complex interweaving of these women's stories, as they echo and revise the day experienced by Woolf's Mrs. Dalloway, that mobilizes the film's commentary on life, death and love. We watch Laura Brown read in 1951 the book that Virginia Woolf writes in 1923 and Clarissa Vaughn enacts (in a parallel manner) in 2001; we witness the framing images of Virginia Woolf's suicide in 1941 (a fourth time in both novel and film): we come to value life more fully, or are invited to do so.

The film's relatively unconventional narrative structure, which adheres to that of the novel, refuses the easy chronological ordering of plot and story elements. It is relevant to note, here, that the film distances itself further from narrative sequencing by avoiding the contextualizing devices of flashback and interior monologue—except for a few voiceovers by Virginia Woolf. Instead it chooses to take advantage of the actors' skillful use of gesture and facial expression, reaction propelling plot more than action. And while one might locate story order within the three intersecting narratives of Laura (the reader), Virginia (the writer) and Clarissa (the editor), there is always the disjunction of the framing images of Virginia (of 1941) entering the river, which allows for resonance but not integration. (No framing occurs in the novel per se, since the river scene only appears in the prologue.) Thus, the spectator confronts a pervading temporal tension.

This temporal tension is intensified by transitions (novel) or abrupt cuts (film) between the three narrative strands, the recurrent ticking and chiming or sounding of clocks (a central motif), and the characters' attentiveness to time (i.e., Clarissa's reiteration of "I'll be back at 3:30"). These aspects of both novel and film insist on the primacy of time, as it functions as a mechanism of order and discipline, as well as emphasizes the tedium of waiting. Time of this kind is oppressive and severe, and epitomizes the hours that Richard Brown must endure (see epigraph). The film's score underscores the persistent weight of time as obligation with its melancholic arpeggios, whose ebb and flow throughout the film recall the opening images of the river and Virginia's (impending) suicide.

But water, i.e., river and music (in the film), as a trope for time, operates in a second way: it offers hope. Virginia's suicide at the river in 1941, which precedes the film's title and introductory credits, is not an end but rather opens onto the unfolding narratives of Laura, Virginia and Clarissa. And the scene's reiteration at the film's conclusion is the promise of a more fulfilling life for Leonard Woolf. Likewise, the use of water in daily routine, i.e., for washing the face or filling vases for flowers, provides instances of continuity between the narratives (often through graphic matches, and sometimes accompanied by a musical sound-bridge). In these instances, time is not bound or linear but expands beyond the limits of any one woman's day to encompass them all. This sense of expansion might be seen to evoke the intensity of the single, surprising moment, which bursts through clock time and, perhaps, exceeds social, i.e., patriarchal, heteronormative, norms/expectations (as well as intervenes in the linear time of narrative convention). The vitality of the moment, i.e., of an illicit kiss, is life-affirming and, therefore, uncontainable and full of possibility.

For the most part, *The Hours* has been highly regarded by critics who have commended it for its faithfulness to the novel and the actors for their powerful performances, particularly Nicole Kidman—although Meryl Streep's performance is especially amazing. There have been a few critics who have found the film to be overly sentimental. Still others have considered Ed Harris' Richard Brown and Jeff Daniel's Louis Waters to be overly effeminized gay men. The film has received numerous award nominations, winning the Oscar and Golden Globe for Best Performance by an Actress in a Leading Role (Nicole Kidman), as well as the Golden Globe for Best Motion Picture and the Seattle Film Critics Award for Best Screenplay (adapted). Additionally, Michael Cunningham and David Hare received the 15th USC Scripter Award, an award that recognizes both author and screenwriter of a film adaptation. At the box office, the film (budget of $25 million) earned $338,622 in its opening weekend (US) and, as of May 2003, had grossed $41.6 million (US).

3
PERFORMANCE

The thing about performance, even if it's only an illusion, is that it is a celebration of the fact that we do contain within ourselves infinite possibilities.

—Daniel Day Lewis, 1990

CTCS 190 LECTURE OUTLINE – WEEK III   **LECTURE 3**

A. **Introduction**
B. **Performance** as visual-aural representation of the script
   1. Dialogue through the <u>voice</u> of the player
      a. Words
      b. Beats and intonation
      c. Pauses and pace
      d. Volume
      e. Silence
   2. Action through the <u>body</u> of the player
      a. Action as content
      b. Posture
      c. Gesture
      d. Business
      e. Facial expression and reaction
        Visual Analysis
   3. Character and other aspects of the film's meaning through dialogue, action and the <u>properties of the player</u>
      a. Properties:
        1. Player's physicality: voice/body/face/eyes/age
        2. Player's personality
        3. Player's talent
        4. Player's mythology: off-screen and on-screen
      b. Persona of the player: comprised of these four properties
      c. Persona of the player in today's screening
C. **The player's importance** in the experience of the film
D. **Type of player**
   1. The non-professional
   2. The actor
   3. The star/star actor
E. **Acting styles**
   1. Pantomime/presentational
   2. Representational/realist
   3. Method acting
   4. University-trained
   5. Improvisation
   6. Star turn
F. **Critical criteria**
   1. Expressive coherence
   2. Ensemble
   3. Relation to setting
   4. Consistency
   5. Conveying thoughts
   6. Playing with/against/behind the beat
   7. Casting
   8. Performance in rhythm
   9. Affect
G. **Director as guide**
H. **Introduction and Screening**

Notes

Notes

WHAT IS ACTING?

from *Acting in the Cinema* (1988) by James Naremore

> The actor can only be said to be reproducing something when he is copying another actor.

> —Georg Simmel, *On the Theory of Theatrical Performance*

The preceding section describes Chaplin as an actor who mimes, mimics, or somehow imitates "real persons."[17] In its simplest form, however, acting is nothing more than the transposition of everyday behavior into a theatrical realm. Just as the language of poetry is no different in kind from the language in a newspaper, so the materials and techniques used by players on the stage are no different in kind from those we use in ordinary social intercourse. This may explain why the metaphor of life as theater is so ubiquitous and convincing.[18] After all, in daily activity we constitute ourselves rather like dramatic characters, making use of our voices, our bodies, our gestures and costumes, oscillating between deeply ingrained, habitual acts (our "true mask") and acts we more or less consciously adopt to obtain jobs, mates, or power. There is no question of breaking through this condition to arrive at some unstaged, unimitated essence, because our selves are determined by our social relations and because the very nature of communication requires us, like Prufrock, to put on a face to meet the faces that we meet. Hence Lee Strasberg's notion that the stage actor does not need to "imitate a human being" is at one level entirely correct: to become "human" in the first place we put on an act.

As a result, words like "drama," "performance," and "acting" can designate a great variety of behavior, only some of which is theatrical in the purest sense. But given the affinity between theater and the world, how do we know this purity? How do we determine the important and obvious difference between performers in everyday life and performers who are behaving theatrically? The answer is not altogether clear, even though we often make such

---

[17] In the preceding section, Naremore analyzed an early Chaplin short, *Kid Auto Race*. Editor's note.

[18] Consider the situation in "real life," as described by Robert Ezra Park: "It is probably no mere historical accident that the word person, in its first meaning, is a mask. It is rather a recognition of the fact that everyone is always and everywhere, more or less consciously, playing a role... It is in these roles that we know each other; it is in these roles that we know ourselves...In a sense, and in so far as this mask represents the conception we have formed of ourselves--the role we are striving to live up to-this mask is our truer self, the self we would like to be. In the end, our conception of our role becomes second nature and an integral part of our personality. We come into the world as individuals, achieve character, and become persons." (quoted by Goffman in *The Presentation of Self*, 19).

On the question of whether acting involves imitation, one of my early childhood memories seems appropriate. (Coincidentally, it belongs to a category of recollection that Freud once termed "screen memory" [III, 303-221.] I can recall asking my parents, at the age of four or five, whether the people in movies were really kissing. The question involved a moral dilemma, and it revealed a paradox: in fact, actors both do and pretend, sometimes at one and the same moment-hence the potentially scandalous nature of their work. In certain contexts, their actions can become *too* real, breaking the hold of illusion. For instance, film reviewer Vincent Canby was disturbed by a scene in *Devil in the Flesh* (1987), in which Maruschka Detmers performs fellatio: "One's first response [is], 'Gee whiz, they're actually doing it!' Then one begins to wonder how it was staged.... It's a recorded, documented fact, which destroys the illusion as thoroughly as hairpieces that don't fit." ("Sex Can Spoil the Scene," *New York Times*, 28 June 1987, 17.)

distinctions, and even though the basis on which we make them is crucial to the study of acting as an art or as a vehicle for ideology.

One solution to the problem has been offered by Erving Goffman, who defines theatrical performance as "an arrangement which transforms an individual into...an object that can be looked at in the round and without offense, and looked to for engaging behavior by persons in an audience role".[19] The "arrangement" of which Goffman speaks may take a variety of forms, so long as it divides people into two fundamental groups, designating some as performers and others as watchers. Its purpose is to establish an unusually high degree of ostentation, a quality the actor Sam Waterston has called "visibility": "People can see you...all the lights are turned out, and there is nothing else to look at".[20]

This showing (or showing off) is the most elementary form of human signification, and it can turn any event into theater. For example, the New York performance artists of the fifties and sixties were able to stage "happenings" by standing on a street corner and waiting for an auto accident or any chance occurrence that their role as audience would transform into a show; their experiments demonstrated that anyone—a juggler, a dancer, or an ordinary passerby—who steps into a space previously designated as theatrical automatically becomes a performer. Furthermore, not much conscious artistic manipulation or special skill is required to provide some kinds of "engaging behavior." When art theatricalizes contingency, as in Kid's Auto Race, John Cage's music, or Andy Warhol's movies, it puts a conceptual bracket around a force field of sensations, an ever-present stratum of sound, shade, and movement that both precedes meaning and makes it possible. Julia Kristeva seems to be talking about such a process when she refers to a "geno-text" or an "other scene" made available to communication by "significance" a preverbal activity she equates with the "anaphoric function." "Before and after the voice and the script is the anaphora—the gesture which indicates, establishes relations and eliminates entities".[21] Meaningless in itself, the anaphora is a purely relational activity whose free play allows meaning to circulate, even when meaning is unintended. All forms of human and animal exchange involve anaphoric behavior, and the "arrangement" Erving Goffman calls a theatrical framee could be understood in exactly those terms, as a primary gesture. It might take the form of a stage or a spot on the street; in the absence of these things, it could be a simple flourish of the hand or an indication to "look there." Whatever its shape, it always separates audience from performer, holding other gestures and signs up for show.

The motion picture screen is just such a theatrical anaphora, a physical arrangement that arrays spectacle for persons in an audience role. As in most types of theater, however, the actions and voices in movies are seldom allowed to "mean" by simply displaying themselves. This is especially true when the film involves acting—a term I shall use to designate a special type of theatrical performance in which the persons held up for show have become agents in a narrative.

At its most sophisticated, acting in theater or movies is an art devoted to the systematic ostentatious depiction of character, or to what seventeenth century England described as "personation." Unplotted theatrics can partake of acting, as when rock musicians like Madonna or Prince develop a persona that has narrative implications; but to be called an actor in the sense I am using, a performer does not have to invent anything or master a discipline, so long as he or she is embedded in a story. The following example from the proscenium stage, cited by Michael Kirby, may serve to illustrate the point:

[19] Goffman, Erving. *Frame Analysis*. New York: Harper, 1974, p. 124.
[20] Kalter, Joanmarie, ed. *Actors on Acting: Performance in Theatre and Film Today*. New York: Sterling. 1979, p. 156.
[21] Kristeva, Julia. "Gesture: Practice or Communication?" Trans. Johnathon Benthael. In *The Body Reader*, edited by Ted Polhemus. New York: Pantheon. 1977, p. 270.

Some time ago I remember reading about a play in which John Garfield—I am fairly sure it was he, although I no longer know the title of the play—was an extra. During each performance he played cards and gambled with friends on the stage. They really played, and the article emphasized how much money someone had won (or lost). At any rate, since my memory is incomplete, let us imagine a setting representing a bar. In one of the upstage booths, several men play cards throughout the act. Let us say that none of them has lines in the play; they do not react in any way to the characters in the story we are observing.... They merely play cards. And yet we also see them as characters, however minor, in the story and we say that they, too, are acting.

("On Acting and Not-Acting," Battcock and Nicas, 101)

This kind of "received" acting is fairly typical of theater, but in the movies it has much greater importance, extending even to the work of the star players, who sometimes perform gestures without knowing how they will be used in the story. For example, it is rumored that during the making of *Casablanca* (1942), director Michael Curtiz positioned Bogart in close-up, telling him to look off to his left and nod. Bogart did so, having no idea what the action was supposed to signify (the film, after all, was being written as it was shot). Later, when Bogart saw the completed picture, he realized his nod had been a turning point for the character he was playing: Rick's signal to the band in the Café Américain to strike up the Marseillaise.

A more "scientific" illustration of the same effect is the so-called Kuleshov experiment, in which an actor's inexpressive offscreen glance was intercut with various objects, thus creating the illusion that he was emoting. Kuleshov described the process as if he were a chemist working in a lab: "I alternated the same shot of Mozhukhin with various other shots (a plate of soup, a girl, a child's coffin), and these shots acquired a different meaning. The discovery stunned me".[22] There is, unfortunately, something disingenuous about Kuleshov's account, which has created what Norman Holland calls a "myth" of film history.[23] Even so, the "Kuleshov effect" is a useful term in film criticism, and anyone who has ever worked at a movie-editing table knows that a wide range of meanings or nuances, none of them intended by the script, the playing, or the découpage, can be produced through the cutting. Audiences, too, are aware of a potential for trickery, and a certain genre of comedy or parody foregrounds the process: a recent TV commercial uses close-ups from the original "Dragnet," editing them to make Joe Friday and his partner seem to discuss the merits of a brand of potato chips; a video on MTV shows Ronald Reagan piloting a dive bomber, gleefully attacking a rock and roll band; and Paramount's *Dead Men Don't Wear Plaid* (1982) allows Steve Martin to play scenes with half the stars of Hollywood in the forties.

One reason these jokes are possible is that expression is polysemous, capable of multiple signification; its meaning in a film is usually narrowed and held in place by a controlling narrative, a context that can rule out some meanings and highlight others. As a result, some of

---

[22] Kuleshov, Lev. *Kuleshov on Film*. Trans. and Ed. by Ronald Levaco. Berkeley and Los Angeles: University of California Press, 1974, p. 200.

[23] Holland has pointed out that Kuleshov and Pudovkin, who worked together to produce the famous sequence, disagreed about exactly what it contained. The original footage has not survived, and there is no evidence that it was shown to an innocent audience ("Psychoanalysis and Film: The Kuleshov Experiment," 1-2). The sequence therefore has dubious status as either history or science, although a formal experiment seems unnecessary when movies have always proved Kuleshov's point.

the most enjoyable screen performances have been produced by nothing more than typage,[24] and it is commonplace to see dogs, babies, and rank amateurs who seem as interesting as trained thespians. In fact, the power of movies to recontextualize detail is so great that a single role frequently involves more than one player: Cary Grant acts the part of Johnny Case in *Holiday* (1938), but he performs only two of the character's many somersaults, Rita Hayworth does a "striptease" in *Gilda* (1946), but the voice that issues front the character's mouth as she sings "Put the Blame on Mame" belongs to Anita Ellis.

By slightly extending Walter Benjamin's well-known argument about painting in the age of photography, we could say that mechanical reproduction deprives performance of authority and "aura," even as it greatly enhances the possibility of stardom. Significantly, another of Kuleshov's "experiments" had involved the creation of a synthetic person out of fragmentary details of different bodies—a technique that undermines the humanist conception of acting, turning every movie editor into a potential Dr. Frankenstein. Nevertheless, Kuleshov was intensely concerned with the training of players, and audiences continue to make distinctions between figures on the screen, claiming that some of them are a bit more actorly than others.

Up to a point we can make such claims by simply quantifying the character traits exhibited by the performer. As a test case, notice a brief sequence early in *North by Northwest* (1958), when Cary Grant/Roger Thornhill goes to the Oak Room bar in the Plaza Hotel for a business meeting: Grant arrives late, introduces himself to three men waiting at a table, and orders a martini; after chatting for a moment, he suddenly remembers that he needs to call his mother, so he signals across the room to a messenger, asking that a telephone be brought to the table. The sequence involves a great many players, and we can rank them on an "actorly" scale, ranging from the extras in the background, who are rather like decor or furnishings for the hotel set, to Grant himself, who brings a fully shaped star image into the film and acts as the central agent in the story. Between these extremes are the messenger boy, who must respond to Grant's signal, and the three businessmen around the table, who are given a few lines of dialogue. One of these men, however, is different from the others. For some reason—perhaps for the sake of verisimilitude, perhaps out of sheer playfulness—he has been allowed to cup a hand over his ear, lean over the table, and frown in bafflement because he cannot follow the conversation. His gestures, unnecessary to the cause-effect chain of the story, make him a slightly more identifiable character than his companions, and in one sense more of an actor.

In a more obvious form, acting in movies involves still another quality—a mastery, skill, or inventiveness that is implied in the normative use of the word performance. In fact all types of art or social behavior are concerned at some level with this sort of parading of expertise. Writing about Balzac, Roland Barthes remarks that "the classic author becomes a performer at the moment he evinces his power of conducting meaning"[25]. One might say the same thing of a modernist like James Joyce, or of Barthes himself, whose verbal skill is foregrounded on every page and whose intellectual tours de force made him a celebrity. In literature, we can even speak of a "performative" sentence, as on the opening page of *Moby Dick*:

> Whenever I find myself growing grim about the mouth; whenever it is a
> damp, drizzly November in my soul; whenever I find myself pausing before
> coffin warehouses, and bringing up the rear of every funeral I meet; and
> especially whenever my hypos get such an upper hand of me, that it requires
> a strong moral principle to prevent me from deliberately stepping into the

---

[24] *Typage*, a term coined by Soviet directors in the twenties, should not be confused with "type casting." Typage depends on cultural stereotypes, but, more important, it emphasizes the physical eccentricities of actors (often, by preference, nonprofessionals). Kuleshov argued that "because film needs real material and not a pretense of reality... it is not theater actors but 'types' who should act in film—that is, people who, in themselves, as they were born, present some kind of interest for cinematic treatment.... A person with an ordinary, normal exterior, however good-looking he may be, is not needed in cinema" (63-4).

[25] Barthes, Roland. *S/Z: An Essay*. Trans. Richard Miller. New York: Hill and Wang, 1974, p. 174.

street, and methodically knocking people's hats off—then, I account it high
time to get to sea as soon as I can.

Melville keeps the sentence in play, stringing out parallel constructions like a singer
holding his breath, until that final moment when the period brings us to rest beside the sea. To
read his words, we need to employ skills of our own, mentally repeating the rhythms, or perhaps
interpreting them aloud so that our vocal cords participate in a dance of meaning. Oratory and
most kinds of theatrical acting involve similar effects, and for that reason star performances in
movies are often structured so as to give the audience a chance to appreciate the player's
physical or mental accomplishments. Film problematizes our ability to measure these effects
simply because it allows for so much manipulation of the image, throwing the power of
"conducting" meaning into the hands of a director; nevertheless, one of the common pleasures of
moviegoing derives from our feeling that an actor is doing something remarkable. Garfield
playing poker, Bogart nodding his head, a minor player in a crowded scene—all these are
clearly different from Chaplin/Hinkle in *The Great Dictator* (1940), bouncing a globe around a
room in a long shot, executing a brilliant comic ballet while dressed as Hitler...

RHETORIC AND EXPRESSIVE TECHNIQUE

from *Acting in the Cinema* (1988) by James Naremore

> Must not anyone who wants to move the crowd be an actor who impersonates himself? Must he not first translate himself into grotesque obviousness and then present his whole person and cause in this coarsened and simplified version?
>
> —Friedrich Nietzsche, *The Gay Science*, 1882

> 1 would almost say that the best screen actor is the man who can do nothing extremely well.
>
> —Alfred Hitchcock, "Direction," 1937

The quotations above indicate how much our conception of acting has changed during the past century. Hitchcock's remark sounds a good deal like Spencer Tracy's famous advice to his fellow players: "Just know your lines and don't bump into the furniture." Charmingly unpretentious as Hitchcock and Tracy may sound, however, they are quite misleading. All performing situations employ a physics of movement and gesture that makes signs readable; in this sense Nietzsche's observation that actors translate their person into a simplified version still holds true. The actual work for people who appear in movies or television seems to involve a compromise between "obviousness" and "doing nothing." Spencer Tracy was a master of such practical considerations, and as a result his behavior in films differs from ordinary social interaction.

At its simplest level, the activity of any performer can be described in terms of a mode of address and a degree of ostensiveness. For example, in most circumstances of everyday communication the interlocutor's gaze is directed toward an individual or a small group in the immediate vicinity; no special energy is required for the "presentation of self," and considerable latitude is allowed for insignificant lapses, irrelevant movement, or glances away from the audience. In theatrical events, the voice and body are subject to a more rigorous control. Thus in oratory, the performance is formalized and "projected"—movements are at once less frequent and more emphatic, and the speaker tries to maintain eye contact by distributing his or her glance around a crowd. By contrast, the typical TV newscast makes its rhetorical strategy nearly invisible, indirectly confirming Derrida's argument about the cultural valuation of "speech" over "writing." The news anchorman is framed in a bust-sized close-up, directing his gaze at the camera; he speaks to a crowd, but he thinks of it as an abstracted, generalized individual with an intimate frontal view. The performance therefore becomes a blend of public speaking and everyday behavior—more formalized, intense, and "sincere" than ordinary conversation but projected less strongly than a talk from a podium. The speaker's balancing act between clear, standardized enunciation (once known as the "telephone voice") and warm, close-up address also requires him to adopt a fairly rigid posture, since any quick movement threatens to disrupt what Goffman has called the "front" for the performance. At this range, even a minute shift of the body could decenter the careful framing, and a glance downward could fill the screen with a bald spot or a meaningless expanse of hair. Hence the player uses a teleprompter, "anchoring" us with a forthright gaze, masking the fact that he is reading. If any part of the machinery were to refuse to collaborate in this rhetoric—if, for example, the camera were to move a few degrees to the left or right, so that Dan Rather seemed to be looking offscreen toward nothing—then we would witness a sudden transformation of naturalized communication into artifice, a revelation that televised speech is simply another form of writing.

On television variety or talk shows of the Carson type, both the degree of ostensiveness and the mode of address can change rapidly, moving from vaudeville comedy to intimate exchanges, from showbiz to semidocumentary. In the chatty episodes, players cultivate a shifting gaze, aimed now at the interviewer or interviewee, now at the studio audience, now at the lens of the camera. Whatever the situation, they behave more theatrically than they would in an everyday encounter. The more skillful and eager performers know how to enter a stage and find a mark, how to shake hands with the host without turning their backs to the camera, and how to sit down without "bumping into the furniture" or searching too much behind them for the seat. They know how to align their bodies with the slightly outturned position of the chairs, and for the most part they take care to focus their attention on the center of theatrical interest, seldom turning to look randomly at the monitor or the crew. During conversations they usually take turns speaking, treating the camera with the good manners of polite society, as if they were drawing it into the circle of talk with brief glances toward the lens. The trick behind their act is to stage a "natural" give-and-take that is tightly framed, directed at several potential audiences, and viewed somewhat obliquely.

Dramatic theater involves still another strategy, marked by two broadly different playing styles. Imagine two ways of staging *Hamlet*: in the first, the actor places his hand to his brow, turns slightly away from the audience, and mutters "To be or not to be" as if speaking to himself. In the second, the actor poses the question with full rhetorical force, remaining in character but looking directly at the audience like an orator who is genuinely baffled by the philosophical issue. These two styles—the representational and the presentational—can make up a formal dialectic, as they do in Shakespeare, where characters frequently step outside the ongoing action and become commentators. A number of dramatic movies (usually adapted from theater pieces) have employed a similar technique: consider Brando in *Teahouse of the August Moon* (1955), Michael Caine in *Alfie* (1966), Glenda Jackson in *Stevie* (1983), and so on. Likewise, in certain types of vaudeville-inspired comedy the actors use direct address to disrupt illusion: Groucho Marx steps up to the camera and advises us to go out to the lobby for popcorn; Bob Hope turns to the lens and makes wisecracks; George Bums interrupts the action of his TV sitcom to chat with viewers about the plot. In radical or modernist cinema, speeches of the same sort have didactic or perhaps deconstructive implications. Godard's films provide the best-known examples, but notice also *Francisca* (1983), a masterwork by Manoel de Oliveira, which sometimes gives us two versions of an action, first in representational and then in presentational form.

Brecht's quarrel with Stanislavsky had centered largely on a need to restore presentational techniques to the stage (when he and Piscator adopted the term "epic theater," they were borrowing not from a Hollywood press agent but from Goethe, who had used "epic poetry" to designate a technique of narration). For that reason, it is tempting to link presentational rhetoric with activist or "progressive" strategies. We should remember, however, that direct address appears just as often in television commercials or hard-core pornography as in radical drama. In the next chapter I shall have more to say about Godard's particular use of the technique to foster the *Verfremdungseffekt*; for now, I want only to emphasize that narrative movies depend chiefly on representation—in other words, the characters seem to be speaking to one another even though their performance is aimed at an audience beyond the "fourth wall." Different performing methods or styles of blocking can make acting seem more or less presentational, depending on the emotional tone of the players, their movements in relation to the camera, and the degree to which they mimic well-known forms of behavior; nevertheless, screen actors usually pretend that the audience is not present.

This representational rhetoric extends to every aspect of the filmed spectacle. The screen is a picture-frame arrangement rather like the proscenium arch (until fairly recently motion picture theaters were outfitted with curtains that drew apart as the projection began); hence it is common for Hollywood directors to speak of the 180-degree rule as the "stage line," and in arranging a given shot they necessarily think in many of the same spatial terms as a theatrical metteur-en-scéne. For the most part, performance in film, as in theater, is a matter of "acting sideways," so that audiences are given a clear view into every encounter. The essential difference from stage convention, as the British actor Peter Barkworth has remarked, is that "in the theatre you need to widen your performance so the whole audience can see you, whereas for the cameras you need to narrow it down".[26]

In either case, the need to make events at least obliquely visible puts a good many constraints on behavior. Suppose, for example, that a scene on the proscenium stage involves a single player in a standing pose. He or she may take a variety of stances relative to the audience, ranging from full front to full back; the front view is the strongest and "stagiest" position, whereas the full back view is usually regarded as "weak"—a device used to give the platform an added dimension, to conceal or suggest emotions, or to lend an air of verisimilitude. The stance most common in representational theater is a profile, usually of an "open," three-quarter variety, which gives the audience a clear view of the actor's expression while maintaining the illusion that spectators are not present. When another actor is added to the scene, the two players are said to "share" or "give" positions, depending on whether their faces are equally visible: if they line up parallel to the arch, they are in a shared relation; but if they are set on the diagonal, they cannot exchange glances without one player assuming a "weak" stance.[27] Thus players with important narrative or expositional functions usually receive the strong focus of the arrangement, facing more or less toward the auditorium, and crossing movements or changes of position are executed so as to preserve the audience's view.

The chief mark of realistic, psychological drama from the late nineteenth century onward has been the tendency of the actors to turn away, moving out of the strong or shared positions, facing one another on the diagonal so as to make the stage seem less "rhetorical," more "natural." Hence the Moscow Art Theater's famous production of *The Seagull* in 1898 opened with the actors standing with their backs to the audience, and the American tour of the Abbey Theater in 1911-12 was heralded by critics because the company frequently played to the rear of the stage; at about the same time, Mrs. Fiske created a sensation by speaking with her back turned or by walking into dark corners at highly dramatic moments.

Roughly contemporary developments in cinema can be understood similarly as the creation of cinematic strategies to conceal the fundamental "staginess" of acting. As Janet Staiger has shown, a full-scale change toward the rhetoric of psychological realism occurred in Hollywood between 1908 and the mid-teens, when the industry shifted to a director-centered mode of production and began to manufacture feature-length dramatic films that took their subject matter, aesthetic values, and talent from the increasingly intimate and naturalistic New York stage.[28] By contrast, the "primitive" cinema had been devoted to straightforward action sequences, paying little or no attention to the psychological motives of characters. Except in

[26] Barkworth, Peter. *About Acting.* London: Seker and Warburg, 1984, p. 52.
[27] Naremore adapted these terms from a textbook, *An Introduction to Acting,* by Stanley Kahan (Boston: Allyn and Bacon, 1985).
[28] Staiger, Janet. "The Eyes are Really the Focus: Photoplay Acting and Film Form and Style" *Wide Angle* 6, no. 4 (1985), p. 18.

kissing scenes, portrait shots, or occasional inserts, the camera was positioned at a distance, so that figures on the screen approximated proscenium scale and the spectator seemed to occupy an orchestra seat. Performers in these early films sometimes behaved with easygoing restraint; in general, however, they moved parallel to the camera, stood in three-quarter profile when they addressed one another, and gesticulated vividly to compensate for their relative distance from the audience. (Edwin Porter's *Uncle Tom's Cabin* [1903] is a good example of the technique, as is F. S. Armitage's somewhat more realistic *The Nihilists* [1906].) Sometimes, too, they adopted a rudimentary sign language in place of intertitles; Kristin Thompson has noted that an actor in the earliest films might signal his desire for "just one drink" by pointing to himself, holding up one finger, and then miming the action of drinking. Thompson calls the technique "pantomime"[29], but a better term would be "codified gesture," because the actors were relying on a sort of writing with the hands rather than on the culturally transmitted, broadly expressive gestures of most nineteenth-century theater.[30]

The first step in facilitating the change toward psychological realism was to shorten the distance between actors and camera. Prior to 1909, scenes were usually played up to a line drawn perpendicular to the lens axis at a distance of twelve feet, with the camera set at eye level; soon afterward, a "nine-foot line" came into vogue, so that the standard group shot framed the upper three-quarters of the actors' bodies, with the camera at chest height.[31] The screen now seemed a Bazinian mask, suggesting a world beyond its edges and giving the spectator a sense of being in the theatrical space. The new arrangement (called "the American foreground" by some producers and later dubbed the plan américain by the French) facilitated a wider, more subtle range of gesture and allowed greater variety in the staging of entrances and exits. Actors could turn their backs when they moved into the foreground; eventually they walked on and off from behind the camera, something they had done previously only in films shot outdoors. By these means, the movements of players could be rigorously subordinated to a narrative economy: as Chaplin remarked, "you don't want an actor to walk an unnecessary distance unless there is a special reason, for walking is not dramatic".[32] Equally important, the actors could now pose in conversational situations, allowing the camera to focus on extended emotional exchanges between two characters at close quarters.

Griffith's later work depended heavily on these medium shots, and on "cut-ins" for tight framings of faces and details. In general, however, when his players conversed, they stood parallel to the camera in shared relationships. Subsequent directors relied more on the shot/reverse shot combination, which allowed actors to remain still, their bodies largely out of sight, while the camera selected whose face was "given." With this technique, a certain amount of visibly rhetorical blocking could be eliminated, and the smallest psychological nuances could be acted in a pattern of action and reaction. Once the system of interlocking eyeline matches and "cinematographic" camera angles was in place, the actor could play a given shot in any relation to the camera and still seem to be working in representational form. The camera was no longer simply an audience; it had become a kind of narrator, so that it could momentarily take up the position of a player in the scene, looking another player in the eye.

Realistic découpage made the most extreme frontal stances seem naturalistic, and the talkies ultimately provided everything else that was necessary to "transparent," fully representational performances. Directional microphones, multitrack sound editing, looping, sound mixes—all these devices were ultimately employed to render intimate, low-key behavior in ways that would have dazzled Stanislavsky. The highly artificial conventions of the sound

[29] Bordwell, David, Janet Staiger, and Kristin Thompson. *The Classical Hollywood Cinema: Film Style and Mode of Production to 1960.* New York: Columbia University Press, 1985, p. 189.
[30] A similar distinction between "pantomime" and "codified gesture" may be found in Betty and Franz Bauml, *A Dictionary of Gestures*, 1.
[31] Salt, Barry. *Film Style and Technology: History and Analysis.* London: Starword, 1983, p. 106.
[32] Chaplin, Charles. *My Autobiography.* New York: Simon and Schuster, 1964, p. 151.

mix even allowed viewers to spy on "private" behavior in the midst of "public" settings: as one of countless examples that could be chosen, notice the scene early in William Wyler's adaptation of the popular Broadway play *The Heiress* (1949), where a quiet, shyly flirtatious conversation between Montgomery Clift and Olivia de Havilland can be heard in the midst of a party, while an orchestra is supposedly playing for a crowd of dancers nearby.

Prior to the full advent of sound, however, the movies had already achieved something akin to a Stanislavskian ideal, as in the performances of Eleanor Boardman in *The Crowd* (1925) or Louise Brooks in *Diary of a Lost Girl* (1929). The most important technical device in fostering this naturalism was the close-up, which became a perfect vehicle for what Stanislavsky had called "gestureless moments." Here is V.I. Pudovkin, commenting on behavior in portrait shots:

> Stanislavski felt that an actor striving towards truth should be able to avoid the element of *portraying* his feelings to the audience, and should be able to transmit to it the whole fullness of the content of the acted image in some moment of half-mystic communion. Of course, he came up against a brick wall in his endeavors to find a solution to this problem in the theater.
>
> It is amazing that the solution to this very problem is not only not impracticable in the cinema, but extreme paucity of gesture, often literal immobility, is absolutely indispensable in it. For example, in the close-up, in which gesture is completely dispensed with, inasmuch as the body of the actor is simply not seen.[33]

Nowhere is the romantic idealism underlying Stanislavskian aesthetics more apparent than in this quote, where the close-up is regarded as a mirror of the soul; Brecht, of course, would have argued that actors are always and everywhere "portraying," and that they ought to be forthright about the process. Pudovkin writes as if "truth" could be seen shining transparently through faces, forgetting that the muscular arrangement of the eyes and mouth are themselves a form of gesture, even when the actor is "living the part." And yet Pudovkin is correct when he describes typical film acting as a relatively passive phenomenon—not only because the meaning of expressions can be determined by editing, but because the camera takes on a rhetorical function when it selects details or changes the scale of an image.

The camera's mobility and tight framing of faces, its ability to "give" the focus of the screen to any player at any moment, also means that films tend to favor reactions. On stage or in the standard middle-distance shot of a movie, the eye of the spectator automatically follows whoever moves or speaks; but in film it is possible to cut away, focusing on a relatively immobile bystander. As a result, some of the most memorable Hollywood performances have consisted largely of players isolated in close-up, responding nonverbally to offscreen events: William Powell trying to maintain his decorum while Mischa Auer acts like an ape in *My Man Godfrey* (1935); Brandon de Wilde gasping in bug-eyed awe at Alan Ladd's fast draw in *Shane* (1953); James Stewart squirming in helpless anxiety as he watches Grace Kelly being manhandled in *Rear Window* (1954). In each of these cases, one character becomes audience for another; the close-ups usually involve intense, rather exaggerated facial expressions, but in one sense the actors could be regarded as "doing nothing extremely well."

The "gestureless" form of classic cinema nevertheless involves a good many physical problems for the actors. Tight framing requires them to cultivate unusual stillness or restraint; in two-shots, for example, they often stand closer together than they would in actual encounters, sometimes working from ludicrous positions that look perfectly natural to the

---

33 Pudovkin, Vsevold. *Film Technique and Film Acting: The Cinema Writings of V.I. Pudovkin*. Trans. Ivor Montagu. New York: Bonanza Books, 1949, pp. 334-5.

camera. Occasionally a small mannerism or emotional reaction that would be automatic in real life can utterly destroy a scene, so that players move counter to their normal instincts. Hume Cronyn has recalled how he learned this lesson in a scene from Hitchcock's *Shadow of a Doubt* (1943):

> During the meal, I said something upsetting to the character played by Teresa Wright. She turned to me with unexpected violence. I stood up in embarrassment and surprise and automatically took a step backward. However, at the point of the rise, the camera moved in to hold us in a close two-shot, and to accommodate it—that is, to stay in the frame—it became necessary for me to change that instinctive movement so that when I got up from the chair, *I took a step toward the person from whom I was retreating....* I was convinced that the action would look idiotic on the screen, but I was wrong... I had to admit that the occasion passed almost unnoticed even by me.[34]

The filming of physical actions can become so complex that the set has to be dotted with gaffer's tape indicating where the simplest movements must start or end. Even such details as the tilt of a head or the position of a hand are matters of great concern, and the combined action of camera and players in the longer takes creates problems of timing and body placement equivalent to those of a formal dance. Later in this book, I comment on one such scene in *Holiday* (1938), where Katharine Hepburn descends a staircase at a crowded wedding reception, urgently searching for Cary Grant. The action is viewed from a considerable distance, yet Hepburn's alternating expressions—friendly smiles and worried glances around the room—are always visible; throughout the shot she remains at the center of the composition, her dark dress contrasting with the white walls, her quick descent set against the upward flow of massed bodies, her face bobbing into full view at strategic moments between the shoulders of extras.

Movie actors therefore learn to control and modulate behavior to fit a variety of situations, suiting their actions to a medium that might view them at any distance, height, or angle and that sometimes changes the vantage point within a single shot. Different directors have exercised authority over these patterns in different ways—some, like Hitchcock, relying heavily on reaction shots, others, like Hawks, cultivating a looser, middle-distance framing and a greater sense of spontaneous interplay. In all films, however, the behavior of players is designed to make significant faces and gestures visible, important dialogue audible. Hence the average two- or three-figure composition will involve a "shared" position, with the actors in three-quarter profile to the camera; larger groupings will be arranged so that figures on the outer fringes of a crowd stand to the sides of the frame, their faces turned slightly toward the lens, leaving an open space for the sight line of a hypothetical viewer. David Bordwell has described the technique as a "classical use of frontality." The result, he notes, "is an odd rubbernecking.... Standing groups are arranged in horizontal or diagonal lines or in half-circles; people seldom close ranks as they would in real life"[35]. Once again, directors have different ways of managing these ensembles. John Ford's *The Man Who Shot Liberty Valance* (1962) is blocked in shallow, one-dimensional fashion, so much like a high-school play that it looks almost Brechtian; by contrast, Orson Welles's *Touch of Evil* (1958) is filled with decentered arrangements, extreme diagonals, and figures who pop in and out of distant comers. And yet the problem for actors in both films is much the same: they must respect the principle of "frontality," playing within the sight line of a camera, never letting their actions disintegrate into truly random, contingent behavior.

---

[34] Kahan, Stanley. *Introduction to Acting*. Boston: Allyn and Bacon, 1985, pp. 297-8.
[35] Bordwell, David, Janet Staiger, and Kristin Thompson. *The Classical Hollywood Cinema: Film Style and Mode of Production to 1960*. New York: Columbia University Press, 1985, p. 51.

The job of making expression visible is further complicated by the fact that people in films do more than just stand, talk, and maneuver themselves into different arrangements. An important principle of realist acting, borrowed from theater, is to devise situations in which the characters talk about one thing while doing something else. Lombard and Powell wash dishes as they discuss their future in *My Man Godfrey*; Hepburn and Tracy give one another a massage as they debate courtroom ethics in *Adam's Rib* (1949); Kirk Douglas and Mitzi Gaynor dance the twist as they have a quarrel in *For Love or Money* (1963), and so forth.[36] If the script does not actually call for some combination of doing and talking, the better actors usually try to invent business, or they sometimes use the simplest action as a rhythmic counterpoint to speech (one of Olivier's favorite tricks was to walk slowly while talking quickly, or vice versa). Some situations create special problems: a small book could be written about eating scenes in movies, showing how actors regulate their biting, chewing, and swallowing, or only toy with the dish to accommodate dialogue.[37] By the same token, scenes involving kissing, fighting, and social dancing always put complicated rhetorical demands on the participants, turning them into virtual marionettes.

And though it is true that movies have helped to foster a restrained, intimate style, it is wrong to assume that "good" film acting always conforms to the low-level ostensiveness of ordinary conversation. As a general rule, Hollywood has required that supporting players, ethnic minorities, and women be more animated or broadly expressive than white male leads. The intensity of behavior also varies somewhat between genres, and a great many nonmusical films involve the actors in "putting on a show"—consider the music hall sequence at the beginning of *39 Steps* (1935), or the "Tonight Show" monologue delivered by Robert De Niro at the end of *King of Comedy* (1983). The most ordinary settings can involve highly theatrical moments, indications of the way "staginess" interpenetrates everyday life: in *Old Acquaintance* (1946), Miriam Hopkins plays a neurotic, self-dramatizing novelist who constantly wrings her hands and holds her brow like a heroine of Victorian melodrama; and near the beginning of *Mean Streets* (1976), Robert De Niro enters a neighborhood bar with all the brassy, outrageous showmanship of a burlesque comic. In fact a single role in a film can involve an extraordinary range of actorly energy—at one moment Charles Foster Kane is whispering "Rosebud," his mouth filling the entire screen, and at the next he is a tiny figure at the end of a hall delivering a campaign speech; in one scene he holds an intimate tête à tête with Susan Alexander, and in another he screams from the top of a stairwell, threatening to "get" Boss Jim Gettys. Some films pitch the entire performance at the level of a quiet, personal interaction, as in the conversation between Wally Shawn and Andre Gregory in *My Dinner with Andre* (1980)—a middlebrow philosophical movie that is deeply concerned with the ideology of "being" instead of "acting." Other films play everything at full tilt: both *The Man Who Shot Liberty Valance* and *Touch of Evil*, despite their differences, are acted with a volume and intensity suitable to a fair-sized theater. For the purpose of analysis, therefore, it is better to speak of the specific performing circumstances required by a given movie, acknowledging a shifting cinematic rhetoric that allows room for the full spectrum of behavior.

In general, naturalistic styles of performance try to conceal or modify all the rhetorical devices I have been describing. Actors in "ethnic" films like *The Godfather* (1972) or in middle-class domestic dramas like *Heartburn* (1986) tend to slop down food and talk with their mouths

[36] The technique is enshrined in a modest little scene in *The Bad and the Beautiful* (1953), when movie-producer Kirk Douglas gives aspiring star Lana Turner a lesson in acting. In the movie-within-the-movie, Turner plays a young woman in a tobacco shop, looking over a paper back novel as Gilbert Roland enters to buy a pack of cigarettes. Roland stares at her and she glances up from the book to ask, "See anything interesting?" The director yells "cut," and Douglas takes Turner aside, whispering something we cannot hear. The scene is shot again, and this time she makes her line more provocative by continuing to read as she speaks.

[37] For a particularly instructive example of the rhetoric of eating in films, notice the scene *in Desk Set* (1957), when Tracy gives Hepburn an IQ test as they both munch on sandwiches. At appropriate moments, Tracy leaves a shred of food visible on his lips, and Hepburn makes a great show of trying to talk around a stuffed mouth.

full. Likewise, they occasionally turn away from the camera, speak softly and rapidly, repeat words, slur or throw away lines, sometimes ask "Huh?" or let dialogue overlap.[38] To achieve the effect of spontaneity, they preface speeches with meaningless intensifiers or qualifiers—a technique especially apparent on television soap operas, where nearly every remark is preceded with "look," "now," or "well." Naturalistic actors also cultivate a halting, somewhat groping style of speech: instead of saying "I am very distressed," the actor will say "I am dis-...very distressed." By the same logic, he or she will start an action, such as drinking from a glass, and then pause to speak before carrying the action through.[39]

Because naturalistic filmmakers are enamored of what William Gillette called "the illusion of the first time," they also encourage a good deal of improvisation, trying to create situations where the actors will be forced to fumble along, or where one player will do something unexpected, forcing the others to react spontaneously. In one sense, of course, there is no such thing as improvisation in movies because everything is recorded and subject to manipulation; nevertheless, certain directors (Hawks, Cassavetes, Altman) have encouraged their casts to develop scenes as the cameras roll, and players sometimes transform mistakes into clever pieces of business, just as they do on the stage.[40] Even when they improvise in this restricted sense, however, actors usually observe the rules of classical rhetoric, aiming everything obliquely toward the camera. When they develop their own lines, they tend to lapse into monologue, playing from relatively static, frontal positions with a second actor nearby who nods or makes short interjections. (See Jane Fonda's rambling talks with her psychiatrist in *Klute* [1971], or Robert De Niro's long, comic explanation of his gambling debts to Harvey Keitel in *Mean Streets*.) Thus naturalism, which began as an attack on rhetoric or "staginess," remains in the end an orderly, formal construction, never radically challenging the conventions of proscenium drama.

Consequently, even when naturalistic movie actors appear to be doing nothing, they are often quite busy. As one last example, consider *Father of the Bride* (1950), in which Spencer Tracy plays the role of a suburban paterfamilias who sometimes has trouble remembering his lines and avoiding awkward contact with the furniture. At his daughter's wedding ceremony, Tracy's character has to speak two words, step backward a couple of paces, and sit on an empty church pew. On the eve of the wedding, he dreams that he cannot speak, that the church floor has turned to rubber, and that the audience is laughing wildly at his helpless condition. Meanwhile Tracy the actor, impersonating this beleaguered fellow, has to perform a variety of complex rhetorical tasks. Occasionally he speaks directly to the camera—as in the opening shots, where he addresses us while slumping back in an armchair and wearily removing his

[38] The technique of overlapping dialogue seems to have been popularized by Alfred Lunt and Lynn Fontaine on the Broadway stage in the twenties. It was quite standard at the beginning of the talkies, but some of the early sound technicians advised actors against it. Mary Astor has commented on those days: "In [*Holiday* (1930)], it was impossible to 'overlap,' which is natural in conversation... the sound man was king. If he couldn't hear it, we couldn't shoot it.... You couldn't talk and pace up and down. For example, if the action started with you standing beside a table and then included a move to a chair by the fireplace, you could speak into a mike at the table, but you couldn't talk on the way over; you'd have to wait until you sat down—where there was another mike in the fireplace" (quoted in Leyda, 16).
[39] One recent example of these naturalistic rhetorical qualities is Woody Allen's *Hannah and Her Sisters* (1986)—a profoundly Stanislavskian movie, despite its comedy and its occasional use of intertitles. (Significantly, Allen's script alludes to Chekhov, the Moscow Art Theater's favorite playwright, and with a friend, one of Hannah's sisters starts up a business called "The Stanislavsky Catering Company.") The film depends on an ensemble of actors who are sharply attuned to the manners of a specific New York social set. In two-shots, one of these players either delivers crucial lines from a "closed" position or steps briefly out of sight; likewise, some of the most intimate conversations are staged in parks or city streets, with the microphone capturing every low-key word while the actors are viewed as tiny figures in the distance.
[40] Katharine Hepburn accidentally broke a heel off her shoe during a scene in *Bringing Up Baby* (1938), and transformed the mishap into a comic walk that remains in the film. George C. Scott slips on the floor during a big speech in *Dr. Strangelove* (1963), and simply turns the fall into a somersault, popping up to finish his sentence. A minor instance of this sort of "playing through" is a scene in *Chinatown* (1974), when Jack Nicholson can't get his cigarette lighter to function. Director Roman Polanski chose to preserve that take, not only because it lends a quality of verisimilitude, but because it makes us vaguely aware of the actor behind the performance.

shoes. Elsewhere he plays fully representational scenes that involve talking about one thing while doing something else: he has an argument with Elizabeth Taylor as he eats ice cream, and then patches up the quarrel during a midnight snack, as he munches bread and butter. During the climactic wedding reception, his character is trapped in the kitchen, trying to mix dozens of different drinks for the guests while making small talk. Throughout the scene, Tracy verges on slapstick comedy, fumbling with ice cubes and glasses, spraying a bottle of coke on himself as he tries to open it—all the while timing every joke and registering every pained expression with exactly the proper ostensiveness. We might say that the effectiveness of his performance, and of good naturalistic playing in general, consists in part of an ability to suggest disorder by means of orderliness—thereby letting us see the distance between a character who is awkward and a player who is in full theatrical control.

• • •

[....] Circus acrobatics, vaudeville comedy, and jazz music have all contributed to the way people stand and move in films, and various twentieth-century schools of acting have fostered their own styles. Meyerhold and the Soviet avant-garde of the twenties, under the influence of Marxism, Taylorism, and early Hollywood,[41] tried to create gymnastic actors who would evoke "the skilled worker in action". Meanwhile the Stanislavskians felt that players should be relaxed and open to sensation, as loose as animals in the wild. Sometimes they supported their instruction with Rousseauistic appeals to the "natural man," as when Richard Boleslavsky contrasts the ideal actor with people in the street:

> Let us take a look back at our childhood: on the way we were taught to carry ourselves, the conventionality of our clothes and shoes; on the unnatural way of our modern locomotion compared to the one indicated by nature itself. Think of rush hour in streetcars or subways, when we travel for hours suspended like grapes...and you'll understand how much energy we are wasting and how far we are removed from the free body of an ancient Roman or an animal. Compare the free stride of a savage with the walk of a modern girl.[42]

The Meyerholdian actor and the Stanislavskian actor therefore worked from different physical assumptions, and they could look as opposite from one another, even in repose, as Buster Keaton and Marlon Brando.

A still more crucial influence on the physical quality of acting in this century relates to two broadly different techniques for producing expressions. At one extreme, the actor develops the body as an instrument, learning a kinesics, or movement vocabulary; at the other, he or she is encouraged to behave more or less normally, letting gesture or facial expression rise "naturally" out of deeply felt emotion. Professional players have always spoken about the value of both skills, but as I have indicated, modern dramatic literature strongly favors the second. To explain the difference between the two, critics and players usually resort to an inside/outside antithesis fundamental to Western thinking. Thus Olivier, who defines acting as "the art of

---

[41] Frederick Winslow Taylor was the first American efficiency expert, and his studies of industrial movement were imitated to a certain degree in the Soviet Union during the period of the NEP. A satiric biography of Taylor ("The American Plan") can be found in John Dos Passos's *The Big Money* (1935). On the influence of Hollywood in early Soviet avant-garde acting, see Sergei Gerassimov, "Out of the Factory of the Eccentric Actor": "Grigori Kozintsev taught the principal matter, called 'cine-gesture.' It was based on the mathematical precision of American comic and detective films. The actor was required not to 'feel.' The very word 'feeling' was only ever pronounced with derisive grimaces accompanied by scornful laughter from the whole troupe" (Schnitzer and Martin, 114).

[42] Cole, Toby and Helen Krich Chinoy, eds. *Actors on Acting.* New York: Crown, 1970, p. 513.

persuasion," has remarked almost apologetically, "I'm afraid I do work mostly from the outside in... I think personally that most film players are interior people".[43]

The modern stress on "interior" work becomes especially evident in English theater around 1890, in the debates over Diderot's paradox that broke out when the playwright William Archer published *Masks or Faces? A Study in the Psychology of Acting* (1888). Attempting to overturn Diderot's famous argument that actors are unaffected by the emotions they portray, Archer interviewed a number of professional thespians and found that nearly all of them were quite emotional, "living the part" to some degree. The real significance of Archer's research, however, was not its attack on neoclassical "reserve," or its proof of a relatively unimportant point. Actors have always been caught up in the passions of drama, and there is every reason to suppose that they felt their emotions as deeply in the nineteenth century as they do today. At bottom, Archer was concerned less with emotionalism than with what theater historians now call the mimetic or "pantomime" traditions performance technique that relies on conventionalized poses to help the actor indicate "fear," "sorrow," "hope," "confusion," and so forth.

"Pantomime" in this sense has something in common with the techniques of silent performance, but it is a much broader concept, indicating a whole attitude toward the mechanics of gesture. As Benjamin McArthur has pointed out, for most actors in the nineteenth century, "each emotion had its appropriate gesture and facial expression, which were passed down from one generation to the next.... Books were written analyzing, classifying, and breaking down gestures and expressions into their component parts".[44] Until fairly recently, the old "cookbook" tradition seemed almost to define acting. "The fundamental concept of codified pantomime," John Delman has remarked, "is several thousand years old, while the modern tendency to laugh off all codes and conventions is younger than the memory of living men".[45]

In place of pantomime, Archer was tentatively, almost covertly proposing a naturalistic style; inspired by Ibsen and a new wave of European dramatists, he was promoting the notion that acting should be less flamboyant and contrived, more attuned to the psychological dynamic of everyday life. Repeatedly, he insists that actorly emotions should not be "imitated": "We weep our own tears, we laugh our own laughter.... Therefore I think there is a clear distinction between mimicking tricks or habits and yielding to emotion or contagion. Roughly speaking, one is an affair of the surface, the other of the centers".[46]

Archer is symptomatic of a so-called revolutionary trend, a shift from a semiotic to a psychological conception of performance that began with the rise of drawing-room dramas in the 1850s, but that can be localized in the period between 1880 and 1920. The development of this more or less subjective approach was uneven; it left certain marks on Griffith and the movies (Griffith had in fact acted Ibsen on the stage before becoming a film director), but its full-scale arrival in America was delayed. Louise Brooks recalls how affected her contemporaries in New York theater:

> In the twenties, under the supervision of old producers like David Belasco, stage direction dated back to the feverish technique of the English theatre before the plays of Ibsen, Chekhov, and Bernard Shaw revolutionized it, introducing what Lytton Strachey called "a new quiet and subtle style of acting, a prose style." In New York, we began to realize how bad our directors and actors were when the new young English stars began to appear on Broadway. There was Lynne Fontaine in *Pygmalion*, Roland Young in *The Last of Mrs. Cheney*, Leslie Howard in *Berkeley Square*, and Gertrude

[43] Cole, Toby and Helen Krich Chinoy, eds. *Actors on Acting*. New York: Crown, 1970, pp. 410-11.
[44] McArthur, Benjamin. *Actors and American Culture, 1880-1920*. Philadelphia: Temple University Press, 1984, p. 171.
[45] Delman, John, Jr. *The Art of Acting*. New York: Harper, 1949, p. 241.
[46] Cole, Toby and Helen Krich Chinoy, eds. *Actors on Acting*. New York: Crown, 1970, pp. 164-65.

Lawrence and Noel Coward in *Private Lives*. These marvelous actors of realism spoke their lines as if they had just thought of them. They moved about the stage with ease. And they paid attention to-they actually heard-what other actors were saying.[47]

The single most important exponent of the new, "quiet" naturalism is of course Stanislavsky, who was not conscientiously studied in America until the late twenties, but who, in the very year that William Archer's book was published, had begun his work at the Moscow Art and Literary Society. It is difficult to find a single individual of comparable importance who stands for the older, pantomime tradition, but a leading candidate is François Delsarte (1811-71), a Parisian elocutionist who made one of the earliest attempts to codify expressive gestures for actors and public speakers. Even though Delsarte's fragmentary writing is now virtually unknown, his way of thinking about "performance signs" helped determine American acting at the beginning of the century. His influence persisted alongside psychological realism during the period of silent cinema, and in some ways he deserves reconsideration in our own time.

Delsarte paid a good deal of attention to what he himself called the semiotic function of gesture (a term he took from Locke, and used well in advance of either Peirce or Saussure). His work led to prescriptive, formulaic descriptions of actorly poses, as when he tells us that "conscious menace—that of a master to his subordinates—is expressed by a movement of the head carried from above downward," or when he claims that "any interrogation made with crossed arms must partake of a threat".[48] Rules such as these are based on a crude faculty psychology, and they ignore the contextual determinants of meaning; nevertheless, most writers on acting in the nineteenth century adopted a similar approach. (Two important manuals in English were Henry Siddon's *Practical Illustrations of Rhetorical Gesture and Action* and Gustave Garcia's *Actor's Art*, both published in 1882 and filled with pictures of typical poses and gestures.) Furthermore, Delsarte had a significant impact on public life at the turn of the century-especially in the United States, where his disciples enjoyed a tremendous vogue.

Delsarte's teaching had been imported to America by Steele MacKaye (1844-94), the manager of New York's Madison Square Theater and the immediate predecessor of David Belasco. The elaborate melodramas MacKaye staged in his specially constructed "Spectatorium" prefigured the silent epics of Griffith,[49] and his Delsarte-inspired technique of "Harmonic Gymnastics" became the principal method of formal instruction for American actors between 1870 and 1895. In 1877 he established a conservatory called the New York School of Expression; in 1884, together with Franklin Sargent, he founded the Lyceum Theatre School, which evolved into the American Academy of Dramatic Arts. Soon afterward, similar conservatories began to spring up in major cities as far west as St. Louis,[50] and a "Delsarte System" of public speaking was in wide popular use from then until the 1920s. Throughout that period, advertisements called upon "every elocutionist, every singer, every teacher, and every other cultured person" to use Delsarte "recitation books" as a means "of acquiring grace, dignity, and fine bearing for society people".[51] Ultimately, the "Delsarte Movement" was so deeply embedded in the culture that a good many actors could be described as Delsartean whether or not they ever studied him—just as middle-class Americans once behaved according to Emily Post whether or not they actually read her advice.

At its best, this tradition could produce dazzling results. I would argue, for example, that the expressive behavior of the entire cast in *The Phantom of the Opera* (1925) owes to Delsarte's

---

[47] Brooks, Louise. *Lulu in Hollywood*. New York: Knopf, 1983, p. 61.
[48] Cole, Toby and Helen Krich Chinoy, eds. *Actors on Acting*. New York: Crown, 1970, pp. 189-90.
[49] Vardac, A. Nicholas. *From Stage to Screen: Theatrical Method from Garrick to Griffith*. Cambridge, Mass.: Harvard University Press, 1949, p. 151.
[50] McArthur, Benjamin. *Actors and American Culture, 1880-1920*. Philadelphia: Temple University Press, 1984, pp. 100-101.
[51] Cole, Toby and Helen Krich Chinoy, eds. *Actors on Acting*. New York: Crown, 1970, p. 187.

vision of the theater. David Thomson has observed that Lon Chaney "moves with a stunning languor, as if he knew of Conrad Veidt in Caligari." But an even more likely influence on both Chaney and his co-star, Mary Philbin, is the supple, demonstrative, highly codified style of pantomime that dominated the previous century and remained in use to a greater or lesser degree throughout silent movies.

Despite its frequent beauties, however, the pantomime style was linked with attempts to perpetuate bourgeois "deportment," and the recommendations of its teachers could frequently lead to stilted, pretentious behavior. To appreciate how bad the technique could become, one need only glance at *Lessons in the Art of Acting* (1889) by Edmund Shaftesbury, one of Delsarte's many American imitators. On his title page Shaftesbury announces "a Practical and Thorough work for all persons who aim to become Professional Actors, and for all Readers and Orators who desire to make use of the power of Dramatic Expression, which is the True Element of Success in the Pulpit, at the Bar, and on the Platform." In his introductory remarks, he comments on the "Delsarte Method," which he says was "accompanied by an irrational craze some years ago, and is still advocated by persons who spent large amounts of money to acquire it, for the purpose of afterward teaching it"[52]. Announcing that he has studied Delsarte himself and found "many excellences, and some defects," he proceeds to offer his own guide, which includes 106 illustrations of "Dramatic Attitudes" for the actor....

A more interesting writer of this sort is the Frenchman Charles Aubert, whose training manual, *The Art of Pantomime*, was translated into English in 1927. Aubert occasionally addresses himself to silent film actors; he never mentions Delsarte, but he draws heavily on the semiotic approach, producing an illustrated list of positions for the legs, the shoulders, the chest, the abdomen, the arms, the hands, and the facial muscles-each attitude signifying a range of possible meanings. Thus if a man stands with his weight on both feet, his thumbs hooked into the armholes of a vest, the pose indicates "Assurance, Independence, Gay Humor, and Self-content",[53] If he folds his arms across his chest, one supporting the other, he suggests "Expectancy, Reflection".[54] If he grasps both hands to his head, the possible meanings are "What shall I do? All is lost; My head hurts: Despair. It will drive me crazy"...[55]

By the time Aubert's book was published, the theoretical commitment to pantomime was disappearing from American theater and films; even Chaplin often parodied Delsartean gestures for comic effect... Clearly, a massive cultural change had been wrought by the postwar economy, by the proliferation of naturalistic literature, and by the growing interest in various psychological determinants of behavior. Nietzsche, Freud, Bergson, and William James had influenced social thought, and dramatic literature as a whole was becoming increasingly introspective. Now more than ever the emphasis in training performers fell being instead of mimicking; the gestures of the actor were supposed to grow out of his or her feelings rather than the other way around. Mae Marsh, who published a short book entitled *Screen Acting* in the early twenties, helps illustrate the trend:

> *While we were playing* Intolerance.... *I had to do a scene where, in the big city's slums, my father dies.*
>
> *The night before I did this scene I went to the theater-something, by the way, I seldom do when working-to see Marjorie Rambeau in* Kindling.
>
> *To my surprise and gratification she had to do a scene in this play which was somewhat similar to the one I was scheduled to play in* Intolerance. *It made a deep impression on me.*

[52] Shaftesbury, Edmund. *Lessons in the Art of Acting: A Thorough Course.* Washington, D.C.: Martyn College Press, 1889, p. ii.
[53] Aubert, Charles. *The Art of Pantomime.* Trans. Edith Sears. New York: Henry Holt and Co., 1927, p. 41.
[54] *Ibid.,* p. 42.
[55] *Ibid.,* p. 45.

As a consequence, the next day before the camera...I began to cry with the memory of Marjorie Rambeau's performance uppermost in my mind....

Mr. Griffith, who was closely studying [the rushes], finally turned in his seat and said:

"I don't know what you were thinking about when you did that, but it is evident that it was not about the death of your father."...

We began immediately upon the scene again. This time I thought of the death of my own father and the big tragedy to our little home, then in Texas. I could recall the deep sorrow of my mother, my sisters, my brother, and myself.

This scene is said to be one of the most effective in "The Mother and the Law."[56]

A rudimentary form of "affective memory" had long been used by actors, but movies and the new literature made it seem essential. And because players ceased to think in terms of a repertory of gesture, the various nineteenth century guides to acting gradually took on a merely historical interest, ultimately constituting what Richard Dyer calls a "record of melodramatic performance practice".[57]

Certain aspects of the pantomime tradition were of course sustained by silent film, but its last flowering is probably in German expressionism, which devised an approximately Delsartean technique via a different, modernist aesthetic. "The melody of a great gesture," Paul Komfield wrote in his *Nachwort an den Schauspieler* (1921), "says more than the highest consummation of what is called naturalness." This credo is evident in *Metropolis* (1926), where the gestures of the various characters are intended to support a political allegory in the boldest, most elemental way....Alfred Abel, as the industrialist's liberal son, beats his breast, looks heavenward in "feminized" spiritual agony, and crucifies himself on a factory machine; Rudolph Klein-Rogge, as the mad scientist, leans forward threateningly and swoops his talonlike hands in triumphant arcs; Brigitte Helm, as the "good" and "bad" Maria, alternates between prayerful entreaties and sinewy, erotic enticements. Of all the characters, Gustave Froelich, the master of Metropolis, is the most inexpressive; nevertheless, he occasionally raises a hand to give a sinister order, and by the end of the film we see him in anguish, clasping both hands to his head....

In most films, actors need to produce vivid expressions in brief shots which are photographed out of sequence, and when asked to register "fear" or "pain" in close-up they look rather like one of Aubert's drawings. Peter Lorre was roughly correct when he described the work of movie acting as "face-making." For example, Hitchcock's most "cinematic" montages—the shower murder in *Psycho* (1960), the cropdusting sequence in *North by Northwest*—elicit grimaces, postures, and movements that function like elemental signs. In fact, as I shall argue later, no less a movie star than Cary Grant could be described as a consummate modern practitioner of vaguely Delsartean technique; more specifically, Grant was the sort of actor Kuleshov had in mind when he devised pantomimic "études" for students, training them to render simple, crisp expressions for the camera.

All of which suggests that the nature of acting may have changed less than we think. John Delman comments, "No doubt the nineteenth century, in its eagerness to perfect the traditional language of pantomime, reduced it to absurdity; but that does not lessen the truth

---

56 Marsh, Mae. *Screen Acting.* Los Angeles: Photo-Star Publishing, n.d., pp. 76-9.
57 Dyer, Richard. *Stars.* London: British Film Institute, 1979, p. 156.

that bodily action, simplified by selection, moderately exaggerated, provides a language of expression more universally intelligible than words".[58] In fact, actors continue to practice the rhetoric of conventionalized expression; most of them simply explain their craft in a different way, exchanging new gestures for old. Recognizing this phenomenon at the turn of the century, Yeats joked that when "educated modern people" are deeply moved, "they look silently into the fireplace." Theater historian Michael Goldman makes a similar point when he writes, "The inner space that Ibsen and his successors were concerned with had to be charted by a repertory of pauses and indirection, by small details of gesture and expression.... The construction of plays, the technique of the actors, the age's growing interest in psychological science and detection of all sorts, invited the audience to listen for movements beneath the characters' public performance."

The result is not only a slightly different set of poses and small gestures, but a greater emphasis on the idiolect of the performer. James Stewart, for example, is an expert pantomimist, but whenever he wants to register "anguish" in close-up he relies on a personal habit rather than a standardized expressive vocabulary. Inevitably, at the point of his greatest trauma, he will raise a trembling hand to his open mouth, sometimes biting at the flesh....

Individual mannerisms aside, a book rather like the ones by Shaftesbury and Aubert could be written to illustrate the standard expressions in contemporary naturalistic cinema. Consider Meryl Streep's close-ups in *Sophie's Choice* (1983), which are filled with lip biting, sidelong glances, and halting speech delivered in an almost whispered register. Doubtless Streep works mostly from the "inside," employing a Stanislavskian method; nevertheless, her movements are carefully orchestrated, consisting mainly of the readable formulas of twentieth-century interpretation, raised to the level of old-fashioned melodramatic eloquence. At the same time, we can make two rather tentative formal distinctions between her practice and the older tradition. Unlike the typical nineteenth-century performers, who tended to arrange their faces in a picture to indicate "grief," Streep tries to register a repressed emotion, so that her look communicates something more like "grief held in check by an attempt to remain calm." In addition, she signals a good deal of what William Archer called "emotional contagion," chiefly by means of blushes and a visibly pulsating blood vessel in her neck—a purely biological language, intended to convince us that she is not simply imitating passion, but responding from her central nervous system. (Because biological symptoms are important to naturalism, film actors have often submitted their bodies to their roles in quite fundamental ways: Agnes Morehead's hysterical breakdown near the end of *The Magnificent Ambersons* owes its power partly to Orson Welles's having shot the scene over and over, until Morehead was truly exhausted; and Ingmar Bergman has claimed that during Bibi Andersson's description of an "orgy" in *Persona* [1966], he wanted the audience to see Liv Ullmann's lips distending with desire.)

We make an error, therefore, if we assume that theorists like Delsarte and Aubert are relevant only in the realm of arcane histrionics. Ironically, Delsarte's writings have exerted two sorts of influence—one on the theater and oratory of his own day, and the other on training techniques for the twentieth century avant-garde. Kuleshov remarked that "for the work of the face and all the parts of a human being, the system of Delsarte is very useful, but only as an inventory of the possible changes in the human mechanism, and not as a method of acting."[59] In the same qualified way, Delsarte's studies of gesture and expression helped to shape Ruth St. Denis's choreography, indirectly fostering modem dance, and were acknowledged as a source for the "physical theater" of Artaud and Grotowski. Although Delsarte was very much a part of the romantic movement, he had foreshadowed the modemist dehumanization of art; and if we put

---

[58] Delman, John, Jr. *The Art of Acting*. New York: Harper, 1949. p. 241.
[59] Kuleshov, Lev. *Kuleshov on Film*. Trans. and Ed. by Ronald Levaco. Berkeley: University of California Press, 1974, p. 107.

aside certain uses of his teaching, particularly the American attempt to instruct public speakers in genteel manners, he seems curiously advanced.[60]

Perhaps not surprisingly, the most unorthodox filmmakers have intentionally drawn from the mimetic tradition, departing from it chiefly in their attempt to divest performance of emotional and rhetorical unity. Thus Robert Bresson, a radical idealist, devotes much of his *Notes sur le cinematographe* to advocating a form of "automatism." As Mirella Affron has noted, Bresson thinks of his largely amateur players as "models," and he never makes upon them "the conventional demands of dramatic expression; that they cry, for example. He asks them instead...to wipe away nonexistent tears, to find not the gesture through the feeling, but the feeling through the simplest and most stylized of gestures".[61] Repeatedly, Bresson emphasizes that acting should be seen as a simple labor: "Let people feel the soul and heart in your film, but let it be made like a work of the hands".[62] An attitude such as this is both old and new. It runs strongly against the grain of mainstream performance, but it has something in common with an earlier era, when actors were regarded as rhetoricians and interpreters, building character out of expressive movement. There is a sense, therefore, in which old-fashioned pantomime can feed our thinking about newer performance techniques, broadening the potential of dramatic films and helping us to understand the complex language of emotion.

---

[60] Kirby, E.T. "The Delsarte Method: Three Frontiers of Actor Training." *Drama Review* 16, no. 1 (March 1972), pp. 55-6.
[61] Affron, Mirella Jona. "Bresson and Pascal: Rhetorical Affinities." *Quarterly Review of Film Studies* 10, no. 2 (Spring 1985), p. 124.
[62] *Ibid.*, p. 125.

A DREAM OF PASSION:
THE DEVELOPMENT OF THE METHOD

by Lee Strasberg, from *Star Texts* (1991), edited by Jeremy Butler

The one man most responsible for the Method becoming the dominant method of screen acting in the United States was Lee Strasberg: popularizer of the term "the Method," cofounder of the Group Theatre (1931-36), artistic director of the Actors Studio (starting in 1951), and chief proponent of the Method in the United States from the 1920s until his death in 1982. Strasberg refined, synthesized, and eventually disseminated the teachings of Stanislavski and Stanislavski's students: Eugene Vakhtangov, Richard Boleslavski, and Maria Ouspenskaya. Strasberg brought the Method to the masses, as it were, through his Actors Studio students (Marlon Brando, Julie Harris, Montgomery Clift, James Dean, and others) and colleagues-most significantly, director Elia Kazan, who cofounded the Actors Studio. Brando, under the direction of Kazan in *A Streetcar Named Desire* (1951) and *On the Waterfront* (1954), came to epitomize Method acting in the public's mind.[63] To be accurate, however, Brando and the rest of the 1950s wave of Method actors were not the first incursion of the Method in Hollywood. In the 1930s, Boleslavski carted Stanislavskian precepts to Hollywood and used them in the direction of actors such as Marlene Dietrich, Charles Laughton, and the Barrymores. But still, it was not until the Method's impact on film acting in the 1950s that it mutated from an arcane procedure for training theatrical actors into a generally recognized element of popular culture.

In the United States this popular-culture assimilation of a watered-down Method was a phenomenon of the same post-World War II fascination with the hidden drives of the unconscious that fostered a popular interest in Freud. Strasberg himself aspires to the level of psychologist in the following excerpt from *A Dream of Passion*—a posthumously published (1987), autobiographical account of his life with the Method. Alluding to several psychologists, Strasberg explains the importance of improvisation to the central concept of "affective memory," the process of contacting one's memories of emotions in order to channel them into a role. Affective memory originated in Stanislavski, was nurtured by Boleslavski, Strasberg's teacher at the American Laboratory Theatre in the 1920s, and was further refined by Strasberg. Strasberg divides affective memory into the recall of sensations (sights, sounds, smells, and so on) and that of feelings (horror, sadness, pleasure, and so on). The actor, he explains, uses the former, his or her sense memory, to stimulate the latter, his or her emotional memory, which can then be used in the context of a particular character. The Method, he concludes, is "the procedure by which the actor can use his affective memory to create a reality on stage."

· · ·

---

[63] Although Brando is clearly identified with the Method, he is less a product of the Actors Studio—where he studied but briefly—than he is of the Stanislavskian teachings of Stella Adler, a Group Theatre member who broke with Strasberg in 1934 over his interpretation of Stanislavski.

The Method is sometimes accused of making problems for the actor that never existed. Problems and difficulties have always existed; only their solutions and the discovery of methods to train the actor are modern.

The two areas of discovery that were of primary importance in my work at the Actors Studio and in my private classes were improvisation and affective memory. It is finally by using these techniques that the actor can express the appropriate emotions demanded of the character.

When the French director Michel Saint-Denis visited the Actors Studio and saw an improvisation, he was amazed. He seemed unaware of the fact that it was a basic element in Stanislavsky's procedures, and that we had already used improvisation in productions of the Group Theatre. There is, of course, no chapter on improvisation in Stanislavsky's work; yet the études that he describes were improvisations, used not only in the process of training, but in the actual process of production. Vakhtangov also used the études in an extraordinarily imaginative way.

Improvisation today seems to be considered either as a verbal exercise or a game that is supposed to stimulate the actor. A good deal of what is thought of as improvisation as an exercise in verbal invention is illustrated in some of the fine work of the Second City. Improvisation is also mistaken as a paraphrase of the author's words. Both of the approaches have little to do with the primary value of improvisation to the actor's training, by which I mean exercises related to an exploration of the actor's and the character's feelings.

Improvisation is best known in the theatre through the work of the commedia dell'arte actors who performed across Europe during the sixteenth, seventeenth, and eighteenth centuries. Besides their use of stock characters, established through masks and costuming, the troupes elevated improvisation to a creative and natural level. With only an outline of the play's plot posted on the edge of the stage wings, the commedia performer was expected to fill in the unwritten dialogue and actions with set speeches, often in colloquial language, and standard comic routines. This procedure produced a kind of naturalness and spontaneity that we associate with twentieth-century acting. Everything, even totally memorized speeches, assumed the impression of spontaneity, since no actor was exactly certain what his partner might say or do within the plotlines of the scenario. Commedia audiences sensed this new feeling, and ultimately this led to new ways of writing and staging plays. Certainly Shakespeare's and Moliére's work is indebted to the influences of the commedia dell'arte actors: there is a freedom and freshness in their dialogue and in their use of colloquial speech.

Another great contribution of commedia dell'arte is in the development of realistic and believable characterizations on stage. A great deal of what was achieved by the commedia in this area was lost in succeeding periods and did not return to the stage until David Garrick, and later Edmund Kean, reinstated a naturalistic style.

Improvisation is essential if the actor is to develop the spontaneity necessary to create in each performance "the illusion of the first time."

Stanislavsky had correctly discovered that a major problem in acting derives from "anticipation." Everything the character is supposed to be aware of, what he will be asked, what he will be told, events that are supposed to surprise him, even his responses—these things the actor already knows. Regardless of the skill with which the actor may pretend not to know what will occur next on stage, his normal scenic activity is actuated by his memory-by his carefully prepared and memorized words and motions. This leads, even at its best, to an "indication" of what is supposed to be taking place.

The actor will say in character, "I don't understand," and will therefore pretend not to understand. But a real character who says, "I do not understand," is at that moment actively trying to find out what it is that is being said. Thus, the actor may suggest the results, while the character is actually concerned with thinking and discovering what it may possibly mean. An actor will ask, "Who are you?" and naturally wait for the reply. A real character, while perhaps waiting for an answer, is actively concerned with trying to discover who the person is. The face might look familiar or unfamiliar, he might confuse him with another individual, etc. When a character says, "I don't know where to go," he is usually concerned with where he might go. But an actor simply suggests that he doesn't know where to go without solving his dilemma.

A real character has a continuous aliveness, a continuous process of thought and of sensory and emotional response. This goes beyond the line of dialogue already supplied to him by the author. To stimulate a continuous flow of response and thought within the actor is the primary value of improvisation. Many actors believe that they truly think on the stage. They do not accept the premise that their thought is tied only to the memorized lines of dialogue. In the process of training or of rehearsal, I will often deliberately change objects, partners, or other details and demonstrate to them that they go right on doing and saying what they have prepared to do. Often an actor enters a scene and, because he already knows the outcome, is playing toward that end. By improvising, the actor finds a way to play the scene more logically and convincingly, not just from his own point of view, but also from the audience's.

In one session at the Actors Studio, I asked an actress to participate in a demonstration. I suggested that she choose a scene from a production in which she had actually appeared and that had presented some difficulty she would like to investigate.

She chose the scene in *The Three Sisters* where Masha confesses to her sisters that she's in love with the Colonel. She preceded the scene with an improvisation in which she appeared to open a door and enter a space that seemed somewhat confined. Then she knelt to pray. The relevance of this improvisation to the scene which was to follow was unclear. Then she finished the improvisation and exited. She then entered the set in which she was to connect the exercise to the play. She sat down on the sofa and picked up a pillow she lightly played with and seemed to embrace. Then she uttered the first line of the actual scene, "Sisters, I have something to confess.... I love that man." The reality with which she rendered the scene was startling in its naturalness and vividness. A mixture of tears and laughter spontaneously poured from her.

After she finished the scene, she explained what had just happened. She described her experience when she was first asked to accept the part and read the script. It was when she came to this scene in the play that she decided to do the role. She did not question her decision, nor was she aware of what motivated her. In the actual performance, however, she was never satisfied; nor were the critics and audience.

She had had difficulty in arriving at any personal experience that might be connected with this particular event. She could find no direct parallel in her own life. She remembered her original response when she first read the script and wondered what motivated her decision to play the role in the first place. She then realized something she had completely forgotten. When she was a child of six, she was forced to go to confession. She had little to confess, but the nun told her a story which moved her deeply. The Lord sent Saint Peter down to earth to bring back the most beautiful thing he could find. When Saint Peter returned, what he had brought back was unacceptable. He was sent back to find something more suitable, but again what he brought back was insufficient. Finally, he returned and extended a closed fist. As he opened his hand, there was a single tear. It was a tear of a child at confession, and the Lord accepted this as being the most beautiful thing Saint Peter could have brought back. This story had made a deep impression on her.

After hearing that story, she would try to force a tear at confession, with very little success. She would make up stories that might possibly bring some tearful response from her, but to no avail. She suffered because she had nothing to confess. This is what she had found in trying to analyze her own response to this scene. It was this memory that had unconsciously affected her decision to do the part. In the improvisation at the Actors Studio, the re-creation and acting out of this event made a perfect preparation for what otherwise had proven a difficult scene.

Improvisation leads not only to a process of thought and response, but also helps to discover the logical behavior of the character rather than encouraging the actor "merely to illustrate" the obvious meaning of the line. Actors are often confused by the fact that during scenes for which they were praised, they were aware of having thoughts unrelated to the play.

As I've said before, it does not matter so much what the actor thinks, but the fact that he is really thinking something that is real to him at that particular moment. The make-believe thinking that may coincide with the play is not real enough, though it may be sufficient to fool the audience. This is what we sometimes mean when we refer to acting as being only "indication."

The second major area of my work involves affective memory.... Boleslavsky divided affective memory into two categories: analytic memory, and the memory of feeling. Analytic memory is trained and developed by exercises involving imaginary objects; in our work we call this aspect of affective memory sense memory. The second category that Boleslavsky described was the memory of feeling, which we call emotional memory. My work at the Actors Studio and in my private classes revolved around emotional memory as part of the actor's training. (The generic term affective memory is often confused with the term emotional memory, but emotional memory pertains specifically to the more intense reactions of an emotional response. Stanislavsky and his circle often used the term affective memory to mean what we call emotional memory, the memory of feeling. In the following discussion, the terms are used to mean the same thing.)

The term affective memory was taken by Stanistavsky from a work by the French psychologist Theodule Ribot, *The Psychology of the Emotions.* This book was translated into Russian in the 1890s. (A copy of the book is in Stanislavsky's library.) Ribot noted in his chapter "The Memory of Feelings" that there had been numerous studies into the nature and the revivability of visual, auditory, tactile-motor, and verbal images, but that the question of the emotional memory remained nearly untouched. Our emotions and passions, like the perceptions of sight and hearing, can leave memories behind them. It is clear that these memories are provoked in life by some actual occurrence. His concern was whether or not these "emotions formerly experienced can be revived in the consciousness spontaneously or at will, independently of any actual occurrence which might provoke them."

Ribot in no way questioned the presence of emotional memories. He questioned only the extent to which these are capable of being revived at will. Many critics, unfortunately, have confused the existence of emotional memories with the difficulty that most people have in recalling them at will. It is precisely this problem of recall that was of major significance to Stanislavsky because of its application to all schools or styles of acting.

Ribot cited his own investigations in which he asked a variety of people to revive or recapture an emotional memory. In one of his studies, a young man of twenty made an effort to remember the feeling of ennui that he had experienced on his first day in the barracks. The young man shut his eyes and abstracted his thoughts. He first felt a slight shiver down his back, a feeling of something unpleasant that he would prefer not to have felt again. This uncomfortable feeling was connected with a vague sensation that did not firmly materialize. He then visualized the barrack yard where he used to walk; this image was replaced by that of a dormitory on the third floor. Then he saw himself seated at a window, looking through it, viewing the entire camp grounds. While the image soon disappeared, there remained a "vague idea of being seated at a window and then a feeling of oppression, weariness, rejection and a certain heaviness of the shoulders." Throughout, the feeling of ennui persisted.

Ribot noted that a characteristic peculiar to affective memory is the slowness with which it developed. Actually, I discovered that after sufficient exercise, the recall can be accomplished in one minute.

Ribot's discoveries obviously played a great role in Stanislavsky's growing awareness of the actor's unconscious procedures during the creative process. This presented a solution to a problem that had previously evaded comprehension: What happens when the actor is inspired, or what is the nature of the actor's inspiration?

Memory can be divided into three categories. First, there is mental memory, which can be easily controlled. We try to remember where we were yesterday at this particular time, and most people will be able to do so. The second kind is physical memory, which teaches us how to control our muscles. During the process of learning, we are quite conscious of what we are doing, but after we have achieved it, it continues to be repeated automatically by memory. For example, at the age of five, my son David grandly announced that he was able to tie his shoelaces. It took five years to train his muscles to deal with that task. After a while, tying his shoelaces became habit; the memory functioned automatically. The third kind of memory is affective memory. It consists of two parts: sense memory and emotional memory.

Affective memory is the basic material for reliving on the stage, and therefore for the creation of a real experience on the stage. What the actor repeats in performance after performance is not just the words and movements he practiced in rehearsal, but the memory of emotion. He reaches this emotion through the memory of thought and sensation.

Psychologists disagree on the actual nature of emotion: What takes place psychologically? In what area is an emotion localized? How are emotions stimulated? How are they expressed? Many of these questions have not been answered sufficiently.

A startling study on the presence and the working of affective memory (both sense memory and emotional memory) is the work of a Canadian brain surgeon, Dr. Wilder Penfield. In the course of surgically treating patients who suffered from epileptic seizures, he stumbled on the fact that electrical stimulation of certain areas of the brain occasionally produced a state in which the patient "relived" a previous experience. On first encountering these flashbacks in 1933, he was incredulous. A young mother told him she was suddenly aware of being in her kitchen, listening to the voice of her son playing in the yard. Each element of the original experience was reproduced: the neighborhood noises, the passing motor cars. Another patient relived an experience in a concert hall; each individual instrument was clearly defined.

In an effort to confirm his findings, Dr. Penfield was interested in further exploring the source of these sensations. He restimulated the same point thirty times. In each instance the subject "relived" the experience. Dr. Penfield called such responses "experiential." In real life, this process is stimulated by some conditioning factor that arouses it. For example, when someone tells you that he met a particular individual whom you have strong feelings toward, your heart starts pounding. You will find yourself reacting merely to the mention or suggestion of that person, even in his absence.

While mental or physical actions can be controlled at will, emotions cannot. You cannot tell yourself to be angry, to hate, to love, and so forth. Conversely, you cannot tell yourself to stop feeling any of those emotions once they are aroused. It is in this area that the startling methods of Boleslavsky and Madame Ouspenskaya have made the greatest contribution in acting.

The "inspiration" I had noted in my earlier years had occurred when a great actor worked unconsciously and was able to relive an overwhelming experience and express it in performance. I have spoken of Ben-Ami's inspiration in John the Baptist. But these actors were not always able to repeat the experience at will. Recreating or reliving an intense emotional experience at will was at the core of our work.

The actor trains himself to control "inspiration" through an "emotional-memory" exercise. To try to recapture or relive an experience, the actor needs to be first of all relaxed, so that there is no interference between the activity of the mind and the other areas that are being induced to respond. I discovered that the presence of mental or physical tension is often the result of anticipating the way in which the emotion should happen, and thus interferes with the spontaneous flow of sensation.

It is not necessary to go through the hours or days it took for an event to develop. The actor starts five minutes before the emotional event took place. The correct process of inducing a response is through the senses. He tries to remember where he was. Say he was in the yard. The actor cannot simply think in generalities. The yard is composed of many objects that he sees, hears, touches, and so forth, to which he assigns the word yard. Only by formulating the sensory concreteness of these objects can the emotions be stimulated. It is not sufficient to say, "It was hot." Rather, the actor must define precisely in what area he experienced the particular heat he remembers; the actor localizes the concentration in that area to create not just a memory but a reliving of that particular moment. The actor remembers what he had on: the sight, texture, or sensation of that material on the body. The actor tries to remember the event that caused the emotion, not in terms of the sequence of the story, but in terms of the various senses that surrounded it. If another individual was involved, he must be experienced in terms of sense memory as well.

As the actor comes closer to the moment of intense emotional reaction, the body will often exert a counter tension to stop it; nobody likes to relive intense experiences. When the actor arrives at the moment of high intensity, he must be able to stay with the sensory concentration; otherwise, the actor's will is out of control and he may be carried away by the emotional experience.

I have seen much fear on the part of many people when they first faced the problem of performing the emotional-memory exercise—fear of being carried away, as they put it, and of not being able to be pulled back, a fear which is perfectly natural because the human being is doing something that he is not accustomed to, and anything new is frightening. This is also a fear of losing control. The whole point of the emotional-memory exercise is to establish control over emotional expression. For this reason, the emotional memory work is preceded by extensive preparation work.

The fundamental work of the actor—the training of his internal skills-is preceded by the development of the actor's relaxation and concentration. Work in concentration leads to the development of the ability to use the senses not only with actual objects, but with imaginary objects....

CRITICAL FILM ANALYSES

NOW, VOYAGER (1942)

Philantha Kon

Warner Bros. Pictures, Inc. Produced by Hal B. Wallis. Directed by Irving Rapper. Screenplay by Casey Robinson. Base on the novel by Olive Higgins Prouty. Music by Max Steiner. Musical direction by Leo F. Forbstein. Photographed by Sol Polito. Art direction by Robert Hass. Edited by Warren Low. Gowns by Orry-Kerry.

CAST: Bette Davis (Charlotte Vale), Paul Henreid (Jerry Durrance), Claude Rains (Dr. Jaquith), Gladys Cooper (Mrs. Henry Windle Vale), Bonita Granville (June Vale), Ilka Chase (Lisa Vale), John Loder (Elliot Livingston), Lee Patrick (Deb McIntyre), Franklin Pangborn (Mr. Thompson), Kathenne Alexander (Miss Trask), James Rennle (Frank McIntyre), Mary Wickes (Dora Pickford), Janis Wilson (Tina Durrance), Michael Ames (Dr. Dan Regan), Charles Drake (Leslie Trotter), Frank Puglia (Manoel), David Clyde (William). Running time: 118 minutes. B/W

> Bette Davis didn't look like anybody else, didn't walk like anybody else, didn't talk like anybody else. Her eyes were enormous, her stride started at the waist; her speech was all unexpected stresses and sudden plosives. Professional mimics loved her, the way they loved James Cagney and Edward G. Robinson. Like them, she was sui generis, irresistible to the imitator. Like them, she was an extraordinary performer.[64]

Critics and others who have studied the acting art say there are two kinds of successful actors and actresses: those who project by craftmanship an image to which the public reacts favorably, and those who project such an image by the sheer force of personality.[65] The danger of such generalities is that they are not true in all cases, but in the case of Bette Davis, this particular generality holds doubly true. Davis succeeded at first by projecting an image which was the essence of personality, and survived as a star because she was intelligent and hard-working

---

[64] *New York Times* editorial (10/89) from Ringgold, Gene. *The Complete Films of Bette Davis*, New York: Carol Publishing, 1990, p. 196.
[65] Henry Hart, "Foreward" from Ringgold, p. 7.

enough to learn the acting craft. The career of Bette Davis is a distinguished one. Her contributions to motion pictures are even more impressive when consideration is given to the personal misfortunes and professional disappointments which profoundly affected her life but were never severe enough to frustrate her determination to become an actress and a great film star. After proving her acting ability on New York stages, Davis had the courage to crash Hollywood in the early years of talking pictures when glamour and physical beauty were prerequisites for female stardom (and of which many of her employers thought she had neither). She survived because of her ability to craft a persona, to mesmerize the audience by her performances; through sheer force of personality, she could make us think she was beautiful, make us cry for her, and make us hate her.

Her popularity with women in particular revolved largely around the way in which in her every role, audiences sensed an exemplar of the "new woman." Hence, in addition to watching a good acting performance, women saw one of their own confront the male with power, rebellion, confidence, a new independence. The roles she sought to play in motion pictures which have brought her the greatest acclaim have all been variations of the free-thinking, emancipated woman. We observe this clearly in *Now, Voyager* as Davis, in the role of Charlotte Vale, portrays an initially vulnerable, sensitive spinster manipulated by those around her who ultimately comes to exhibit strength, confidence, and newfound independence.

Bette Davis convinced producer, Hal Wallis, that she was most fit for the challenging role as neurotic spinster Charlotte Vale in *Now, Voyager*. She proved herself right as her interpretation of the complex character earned an Academy Award nomination in 1942. *Now, Voyager* crystallizes the dilemma of women facing the consequence of having won their emancipation and not being too certain it was a victory after all. It is a tragically romantic female melodrama (and a personal study of the sort which Davis claims as her forte) about a repressed "ugly duckling" who is emotionally crippled and enslaved by her tyrannical mother and on the verge of a nervous breakdown. She undergoes therapy, learns to stand on her own feet and to face the world, and is transformed into a chic and attractive woman under the ministrations of Dr. Jaquith (Claude Rains), a psychiatrist recommended by her sister-in-law. Davis highlights Charlotte's progress to emotional maturity with the decision and accuracy of an assured actress.

It is Davis' ability to convey the psychological aspects of the transformation from an ugly duckling to a beautiful swan that makes her role as Charlotte both challenging and impressive. We see this both in her costume and body language. As insecure and unattractive Charlotte, Davis wears dowdy dresses that hide her heavier figure. She also walks and talks as if trying to hide her face and body. After her three month "makeover," Davis wears fashionable and figure-flattering clothing to show off her slimmed-down figure and characteristically walks with her hips. Charlotte's transformation is further seen in being given the "business" of constantly holding and smoking cigarettes openly and confidently in contrast to her earlier days of hiding them in her room from her mother. Davis was of course known for the use of her eyes as part of her performance style: they signified intensity and passion at key moments of dramatic tension in the narrative.[66] Her eyes in *Now, Voyager*, initially concealed by her heavy brows and glasses signifying vulnerability, are exposed after her "makeover" to suggest a certain kind of femininity, in this case a rebellious one which represented a challenge to her mother's authority as well as a seductiveness and resistance to the men who loved her. Many have claimed that her skill as a performer is so artful, she has advanced feminism on the screen to a zenith where many men, as well as women, have found her fascinating.[67] She offers the spectator fantasies of power outside his or her own experience. Particularly, the qualities of confidence and power are remembered as offering female spectators the pleasure of participation in qualities they

[66] Stacey, Jackie, *Star Gazing*, London: Routledge, 1994, p. 162.
[67] Ringgold, p. 11.

themselves lack and desire. Her fans describe the phenomenon of seeing a genuine realist performing her job so well she has been able to make the most mediocre Hollywood fantasy seem intelligent. It is her ambition, will power, and mastery of craft combined with intelligence which are the vital components of a screen image unique enough to survive nearly five decades of social and economic evolutions. Davis knew how to compete in a masculine industry with a strength beyond her gender.

Now, Voyager was one in a decade in which her films were all of superior quality, all commercially successful, and often critically acclaimed. Her decline resulted from an inability to find suitable scripts that would add new dimensions to her already encompassing acting range and additional prestige to her already established legend. Critics claimed that her potency and acting economy had been replaced by all-too-familiar devices and mannerisms (the famous bug eyes, disdainful slash of a mouth, the ambulatory elbows, wet-nail-polish gestures, the distinctive pelvic walk, her omnipresent cigarettes, and clipped speech patterns). The distinctive personality that had fascinated so many had transformed itself into a caricature.[68]

Davis' extensive career consists of over 80 films, including 2 Academy Awards (one for *Dangerous* in 1935 and for *Jezebel* in 1938), Academy Award nominations for 8 other films (in addition to *Now, Voyager* in 1942, *Dark Victory* (1939), *The Letter* (1940), *The Little Foxes* (1941), *Mr. Skeffington* (1944), *All About Eve* (1950), *The Star* (1952) and *What Ever Happened to Baby Jane?* (1962), and television work in the 1970s and 1980s before her death on October 6, 1989.

---

[68] *Ibid.,* p. 73.

THE CORN IS GREEN (1945)

Jaime Nasser

Credits: Produced by Jack Chertok and Jack L. Warner. Directed by Irving Rapper. Screenplay by Frank Cavette and Casey Robinson. Based on the play by Emlyn Williams. Photographed by Sol Polito. Musical score by Max Steiner. Costumes by Orry-Kelly. Make-up by Perc Westmore. Art-direction by Carl Jules Weyl. Set Decoration by Jack Chertok and Fred M. MacLean. Sound by Robert B. Lee. A Warner Brothers First National Picture. Running time 115 minutes. Released March 1945.

Cast: Bette Davis (Miss Moffat), Nigel Bruce (Squire), Rhys Williams (Mr. Jones), Rosalind Ivan (Mrs. Watty), Mildred Dunnock (Mrs. Ronberry), Arthur Shields (Glyn Thomas), John Dall (Morgan Evans), Joan Lorring (Bessie Watty), Gwyneth Hughes (Sarah Pugh), Billy Roy (Idwal Morris), Thomas Louden (Old Tom), Jack Owen (Tudor).

-"You go one step further toward that door you son of a bitch and you're fired!"

-"Only Jack Warner can fire me, Bette, you know that. But he won't have to: I quit. I've had enough of your tantrums and sadistic bullying."

-"Listen, you no-talent third-rater, you ought to go down on your knobby knees in gratitude that you're directing a Bette Davis picture!"

-"I'm not directing Bette, you are."[69]

Bette Davis and director Irving Rapper exchanged these words during the filming of *The Corn is Green.*

As we have discussed in this class before, a film does not have one single author. Producers, writers and stars (among others) have strong influences that affect the finished text. Bette Davis was always concerned with every detail of her films, large and small. Davis, as a Warner Bros. star was well known for fighting with directors and studio executives and doing everything possible to have her way on the set regarding the characters she portrayed. *The Corn is Green* was no exception. At the time the film was in production, Davis was (arguably) at the peak of her career and popularity. She was very well aware of her power to attract audiences and that this power also meant that a bad Bette Davis film would be blamed on Bette Davis. The studio wanted Bette to play Miss Moffat close to her own age. However, Bette preferred to wear a gray wig and thirty pounds of padding to her clothes to give herself a middle aged frumpiness that seemed to her more suitable to her character. Davis always relied and depended on heavy make-up, costumes and lighting in order to render realistic performances. [70]

[69] Spada, James. *More than A Woman: An Intimate Biography of Bette Davis.* New York: Bantam Books, 1993, p. 218
[70] Ibid., p. 219

The studio tried to put up a fight but ended up conceding to her wishes. After the film was finished, the studio was reluctant on how to handle the advertising for the film. They weren't sure that audiences would flock to see the story of an old teacher. Perhaps in an effort to spice things up, the poster for the film showed a contemporary picture of a seductive Davis (see the last page) with the slogan: "In her heart of hearts she knew that she could never hold him." Davis' vision conflicted with the interests of the studio. A film critic for Picture Post captured this conflict:

> As the schoolmistress in *The Corn is Green*, only Bette Davis, I think, could have combated so successfully the obvious intention of the adaptors of the play to make frustrated sex the mainspring of the chief character's interest in the young miner. This would have pulled down the whole idea of the relationship into something more simple and more banal... than the subtle representation she insisted on giving.[71]

Despite all the antagonism in the set, the changes that Bette made to her character proved successful. Bette had a theory: the best films are made amid creative conflict.[72] Her theory proved right once again, the film was considered a success and posted a profit of 2.2 million dollars the year it opened; it also received a good critical reception. The tension that existed between Davis' interpretation of the character and the studio's desire to market the film (based on Davis' strong sexuality and dominant personality) has to be taken into account when discussing how a player's performance enters into the meaning of the text.

It is through the re-telling of anecdotes such as this one that the boundary between Bette Davis' on screen and off screen mythology is blurred. Virtually all books that pretend to study Bette Davis, such as autobiographies, performance studies,[73] etc. will inevitably contain anecdotes like this one regarding her explosive personality on and off the set. It is as if audiences long to bring to life the characters that Davis is most well-known for: "the dominant, ambitious and liberated woman." Some of the most well known characters that she plays in these types of films include Judith Traherne in *Dark Victory* (1939), Julie Marsden in *Jezebel* (1940), Leslie Crosbie in *The Letter* (1940) among others. However, Bette Davis is not only known for these roles but her range as an artist goes far beyond that. Davis also starred in roles where she played a suffering martyr in the late 30's and into the 40's, such as Miss Lilly Moffat in *The Corn is Green*. Released in March 1945, the film is based on Emlyn William's play about a sixty-year-old school teacher in Wales at the turn of the century who sacrifices everything to help a poor miner's son in order to prepare him for a scholarship examination at Oxford that, if he passes, will help lift him out of his life of poverty. One also has to acknowledge that Davis' representation of the martyr Lilly Moffat is also colored by her own persona of the dominant and ambitious woman. In this film, her strong personality is put to the service of society and the nation and one could therefore argue that the film negotiates, in the context of the end of World War II, the depictions of the liberated woman (which Davis is most famous for) with the anxieties related to the return of the men from the battlefield.

At the time, World War II was coming to an end and soldiers were returning home from the battlefields in Europe. Women had taken over jobs typically done by men in the US and now they were supposed to go back to their duties in the home. Women had a taste of what it was like to work outside the home, and even though a number of them might have been glad for things to get back to "normal," it is needless to say that not all women were happy to leave their jobs in order to go back to the home. The role of women in society was being contested and the

---

[71] Ringgold, Gene. *The Films of Bette Davis*. The Citadel Press, New York: 1966. p. 133

[72] Spada, James. *More than A Woman: An Intimate Biography of Bette Davis*. New York: Bantam Books, 1993, p. 227

[73] "Performance studies" or books that pretend to study actors and/or actresses with similar depth as required by CTCS 190 are extremely rare.

"women's films" of the 30's and 40's were there to stress these issues out on the silver screen. Most of Bette Davis' characters have often been described as the exemplar of the "the new woman," a female who appeared to confront and defy male power, with a rebellious attitude and often using her sexuality as a tool to achieve her goals. Bette Davis' strong personality is very much a part of her representation of Miss Lilly Moffat. With the premise that films about the past are more about trying to deal with the present, one could try to understand the function of this film in the context of the end of World War II. Moffat utilizes her strong convictions, will and knowledge for the betterment of Glancermo, more specifically, the film focuses on her efforts to help Morgan Evans get a scholarship to Oxford in order for him to become a man that could later serve not only his town but his country (as Moffat explains to him throughout the film). Whereas Davis' previous films depicted a strong woman fighting for her own needs and desires explicitly against men in a male-dominated society, *The Corn is Green* shows a strong woman putting her strong personality, wisdom and knowledge to the service of the nation by helping a young man who in her own mind has the ability to change the world. One could therefore argue that this film negotiates Davis' previous performances as "transgressive" and defiant, with the return of men from the war, and the need to curb the gains of women in the previous years and to stand back behind the men in order to better the nation.

As stated previously, most of Bette Davis' characters have often been described as the exemplar of the "the new woman," a female who appeared to confront and defy male power, with a rebellious attitude and often using her sexuality as a tool to achieve her goals. Even though Miss Moffat's character is mostly known for her self-sacrifice and suffering, Davis performance presents her as a strong woman that must have her way no matter what without deploying her sexuality as a weapon to achieve her goals. It is pertinent to take a look at a scene early in the film when Miss Lilly Moffat finds out that Glancermo has a high illiteracy rate and decides to take matters in her own hands by starting a new school. She enlists the help of Miss Ronberry (Mildred Dunnock) and Mr. Jones (Rhys Williams). In the scene, Miss Moffat presents her project with such confidence that even though it sounds outrageous for the small town, Ronberry and Jones agree to help her without question.

Shortly after her arrival into the town, Miss Moffat hears from Mr. Jones that most children in Glancermo work in the mines starting at a very young age and that their parents don't require them to attend school. Miss Moffat decides that things need to be changed. "When I was quite a young girl, I looked at the world straight in the eyes and decided I didn't like it. I saw poverty and disease, ignorance and injustice and in small ways I've always done what I could to fight them." It is relevant to point out that Davis does not say these lines as if she was some sort of wonder woman planning to save the world, but as if it was "a matter-of-fact" and very nonchalant. She says them at a steady speed and volume with no long pauses, only those necessary to differentiate between each sentence. As she utters these lines, Davis walks towards the house in steady footsteps with an upright posture, her chin up, holding some flowers with both hands at the lever of her waist as Mr. Jones and Miss Ronberry follow her. "So now that I have the fortune to come to this house with a little money, what could I do better than to continue to fight them? Especially with you two to help me- Oh Watty, could you put these in water?" Davis says those lines as she sits at the table, always keeping her upright posture and hands the flowers to Mrs. Watty. Notice how Davis never asks Jones or Ronberry if they wish to help her, but instead asks Mrs. Watty to put the flowers in water as if it was obvious they would help her. Her actions convey the sense that the favor she is asking is nothing out of the ordinary, when in fact starting a new school in a town like Glancermo would be a life-changing experience. At this point, Jones and Ronberry stand speechless. Miss Moffat asks them to sit down and proceeds to tell them that their lives (despite some minor accomplishments) have been completely meaningless. Therefore, it is in order that they join her in this endeavor. They are never given any other choice. Through out the conversation, Davis keeps the same steady speed and volume. As she talks to Ronberry and Jones she proceeds to pour some tea. Notice how she uses the props on the table, specifically the teapot, sugar, cups and saucers. Even though it is very subtle, it is important to note how she handles them, steady with confidence and without hesitation as she presents her wild project to two people she just barely met and who sit speechless next to her. Furthermore, her chin is always up, her head straight and more importantly, her eyes which are perhaps the most important Bette Davis facial feature move steadily from the tea that she is preparing to the people she is convincing, as if the task of convincing Ronberry and Jones to start a new school is not anymore difficult than preparing a cup of tea (notice how Moffat pours hot water from the teapot as she convinces Ronberry and proceeds to add sugar to the tea while she deals with Jones).

Even though Bette Davis' performance in this film is different from most of her most popular films where she plays a rebellious woman with a strong sexuality, her sexuality was something that studios hoped to cash in (as discussed earlier with the poster). What is certain and perhaps most significant is that, due to the immense popularity of Bette Davis' performances and her appeal, one cannot simply reduce her films in which she portrays a strong woman, as either a) overtly positive exemplar of the emancipation of women in film, or b) moral stories about what is conceived to be woman's place in society (according to traditional values and beliefs). It is often the case that, as a number of scholars have argued, that women that use her sexuality to achieve a goal are punished by the film's narrative, those who don't have to do so by restraining or even sacrificing their sexuality. I would argue that Betty Davis' performances and characters should perhaps be appreciated as "struggle," in which (even though) traditional values usually prevail within the narrative, these become contested and debated off-screen. Bette Davis' persona is often constituted in "real life" as trying to exercise the values of the "new woman" she portrays in many of her films even though she is in a hostile, male dominated environment. Her hardships are usually described through accounts of her personal problems: She is often described as a woman who is fighting to gain control of her own life, personal and professional. A big part of the myth-making process involves the role of fans, readers and writers who rejoice in learning in great detail as to how the actress challenged directors and studio heads throughout her career (such as the quote I included at the opening of this paper). As if by reading the many details of her off-screen "performances," would bring those characters alive and make us believe that outside of the Hollywood narrative, Hollywood's "new woman" did exist, without being punished or sacrificing their sexuality.

ALL ABOUT EVE (1950)

Mary Kearney

Twentieth Century-Fox, 1950. Producer: Darryl F. Zanuck. Director: Joseph L. Mankiewicz. Screenplay adapted by Mankiewicz from Mary Orr's 1946 short story, "The Wisdom of Eve." Director of Photography: Milton Krasner. Music: Alfred Newman. Art Direction: Lyle Wheeler and George W. Davis. Set Decoration: Thomas Little and Walter M. Scott. Editor: Barbara McLean. Wardrobe Direction: Charles LeMaire. Costumes for Bette Davis: Edith Head. Orchestration: Edward Powell. Makeup: Ben Nye. Special Photographic Effects: Fred Sersen. Sound: W. D. Flick and Roger Herman. 138 minutes.

CAST: Bette Davis (Margo Channing), Anne Baxter (Eve Harrington), George Sanders (Addison DeWitt), Gary Merrill (Bill Simpson), Celeste Holm (Karen Richards), Hugh Marlowe (Lloyd Richards), Thelma Ritter (Birdie Coonan), Gregory Ratoff (Max Fabian), Marilyn Monroe (Miss Caswell), Barbara Bates (Phoebe).

> I don't take the movies seriously, and anyone who does is in for a headache.... Honestly, every time I go to a preview of one of my pictures I wonder how soon they'll get wise and fire me. If they do, I'll probably go back to the theater, where I got my start.[74]

Quoted shortly after receiving her first Academy Award for Best Actress, Bette Davis made the above statement while taking an unauthorized vacation from the Warner Brothers' production of *The Golden Arrow* in March 1936. Threatening to leave Warner Brothers and Hollywood and return to Broadway if she did not receive a new contract worthy of an Oscar winner, Davis's comment signaled the beginning of an eighteen year battle that opposed Davis's perceptions of herself as an Academy Award-winner "worth her weight in gold" and Warner Brothers' primary understanding of her position within the studio as a contract player (albeit a sure draw at the box office). However, as Barbara Leaming suggests, Davis's success in the Hollywood film industry is perhaps best attributed to this unique combination of this actress's incredible drive towards stardom and Warner's relentless factory-like approach to filmmaking. Pumping out four to five Bette Davis pictures every year, the studio virtually guaranteed that this rising star would have no competition on the silver screen.

　　Originally trained as an actress for the stage, Davis left the theatrical world behind after a short but successful career on Broadway (much as the young actress does at the end of *All About Eve*). Lured to Hollywood by a talent scout for Universal Studios in 1930, Davis was offered a three-month contract and a weekly salary of $300, but decided to return to New York

---

[74] Barbara Leaming, *Bette Davis: A Biography* (New York: Simon & Schuster, 1992) 102.

after several disappointing performances in her first films. But before her bags were packed, Davis received a screen test offer by Warner Brothers, the success of which helped launch her career as a movie star. It would only be three years later, with twenty-one films under her belt, that Davis would attract the full attention of the Hollywood film community with her portrayal of Mildred Rogers in RKO's *Of Human Bondage*. Indeed, her performance in that film was considered so phenomenal that when Davis received her first Academy Award in 1935 for her more mediocre performance in *Dangerous*, many considered it a consolation prize for the injustice done to her when the Academy failed to nominate the young actress the previous year.

While popular notions of progress might encourage us to believe that there has been an evolution of female characters in film, the "women's films" of the 1930s and 1940s which Davis starred in were characterized by assertive, independent, sharp-witted women who resisted and often opposed—in many ways, more so than today—dominant notions of appropriate feminine behavior and the traditional roles of wife and mother. Although the filmic narratives of that time period often resolved this conflict by punishing the independent woman for her "transgressions," many of Davis's characters resisted such strategies. Indeed, it was this strong-willed, intelligent, independent female persona that Davis refined and projected so well in roles such as Julie Marsden in *Jezebel* (for which she received her second Academy Award in 1938), Judith Traherne in *Dark Victory* (1939), Leslie Crosbie in *The Letter* (1940), Regina Giddons in *The Little Foxes* (1941), and Charlotte Vale in *Now, Voyager* (1942). Characterized in the media as a bitchy, self-reliant, ambitious go-getter, it was this "Battling Bette" persona which brought women to the movie theaters in droves during World War II.[75]

However, the role of the ambitious, independent woman was not the only type of character played by Davis during this period. Indeed, it could be argued that her role as the suffering but strong martyr in films such as *The Sisters* (1938), *The Old Maid* (1939), *The Great Lie* (1941), *Old Acquaintance* (1943), and *The Stolen Life* (1946) was a more realistic portrayal of feminine experience during the war years. Compelled to fill positions and responsibilities left vacant by men who had gone off to fight in the war overseas, many American women found comfort in Davis as a role model of female strength and endurance.

As U.S. society returned to a middle-class, male-dominated ideology after the war, however, the women who had challenged traditional notions of feminine propriety by seeking jobs outside the home and lives outside marriage were coaxed out of their independent positions and firmly resituated in the more "appropriate" role of domestic femininity. It is in this 1950s post-war context—rather than the period of the late 1930s and 40s (the period during which Davis's career peaked)—that we must consider a film such as *All About Eve* and Bette Davis's portrayal of the fading stage star Margo Channing.[76] Instead of Davis acting in the role of the assertive single woman who "drops things on her way up the ladder so she can move faster" or the martyr who is sinned against yet endures, we have Davis portraying a combination of these two personae. As Davis so brilliantly communicates in one of the film's best monologues, Margo Channing is a 1950s' "female in crisis" who struggles to maintain a grip on her career as well as her personal life in the face of a friend's deceit and her own paranoia about growing old.

---

[75] Davis's persona as a strong, successful woman was further cemented when she was elected the first female president of the Academy of Motion Picture Arts and Sciences in 1941, a position she resigned from two months later when she felt she was being used as a figurehead. Her popularity among women increased even more when Warner Brothers finally agreed to the formation of Davis's own production company, B.D. Inc., one of the first independent production companies to be headed by a woman. (Unfortunately, Davis dismantled B.D. Inc. in 1947 after she virtually sabotaged the production of its only project, *Stolen Life*, in 1946.)

[76] According to Leaming, the Margo Channing role was originally intended as a vehicle for actress Susan Hayward. Although producer Darryl F. Zanuck decided to sign Claudette Colbert for the role instead (after first considering Marlene Dietrich, whom writer/director Joseph L. Mankiewicz rejected), Colbert withdrew from the project due to illness shortly before production on the film was to begin. Davis was signed as her replacement only after Gertrude Lawrence and Ingrid Bergman were considered for the part.

It goes without saying that there are many similarities here with Billy Wilder's *Sunset Boulevard* which was also released in 1950. Perhaps the first films to reveal and explore the intricate relationship of female ambition, physical beauty, age, and self-esteem, both narratives focus on the story of an older actress who finds it increasingly difficult to maintain control of her physical appearance and the devastating effect age has upon both her career and her relationship with a younger man. But while Norma Desmond of *Sunset Boulevard* comes across as a grotesque, deranged vampire who drains the vibrancy and talent from her young lover in order to stage her comeback and regain her star stature, Margo Channing of All About Eve remains more humanly neurotic as she attempts to guard both her younger lover and her career from the overly ambitious clutches of a younger woman. Thus, unlike *Sunset Boulevard* which shows the monstrosity connected with has-been stars, *All About Eve* allows Margo the possibility of gracefully reconciling her need to live as a person (as well as an older woman loved by a younger man) with her desire to exist as a star.[77] What is clear in both films, however, is the profound comment made on the tragic dependency of female success and self-confidence on youthful beauty rather than talent. (It is sadly ironic, therefore, that the "dumb blonde" role Marilyn Monroe portrays in *All About Eve* is the stereotype she would spend her life trying to overcome.)

It is in the opening scene of the film that Davis's phenomenal manipulation and control of non-verbal communication (learned as a young woman under the instruction of Martha Graham) are first brought to our attention. Through sublime camerawork that focuses on her unique eyes, the film introduces Margo (and Bette) to us in a manner fit only for a star:

> For a moment her heavily lidded eyes remain downcast, tantalizingly inaccessible—until the [narrator] recalls Margo's first stage appearance. Thereupon Bette slowly, majestically looks up, a spare gesture of astonishing power and intimacy.... One can think of few other screen actresses since the silent era capable of making so exhilarating an entrance by means of the eyes alone.[78]

In just three shots, each of which show a different position of her eyes, Davis communicates to us Margo's power as a star, her independence as a woman, and her deep contempt for Eve Harrington (Anne Baxter) who, instead of Margo, is receiving the highest honor the theatrical world can bestow.

Later in the film—just before the party scene which includes the famous "Fasten your seat belts" line—Davis again uses subtle gestures to communicate to us the frustration Margo experiences as she begins to believe that Eve is pursuing both her career and her younger boyfriend, director Bill Simpson (Gary Merrill). After discovering Bill and Eve engaged in a deep conversation from which she has remained excluded, Margo dashes quickly downstairs to interrupt them. But before they can see her and witness her frenzied state, Margo pauses to compose herself on the steps, and we watch as the tumultuous emotions she is experiencing inside radiate downward and are shaken out of her fingers. (Pay close attention to Davis's fingers in this film, especially when she is smoking cigarettes; rarely has a performer communicated emotion so subtly with a body part other than the eyes.)

After Margo dismisses her young progeny and begins a heated discussion with Bill about Eve, she flits nervously about the room making sure it is ready for her guests that evening. Pacing agitatedly as Bill assures her that there is nothing to worry about, Margo is drawn repeatedly to a covered candy dish whose contents she attempts to resist. Finally, just as Bill is pointing out the insecurities which cause her to doubt his affections and Eve's intentions, Margo

---

[77] Davis's caricature of Tallulah Bankhead here in a film about the reproduction of stars should not go without notice, for Davis performed in film many of the characters Bankhead successfully portrayed on the Broadway stage.
[78] Leaming, 224.

succumbs to the tension that has been building, grabs one of the candies, and flings it into her mouth, ostensibly relieving her frustration (as well as our own). However, when Eve enters the room only seconds later to ask for further instructions from her idol, Margo—the loquacious, sharp-tongued actress—is left speechless with her mouth full. With this one simple action, Davis has expertly revealed to us the nature of the aging actress's deepest fears: Margo's paranoia of growing old has become a hard pill to swallow.

These examples of Davis's non-verbal acting are not meant to suggest that it was only her superb use of gesture that made this actress a great star, for it is the expert delivery of dialogue in her scratchy, smoker's voice with its distinct "Yankee" accent that punctures scenes and draws our attention to Davis. An arched eyebrow, a flared nostril, a tossed head, the flourish of an arm only bolster the profound effect of her quick, sharp tongue. Indeed, Davis's delivery of Margo's quips has made Joseph L. Mankiewicz's dialogue some of the best remembered lines to have ever emerged from Hollywood.[79] As Davis told writer/director Mankiewicz on the set of *All About Eve*, "Now you know as well as I...that there is nothing more important to an actress, nothing she wants more, than a well-written part—and a director who knows what he wants, knows how to ask for it, who can help her provide it. This is heaven...."[80]

For her portrayal of Margo Channing in *All About Eve*, Bette Davis received the New York Film Critics award for Best Performance in 1950. Although Davis was nominated for a Best Actress Oscar for this role, the vote was split due to Anne Baxter's insistence that she also be considered in the Best Actress category (instead of the Supporting Actress slot). (They both lost the Oscar to Judy Holliday who starred in *Born Yesterday*.) Similarly, the vote for Best Supporting Actress was split due to the simultaneous nominations of Celeste Holm and Thelma Ritter for this award. *All About Eve*, however, received not only the Palme d'Or (best picture award) at the Cannes Film Festival but six Academy Awards: Best Picture (Darryl F. Zanuck), Best Director (Joseph L. Mankiewicz), Best Screenplay (Joseph L. Mankiewicz), Best Supporting Actor (George Sanders), and Best Costumes (Charles LeMaire and Edith Head). In addition to the actresses' Oscar nominations, Milton Krasner received a nomination for Best Cinematography, and Alfred Newman received a nomination for Best Music.

When Bette Davis received the American Film Institute's Lifetime Achievement Award in March 1977 at the age of 68, she indicated that the character of Margo Channing in *All About Eve* had been her greatest role.

---

[79] Ironically, Mankiewicz's film about the world of theatre became the source material for a Broadway musical, *Applause* (1970), which starred film actress Lauren Bacall.
[80] Joseph L. Mankiewicz with Gary Carey, *More About All About Eve* (New York: Random House, 1972) 89.

The Quiet American (2002)

Paul N. Reinsch

CREDITS. *Director: Phillip Noyce. Producers: Staffan Ahrenberg and William Horberg. Executive Producers: Moritz Borman, Guy East, Anthony Minghella, Sydney Pollack, Chris Sievernich, Nigel Sinclair. Screenplay: Christopher Hampton and Robert Schenkkan. Based on the novel by Graham Greene. Cinematography: Christopher Doyle. Editing: John Scott. Production Design: Roger Ford. Art Direction: Ian Cracie and Jeffery Thorp. Set Decoration: Kerrie Brown and Duc Tho Nguyen. Original Music: Craig Armstrong. 101 minutes. MPPA rating: R.*

CAST. *Michael Caine (Thomas Fowler) Brendan Fraser (Alden Pyle) Do Thi Hai Yen (Phuong) Rade Serbedzija (Inspector Vigot) Tzi Ma (Hinh) Robert Stanton (Joe Tunney) Holmes Osborne (Bill Granger) Quang Hai (General The') Ferdinand Hoang (Mr. Muoi) Pham Thi Mai Hoa (Phuong's sister) Mathias Mlekuz (French Captain)*

> A film actor must be sufficiently in charge of his material and in tune with the life of his character to think his character's most private thoughts as though no one were watching him – no camera spying on him.
>
> – Michael Caine [81]

James Naremore's *Acting in the Cinema* – which is excerpted in the *Reader* – is one of the few useful critical works about screen acting. Though film studies has expanded each year in its address to the myriad issues regarding films, acting remains unfortunately neglected. Michael Caine's non-academic work, *Acting in Film*, though designed primarily as a guide for actors, also functions as a discussion of the unique opportunities and difficulties which are products of film acting. Caine speaks from years of experience acting for the screen; he has worked in the movies since the mid 1950s. And Caine has worked steadily, adeptly appearing in everything from thrillers to comedies, lending his insolent grin and Cockney accent to a variety of characters. Though at times criticized for his choice of roles, Caine takes his job seriously and in the last few years his peers and film critics have lauded his performances. His work in *The Cider House Rules, Little Voice*, and today's film *The Quiet American* has brought him renewed acclaim.

In *The Quiet American*, Caine has the difficult task of portraying English newspaper correspondent Thomas Fowler. He does this by being "in tune with the life of [the] character," and becomes Fowler rather than simply playing him for an audience. Fowler is bound in marriage to a woman he does not love and who will not, for religious reasons, grant a divorce, and bound in love to a woman whose land is at war. He is stationed in Vietnam in the early

---

[81] Caine, Michael. *Acting in Film: An Actor's Take on Movie Making*. New York: Applause, 1990. p. 3.

1950s, documenting the widening conflict between French colonial forces and the rising tide of communists. He meets Alden Pyle, the titular quiet American, sent, he says, on an aid mission. The two men become friends, despite or perhaps because of their obvious differences. Pyle is drawn to Fowler's lover Phuong as well as to his goal of improving life in the country. Fowler is intrigued by Pyle's combination of earnestness, innocence, and ignorance, traits which to the worldly reporter are the marks of a uniquely American sensibility. The film, and the Graham Greene novel on which it is based, is about the relations between people and nations. In film and novel, the personal and political are seen to be one. Fowler has built up a wall of indifference which seemingly only Phuong can penetrate. His efforts to remain in Vietnam, despite his newspaper's attempts to bring him back to England, and the duplicitous actions of Pyle, gradually erode Fowler's self-imposed distance from the people and events around him. Caine, over the course of the film, reveals a man coming to terms with his own complicity for the world which he is paid merely to observe.

The first shot of the film depicts the conflict between surface and deep content, beauty and horror, as the camera tilts downward from a peaceful, beautiful harbor at night to a corpse floating in the water. The corpse is Pyle, the quiet American, whose attempts at improving life in Vietnam wrought quite the reverse. Fowler sees numerous corpses as part of his job and writes about them. But he is responsible for this corpse, more responsible than he is willing to admit. The film functions partially as a mystery: who killed Pyle and who is Thomas Fowler? Pyle is Greene's fictional representation of the real men who intervened in the affairs of Southeast Asia to combat the growth of communism in the area. While fighting the Korean War, Americans were also active in Vietnam, funding the French attempts to suppress the communist forces. Fowler, Greene's mouthpiece, disagrees with the Americans' methods, if not their politics. And eventually he must act. As Fowler's assistant Hihn says, in a line taken directly from Greene's novel: "Sooner or later one has to take sides. If one is to remain human."

Director Philip Noyce and Michael Caine have managed to put Greene's world on the screen, something many others have failed to pull off. Perhaps no novelist, particularly among those who wrote in English, chronicled the 20th century with more precision and concern than Greene. The author struggled with his Catholic upbringing for the whole of his long life. He worked as an editor for a newspaper, a film critic, and for the British Foreign Office all while pouring out his own concerns and fears into his characters. Greene traveled at seemingly every opportunity and used his experiences abroad for his fiction. Works such as The Power and the Glory, and The Heart of the Matter, along with *The Quiet American*, demonstrate his interest in what is universal and what is particular about human relationships and cultures.

Greene famously labeled his work as falling into two categories: serious work (such as those listed above) and "entertainments." His "entertainments" – novels of international espionage and suspense – have much more easily been transferred to the screen than his more serious work. Fritz Lang's Ministry of Fear and Carrol Reed's The Third Man are but two examples of successful film adaptations of Greene's work. Joseph L. Mankiewicz's 1958 film of *The Quiet American*, on the other hand, is typical of how the serious work has historically fared (excepting Neil Jordan's The End of the Affair in 1999). Though not a disaster it is decidedly not a representation of Greene's work. Greene was not pleased with the film and wrote: "Mankiewicz . . . made it into a propaganda film for America in Vietnam, when it had been an attack on the American influence in Vietnam." Elsewhere he continues: "the book was based on a closer knowledge of the Indo-China war than the American director possessed and I am vain enough to believe that the book will survive a few years longer than Mr. Mankiewicz's incoherent picture."[82]

Greene's novel has endured beyond the 1958 film and has certainly not been superseded by Noyce's work. Yet Caine's performance as Thomas Fowler may prove definitive. Caine slowly

---

[82] *The Graham Greene Film Reader.* ed. David Parkinson. New York: Applause, 1995. pp. 543, 443

reveals the inner turmoil of Fowler with discrete actions and phrasings. Eventually it boils to the surface when Phuong leaves him for Pyle. Fowler barges into Pyle's office yelling hysterically before collapsing and sobbing uncontrollably in the bathroom. This is one of the few moments where Caine is not primarily responding to his fellow actors. In his book, Caine states: "In movies, it is reaction that gives every moment its potency."[83] Particularly in the first half of the film, but truly throughout, Caine reacts to his fellow actors and the events which occur around Fowler. The character is not passive, but withdrawn and watchful and Caine's performance matches Fowler's identity perfectly.

Much of Caine's work in the film is captured in unflinching closeup, permitting, even daring the audience and camera to read his face. When working in closeup, Caine advises actors: "Just rely on your character's thought processes and your face will behave normally."[84] Note the scene where Folwer and Pyle settle in to the watch tower after the car has run out of gas. The two men sit in silence until Pyle says that he wonders what Phuong is doing. Folwer's demeanor is subtlety warm and reflective as he describes how Phuong's spends her days. When Pyle asks if Fowler has known a lot of women, he responds: "one starts out promiscuous and ends up being like your grandfather: faithful to one woman." Caine's delivery of the line is deceptively simple both visually and aurally but one can see Caine thinking; he is realizing what Phuong means to him. In *The Quiet American* we can see Caine live by his own advice. Caine and Fowler both think onscreen, rendering every blink and glance laden with meaning. His work is careful and precise, and seems less like acting than being. Additionally in this scene Caine's onscreen mythology (established in Alfie and other films) of the English rake deepens his performance. Caine speaks as an aging man who has lived a full life and lends his own experience to his depiction of Fowler.

The Quiet American was platform released domestically and found an audience. Unfortunately its gross of nearly 13 million fell considerably short of its budget of 30 million. The film was reviewed favorably and received several nominations. Caine was nominated for numerous awards for his performance, including the Academy Award, the BAFTA, and the Golden Globe. Director Philip Noyce was also honored with awards and nominations, some which also acknowledged his other effort of 2002, *Rabbit-Proof Fence*, a film about the government's misguided attempts to relocate aboriginal children in his native Australia.

---

[83] Caine, p. 11
[84] Caine, p. 61.

4
VISUAL DESIGN

The image is indivisible and elusive, dependent upon our consciousness and on the real world which it seeks to embody. If the world is inscrutable, then the image will be so too. It is a kind of equation, signifying the correlation between truth and the human consciousness, bound as the latter is by Euclidean space. We cannot comprehend the totality of the universe, but the poetic image is able to express that totality.

—Andrey Tarkovsky, *Sculpting in Time*

CTCS 190 LECTURE OUTLINE – WEEK IV   **LECTURE 4**

A. **Elements of visual design:**
  1. Costume, hairstyle, makeup
  2. Decor
      a. Set (studio-built, location, and computer generated)
      b. Set dressing
      c. Prop
  3. Lighting
      a. Three-point lighting system
      b. Direction of light
      c. Quantity of light
      c. Film stock
      d. Film gauge
      e. Filters
  4. Color
      a. Components and uses
      b. Black and white vs. color
  5. Title design
      a. Representational
      b. Abstract
  6. Special effects
      a. Makeup
      b. Mechanical
      c. In-camera
      d. Post-production/computer-generated images
B. **Visual design as a part of film space**
C. **Functions of visual design:**
  1. Direct attention to or away; lighting as molding objects and establishing depth
  2. Shaper of story's setting (spatio-temporal dimensions)
  3. Mood and atmosphere
  4. Delineation of character
  5. Objective correlative: projection of a state of soul
  6. Visual motif
  7. Enunciator of subject, theme, and conflict
  8. Character and plot catalyst
  9. Color
      a. Metaphoric associations
      b. Relation to spectator
  Visual Analysis
  10. Title design as anticipation of thematic values or in-medias-res function
D. **Introduction and Screening**

Notes

Notes

MEET ME IN ST. LOUIS (excerpts)

From *Vincente Minnelli and the Film Musical* (1977) by Drew Casper

The structure of Meet Me in St. Louis—four faded seasonal photographs of the Smith house on Kensington Avenue, St Louis, circa 1900—relates that the film is a memory and establishes the awesome and nostalgic tone of the entire piece.

Moving into Kensington Avenue and this world as each photograph fills with color, blows up, and comes alive, the film set itself up as a contrast with one's own world. This vanished, almost mythic past is a fantasy burgeoning from the seeds of remembrance and counterpointing present reality. Here is a world of a family that spans all ages from the tot Tootie to Gramps, of homemade ketchup, corned-beef-and-cabbage nights, and chocolates in lavender tine boxes topped with a pink satin bow. Young ladies heat water on the kitchen stove to clean their tresses. Pictures of butterfly wings grace the walls. An ice wagon hobbles down the street. "Clang, clang, clang [goes] the trolley." The measure has three beats. Rituals, like grace before meals, bon voyage parties where a trumpeter performs a solo and the "welch rabbit is ginger peachy," Halloween, Christmas, and of course, the commemoration of the Louisana Purchase are kept. Boys do not like girls with the bloom rubbed off. When a lad in New York telephones a girl in St. Louis, the urgency and financial expenditure are expected to indicate nothing less than a proposal. A girl is in love with the boy next door. The family's happiness takes precedence over financial gain.

Within the film itself, the venture from reality to fantasy is undertaken. In mid-summer, the Smiths anticipate (a form of hope), project, and envision the fair, still seven months away, and their city which will be transformed because of the fair. Esther [Judy Garland] and John [Tom Drake] are part of an outing to the fairgrounds in late summer. On Christmas Eve, Mr. Smith [Leon Ames] makes extravagant predictions about the future of the city. With the Smiths' springtime visit to the fair, their expectation is rewarded, their vision comes true. St. Louis is transformed.

Esther's reality of being a high school senior with "too much bloom" leaves something to be desired and that something is John Truett. "The Boy Next Door" and "Over the Bannister Leaning" are daydreams and picturesque poses. These pretences are much more professionally crafted than that wispy, half-baked pose on the porch's wooden rail with a rose almost kissing her cheek opposite John smoking his pipe on the lawn. With John's proposal, elicited by her, Esther's reality is transcended.

Tootie [Margaret O'Brien] imagines all the time—her doll with the four fatal diseases, and the entire trick-or-treat sequence from Mr. Bankoff's murder to John's assault. With here, it is not a question of making but sustaining a fantasy.

"You and I" of Mr. and Mrs. Smith is a wedding-day reminiscence. The song's lyrics paraphrase the wedding vows. The tune approximates Wagner's Lohengrin. Their duet transports them (they are oblivious to their family's intrusion during this memento) to a state different from the one they inhabit in the film's opening two-thirds where he barks and she submits, where her feelings are overlooked in his decision to move to New York. For the rest of the film, they exist in a new way, eloquently imaged in their ardent, tender kiss and embrace, her uncontrollable tears of joy, and his soft hushes on Christmas Eve. The fantasy of their first days together is renewed.

Décor:

Not a single Minnelli interview desists from the topic of the décor's importance and integration in his work: "The decors are enormously important to me."[85]

> [Décor] flows from the subject. It renders in dramatic terms the time and space where people live…Ideally, it is the projection of the characters…You are not able to separate the character from his milieu, to arbitrarily isolate the character by a close-up. The character's surroundings, his way of life, the chairs on which he sits, the house where he lives, all is a part of his personality. It is the history of this man. It is as others seem him…[86]

> The characters are so much more real when they are surrounded by an environment that helps to dramatize them. You don't see people isolated, you see them in their surroundings.[87]

> I do a great deal of research and try to find the style and color sense for that particular film. Then it's a matter of the way you compose with the camera or the movement of the camera, trying to make something that fits that particular film.[88]

> The characters are much better when they're surrounded by their own things. You don't see people isolated. You see all around them their effects. The objects that surround them are important.[89]

…From these quotes, the director's methodology with regard to décor, which applies to spectacle's other elements as well, emerges as a process of researching the story's subject and its spatial-temporal context, using the dramatic elements as the criterion for the décor's selection, which is then worked out with collaborators, and lastly, translating it filmically.

Painting is one of the prime sources of research for Minnelli, a Sunday painter himself and an habitue of the gallery. "The look of [St. Louis] was based squarely on period shots of the town"…and American Gothic painters. "Of course, the fair had a look of its own. There was plenty of material on that."

…Décor's most obvious function is, of course, as a carrier of context, as a shaper of the story's spatial-temporal dimension. Everyone lives in a world of a certain shape. Minnelli shows up that shape…

But Minnellian décor usually goes beyond this function by creating a spatial-temporal atmosphere which has something to do with the olfactory, tactile, kinesthetic sensations as well as the visual and aural ones and a spatial-temporal mood which has something to do with sentiment or emotion…St. Louis's summer is rich, indolent, carefree with possibility; autumn—spare, chilly, ominous; winter—still, expecting, velvet; spring—fluid, sweet, joyful…

Décor delineates character…During the elder sister's ode to the fair in barbershop harmony, Esther, standing behind Rose [Lucille Bremer] seated at the piano, places her hands

---

[85] Bitsch and Domarchi, "Entretien avec Vincente Minnelli," p. 10.
[86] Domarchi and Douchet, "Renontre avec Vincente Minnelli," p. 6.
[87] Diehl, "The Directors Go to Their Movies," p. 5.
[88] Serebinsky and Garaycochea, "Vincente Minnelli Interviewed in Argentina," p. 24.
[89] Personal Interview, February 7, 1973.

on her sister's shoulders. A bust of a couple positioned exactly as the two sisters embellishes the piano top. This pithy detail clues one in on the girls' pose while deepening the story's context—people of this period, especially impressionable maidens, copied the art of the times...

Décor projects states of soul. Autumn and the swirling leaves and dust, the wiry branches of the black trees, the raging bonfire, the horrific masks, the imposing columns of Bankoff's porch express Tootie's wild and sinister imaginings...

One piece of décor continually props up in a Minnelli musical—the window frame and its extension, the balcony ledge. Besides providing a frame to the composition, in which case it functions purely aesthetically, this image crystallizes plot, conflict and theme. The window frame and balcony ledge, situated yet opening onto a view, prospective, or horizon like some wharf on the infinite, contains the dialectic of immanence-transcendence, present-future, reality-fantasy...

Esther's two daydreams, "The Boy Next Door," and "Have Yourself a Merry Little Christmas," are delivered at window ledges. John is on the other side both times. Through the trolley's windows, Esther pines for her beau. From the bedroom window, Mr. Smith gazes below at Tootie pummeling the snowmen. This incident triggers his decision to remain in the Midwest. Also, the border of the photographs that open each section of the film is a metaphorical equivalent of the window frame.

Color:

Décor, costumes, and lighting are the carriers of color in Minnelli's work. Color is important and essential because it not only records, but reveals as well. It builds a scene in terms of spatial-temporal dimensions, atmosphere, mood, and character...

Color is also an integral part of the film's structure. It flows throughout a Minnelli musical like visual music, affecting one's emotions precisely as music affects them. This use of color is an emotional expression of the plot, conflict, characters, and theme.

St. Louis's four seasons are designated by specific colors—summer's reds and roses, autumn's oranges, yellows, browns, winter's deep blues and fuscous, and spring's white. The darkening of the values parallels the dimming of the family's hope of attending the fair. When all seems lost, the color is drained from the frame. Mr. Smith, in an ebony smoking jacket, leaves the window from which he witnessed Tootie's destruction of the snowmen in the black night. He rambles through Agnes' bedroom in darkness, descends the steps to the parlor, and comes to rest in an indigo chair. Brown barrels of paper-wrapped objects sling jagged shadows across the room. Even the walls have square areas, lighter than the rest, where colorful pictures used to hang. He strikes a match to light a cigar and keeps the orange flame burning, suggestive of the light in his head or idea (the use of the prop as dramatic point). The camera dollies in and the scene is suddenly suffused with light and warmth. The flame burns his finger. He shouts, "Anna," rises, and turns up the desk lamp. The family in variously-hued frocks resembles a crazy quilt on the steps. Gramps [Harry Davenport] turns up the gas jets. The climax comes when the Smith family is assured of being in St. Louis for the fair and color rushes through the house like blood through a once-frozen body. The dazzling white of the next sequence, denotes newness and renovation.

Musical Sequence: "Meet Me in St. Louis"

St. Louis's opening musical sequence, one of the most fluent in all film musicals, touches almost every dramatic base. It advances the plot by introducing and delineating the house and its members, establishes the conflict, and provides context and mood. A framed, faded photograph of an old suburban neighborhood with white filigreed mansions and wide lawns turns into color, growing larger and larger until it bursts its edges and begins to breathe, move a bit, and finally, come to life. A horse-drawn beer wagon with two boys fighting atop the yellow barrels creaks up the street while a shiny red motor car hoots in the opposite direction (America is on the verge of the scientific age). Passersby saunter beneath the emerald trees and bicyclists pedal every which way, among whom is Lon turning into a red-roofed Victorian residence with barbershop-striped awnings.

Cut to Lon [Hank Daniels] depositing groceries on the kitchen table where his mother and the maid are absorbed in making ketchup. While thumbing through the latest Sears and Roebuck catalogue, he offhandedly hums the fair song. Enter Agnes [Joan Carroll], dripping wet from a late afternoon swim, who is warned by mother: "Don't track up the floor now." Putting on clodhoppers, she replies: "I won't," and begins the lyrics of "Meet Me in St. Louis" in the kitchen, continues through the parlor where she sneezes on the word "fair" (quite a natural piece of business), up the staircase, along the upstairs corridor, all against the clump-clump rhythm of the shoes. At the bathroom door, which is locked, she jumps back as Gramps starts the song over her feeble, shaky rendering of the second "Louie" near the song's close due to her fright.

Cut to Gramps concluding a shave in the bathroom where he extends the natural pause after the first line of the song with: "I'll be out in a minute, Agnes." Overlapping her, "All right, Gramp," he continues the song: "Meet me at the fair."

Cut to Gramps prancing out of the bathroom which Agnes enters, down the corridor, and into his room where he tires on different hats before his dressing mirror, while improvising some lyrics: "...we coochie coochie coochie / We'll be a tootsie-wootsie / Meet me in the fair," and substituting others with la-las and de-das. From below his open window, the correct lyrics are heard, faintly at first but quickening in volume. Glancing below, Gramps watches a tennis party, among whom is Esther, approaching a horse and buggy. Amid cheers, laughter and adieus, they chant the song's last lines before depositing Esther on the curb stone.

CRITICAL FILM ANALYSES

ROSEMARY'S BABY (1968)

Harmony H. Wu

1968 Paramount release of a William Castle production. Director: Roman Polanski. Screenplay: Roman Polanski, from the book Rosemary's Baby by Ira Levin. Director of Photography (Technicolor): William Fraker. Editors: Sam O'Steen and Bob Wyman. Music: Christopher Komeda. Production Design: Richard Sylbert. Costume Design: Anthea Sylbert. Art Director: Joel Schiller. Make-up: Allan Snyder. Hair Styles: Vidal Sassoon, Sydney Guilaroff, Sherry Wilson. Sound: Harold Lewis. Assistant Director: Daniel J. McCauley. MPAA Rating: R. Running time: 134 minutes.

CAST: Mia Farrow (Rosemary Woodhouse), John Cassavetes (Guy Woodhouse), Ruth Gordon (Minnie Castevet), Sidney Blackmer (Roman Castevet), Maurice Evans (Hutch), Ralph Bellamy (Dr. Sapirstein), Charles Grodin (Dr. Hill), Patsy Kelly (Laura-Louise), Victoria Vetri (Terry Gionoffrio), Phil Leeds (Dr. Shand), Tony Curtis (voice of Donald Baumgart).

"This is no dream! This is really happening!" Rosemary cries in the midst of the surreal sequence in which she 'dreams' the devil rapes and impregnates her. It is precisely the tension between knowing what is real and what is not that drives *Rosemary's Baby* forward, in spite of not much happening in terms of plot.

From the opening title sequence, in which a female voice eerily sings a wordless lullaby, director Roman Polanski positions the viewer in a space that is wholly real: the rooftops of the old brownstones in Manhattan. Through masterful direction and camerawork, Polanski and USC alumnus William Fraker probe the surface of familiar reality to find what sinister lurks below.

Most of the "action" in this horror film takes place in Rosemary and Guy Woodhouse's new apartment in the Branford building, which became vacant after its previous tenant, an old woman with a strange collection of herbs in her indoor garden, died after falling mysteriously into a coma. After deciding to rent the place, the Woodhouses' old friend Hutch informs them that Branford was known as "Black Branford" before the War, because of the macabre events that took place there, including the murder of devil worshiper Adrian Marcato in the lobby and the eating of children by the Trench sisters. Dismissing such stories and the implication of bad karma, Guy and Rosemary move in, re-decorating the dark and heavily curtained apartment with white paint and bright yellow curtains and furniture.

The genius of the film is in its presentation of a brightly lit world that is prettily papered and painted, in which something is not quite right. Through the subtlety of suggestion, Polanski makes a simple wall, blank except for its cheery yellow paper, positively creepy, and a plain broom closet downright scary. Fraker's camera snakes through the halls of the apartment at a low angle, tracking just ahead of the characters who weave in and out of the rooms. When Rosemary and Guy first move in, a still camera watches them enter the apartment at the other end of the hall. As they walk toward the camera, bodies looming larger, heads and shoulders disappear, introducing a vaguely disconcerting atmosphere. This mood is only heightened by the stark scene of their first sexual encounter in their new home: seated cross-legged on the barren floor of their empty living room, with only the low light of a single lamp and the dim glow from the windows, Rosemary and Guy undress silently and separately. Instead of moving in for a more intimate shot, the camera at first keeps its distance, again signaling that in spite of this attractive young couple's appearances, something is amiss in this marriage.

Careful attention to the color palette and costume heightens the seeming picture-perfection of Rosemary's world. Rosemary, like her dream apartment, appears in yellows and navy, seeming at times like a fragile doll in a lovingly decorated doll-house. Minnie Castevet, their elderly nosy neighbor who along with her husband Roman has devilish designs on Rosemary's womb, by contrast is costumed in bright mismatched colors, presenting a garish figure, which is made comically obvious in the POV shot in which Rosemary peers through her peephole to find a distorted and grotesque Minnie trying to peer back on the other side.

Hairstyle and makeup are also used to maximum effect in Rosemary. While at the beginning of the film Rosemary sports girlish pony-tails and bangs, soon after discovering she's pregnant, she gets what is possibly one of the most famous screen haircuts—a very short pixie cut. This dramatic change in the star's appearance midway through the film signals a narrative shift too: not only does her new boyish 'do suggest an unconscious rejection of her new role as mother, it also marks the point where Rosemary's bodily health begins its rapid decline. Her severe hairstyle draws attention to the angles of her face, which are made deeper and darker with makeup, making her illness-in-pregnancy all the more visually alarming. In stark contrast to the usual glow of mothers-to-be, Rosemary becomes increasingly sick, pale, and skinny, and in spite of the Castevets', Dr. Sapirstein's, and Guy's statements to the contrary, the viewers know something is wrong.

Much as, narratively speaking, the Branford houses dark secrets behind its doors, Polanski and Fraker worked together to recreate that effect cinematically. The architecture of the Branford set is brilliantly exploited (Rosemary was shot on location for two weeks in Manhattan for exteriors; the rest was filmed on Stage 12 of Paramount's Los Angeles lot). [90] In Visions of Light, a documentary on the art of cinematography, Fraker describes how Polanski asked for a shot of Minnie on the phone in the bedroom from Rosemary's POV in the living room. Having set up a lovely shot with Minnie framed beautifully by the doorway, Fraker goes on to describe how Polanski rejected the shot and moved the camera over little by little until he said it was perfect. The shot Polanski created had Minnie's face and half her body obscured by the doorjamb. The genius of this move only came to Fraker at the screening of the film—when the shot appeared, the audience, he relates, craned their necks in an effort to see around the door jamb.

Using only a 25mm lens for the whole film (except the one peephole shot), Fraker was able to work around the narrow halls and doorways to develop a familiarity of the apartment, which is itself much like a character in the film. Unusual frame compositions and depth of field

---

[90] Barbara Leaming, *Polanski: A Biography — Filmmaker as Voyeur.* New York: Simon & Schuster, 1981, p. 86.

are used to emphasize the increasing emotional distance growing suspicion between Guy and Rosemary. Their conversations are often shot with one of the two in the foreground, to one side of the screen, and the other in another room, on the other side of the frame, far in the background. There are also several shots in which the back of a character's head looms large in the frame, while his/her conversant stands in medium shot facing us (quite distinct from the more normal "two-shot"). Shots like this work together with architecturally composed shots, like with the door jamb, creating that tension and desire on the part of the viewer to see what s/he's missing.

Rosemary's Baby was the Polish director's first American film. He was called to the project based on previous works such as *Repulsion* (1965), after B-horror film director and producer of *Rosemary* William Castle, who purchased the rights to Ira Levin's novel for $150,000 after Alfred Hitchcock passed, decided that the material needed a different stylistic touch from the one Castle himself would provide.[91] Polanski was signed for a flat $150,000, with no back-end profits from returns. Polanski adapted the novel to screen himself with art director Richard Sylbert (uncredited), sketching out in the most careful detail the elements of set and costume design,[92] which undoubtedly in part accounts for the amazing visual coherency of the film. Though Polanski originally wanted Jane Fonda or Tuesday Weld (depending on where you read) to star as Rosemary, and Robert Redford as Guy, a Paramount lawsuit made the latter impossible to cast, and when Polanski met Farrow, he knew she was perfect.[93] The role launched the young actress's budding career, although she was already famous for being Frank Sinatra's wife. It has been suggested that Sinatra couldn't stand his naïf bride's (the 23-year-old Farrow was 30 years Sinatra's junior) developing independence and stardom, for he served a dismayed Farrow divorce papers on the set of *Rosemary's Baby*.

Paramount executives continually hounded Polanski about going over budget, and in the end, the film was $400,000 over its $1.9 million budget.[94] In spite of a "C"/condemned rating from the National Catholic Office for Motion Pictures (for "the perverted use which the film makes of fundamental Christian beliefs and its mockery of religious persons and practices"[95]), however, audiences flocked to the film and Paramount more than recouped its costs with the film grossing over $30 million.[96] Reviews ran the gamut from unbounded praise to disappointment and confusion. *Variety* called the film "exhilarating" with "hot, sustained [box office] profits" (May 29, 1968), while *Films in Review* called it "gabble," and expressed surprise that audiences believed, contrary to the reviewer's point of view, that the film is "seriously about witches," suggesting somewhat patronizingly instead that the film is "about the delusions women nurture before and after they give birth" (Aug.-Sep. 1968). Singling out Farrow's exceptional performance, Renata Adler of *The New York Times* also considers the question of the film's "reality," but concludes that "it is almost too extremely plausible." Although the review states the film "has nothing to be excited about," this is more in reference to the film's stylized and highly cinematic rendition of the generally more over-the-top horror genre film, stating that "the good side of that is that you can see the movie, and like it, without risking terrors or nightmares" (June 13, 1968). Ruth Gordon won the Oscar for her supporting role as Minnie Castevet.

In retrospect, *Rosemary* seems to have inspired the cinematic cycle of "devil children" films, with the most notable examples being *The Exorcist* and *The Omen*. Perhaps especially in comparison with its "devil spawn" progeny, *Rosemary* remains today a horror film of exquisite subtlety and stylistic beauty and control.

---

[91] Leaming, p. 82.
[92] *Ibid.*, p. 84.
[93] *Ibid.*, p. 84.
[94] Roman Polanski, *Roman*. New York: William Morrow & Co., Inc., 1984. p. 274.
[95] Quoted in Ivan Butler, *The Cinema of Roman Polanski*. New York: A. S. Barnes & Co., 1970. p. 161.
[96] Leaming, p. 84.

BABETTE'S FEAST (1987)

Broderick Fox

1987. A Just Betzer/Panorama Film International production in cooperation with Nordisk Film and the Danish Film Institute. Claes Kastholm Hansen, Executive Producer. Just Betzer and Bo Christiensen, Producers. Gabriel Axel, Director. Gabriel Axel, Screenwriter. Adapted from a story by Karen Blixen (Isak Dinesen). Henning Kristiansen, Director of Photography. Sven Wichman and Jan Petersen, Production Designers. Annelise Hauberg, Pia Myrdal, and Karl Lagerfeld, Costumes. Lydia Pujols, Bente Møller, and Elisabeth Bukkehave, Make Up Artists. Finn Henriksen, Editor. Michael Dela and John Nielsen, Sound Design. Per Nørgaard, Original Music. Jan Pedersen, Gastronomic Advisor. Eastmancolor. 103 Minutes.

CAST: Stéphane Audran (Babette). Birgitte Federspiel (old Martina), Vibeke Hastrup (young Martina), Bodil Kjer (old Philippa), Hanne Stensgard (young Philippa), Jean-Philippe Lafont (Achille Papin), Gudmar Wivesson (young Lorenz Lowenhielm), Jarl Kulle (old Lorenz Lowenhielrn), Bibi Andersson (Lady from the Court), Bendt Rothe (Old Nielsen), Ebbe Rode (Christopher), Lisbeth Movin (The Widow), Preben Leerdorff (The Captain), Poule Kern (The Vicar), Axel Strøbye (Coachman), Ebba With (Lorens' Aunt), Erik Petersen (Young Erik), Holger Perfort (Karlsen), Asta Esper Andersen (Anna), Else Petersen (Solveig), Finn Nielsen (Grocer). Therese Højgaard Christensen (Martha), Las Lohmann (Fisherman), Tine Miehe-Renard (Loren's Wife), Thomas Antoni (Swedish Lieutenant), Gert Bastian (Poor Man), Viggo Bentzon (Fisherman in Rowing Boat), Cay Kristiansen (Poul, Ghita Nørby (Narrator).

Attempting to penetrate the lucrative American magazine market, Danish writer Isak Dinesen, (aka Karen Blixen, best known for *Out of Africa*) took the advice of a friend: "Write about food. Americans are obsessed with food."[97] The resulting short story, "Babette's Feast," appeared in the June, 1950 issue of *Ladies' Home Journal*. Nearly four decades later, Danish director-screenwriter Gabriel Axel's film version of the story was proclaimed an art house hit by American film critics, winning him the 1987 Academy Award for Best Foreign Film. Yet in an interview for the Spring '88 issue of *Sight and Sound*, Axel remarked, "The film hasn't received a single award in Denmark. No one is a prophet in his own country."[98] Perhaps Dinesen's friend's estimations of American art house appetites hold some truth...

Axel's film version of *Babette* opens with a flat plane of gray sea and sky, zooming out to reveal the rooftops of a late 19th century village on Denmark's remote Jutland Peninsula. A female narrator tells us of two pious elderly sisters, Martina and Philippa, who forsook the extravagances and amenities of the outside world in favor of ascetic living and the continuing of their deceased father's strict Lutheran ministry. Through flashback, the film visualizes each sister's brush with an opportunity to leave abstemious existence in favor of romance, wealth, and prestige. Flashback also explains the presence of their French housekeeper, Babette, who

[97] Nancy Bilyeau. "Hunger Artist," *American Film* (March, 1988): 68.
[98] Jill Forbes. "Axel's Feast." *Sight & Sound* (Spring, 1988): 107.

fled Paris when civil war broke out in 1871. The flashbacks end, the film returning to 1885. After fourteen years, Babette's only remaining link to her native land is a lottery ticket, renewed annually by a friend in Paris. When the ticket comes up a winner, the question becomes whether Babette will remain in the austere village or depart with her small fortune, returning to the material comforts of the outside world.

The film's theme of "repression vs. expression" derives powerful support from a meticulous visual design, juxtaposing the ascetic lifestyle of the Jutlanders against the encroachment of outside-world pleasures and material indulgences. Dinesen's original story took place in the Norway, but scouting the Norwegian coast during pre-production, Axel found its villages too beautiful and idyllic. He changed the setting to Denmark's Jutland Peninsula and built an entire town to his specifications.[99] The resulting village is religious in its adherence to a limited color palette of grays and browns. Narrow, blown-out windows and candlelight predominate as means of lighting the sparse interiors, their simple wooden furnishings and whitewashed walls quickly dropping off into shadow. The villagers wear plain clothing, mostly black and gray, the women's silver hair neatly pinned, their faces pale and without makeup. Even weather is manipulated as a design tool. When it is not raining or snowing, the coastal village remains under gray cloud cover, rendering exterior lighting flat and diffuse.

Introduction to the outside world comes in a cut to a military courtyard, a row of alternating black and white horses stepping in perfect formation before the imposing yellow façade of an official-looking headquarters. Ornate moldings and banisters, period furniture, gowns and jewelry glimpsed at an officer's ball, women's hair in coifed ringlets, men's moustaches carefully waxed and curled--the décor, costuming, hairstyling, and makeup of this outside-world are clearly distinct from the Jutland Peninsula's. Yet compared to other late 80's-early 90's period films (Scorsese's *Age of Innocence*, for example), *Babette*'s depiction of late 19th century "society" is decidedly restrained. The interiors may be brighter than Jutland's, sourced with candelabras, chandeliers, and floor-to-ceiling windows, but the film's color palette opens up only slightly-dark green and pale blue walls, the gleam of brass buttons up the front of navy blue uniforms, rust colored waistcoats. The most striking use of color is carefully saved to coincide and underscore the film's midpoint: Babette receives the letter announcing her lottery winnings from a messenger on horseback, the jacket of his uniform *crimson*.

Special visual attention is afforded to moments of intersection/connection between the film's two worlds. Standing together, faces lit by the glow of a single candle, young Philippa and her Lieutenant are momentarily transported from the surrounding blue darkness of the cottage's front hallway. The finer furnishings of the cottage's sitting room remain largely hidden in shadow throughout the film, save for a singing lesson scene between young Martina and a visiting French opera star. Here, light from the small windows reaches even the furthest wall of the room, glinting off a gold picture frame and the lacquered piano, the understated room and its furnishings imbued with sudden elegance.

With details of her Parisian past still unspoken after fourteen years of quiet service in the sisters' employ, Babette's character serves as a physical manifestation of the conflict between Jutland and the world outside. As such, the film affords her a subtle, but distinct visual treatment of her own. She first appears at the sisters' door on a stormy night, hidden beneath a hooded black cloak, utilizing costuming to establish the air of mystery surrounding her throughout the film. Her subsequent costuming remains in line with that of the other Jutlanders in its simplicity, but her auburn hair and the hint of color on her lips cast Babette in a restrained warmth, distinguishing her from the other women of the village. Bartering with a fisherman on the rocky beach, standing in silhouette against an orange evening sky, Babette is the only principal character repeatedly photographed in direct sunlight, underscoring her importance and centrality as the film's major agent of change. Babette is a ray of light in the

---

[99] *Variety* (March 2, 1988): 4.

otherwise bleak village, the film's visual design hinting at a latent exuberance beneath her reserved exterior.

Careful control and pacing of visual design elements throughout the movie allows the late Minister's anniversary dinner to prevail as both the narrative and visual climax of the film. In his *Monthly Film Bulletin* review Richard Combs describes the banquet as "a set-piece comparable to those in a Hollywood spectacular. The sequence took a fortnight to shoot and employed one of Copenhagen's top chefs, Jan Pedersen of LaCocotte, as its second unit director."[100] The meal's splendor comes from its details, rather than from overt displays of ostentation or color—the glow of candlelight off the white tablecloth, the glint of silver and crystal, the golden fizz of champagne. *Babette's Feast*, a film sparing in dialogue by modern standards, achieves much of its storytelling and thematic expression through a carefully executed visual design that, as Gabriel Axel, himself, notes, is as much about the elements withheld from the screen as it is about those presented:

"I find a similar quality in certain painters, such as Braque or Vermeer. Nothing extraneous, only the essential. In a film, what I look for is the actor's face. Nothing should detract from the actor's eyes, in which everything can be read, whether in long shot or in close-up. In *Babette* there's hardly a story. It's just a series of portraits. And that's my ultimate aim."[101]

EST–OUEST (EAST–WEST) (1999)

Broderick Fox

1999. Sony Pictures Classics, American Distribution. A Co-Production of Le Studio Canal +, CNC, FR3, Gala Films, Mate Productions, NTV-PROFIT, Sofica Sofinergie 5, Studio 1+1, and UGC YM. Régis Wargnier: Director. Yves Marmion, Producer. Rustam Ibragimbekov, Sergei Bodrov, Louis Gardel, and Régis Wargnier: Screenwriters. Laurent Dailland: Director of Photography. Aleksei Levchenko, Vladimir Svetozarov: Art Direction. Pierre-Yven Gayraud: Costume Design. Jocelyne Lemery, Marie-France Taulere, and Mina Matsumura: Make Up. Patrick Girault, Agathe Moro, and Pascal Ferrero: Hair. Hervé Schneid: Editor Guillaume Sciama: Sound Design. Patrick Doyle: Original Music. 120 Minutes.

CAST: Sandrine Bonnaire (Marie), Oleg Menshikov (Alexei), Catherine Deneuve (Gabrielle), Sergei Bodov Jr. (Sacha), Ruben Tupiero (Seryozha, age 7), Erwan Baynaud (Seryozha, age 14), Girigori Manukov (Pirogov), Tatayana Dogileva (Olga), Bogdan Stupka (Colonel Boyko), Meglena Karalambova (Nina Fyodorovna), Atnass Atanassov (Viktor), Tania Massalitinova (Alexandrovna), Valentin Ganev (Vovodya Petrov), Nikolai Binev (Sergei Kozlov), René Féret (French Ambassador), Daniel Martin IV (Turkish Captain), Hubert-Saint-Macary (Embassy Advisor), Jauris Casanova (Fabian)), Joel Chapron (Theater Interpreter).

---

[100] Richard Combs. *Monthly Film Bulletin* (March, 1988): 74.
[101] *Forbes*, 107.

The opening titles of Régis Wargnier's *Est-Ouest's* skim dizzyingly over blue-gray ocean waves, immediately establishing both a color scheme and a visual motif for the film-in the ensuing 120 minutes, cold, desaturated colors will predominate, and water will come to represent hope. Hope certainly fills the hearts and minds of the ship's passengers, Russian émigrés the likes of Alexei, who is returning to his homeland, along with his French wife, Marie, and their son, Seryozha. As the title sequence turns more distinctly representational, cutting to the ship's stately dining room, costume, hair, and set dressing immediately draw audience members back in time to 1946 postwar Europe.

Yet the high spirits of the Golovin family and their fellow passengers will fall hard and fast only moments after the ship has docked at the Russian port. Red, a color initially representative of Western consumption through the ship's dining room upholstery, Marie's lipstick, and the wine raised in a voyage-ending toast, is quickly reassigned to Marie's bloody face after her welcome interrogation, the crimson trimmings on military uniforms, and an abundance of Socialist Party banners—visuals of pain and Stalinist power.

As hinted earlier, the film's color scheme consists predominately of desaturated grays, blues, and greens, underscoring the somber mood and bleak atmosphere of Kiev. Lighting corroborates such sentiments, remaining for the most part, diffuse and flat, adding to the bland, claustrophobic feel of a Socialist state in which five families are forced to share a communal apartment. Weather contributes to both the lighting and color schemes. Exterior scenes are predominately shot under gray cloud cover, reflecting the interior mood of Marie and her draining struggle to find a way back to France.

The consistency of such design makes even the slightest deviation pronounced and important. Colors often turn towards slightly warmer browns and yellows within the relative safety of the Golovin's one-room space. Marie's camaraderie with the young swimmer, Sacha, is one of the only bright things in her life, and the exterior scenes down at the river, where she watches him training, are marked by perhaps the film's most dramatic changes in lighting—simply by virtue of the fact that the sun is permitted to come out, brightening the screen for brief moments and saturating the greens and browns of the riverside foliage.

Such moments of visual design change during Sacha's training sessions are also appropriate, given the motif of water suggested earlier; his swimming talent opens up one of the two possible hopes for Marie's escape. The correlation between water and hope is again underscored, later in the film, when a scene of disappointing news between Marie and the Kiev swimming coach plays out with the two standing in the deep end of an empty, outdoor swimming pool. But all hope is not yet lost; the ocean waves that began the film will return once more, in one of *Est-Ouest's* most dramatic and rousing sequences.

Being a period piece, visual design components are key to establishing the spatial-temporal components of setting. Costume, hair, and makeup go beyond simply establishing a believable postwar Russia, however; they also underscore the grueling passage of some seven years Marie must endure in her quest for escape. Towards the film's end, there is no need for Wargnier to waste screen time delivering scenes of Marie serving her long sentence in a Russian labor camp; her greasy, limp hair and pallid face upon reuniting with her husband and son imply all she has gone through with a single image.

Catherine Deneuve's character, the touring French actress Gabrielle, serves as Marie's second source of hope, and she is fittingly introduced backstage, in full stage makeup and an ostentatious, scarlet costume, underscoring, again, the correlation between red, power, and Western consumption. Her appearances later in the film, out of theater garb, would be unremarkable in any other film, but here, juxtaposed against the poverty and austerity expressed through other characters' threadbare garments and pale visages, Gabrielle's tailored suits, coifed hair, painted lips, and powdered cheeks jump from the screen, emphasizing the separate world in which she exists and to which Marie so longs to return.

Certain pieces of set dressing take on especial significance, becoming key props in *Est-Ouest*. The close-up of Marie's French passport, her only link to her former identity, being torn up by the Russian security officer in one of the first scenes augurs the severity of what is to come with a visual punch no line of dialogue could ever match. Note the repeated appearance of letters in the film and the range of purposes they serve—eliciting a range of emotional associations, providing strong elements of suspense, serving as a structuring element to the work, and exemplifying objective correlative to characters' inner states.

A pile of nondescript, dusty books become central to the story as they are in French (therefore dangerous property) and come to replace Marie's passport as a link to her Western identity and a source of bittersweet comfort. Even a piece of costuming (a pair of sole-trodden, otherwise nondescript shoes) is elevated to prop status, catalyzing perhaps the film's most heart-pounding climactic moment.

Though *Est-Ouest* garnered just under $3 million in U.S. theaters, reviews by American critics were predominately favorable. The film garnered year-2000 Oscar and Golden Globe nominations for Best Foreign Language film, along with four French César noms, winning the Audience Choice Award at both the Palm Springs and Santa Barbara International Film Festivals. Though none of the aforementioned nominations were in categories involving visual design, Wargnier's film certainly exemplifies the range of powerful functions this formal component of mise-en-scène can provide in the production and consumption of a film text.

5
COMPOSITION

Today we can say that at last the director writes in film. The image—its plastic composition and the way it is set in time, because it is founded on a much higher degree of realism—has at its disposal more means of manipulating reality and of modifying it from within. The film-maker is no longer the competitor of the painter and the playwright, he is, at last, the equal of the novelist.

—Andre Bazin, "The Evolution of the Language of Cinema," 1955

CTCS 190 LECTURE OUTLINE – WEEK V   **LECTURE 5**

A. **Composition**
   1. Framing
      a. Aspect ratio
      b. Aesthetic consideration
      c. On-screen vs. off-screen space
   Visual Analysis #1
   2. Staging
      a. Proxemic patterns <u>within the frame</u>
      b. Shape, line, plane and stasis/movement (<u>within the frame</u>)
      c. Balance; dominant and subsidiary contrasts
   Visual Analysis #2
   3. Photographing
      a. Proxemic patterns <u>outside the frame</u> (between spectacle and spectator); focal length of the lens and camera distance
      b. Image size: extreme long shot, long shot, medium shot, medium close-up, close-up, and extreme close-up
      c. Angle
      d. Stasis/movement (of the camera): through space and in a fixed position on a tripod
   Visual Analysis #3
      e. The notion of perspective: physically, psychologically, ideologically
      f. The correlative relationship of space and time
      g. Objective camera; subjective camera (mindscreen)
      h. Distortions of movement: fast motion, slow motion, reverse motion, freeze frame
B. **The Functions of Composition**
C. **Introduction and Screening**

Notes

Notes

TYPES OF CAMERA LENSES AND CAMERA MOVEMENTS

CTCS 190 Document

Camera Lenses

Each lens has its own focal length, which equals the number in millimeters used to express a lens's respective width or length. In other words, a focal length refers to its range of focus (above 50 mm = very "long"; below 50 mm = very "wide")

Fixed Focal Lengths:

1) Normal/middle focal-length lens (approx 50 mm):
   Attempts to reproduce depth relationships much as they are seen by the human eye; tendency to eliminate distortion.

2) Telephoto/long focal-length lens (more than 50 mm):
   Magnifies the size of an object at great distance while it flattens depth relationships; movement toward and away from camera appears to be slowed down when this type of lens is used

3) Wide-Angle/short focal length lens (less than 50 mm):
   Allows the camera to photograph a wide area while it exaggerates and deepens depth relationships; straight lines near the edge of the frame are warped and movement toward and away from the camera appears to be faster when this type of lens is used

   3a) Extreme Wide-Angle lens: Also known as a "fish-eye" lens. It creates a visual effect similar to looking through a crystal ball.

#1, #2, #3 are also called PRIMARY LENSES.

Variable Focal Length:

Zoom lens (with a variable distance as wide as 35 mm and as long as 400 mm):
   Approaches an object within a larger frame to accentuate it; or the reverse, leaves an object within a larger frame to minimalize it; to bring action nearer or keep action farther away; zoom in/zoom out; on occasion it can do this so suddenly like a flash of lightning, we call it a "crash zoom;" but it is not normally used in such a dramatic fashion—mostly center zoom; with zoom lens, image is not as crisp as in a primary lens.

   Use of zoom lens to avoid camera movement; used a good deal in TV (sports events, news broadcasting).

With the use of variable lens, a common technique is to "rack focus." In other words, blur the focal planes in the sequence and force the spectator's eyes to move with those areas of the space that come into sharp focus.

Another technique is to "follow focus." In other words, through the focus ring on the lens, you can follow the action or the object in motion

Camera Movements

Tracking or trucking: forward, backward, or lateral movement of camera

1) Handheld: mounts strapped to operator's waist or shoulders and a special series of springs and counterweights lock the camera fairly steady as the operator moves about.

2) Steadicam: first introduced in the 1976 film *Bound For Glory*. Steadicam was invented by Garrett Brown with engineers from Camera Products, Inc. A Steadicam is a device consisting of a lightweight frame, tension arm, movie camera, and small TV monitor, allowing the camera operator to move around smoothly while filming; like handheld shooting without lack of stability inherent in handheld shooting; creates space, flexibility, mobility, dynamism.

3) Dolly: camera is mounted on a wheeled vehicle that follows action dolly made specifically for the camera and this type of movement it has an attachment for the camera, 2 seats (1 for the camera operator, 1 for the director), wheels that ride on 8–10 foot sections of track that are laid down; these tracks used to weigh over 400 lbs., but now, they are made of light PVC plastic pipe and snap together thus ensuring smooth movements; the camera can also be placed on a bike, wagon, wheelchair which substitutes for a dolly if the production can't afford a dolly or if a dolly is impractical (e.g., too big to use).

4) Crane: airborne shots using a camera mounted on a mechanical are more than 20 feet in length allowing a photographer to descend or ascend in a scene.

   Jib Crane: unlike the traditional cranes, the jib crane allows the cameraman to stay on the ground, as the camera is mounted on a counterweighted arm that can extend up to 25 feet.

5) Aerial: camera on helicopter

CRITICAL FILM ANALYSES

HOW GREEN WAS MY VALLEY (1941)
Philantha Kon

Directed by John Ford. Produced by Darryl F. Zanuck. Screenplay by Phillip Dunne, based on the novel by Richard Llewellyn. Cinematography by Arthur Miller. Film edited by James B. Clark. Music arranged by Alfred Newman, choral effects by Eisteddfod Singers of Wales. Narrated by Rhys Williams. Art Direction by Richard Day and Nathan Juran. Makeup by Gut Pierce. Set Decoration by Thomas Little. Costumes by Gwen Wakeling. Sound by Eugene Grossman and Roger Heman.

CAST: Walter Pidgeon (Mr. Gruffydd), Maureen O'Hara (Angharad Morgan), Donald Crisp (Gwilym Morgan), Anna Lee (Bronwen Morgan), Roddy McDowall (Huw Morgan), John Loder (Ianto Morgan), Sara Allgood (Beth Morgan), Barry Fitzgerald (Cyfartha), Patrick Knowles (Ivor Morgan), Morton Lowery (Mrs. Jonas), Arthur Shields (Mr. Parry), Ann Todd (Ceinwen), Frederick Worlock (Dr. Richards), Richard Fraser (Dacy Morgan), Evan S. Evans (Gwinlyn), James Monks (Owen Morgan), Rhys Williams (Dai Bando), Lionel Pape (Old Evans), Ethel Griffies (Mrs. Nicholas), Marten Lamont (Jestyn Evans). Running time: 118 min, B/W.

Based on a best-selling novel, this saga of Welsh coal-mining life is replete with human interest, romance, conflict, and emotion. It is inspiring and heart-breaking enough to call it a "Hollywood milestone" (*Halliwell's Film Guide*) and "a perfection of screen art...one of the finest pictures ever made" (*Variety*).

Set at the turn of the century, it is seen from a fictional present in which sixty year old Huw Morgan summons the remembrance of happy things past. In first person narrative form, the story is episodically told in reverie, running through a period of years. Huw's fond recollections explore his youth, his cheerful home on a Welsh hillside, his family, and the joys, griefs, struggles, and triumphs of those who lived by the pit. Told from Huw's point of view, the film permits an idealized depiction of the Morgans. In contrast, Richard Llewellyn's novel offers a stark portrayal of the destructive and dehumanizing forces of industrialization. It is about the economic, physical, and moral breakdown of the valley and its people. "It is the story of a good people's doom, the story of how the black coal retrieved perilously from the earth darkens the lives of those who dig it and befouls the verdant valley in which they live."[102] Ford's film reasserts traditional family values for a nation on the verge of WWII, recovering from the Depression and concerned with an insistently organizing labor force.

Huw's voice-over begins the film, telling us that the valley and his family are doomed and that he is leaving the valley which is so unlike the one in his memory. The camera pans from the faceless man to the window in the little room and tracks through it. It opens up the frame spatially and the movement in a right-left direction is backwards, into the past. The film cuts gradually (first a long shot, then a medium shot, and finally a close-up) to an old woman in a static, frozen composition. Her expression is rapt with memory. From this shot, the film dissolves to an unbounded moving long shot of the valley of Huw's memory. The movement of Huw and his father and of the sheep lend the scene a sense of awakening movement, indicating that the life lies in the past, in contrast to the dead present. The bleakness of the first sequence and the sadness of the narrator indicate a tragic point of view. The entire matrix of social relationships in the film is laid out in the first few minutes, aided greatly by the use of shots that establish them. The opening sequence of the film describes a complex setting in detail, introduces us to eight or nine characters, to an entire village, and immerses us in a nostalgic vision of a way of life that will begin to deteriorate in the next sequences.[103]

The constant insertion of the voice-over represents the man stepping in to tell us about the boy's story, both reminding us that it is his story and providing insights into feelings that are felt by the child but interpreted by the man. The flashback structure and voice-over are devices which maintain a specific point of view and function as distancing devices to protect against too directly confronting the Freudian implications (the death of the father which finally allows Huw a place in the visual world of the film) and stark tragedy of the breakdown of the valley and of the family.[104] A large variety of visual devices continually affirm Huw's narrating presence and reminds us that the events that we see are from his point of view. This includes scenes that echo his mood in lighting such as the shadowed corridor on his first day of school; scenes that echo his mood in cutting such as when Huw opens the classroom door and we see crosscutting between Huw and the students at their desks which follows the pattern of Huw's timid attempt to take in the situation; and scenes echo his mood in sets such as when Huw visits married Angharad at the Evans' mansion and the gates and doors are twice their real size.

The frame of the film is enclosed in exteriors by light and composition. Going to and coming from the mine, a line of houses always bounds the side of the frame. We never know what is on the other side of the houses. The mine with its smoke towers and the church with its bell tower define the upward limits of the frame of the town. These structures are composed to constantly appear at the edge of the frame, limiting and defining a boundary. Inside, low ceilings, dark foreground objects, and dark areas confine and limit the frame. Characters are often pressed against the ceiling by an extreme low angle, defining the world of the film captured within the memory of the boy.

Even the relationship between the father and sons is indicated by composition. When talking to his sons, the earlier scenes are constructed as a triangle with Mr. Morgan at the apex and the sons at the lower two angles of this triangle. We recognize Mr. Morgan's greater power position as he stands above them and center frame in this triangular, hierarchical construction. This later shifts as the union's threatened strike sets off the change in the family structure/power relations and the father no longer occupies center frame. The father cannot keep the home isolated from the economic tensions of the mine. The tensions interrupt the

---

[102] Bosley Crowther, "How Green Was My Valley," *The New York Times Film Review* (Nov. 1, 1941).
[103] Henderson, Brian, "Tense, mood, and voice in film," *Film Quarterly* 36:4, pp.4-17, 1983.
[104] Place, J.A., *The Non-Western Films of John Ford*, Citadel Press, Secaucus, 1979.

previously ordered visual balance of the dinner table. In a high angle shot (contrasted to the eye-level shots of the opening dining scenes which were head-on or profile), Ivor rises, compositionally challenging his father's authority. Finally, in a long shot, all the grown sons stand as their parents and Huw remain seated. The polarities are defined as the sons leave the frame (and the house), crippling the composition and isolating the father. He is shot from across the long, empty table, emphasizing his aloneness. Huw, recognizing that he is now alone with his father, sneezes to get his father's attention. When his father acknowledges Huw's presence, Huw contentedly resumes eating, once again confirming to us that we are seeing this from his point of view.

Huw's moments of triumph, in which he is on the verge of becoming a full member of the family in his own right, are often snatched from his grasp as the attention is shifted to someone else. When he comes home with his Latin report, his parents fuss over him for a moment, but then Bronwen upstages him with her visual position in the frame and her talk of her loneliness since Ivor's death. When Huw has gone down into the pit and received his first pay, he takes it to his father who congratulates him; then his brothers, just discharged, enter the frame in a very low angle, upstaging him again and shifting the attention of their father and of the audience away from Huw. At the end, when Huw's dead father is brought up out of the mine, the picture freezes in a balanced and finished composition. Mr. Gruffyd stands on the platform like a comforting angel, and for the first time Huw is a part of the tableau instead of simply observing the rest of his family as they form this moment in his memory. Returning to the Freudian implications suggested in the film, Huw rides out of the mine with his dead father's head resting in his lap. He has taken his father's exact position when his father rode out of the mine with dead Ivor's head in his lap in an earlier scene.

We experience the film through the memory and perception of the now-grown Huw, rendering the experience personal as we share his point-of-view throughout, yearning to participate in the past which ceases to exist as he becomes a part of it. Throughout the film, the scenes become progressively darker in contrast to the warm, safe, balanced, and well-lighted early scenes. Mr. Morgan's death and Angharad's unhappiness follow with increasing blackness as the life of the valley itself deteriorates.

The film was received extremely well and at the Academy Awards it defeated *Citizen Kane* as the Best Picture and Ford defeated Welles, Wyler, Chaplin, Hitchcock, Cukor, and Capra as the Best Director.[105] Something should also be said for the perfect reproduction of a stone colliery, stone houses, and chapel built in the Ventura hills especially for this film.

> **Academy Awards:** Best Picture (Darryl F. Zanuck), Best Director (John Ford), Best Supporting Actor (Donald Crisp), Best Cinematography (Arthur Miller), Best Art Direction (Richard Day, Nathan Juran, Thomas Little); nominated for Best Screenplay (Phillip Dunne), Best Musical Score (Alfred Newman), Best Supporting Actress (Sara Allgood), Best Editing (James B. CLark), Best Sound (Eugene Crossman and Roger Heman). The New York Film Critics presented John Ford their Best Direction Award of 1941.

---

[105] Sinclair, Andrew, *John Ford*, Dial Press, New York, 1979.

THE PARADINE CASE (1947)

Bobby Simmons

Directed by Alfred Hitchcock. Written by James Bridie, Ben Hecht (uncredited), Robert Hichens (novel), Alma Reville, and David O. Selznick. Produced by David O. Selznick. Cinematography by Lee Garmes. Edited by John Faure and Hal C. Kern. Original Music by Franz Wasman. Production Design by J. McMillan Johnson. Art Direction by Thomas N. Morahan. Set Direction by Emile Kuri and Joseph B. Platt. Costume Design by Travis Banton.

CAST: Gregory Peck as Anthony Keane, Ann Todd as Gay Keane, Charles Laughton as Judge Lord Ilorfield, Charles Coburn as Sir Simon Flaquer, Ethel Barrymore as Lady Sophie Horfield (Barrymore received an Academy Award Nomination for Best Supporting Actress for this role), Louis Jourdan as Andre Latour, Alida Valli as Mrs. Maddalena Anna Paradine, Leo G. Carroll as Counsel for the Prosecution, Joan Tetzel as Judy Flaquer, Isobel Elsom as the Innkeeper, John Williams as a Barrister. Technical Specifications: Film negative format: 35 mm. Printed film format: 35 mm. Aspect ratio 1.37: 1. Budget: $4,000,000 U.S. Domestic Box Office: $2,400,000. Length: 125 minutes.

Before taking 190 this semester, had you ever heard of Alfred Hitchcock's *The Paradine Case?* Don't worry you are not alone. With competition like *Vertigo, Rear Window,* and *Psycho,* it's no wonder that this 1947 courtroom melodrama gets little attention in Hitchcock's lexicon of great cinematic accomplishments. Based on actual events, the novel *The Paradine Case* was written by Robert Hitchens, and adapted for the screen by a number of writers, including Hitchcock's wife, Alma Reville, and producer David O. Selznick. The story concerns one Maddalena Anna Paradine (Alida Valli), on trial for the murder of her elderly husband, and her lawyer Anthony Keane (Gregory Peck). In the process of preparing a defense for the distant, but alluring Paradine, Keane falls in love with his client, despite the loyalty and dedication of his wife Gay (Ann Todd). Keane's feelings cloud his approach to the Paradine defense, and threaten not only his client, but also his marriage and career as well.

Although we like to think of Alfred Hitchcock as an auteur with complete control over the films he directed, this was not the case in the early part of his career. Indeed, David O. Selznick was a thorn in Hitchcock's side through the entirety of their working relationship, and *The Paradine Case* was luckily their final effort together. Selznick's participation with the script, and his involvement with particular actors, bound this film in ways that Hitchcock disliked, but had to negotiate within.[106] For example, the thoroughly American Gregory Peck was not Hitchcock's first choice to play British barrister Anthony Keane—he wanted Laurence Olivier.[107] Nor was little-known Alida Valli (credited simply as "Valli" by Selznick in the film)

[106] Leff, Leonard J., Hitchcock and Selznick: *The Rich and Strange Collaboration of Alfred Hitchcock and David O. Selznick* in Hollywood, Weidenfield & Nicholson, New York, N.Y., 1987, pp. 224-264.
[107] Truffaut, Francois., *Hitchcock,* Simon and Schuster, New York, N.Y., 1967, pg. 173.

his favorite to play Mrs. Paradine—Hitchcock eyed Greta Garbo for that role.[108] But Selznick's position on the film and relationship with these actors landed them their roles. Despite his displeasure with the adaptation and casting, Hitchcock nonetheless used his understanding of the story and characters to compose shots and sequences that conveyed the drama of each relationship, each misstep, and each wrenching realization in *The Paradine Case* to his audience.

Just over 15 minutes into the film, Hitchcock takes us to a party where Anthony and Gay Keane mingle with Judge Lord Horfield (Charles Laughton), Lady Sophie Horfield (Ethel Barrymore), Sir Simon Flaquer (Charles Coburn), and his daughter, Judy (Joan Tetzel). The six have dinner together; the men and women split up, and then regroup. As they reconvene, Judge Horfield emerges into the sitting room, puffing cigar smoke, and immediately has his eye caught by Gay Keane, who is seated next to Lady Sophie Horfield. Hitchcock first trains his lens on Judge Horfield walking into the room, flanked by the other characters who are in various states of focus and whose bodies drift in and then out of the frame. The subject of this sequence is clearly the salacious judge.

He notices something, and the film cuts to a relatively swift dolly shot, zeroing in on the Gay's bare shoulder. Hitchcock then returns to Judge Horfield who, without betraying an overt reaction, suggests to his wife that she show the other guests her jewelry, which is located in another part of the room. Hitchcock pulls the camera back from his medium shot of the judge, and pans to the left, revealing Lady Sophie, Anthony Keane, and Sir Simon Flaquer. The judge moves back and to the left until all four are in the same shot. Hitchcock's camera, still moving, then follows the judge left, keeping him in focus in the foreground, and as the other characters recede in the room to see the jewels, Hitchcock keeps them in frame, though steadily more out of focus as they move into the rear corner of the room. Only a parting glance by Judy Flaquer hints at Gay Keane's coming discomfort.

The action now is clearly in the foreground on Judge Horfield and Gay Keane, but the frame still shows the other four characters in the back of the room, out of reasonable earshot. With this series of camera moves and framing, Hitchcock gives us a palpable sense of the depth of the room in the background and the crowded space in the foreground as the judge inches toward poor, upstanding Gay. In the next shot, the judge leans in close to speak with Gay, filling the entire right side of the frame with his bloated head. Although she has the majority of the screen space, Gay is clearly in a defensive posture, trying to fend off the encroaching judge. Hitchcock then goes back to the original shot showing the others in the background, and the judge has moved even closer on the couch to Gay. He picks up her hand and places it on his leg, and then the action cuts to a two-shot of just Gay and the Judge. Despite the fact that the frame shows only the two of them, we perceive what is now the off-screen space where the other characters are interacting, thus amplifying the terse exchange between the two characters on screen. Although their dialog is quite telling of the nature of this interaction, it is the framing, staging, and photography that convey the visceral quality of Gay's experience as a lawyer's wife sitting with a lecherous judge.

Just into the second hour of the film, Maddalena Paradine's murder trial is underway. Anthony Keane is in love with Mrs. Paradine, and suspects that Andre Latour (Louis Jourdan) is a rival for Mrs. Paradine's affections. Latour was the loyal valet to the deceased, and partly out of jealousy, Keane will suggest to the jury that Latour actually murdered his boss in order to have Mrs. Paradine to himself. This strategy, should it work, would both exonerate his client and remove his romantic rival, if only Mrs. Paradine were not so mysteriously opposed to this course of action. Hitchcock again treats us to some compositional choreography, using the frame, staging, and photography to create an emotionally tense and telling sequence.

---

[108] Ibid.

With Latour entering the courtroom, Hitchcock sets up a shot that contains Mrs. Paradine, in focus, in a near close-up on the right side of the screen. In the same frame on the left side and in the background, we see Latour come through a set of doors and into a walkway that runs behind Mrs. Paradine. In a fantastic combination of moves, we see Latour pass from left to right across the screen in the background, while Mrs. Paradine passes from right to left across the screen in the foreground. "We had to do that in two takes," Hitchcock later said. "First, I photographed the scene without her; the camera panned him all around, at a two-hundred-degree turn, from the door to the witness box. Then I photographed her in the foreground; we sat her in front of the screen, on a twisting stool, so that we might have the revolving effect, and when the camera went off her to go back to Louis Jourdan, she was pulled off the screen. It was quite complicated, but it was very interesting to work that out."[109]

This deft piece of camerawork and staging also captures the reactions of Mrs. Paradine, who can only hear Latour's footsteps behind her. While the exact dimensions of the Paradine-Latour relationship are still unclear, it is obvious that each provokes a distinct emotional response in the other. As the camera pans, we see Mrs. Paradine brace herself for Latour's entrance. Her eyes move cautiously around, as if to imagine the sight of Latour walking behind her. As a result of the rotating stool, her lighting changes as he passes behind her and the camera passes before her. As the shot began, Mrs. Paradine's face was lit by a high-key light coming from her right side (our left), cloaking the left side of her face in shadow. As the shot progresses, a fill light gradually illuminates the left side of her face while the right side falls into darkness. The light and shadow washing over her face in this sequence seem to mimic the feeling of blood rushing to and from a face, suggesting that Mrs. Paradine is flush with anxiety. In a critical sequence devoid of dialog, it is the compositional strategy—the framing, staging, and photography of Hitchcock—that conveys this emotional reaction so effectively.

---

[109] Truffaut, Francois, *Hitchcock*, Simon and Schuster, New York, N.Y., 1967, pg. 175-6.

DAYS OF HEAVEN (1978)

Peter Britos

Distributor: Paramount Pictures. Writer/Director: Terrence Malick. Director of Photography: Nestor Almendros. Executive Producer: Jacob Brackman. Producers: Bert and Harold Scheider. Additional Photography: Haskel Wexler, A.S.C. Music: Ennio Morricone. Editor: Billy Weber. Costume Designer: Patricia Norris. Art Director: Jack Fisk.

CAST: Bill (Richard Gere); Abby (Brooke Adams); The Farmer (Sam Shepard); Linda (Linda Manz); The Farm Foreman (Robert Wilke); Linda's Friend (Jackie Shultis); Mill Foreman (Stuart Margolin); Harvest Hand (Tim Scott); Dancer (Gene Bell); Fiddler (Doug Kershaw). Length: 95 minutes.

> It's the magic hour. Actually, it's only about 20 minutes; the time from sunset till complete darkness, and the most beautiful light of the day, when the light is truly magic, because you don't know where it comes from.[110]
>
> —Nestor Almendros

Days of Heaven is a beautifully shot, evocative film about the loss of innocence in America before its entry into the first world war. Set in the wheat fields of the Texas panhandle in 1916, the story centers on three migrant workers and their tragic relationship with a wealthy young land baron (Sam Shepard). After smashing a foreman to the ground in the steel mills of Chicago, Bill (Richard Gere) packs his sister Linda (Linda Manz), and lover Abby (Brooke Adams) on to a train full of itinerant workers headed for the agricultural heartland of the country. There they find employment harvesting wheat under difficult, peasant conditions. Framed early in the narrative as a feudal conflict between the classes, the film slowly takes on epic, if not biblical proportions as the shy land baron falls in love with Abby, and Bill convinces her to marry the dying millionaire.

From the first images the film suggests it be read as a realist parable. The title sequence intercuts period photographs by Lewis Hine with modern re-creations by Edie Baskins, anticipating a documentary-like authenticity. This documentary feel extends to the harvest work scenes and images of industrial machinery belching and threshing as the workers reap the wheat. In keeping with this scope, the film is presented in 70 millimeter panavision and Dolby Stereo, with a masterly score written and conducted by Ennio Morricone (*The Good, the Bad and the Ugly, A Fistful of Dollars, Once Upon a Time in the West, 1900...*).

When it premiered, the film was both lauded as a masterpiece and panned as fluff. Unanimous in praise and derision was the stunning photography of Nestor Almendros (with additional photography by Haskel Wexler). Critics note that the film is full of lyrical camera movement, epic horizons, period costumes, baroque machinery. The shots of vaulted skies and vast wheat fields are composed like painterly tableaux. The use of color and light throughout is exquisite and precise. But critics as well voiced annoyance at the film's elliptical structure, its

[110] From *Nestor Almendros Interview* by Clarke Taylor. Calendar, Sunday, September 17, 1978.

inconclusive or seemingly arbitrary scenes, its lack of dramatic impetus or psychological depth. For instance, the characters of the film are often composed in silhouette against the darkening sky, privileging the importance of the figure as aesthetic device, rather than study in character. Some critics predicted the film's difference in rhythm and dramatic logic from "ordinary" films would put off spectators. Yet much of this sense of fragmentation and vagueness is due to the way the filmmaker makes sense of his material. Less interested in linear cause and effect than the poetics of association, Malick makes heavy use of metaphor and analogy to structure film meaning. In such a system, suggestion is as important (if not more so) than explicit exposition. Images and the way they unfold are loaded with symbolic significance. Interpretation is contingent on connecting seemingly disparate details.

We see this unspoken detail in the foreshadowing of the locusts, and their ultimate association with the "unholy" *ménage à trois*. After the bedroom scene between the farmer and Abby the night of their wedding, we cut to a single locust resting on a leaf. In the very next scene the camera lingers on Bill as he watches his lover and her new husband drive off on their honeymoon. After this, we see him alone in the grand house, which he had so coveted; and then the whole "family" is at the lake, and these are clearly the "days of heaven." But at what price?

In structure and theme, the film has much in common with the story in *Genesis* of Abraham and Sarah entering Egypt, posing as brother and sister. Here too, the Pharaoh who lets Sarah into his house is visited by a plague of locusts. In *Days of Heaven* murderous passions collide in a climax reminiscent of biblical holocaust and retribution. But retribution from what? The duplicity of the lovers? The exploitation of the masses? At the least, the plague of locusts and the accompanying apocalyptic fire represent chthonic forces beyond the control of man. Nature takes on a curious significance here. It symbolizes at once the promise of freedom, and the mechanism of divine purgation. Here the farmer's existential despair is quieted, and the perverse desires of the worker are made fatally manifest. But Malick refuses to spell it out. He holds the spectator at bay with a certain cool detachment. We see this in the film's many long shots, or medium long shots. Close ups are used sparingly, and rarely linger. Ultimately, this is a movie without heroes. Nature is too encompassing and timeless for such conceit.

In short, this is a film about more than beautiful imagery and the overwhelming presence of nature. It is a tale like all of Malick's films about the dark, destructive side of human nature. As in the recent *The Thin Red Line*, Malick explores the interrelated dichotomy between nature and culture. Nature, as mentioned, is itself an ambiguous force. At once vast and teeming with life, a symbol of rebirth, it is as well as symbol of uncontrollable multiplicity and existential desolation. The rapacious culture of Western man, it seems, cannot be reconciled with the generative potential of nature. Humans are destined to slash and burn in pursuit of material desire, while nature inevitably rises again from the ashes of destruction. Interestingly, ambiguity mediates the juxtaposition of nature and culture. This philosophical position is manifest in the editing and composition of scenes. When Bill talks Abby into marrying the farmer, for instance, her face is clouded in shadows. She leaves him in the dark walking into the sunlight towards the farmer across the pond. Then a flock of geese fly by over head, signaling amongst other things, a change of seasons, and the relative banality of the act. Visual juxtaposition rather than dialogue reveal the innermost thoughts and feelings of the characters, as well as the attitude of the filmmmaker. In this sense, the deadpan looks of Gere or Shepard must be understood in context of edited, associational information. Likewise, such scenes as the apocalyptic fire and the hunting of bill near the film's end must be "felt" through the devices of a shaky hand held camera whipping this way and that, or the accelerated tracking and dolly shots that pin in its victim.

Crucial to the narrative structure and "feel" of the film is the voice-over narration and presence of Linda. She provides suturing continuity and a manifestation of adolescent innocence, even as she has a limited impact on the central drama of the story. Her down-to-earth counter-punctual delivery keeps the film from spiraling to the depths and depravity of melodramatic excess. Her function is to keep things in perspective. And yet her ambivalence is palatable: "Sometimes I feel very old. Like my whole life's old. Like I'm not around any more." As well as being distanced, her voice is often filled with naive irony. When Bill's murderous feelings begin to surface because the farmer refuses to die, she refers to his and Abby's pact nonchalantly: "they were kind-hearted. They thought he was going out on his own speed." She is also associated with the bestial forces of nature. She is the first to capture a locust in the fields before the plague; you can also see her trying to capture, and then plucking feathers from fowl; and after the farmer first accuses Abby of amoral relations with her "brother," the next image is of a tiger in a picture book that she is reading. It is also through her eyes that we first experience the coming of the plague as she plucks locusts from the food in the kitchen. Finally, on a not so desolate note, hers is the final voice and image of the film as she walks with her friend down the railway tracks to another, hopefully better destination.

In filming the movie, Director of Photography Nestor Almendros was encouraged by the young Malick to take risks. This was Malick's second film after the well-received *Badlands* (1974) starring Martin Sheen and Sissy Spacek. The crew was taking it badly, says Almendros. "Terrence would want to go on shooting after sunset–into the magic hour, as we called it—but the crew never agreed. We won a few to our cause, but it got worse and worse by the day." The crew was used to working Hollywood style, big lights, filters, gels, grips and gaffers running here and there, moving things around. Now they were trying to figure out who should carry torches, propane burners, and gas lanterns. The Spanish-born Almendros had learned to shoot films in Cuba where he moved at the age of seventeen. In Cuba, minimalist filmmaking was considered a creative challenge. But here, the Hollywood veterans questioned the sagacity of shooting outside with little or no lights. Malick and Almendros were after something different than your typical well-lit three point lighting scheme, and many of the crew felt out of place. As Almendros puts it, "they don't like what they don't understand." But the filmmakers had tools at their disposal that aided in their quest. For instance, they used Panavision fast lenses for many of the open range and bright light shots. Almendros says that "without these lenses the film could not have been made, or it would have been banal." Furthermore, source light was used whenever possible, including existing light, bonfires, furnaces and lanterns.

To take advantage of the last open wheat fields in North America, the film was shot on locations in Alberta, Canada, where as a teenager, Malick had traveled as a migrant harvester from his home in Waco, Texas. Reportedly, it took two to three weeks to shoot the locust scenes. Millions of locusts were imported from farm locations throughout Canada. Ken Middleham a specialist in animal photography was hired to supervise camera close-ups of the locusts. When the Canadian summer refused to give way for crucial winter snow scenes, Almendros had to leave the set due to a prior commitment to shoot Truffaut's *The Man Who Loved Women*. He enlisted Haskel Wexler (Oscar for *Bound for Glory*) to take over for the remaining nineteen days of shooting. It's a credit to Malick's direction that the work of Wexler cannot be distinguished from that of Almendros. For his work on *Days of Heaven*, Almendros won an Academy Award in 1979. He died in 1992 after garnering three more Oscar nominations.

6

TEMPORAL DESIGN

That brings me back to one of the central responsibilities of the editor, which is to establish an interesting, coherent rhythm of emotion and thought—on the tiniest and the largest scales—that allows the audience to trust, to give themselves to the film. Without their knowing why, a poorly edited film will cause the audience to hold back, unconsciously saying to themselves, "There's something scattered and nervous about the way the film is thinking, the way it presents itself. I don't want to think that way; therefore, I'm not going to give as much of myself to the film as I might." Whereas a good film that is well-edited seems like an exciting extension and elaboration of the audience's own feelings and thoughts, and they will therefore give themselves to it, as it gives itself to them.

—*Walter Murch*, In the Blink of an Eye, *1995*

CTCS 190 LECTURE OUTLINE – WEEK VI   **LECTURE 6**

A. **Duration of spatial organization**
  1. Rule
  2. Pace/Tempo/Timing
  3. The shot, scene, and sequence as temporal units
  4. The long take

B. **Relation between shots**
  1. Movement, pace, rhythm
  2. Cutting principles
     a. Spatial contiguity and temporal continuity:
        1. 180° system
        2. 30 degree difference in change of image size and angle
        3. Match shots in terms of formal and thematic properties
        4. Shot/reverse shot
        5. Eye-line match
     b. Spatial discontiguity and temporal discontinuity
  3. Scene building
     a. Theatrical mise-en-scene/mise-en-place
     b. Cutting to continuity
     c. Classical cutting
        1. Primary rules to be observed: perspectivization, displacement, eye contact, introduction and resolution overview
        2. Methods of classical cutting: action/reaction; action/detail of action; cutaway from action; multiple points of view of an action
        3. Crosscutting: same time/same space; same time/different space; different time/same space; different time/different space
  4. Montage
     a. Collision montage
     b. Thematic montage
     c. Hollywood montage
Visual Analysis
  5. The contraction, expansion, freezing, repetition, flashback, flashforward of time
  6. Consecutive vs. simultaneous time
  7. Modes of transition: direct cut, fade-in/out, dissolve, superimposition, wipe

C. **Types of time in film**
  1. Screen time/diegetic time (story's setting: temporal dimension)
  2. Running time
  3. Psychological/experienced time.

D. **Editing and objective/subjective experience of time and space**

E. **Definition of "mise-en-scène"**

F. **Introduction and Screening**

Notes

Notes

TWO FOR THE ROAD (1967)

From *Stanley Donen* (1983) by Dr. Drew Casper

Freddie Raphael had written a movie called *Nothing but the Best* (Clive Donner, 1964). It was a blackly comic variation of *Room at the Top* (Jack Clayton, 1959), in which a young, excessively ambitious English real-estate clerk climbs to the top of the social ladder. I didn't know him but I did know there was a very talented writer behind that movie. So I telephoned him. When we met, I told him I admired his work so much that I'd love to do a film with him. We send each other novels back and forth for a while—nothing that either of us was really pleased with. Eventually he told me he had this one thought for a film. He and his wife had always gone on holiday in the south of France since they were childhood sweethearts. Going to the same places over and over again, he had often thought of passing himself going down the same road. Did it interest me, he asked, doing a movie about a personal relationship of a man and woman and telling the story of their life in five different time bands while they go down the holiday road? I said it sounded wonderful. So with that, we started to work on *Two for the Road*. He wrote a version. We discussed it, He went away and wrote another version, which he sent to me. We worked on it again. Universal was supposed to make the picture, but when I cast Audrey they became disenchanted. In the end Fox put up the money. The casting of Albert Finney came after that. Paul Newman was the first person I approached. [Stanley Donen]

While the incidents in each of the five periods of the couple's ten-year relationship evolve chronologically, the periods are intercut on ironically contrasting visual, verbal, or emotional rhymes.

This contextual structure never loses us along the way and in fact makes the going humorous and suspenseful. It also carries with it a couple of metaphysical implications: the past's intrusion upon the present, the importance of memory or continuity in a relationship, which, though not one of the strongest reasons in the world, does keep people together, as the Fabians, Rhyalls, and Harry and Charlie (*Staircase*) attest to.

With the appropriation of this Resnais-like narrative form, Donen and Raphael at once introduce New Wave technique into the commercial Hollywood film and paid tribute to D. W. Griffith, who pioneered this device as far back as 1916 with *Intolerance*.

The central metaphor of the road unifies the film. Even at hotels and the beach we glimpse the road outside the window or hear vehicles or talk of the road, a particularly apt metaphor for a personal relationship, especially in our day and age. Its rich connotation of advance and retreat, energy and fatigue, continuity and interruption, change and repetition, is easily interchangeable with a metaphysical conception that vividly captures us as a people characteristically on the move. In addition the road is an endemically filmic metaphor, containing a built-in dramatic structure and having an essence of space through time in common with film's. The trope has much to do with the picture's solid construction and fluent pace.

Though the road remains the same in all five periods, the suggestion of circularity or illusion of movement is absent. The semilinear structure and lack of departure and arrival scenes see to that. No, the film insists that the relationship changes even though the two people basically remain themselves throughout. After all, we meet Mark and Joanna in explaining these changes, but instead contents itself with presenting the relationship's ranging moods, through which we glean the inroads getting a little deeper, the cynicism a bit bleaker, and the tolerance of each other a mite more expansive. The film's view of a relationship rings true more often than not. It was extremely influential in bringing about the demythological image of marriage in the American film of the late '60s and early '70s, which refreshingly countered Hollywood's pipe dreams.

Various means of travel, hinting at the couple's economic and emotional status in particular and the manners of the nuclear family in general, also help stitch the pieces together while mirroring the changing relationship. The steamer, their hitchhiking feet, and lifts in assorted trucks characterize the delirious blush of romance; the Manchesters' Ford station wagon presages the suffocation of domesticity; the antique folding-top MG with a "donk" and the Dalbrets' Rolls signify the first years together pregnant with exciting possibilities; their own new red Triumph Herald hints at the dangers of intolerance, and their white Mercedes 230 and airplane, the pallor of the jet set.

Raphael's dialogue is gorgeously crafted: sharply in character, witty fecund with Pinteresque pauses and silences that mean as much as the words and are, above all, so touching.

Marriage, its togetherness and splintering, its passion and coldness, its confrontations and games, is the target here. And the Wallaces' coupling is paralleled and contrasted with other pairs: the frightened, chubby newlyweds, the bickering proprietors, the complacent Manchesters, sundry silent dining partners (a running gag that ironically counters the Wallaces' eating while chatting away during their courtship and early married years), the bored and boring Dalbrets, and the Patmoses, forever on the make. Howard's priggishness and need for efficiency, his Jewish-princess-turned-Wasp wife, and their bad seed, who has neither had nor ever will have one unexpressed thought or gesture in her life, are also given the once over. The script goes on to sneer at jet-set philistinism and vapidness.

This is Donen's most feeling effort since *Indiscreet*, with glints of passion never disclosed before. But lightening the tenderness and pathos, while keeping the incisive satire from turning cruel, are the farcical touches, verbal and visual jokes, and double entendres. In the good old Sennett way, for example, sexual appetite often climaxes in disaster. Whenever the ripostes reach the scathing point, one turns the other's words back on him- or herself and the exchange dwindles to a teasing put-down. (This trait springs from their intimate knowledge of each other and their resenting of the other's knowledge.) Occasionally Mark and Joanna pass each other in different periods of their life in the same shot. (This joke, too, is psychologically accurate in its depiction of similar sight eliciting memory.) While the best double entendre, which is also an allusion to *A Letter to Three Wives* (Joseph Mankiewicz, 1949), takes the form of a train that roars past the window and sends the bed quaking just after Joanna's waking remark, "I dreamt that a train drove slap bang through the room in the middle of the night."

True, the light side does predominate, but not to the extent of bleaching out the film's ambivalent portrait of marriage. *Road* emerges as a gray, if not dark, comedy of romance and manners that consequently expands Donen's horizon.

Hepburn is as nifty as the script. In her third and best Donen round, her Joanna develops from a sharp-eyed yet wistful girl into a hurt and hurting woman. Visual clues, such as clothes and hairstyles, help, but she manages the transition mainly through facial expressions and voice inflections. Though in this seesaw of the sexes her side is slanted toward the sky, her teasing-turned-taunting does sting and her comic timing is perfect.

While conveying Mark's stubborn, narcissistic, and dominating ways, English actor Finney always makes us sense the insecurity within. As written and played, however, the character lacks pastel shading. This makes us favor Hepburn's Joanna although both characters are responsible for their marriage problems.

Albie really can't bear playing a man with pleasant charm. He feels he's letting himself down as an actor if he tries to show charm. He can't believe that that's a quality called for in acting. He wants to play something more startling. He doesn't like to come in and win you with his pleasant ways.

Nevertheless, Hepburn's and Finney's performances do bring the characters to life, but it is the offbeat casting that clinches for us this mutual attraction and volatility of opposites and makes the pairing downright entrancing. The backseat passengers never fail to divert. William Daniels's clipped speech patterns and fussy movements as the efficiency consultant are terrifying hilarious. Everything that comes from Eleanor Bron's haughty, upturned mouth and nasal voice as Cathy is a sneer. Gabrielle Middleton, with Donen's painstaking help, etches a miniature Rhoda; the child's reading of "now" appended to her every command sends shivers down our spines. Claude Dauphin rests on his laurels as the dreary, nebulous Gallic millionaire and in so ding delivers a self-caricature. And Jacqueline Bisset as Jackie is, well, luscious, while Georges Descrières as David gives the impression of being born old.

> We shot all the periods in one spot. Because most of *Road* occurs on a highway on which we had to turn the car around and travel hundreds of miles, I started using two cameras as a time and money saver. Previously, I used only one camera during filming. I found I was adept at this and so, from Road on, I used two cameras on a picture. There were exceptions, of course. For the TV sequence in *Bedazzled*, for example, I used eight to twelve cameras.... As it was, Road was an expensive production. [Donen]

More than anything else, Donen's razor-sharp cutting on dialogue, directions of movement, objects, forms, colors, and moods, which hones the ironic rhyme scheme, energizes the film—a veritable textbook on editing. And the nimble tripping through an entire decade, which this bravura editing ensures, gives rise to still another motif, time's "swift and winged feet."

Furthermore, since Donen regulates the dialogue, the movement of vehicles and passengers, camera movement, shot duration, and cutting to Mancini's lilting, melancholic, and wry score, which never forsakes a traveling rhythm, the film is lyrical and choreographic throughout: Mark and Joanna's relationship is a pas de deux on wheels. This, along with Challis's soft-focus location shooting in late spring and early summer in Panavision, which mirrors the couple's emotional states, is particularly responsible for the film's feeling.

> The score is done after the film. After I hear the score, though, I go back and recut the film to make it work with the score. It took me six months to edit *Road*. [Donen]

In rhythm with Mancini's gently paced title ballad, Binder's animated travel-emblem credits continually advance and recede, move horizontally and vertically, crisscross each other or extend and contract into something else against a black background, which at times doubles for the road's asphalt. When the Hepburn-Finney credit appears, the shape of a rearview mirror expands to hold a fleeting closeup of the actors—another arresting star entrée by Donen. This lovely sequence introduces us to the travelers, established the film's central metaphor, and prepares us for its leaping and rebounding structure as well as its mobile mise-en scène.

Reviews of *Two for the Road* were mixed, although they were more positive than negative. Fox premiered the film at Radio City Music Hall, where it died. After a brief three-week stay—the usual Hall run is six; five, if it is a bomb—it moved uptown to an art house, where it did respectably. The film's shaky start resulted in the studio's insensitive distribution. It did go on to cop the Golden Shell for Best Picture at the San Sebastian Film Festival. The Writers Guild of Britain voted the picture the Best British Comedy Script and Best Original Screenplay. The American Academy stopped at a nomination. Today *Two for the Road* is regarded as one of the best romantic comedy-dramas to come out of Hollywood and enjoys a cult status, viewed again and again by film aestheticians, students, and enthusiasts.

It's a good movie, but I don't think it should have been as sweet as it was.
[Donen]

CRITICAL FILM ANALYSES

THE ADVENTURES OF ROBIN HOOD (1938)

Richard L. Edwards

Produced by Warner Bros./First National Pictures. Directed by Michael Curtiz and William Keighley. Written by Norman Reilly Raine and Seton I. Miller. Cinematography by Tony Gaudio and Sol Polito. Music by Erich Wolfgang Korngold. Costume Design by Milo Anderson. Film Editing by Ralph Dawson. Technicolor photography by W. Howard Greene. Produced by Hal B. Wallis.

CAST: Errol Flynn (Robin Hood/Sir Robin of Locksley), Olivia De Havilland (Lady Marian Fitzwalter), Basil Rathbone (Sir Guy of Gisbourne), Claude Rains (Prince John), Patric Knowles (Will Scarlett), Eugene Pallette (Friar Tuck), Alan Hale (Little John), Melville Cooper (High Sheriff of Nottingham), Ian Hunter (Richard the Lionheart), Una O'Connor (Bess), Herbert Mundin (Much the Miller's Son), Montague Love (Bishop of Black Canon). Running Time: 102 Minutes.

The Adventures of Robin Hood epitomizes the classical Hollywood action adventure film. Errol Flynn turns in a bravura performance as Robin Hood. Flynn performed all his own stunts and this film solidified his status as a "swashbuckling" leading man. One can point to the film's stunning visual design. From the verdant forests to the cavernous castle sets, this film's sets and locales add to the sense of larger than life adventures in 12th century England. Moreover, the film was shot in the expensive three-strip Technicolor process and we can recognize the film's wonderful use of color from costume design to the pageantry of the archery tournament. Yet, when one thinks of the adjectives most commonly used to describe this film, such as "rousing," "exciting," "lightning fast," we find ourselves celebrating the film's temporal design. One of the main ingredients of this classic film's success has to do with its finely tuned editing scheme. Working in conjunction with the musical score, Errol Flynn's engaging athletic performance is only enhanced by the beautifully choreographed, tightly edited action sequences that punctuate this film. We need to look more closely at elements of this film's temporal design, as well as the conventions of classical Hollywood cinema that guide it.

Towards the beginning of the film, the sequence of the Norman feast in Nottingham castle establishes many of the editing conventions used throughout the film. This sequence can be broken into two distinct parts: 1) the beginning of the feast and the entrance of Robin Hood, and 2) Robin Hood's escape from the castle. In the first part, the scene opens with establishing shots that lay out the spatial dimensions of the Great Hall. The ensuing dialogue between Prince John and other members of the court guides the leisurely tempo of the shots. Furthermore, this sequence follows the rules of classical Hollywood editing. For instance, the cuts from Prince John to the Sheriff of Nottingham are based on graphic matches, with both figures similarly framed in medium close-up. Additionally, shot/reverse shots and eye-line matches (e.g. Prince John looking towards the Sheriff in one shot, and the Sheriff looking towards Prince John in the next) establish coherent spatial relations between the characters. After Robin Hood enters the castle, we continue to get graphic and eye-line matches and shot/reverse shots between the main characters. The cuts between shots are motivated by the principal characters acting and reacting to each other and throughout the first part of the sequence, the length of shots is rhythmically steady.[111]

However, the pace of the sequence changes as we approach Robin Hood's daring escape from the castle. Two quick eye-line matches begin to increase the tension in this sequence: we see that Robin Hood is aware that the castle doors are being barred. Furthermore, we get a cutaway shot of the soldiers preparing to move in on Robin. After Dickon (one of the Prince's soldiers) throws a spear at Robin, the editing of the scene changes drastically. First, the sound of the spear hitting Robin's chair coincides with the beginning of non-diegetic music. Throughout the escape sequence, the up-tempo music helps to guide the accelerated pace of editing. Second, the length of shots varies greatly. We get much shorter shots of actions (e.g. Sir Guy throwing a candlestick, sword fighting, etc.) and the relation between shots is based on movement, action and graphic matches. This creates a much faster rhythm for the sequence, and increases the number of edits in the sequence. Thus, as Robin fights his way out of the castle, we often get cuts after he has finished off a soldier with an arrow, or cuts that follow his movement, as when he is sword fighting or when he climbs the wall in the Great Hall. Moreover, we get graphic matches throughout the sequence as when Robin is above the action fighting with soldiers below (e.g. Robin's downward pointing bow and arrow is cut with the soldier's upward pointing crossbows). Furthermore, the excitement of this sequence is increased through the use of crosscutting. While Robin is fighting in the castle, we often cut between his actions and the actions of others in the room, as when Sir Guy is tackled by the soldiers or when we see the pusillanimous conduct of the Sheriff of Nottingham (same time/same space). Once he exits the castle, and the chase continues on horseback, we have crosscuts between him and the soldiers chasing him (same time/different space). This highly choreographed escape sequence has a lot in common with other sections of the film. Whether it is Robin and his merry band setting upon Sir Guy and Maid Marian in the forest, or the tournament sequence, we see that the action sequences use a variety of editing techniques to increase excitement and tension.

As we already noted, sound plays an important part in the editing of films. For example, sound is an integral part of the archery tournament sequence. As Charles Higham notes: "[Erich] Korngold worked very closely with the editor, Ralph Dawson, and the sound department under Nathan Levinson and George R. Groves on the extraordinarily complex tournament scene."[112] Part of the complexity of this scene is in its dual narrative purpose: a crosscutting between the Robin Hood's display of marksmanship at the tournament and Prince John's attempt to capture Robin. Many of the cuts in this scene are motivated by sound and musical cues. Moreover, the music helps guide the rhythm and frequency of the cuts in this sequence. The musical and visual cues also help condense the time of the tournament. Every

---

[111] See Bordwell and Thompson, *Film Art*, for a discussion of rhythmic relations between shots, pages 303-304.
[112] Higham, Charles. *Warner Bros.* New York: Scribner's. 1975. p. 126.

time we cut to a shot of the trumpeteers, a certain amount of time has elapsed that was not necessary to the telling of the story. The time of tournament is condensed to its essentials, and the preliminary rounds, which are not important to the story, are dispatched with quickly in a montage sequence of the participants in the contest.

Thus, another editing technique used in this film is montage. The montages operate to condense time and events in order to move the story along. For example, early in the film, there are two montage sequences that show the Normans robbing and enslaving the Saxons, and another montage sequence that shows the Saxon resistance led by Robin Hood. In both sequences, we are shown only a few brief moments that obviously occur over a long time span. But these montage sequences relay important information (e.g. the Normans' cruelty in collecting the taxes) and help the audience understand why Robin Hood is leading a revolt against Prince John.

The Adventures of Robin Hood had a colorful production history. The film had two different directors, Michael Curtiz and William Keighley. The original director Keighley was removed from the picture eight weeks into production. As Rudy Behlmer notes: "the reasons seem to have been Keighley's too lighthearted approach and the lack of impact in the action sequences."[113] Keighley ended up shooting most of the Sherwood Forest scenes. Michael Curtiz, who previously had worked with Errol Flynn on other swashbuckling adventures[114], was chosen as Keighley's replacement. Curtiz completed the film and shot additional footage "to embellish and punch up [Keighley's] action scenes."[115] Curtiz utilized more camera movement in the footage he shot (for example, remember the moving camera shots that open the Nottingham castle sequence). Thus, when edited together, his shots had more dynamic power than Keighley's. Also, in terms of casting, the role of Robin Hood was originally offered to James Cagney. But when Cagney ran into problems with the head of the studio, Jack Warner, the role was given to Errol Flynn.

At the time of its release, *Robin Hood* was the most expensive film ever made by Warner Bros. Jack Warner approved an initial budget of $1,600,000. The final budget ended up being $2,030,000.[116] Luckily, the film ended up being a tremendous success and the highest grossing Warner Bros. film that year. Besides being a huge financial success, the film also added to the prestige of Warner Bros. studios. The film won multiple Academy Awards. Ralph Dawson won for Best Film Editing, Erich Wolfgang Korngold took home the Oscar for Best Original Score music and Carl Jules Weyl was also a winner for Best Art Direction. The film was nominated as Best Picture of the year, but lost to Frank Capra's *You Can't Take It With You*. In 1995, the National Film Preservation Board added the film to the National Film Registry, further confirming its enduring importance in film history.

---

[113] Rosenzweig, Sidney. *Casablanca and the Other Major Films of Michael Curtiz*. Ann Arbor: UMI Research Press. 1982. p. 30.
[114] *Captain Blood* (1935) and *Charge of the Light Brigade* (1936).
[115] Rosenzweig, p. 30.
[116] Hirschhorn, Clive. *Warner Bros. Story*. New York: Crown Publishers Inc. 1979.

BUGSY (1991)

Chia-chi Wu

TriStar Pictures. Producers: Mark Johnson, Barry Levinson, and Warren Beatty. Director: Barry Levinson. Screenwriter: James Toback. Director of Photography: Allen Daviau, A.S.C. Production Designer: Dennis Gassner. Editor: Stu Linder. Costume Designer: Albert Wolsky. Music Composed, Orchestrated and Conducted by Ennio Morricone. Casting: Ellen Chenoweth. Co-Producer: Charles Newirth. Set Decorator: Nancy Haigh. Running Time: 135 min. MPAA Rating: R.

CAST: Warren Beatty (Bugsy Siegel); Annette Bening (Virginia Hill); Harvey Keitel (Mickey Cohen); Ben Kingsley (Meyer Lansky); Elliott Gould (Harry Greenberg); Joe Mantegna (George); Richard Sarafian (Jack Dragna); Bebe Neuwirth (Countess DI Frasso); Gian-Carlo Scandiuzzi (Count DI Frasso); Wendy Phillips (Esta Siegel).

Sex. Romance. Money. Adventure. I am building a monument to all of them.

—Ben "Bugsy" Siegel from Bugsy

Gangsters tried to copy Hollywood as much as Hollywood tried to copy the gangster. Filmmakers were very impressed by gangsters and the other way around. They were all part of the romantic swirl of American drama.

—Warren Beatty

The opening sequence of Bugsy immediately transports us into an era that bears little resemblance to our own. Dark-hued images with a vintage 40s' look unfold before our eyes. Intercut with abstract titles in black and white, these images slowly fade in and out to give us a "glimpse" of Ben Siegel: saying good bye to his wife and daughters; his silhouette talking to himself, with his face framed by the car's window; purchasing designer shirts and ties; his sexual escapade initiated by an encounter in the elevator, etc. In less than three minutes, Bugsy's character is fully evoked—supremely self-confident and yet neurotically fastidious; romantic and charming but unpredictable and psychotic.

Meanwhile, the idioms of classical editing are fully pronounced in the same sequence. Fade-ins and fade-outs are employed to mark the progress of time. Only the "essential parts" of the action are presented to the viewer. And even though they are just fragments of the whole action, they must be choreographed in a way so that the images flow "seamlessly" and "naturally." For example, the sexual encounter in the hotel comprises only eight shots, with the titles interspersed between them. In the first two shots we see Ben and the woman enter the elevator, followed by a close-up of the woman who responds to Ben's seduction. The camera then cuts back and forth between medium close-ups of them (i.e. shot/reverse shot). This is followed by a close-up of the woman's hand, in a black velvet glove, as she stops Bugsy from re-calling the elevator. The last shot of this encounter is a medium shot of the woman's brassiere lying on the chair, with off-screen space evoked by her "groaning" and Ben's voice. By showing only the essential bits of the action, these eight shots successfully compress time into the linear narrative. Moreover, sound always plays a role in editing. The whole opening sequence is accompanied by an ominous score, created through the use of minor keys which convey an emotional ambivalence toward him. The score connects the disparate activities in which Ben is engaged. The pace of the editing also follows Ben's laconic talk, thus accentuating Ben's character as a quick-witted, dapper womanizer/gangster.

Bugsy chronicles the saga of Ben Siegel's Hollywood and Las Vegas years. The film revolves around his life with Hollywood celebrities and his ambitious project to build the Flamingo Hotel, which paved the way for the gambling Mecca as we know it today. To capture the real mobster on the two-dimensional screen and to compress his life into two hours of screen time, the construction of space and time through editing is crucial. Most of the time editing is motivated by the characters' movements, action, and the progress of the narrative. Inasmuch the camerawork subordinates itself to the presentation of the story, it follows classical edicts of continuity and transparency ("transparent" because the viewers might find their attention more riveted upon the events in the film rather than the cutting devices used). One sequence illustrates this. After Ben mistakes Virginia's brother for her lover and almost kills him, Virginia rushes upstairs in a rage while Ben chases her to tell her about his plan to build the Flamingo Hotel. As if in a screwball comedy, Virginia slams door after door in Ben's face, trying to get rid of him. Note how eye-line match (e.g. Virginia looking down at Ben and Ben looking up at Virginia as they ascend the stairs), and cutting on movement glue the shots together and propel the shifting of space between different rooms in Virginia's house. Also note how sound is used effectively to cue the cutting, as the slamming of the door snaps with the cut, which is also synchronized with the characters opening or closing the doors (cutting on movement). As Virginia finally succumbs to Ben's word, "Flamingo", her nickname to be used for the Hotel, the sequence ends, cut with the closing of the door to the first shot of the next scene.

Throughout the film, the use of editing techniques is in tandem with the forward thrust of the narrative, and it is in the seemingly gap-less, seamless assemblage of shots and scenes that Bugsy's life is "fabricated" and constructed. If the sequence mentioned above is to illustrate the use of filmic techniques to cover short temporal ellipses, the film also uses another classical cutting device for longer temporal ellipses—"montage sequence." *Bugsy* presents two major montage sequences, one of which will be discussed here. When Ben walks out of Jack's house after forcing Jack to relinquish his control of his racket, music suddenly soars and a montage sequence starts. A series of images that are not necessarily connected spatially or temporally are juxtaposed with each other to convey the elapse of a period of time. These images connote Ben's immersion into Hollywood's celebrity culture—the operation of Ben's "business" in casinos; singers at the club singing "Accent-Tchu-Ate The Positive," which at the same time underscores the sequence; Ben seeing gangster films with George at the movie studio; newspaper headlines on Ben's controversy; Ben dancing with various elegant women etc. These images are swiftly joined together by the use of dissolves, fades, and superimpositions, at the same time punctuated by shots (and sound) of Virginia hanging up the phone, signifying Ben's failed attempts at courtship.

Yet editing not only compresses time into the linear time scheme of the narrative or articulates coherent spatial relations between characters, it also heightens dramatic effects and enhances the meaning of the images. When Ben brutalizes Joey (Virginia's ex-boyfriend) over an insult to Virginia, witness how it is intercut with Charlie Luciano dancing with his wife. By cross-cutting between Ben and Charlie (same time, same place cross-cutting), the percussive, discordant music that Charlie Luciano and his wife dance to is overlaid with Ben's relentless, snappy punches falling on Joey. As the music underscores the rhythmic intensification of both actions, dancing and beating, it highlights Ben's homicidal violence to its greatest effect. It also serves as an example of collision montage, in that it juxtaposes shots with diametrically opposed thematic elements with a strong ironic overtone.

As an epic gangster film, *Bugsy* not only fleshes out the life of the "real" mobster Ben Siegel but also self-consciously bespeaks the history of the genre on the "reel." First, the film retains the mythology of the gangster as the tragic hero, despite some comic moments. It reiterates the hero's inevitable downfall as ironically created by the optimism of the American Dream—man as a self-made individual, a dreamer who may not respect money but believes in the pursuit of happiness conceived only in terms of material wealth and success. Ben as a "Dreamer" becomes an aural motif in the film. It resonates with another aural motif "twenty dwarves took turns doing handstands on the carpet" and the song "Accent-Tchu-Ate The Positive", articulating Ben's desire to "speak properly," to go straight and to make his operation "legitimate." Yet the fact that Ben would legitimize his business by "any" means indicates the impossibility of drawing the line "between crime and celebrity, blood and money."[117] The gangster indeed embodies the American Dream as well as its perversion. His tragedy, in Robert Warshow's words, speaks to the contradictions between individualism and the ideals of equality in American capitalism, connoting a denial of "happier American culture."[118]

Second, by thematizing Ben's fascination and connection with Hollywood, the film constantly reminds us that the "gangster" is always experienced as cinema, although these gangster narratives might have their real world counterparts. This is evident in Ben's own experiences of the gangsters on the screen, when Ben and George are watching the gangster films in the movie studio. Such self-reflexive sensibility is also inscribed in our own experience of Ben, when we see Ben's images projected on his home screen, which is circumscribed by our theater screen; or when we see the courtship play out "literally" on a movie set, and then in the light of a home projector, with the lovers in silhouette on the screen. The film (Ben's screen test) within the film (the film we are watching) or the lovers' silhouette on the home screen prompt our awareness that what we are seeing is not so much a "realistic" representation of the real-life gangster, as Hollywood's own fascination and its myth-making process. The last scene can be considered as the film's statement on itself as a gangster film. Ben is brutally murdered while he is watching his own screen test at home. Bullets penetrate his body and shoot down his projector. Yet even if the gangster drops dead, the projector keeps running, projecting a distorted, talking image of Ben.

Bugsy collected eight Golden Globe nominations and won the best picture (drama). It won three Academy Awards, for production design, set decoration, and costume design. Warren Beatty was also nominated for best actor for Oscar, but lost it to Anthony Hopkins (*The Silence of the Lambs*). The film cost approximately $32 million, and grossed around $49 million within six month of its initial release, from December 1991 to May 1992.[119]

---

[117] "If Gatsby Had Been a Goodfella," *Newsweek* (December 16, 1991): 51.
[118] Robert Warshow, "The Gangster As Tragic Hero," in *The Immediate Experience* (New York: Atheneum Books, 1970), 129-131.
[119] *Entertainment Weekly* (November 25, 1991), 1.

CARLITO'S WAY (1993)

Chia-chi Wu

Universal Pictures. 1993. Producers: Martin Bregman Willi Baer, Michael Bregman. Director: Brian De Palma. Screenwriter: David Koepp. Executive Producers: Louis A. Stroller Ortwin Freyermuth. Director of Photography: Richard Sylbert. Production Designer: Stephen Burum. Editors: Bill Pankow, Kristina Boden. Music Supervisor: Jellybean Benitez. Music: Patrick Doyle. Costume Designer: Aude Bronson-Howard. Casting: Bonnie Timmermann. Art Director: Gregory Bolton. Based on the novels "Carlito's Way" and "After Hours" by Edwin Torres. Running Time: 141 mins. MPAA Rating: R.

CAST: Al Pacino (Carlito); Sean Penn (Kleinfeld); Penelope Ann Miller (Gail). John Leguizamo (Benny Blanco); Ingrid Rogers (Steffie); Luis Guzman (Pachanga); Jorge Porcel (Saso); Joseph Siravo (Vinnie Taglialucci); Viggo Mortensen (Lalin). Richard Foronjy (Pete Amadesso).

The film opens with the end of the story, when the gun is fired directly at Carlito, who immediately collapses into semi-consciousness. At this critical moment of Carlito's life, a moment presumably of panic, rush and hustle, De Palma, however, undermines the urgency of the moment and manipulates time to dramatic effects. Proceeding in slow motion, the opening sequence places us in Carlito's awry point of view as well as his delirious state of mind. The soundtrack also gives us Carlito's subjective experience as he talks to us/himself at a sluggish pace, underscored by the melancholy of stringed instruments, and the muffled noise of a crowd. The extension of time and the pan of the camera follows Carlito's final glimpse of the tourist poster with the slogan "Escape to Paradis." This accentuates the inevitable downfall of the gangster, replaying a familiar motif of the gangster genre—the alienated, tragic figure who can transcend social confines only in his own death.

Starting in the 60s, De Palma has proved himself as an auteur fully exploring the potential of the camera. Many of his films have reinvigorated cinematic conventions, revolutionized genres, and have become cult classics—*Dressed To Kill* (1980), *Blow Out* (1981), *Scarface* (1983), *The Untouchables* (1987), to name just a few examples. His virtuosity in scene construction and camera movement often lends his oeuvre to an analogy with that of Alfred Hitchcock, as both have (re-)formulated the grammar of cinema in American film history. Even when his films generate controversy around censorship, social or moral issues, De Palma's critics always allege that he has few peers when it comes to his visual style and his capability to convey a story only with his camera, without the support of elaborate acting or dialogue.

De Palma's trademark in scene construction—the construction of space and time onto the two-dimensional screen through editing—is illustrated in the first shoot-out sequence. After Carlito and his cousin enter the room, note how De Palma establishes coherent spatial relations between characters by the use of shot/reverse shot and Carlito's eyeline match (e.g. the shot showing Carlito looking at something off screen, followed by a shot of what he is looking at—the door of the restroom). When Carlito senses danger lurking behind the door, De Palma employs crosscutting (same time, same space) between one side of the room, where his cousin is doing "business" with a black gangster, and the other side of the room, where Carlito tries to save himself and his cousin by pretending to teach other hoods a new trick on the pool table. Meanwhile, when cutting to Carlito, De Palma presents him in 360 degree camera movement, highlighting Carlito's desperation and panic. The pace of editing gradually escalates, diegetic music growing louder and louder; the fight erupts contemporaneous with the launching of Carlito's cue ball and the coming out of the assassin from behind the door. Frenetic cuts place us on a roller coaster ride of extreme violence and gore. In 30 seconds of fright and flight, De Palma subtly clashes screen directions between the shot showing the assassin's movement from left to right, reflected on the sunglasses, and the shot showing the flight of the ball from right to left. This is an example of *collision montage*, which juxtaposes shots with diametrically opposed formal or thematic elements. This highly choreographed action glues the quick cuts together, meanwhile using *graphic match*, especially between the assassin's slashing of the cousin's neck and Carlito's drawing of another gangster's gun.[120]

The editing is made as sharp as the slashing of the human body. The cutting device of shot/reverse shot becomes synonymous with gun shots. Bullets and blood are discharged from bodies and weapons, as the characters "dance" to the rhythm of camera movement and editing, while the protagonist emerges totally unscathed. All of these constitute a familiar aesthetic experience for fans of Martin Scorsese, De Palma, John Woo; one of *beautiful violence*, a violence rendered so beautiful and stylized that it is experienced as desirable and pleasurable, totally removed from any "real" sense of violence in our daily life. Intriguingly, beautiful violence articulates the film medium in a paradoxical way. On one hand, as *Carlito's Way* demonstrates, camera movement and editing are mostly motivated by characters' action and movement (e.g. tracking shots, cutting on action, etc.). Inasmuch as the camerawork subordinates itself to the presentation of the story, it can be seen to follow classical edicts of continuity and transparency ("transparent" because the viewers might find their attention more riveted upon the events in the film than the filmic techniques used). On the other hand, when the action is so flawlessly choreographed, flow of shots so seamless, violence so stylized, De Palma's fight scenes become an ostentatious display of filmic techniques themselves, a demonstration of cinema's specificity, its ability to manipulate time and space to render an experience of violence that is otherwise unimaginable. In other words, even though the use of filmic techniques is in tandem with the progress of the narrative, it is in the "seamless" and "smooth" flow of the action that the constructed-ness and artifice of cinema are highlighted. It is in the impeccable assemblage of the shots that the violence appears "believable" but at the same time hyperbolic and excessive, therefore constantly reminding the viewer that only cinema can animate and envision movement and violence in such grace and frenzy.

The climactic sequence at the end once again exemplifies this: the seemingly "spontaneous," "natural" flow of shots were conducted in such a breathless fashion, in a bravura that it eventually calls attention to its own intricate and meticulous design. In this sense, De Palma pronounces the idioms of classical editing while extending it to the fullest. In this sequence, the Italian gangsters (Vinnie Taglialucci, Big Guy, and two others) chase Carlito from the disco through the subway to the train station. This is intercut with Carlito's girlfriend, Gail, waiting anxiously at the train station (same time, different space crosscutting). Meanwhile the temporal structure of the sequence is marked by the clock at the train station, progressing toward 11:30, the time by which Carlito must catch the train to escape the gangland he has been mired in.[121] The rules of continuity editing successfully stitch the chase scenes together. Notice especially the scene in the subway as Carlito and the gangsters move from car to car on the subway, coherent screen direction, cutting on movement (both inside and outside the

---

[120] When the filmmaker links shots by graphic similarities, in terms of shape, color, overall composition, or movement, it is called a graphic match. See Bordwell and Thompson, *Film Art: An Introduction*, 7th edition (New York: The McGraw-Hill Companies, Inc., 2003), 297.

[121] The 11:30 pm appointment also serves as a classical narrative device, a *deadline* that drives the narrative toward its closure, dependent upon whether the protagonist can achieve his goal or not. See Bordwell and Thompson, pp. 108-110.

subway car), the staging of 180 degree line and eye-line match deftly link shots and propel the shifting of spaces. Later, after Carlito embarks upon the stairs of the train station but is kept by the gangsters from getting close to the train, De Palma engages a sophisticated traveling shot (tracking shot) that is completely synchronous to the characters' movement. It first swishes along with Carlito's running around; later leaving Carlito and moving agilely down the escalator to close in on Vinnie. It then follows Vinnie going up the escalator. This two-minute long take enacts a dynamic mise-en-scene charged with suspense and tension without a single cut.

Following this long take, De Palma breaks the rhythm by cutting rapidly between Vinnie (moving up on the escalator), Big Guy (above the escalator), and Carlito (hiding and moving down on another escalator). The rhythm of cutting follows the ominous music on the soundtrack, suggesting an inevitable shoot-out on the escalators. The final shoot-out scene, like the first one mentioned earlier, is so well orchestrated that it flows smoothly through quick cuts without calling attention to the device of cutting itself. However, it is also self-reflexive in another sense. With its setup of escalators at a train station, it is reminiscent of the climax sequence from *The Untouchables*, which is in turn an homage paid to the Odessa Steps sequence of Sergei Eisenstein's *Battleship Potemkin* (1925). Eisenstein's films and writings on montage laid down the theoretical foundation of editing and have exerted great influence on American filmmakers. Moreover, the reference to The Untouchables also harks back to the peak of De Palma's oeuvre in the 80s, when De Palma's turned out many films that won critical acclaim.

Sound also plays an important role in editing. It can cover over the change of scenes. De Palma hardly uses transition devices such as dissolves, fades in/out, superimposition, etc., but instead cues the transition of shots through sound. For example, in the beginning of the film, as Carlito is released on parole and excitedly talks to his lawyer, his shouting of "Yes!" is cleverly transposed to the loud Latin music of the next dance scene. The recurrent use of Carlito's voiceover sometimes serves a similar function. At other times, sound underscores the rhythmic intensification of action and provides the beat for editing. In the first gun fight sequence of the film, the snappy, unnerving music breaks out with the fight but comes to a sudden stop with Carlito's slamming of the door, recalling "the urgent strains of Bernard Hermann's work for Hitchcock."[122]

The film begins and ends with the same sequence of Carlito being shot. Thus the bulk of the film is an extended flashback of Carlito's life. The manipulation of temporal order, the repetition of the same event, and the use of slow motion in the end serve to convey a strong sense of doom and Carlito's existential alienation. Indeed, the sense of inevitable failure and isolation have characterized countless gangsters on the American screen. As a film reviewer comments with good humor,

> As we are told more than once, Carlito Brigante gained his education almost entirely on the streets of Spanish Harlem. That is too bad. If he has spent more time at home watching the old *Late Show*, he would have known from the early gangster movies (especially James Cagney's) that there comes a moment in any criminal career when it becomes impossible to go straight, no matter how much you want to. It's an image problem with tragic dimensions.[123]

Carlito's Way is a boxoffice hit, grossing $34,600,717 within two month of its initial release, from November 1993 to January 1994.[124]

[122] Duane Byrge, "Carlito's Way," *Newsweek* (November 8, 1993): 13.
[123] Richard Schickel, "Gangsta Rapping," *Time* (November 15, 1993).
[124] Art Murphy's 1994 Boxoffice Register, in CNTV Library.

7
SOUND DESIGN

Sound has always been important to me. I'm a firm believer that it's 50% of the experience, and it's the neglected 50%. I've always made a practice of putting a great deal of effort and creativity into my sound tracks, hiring my sound editors before we start shooting the picture. They're on through the whole picture and have a lot more input and creative control in continuity—meaning the sound editors actually have discussions with the sound recorders on the set and that sort of thing. So there's a lot of communication that goes on about what is necessary. Sound editors are very involved in the mix. Up here we call them sound designers.

—George Lucas, 1993

CTCS 190 LECTURE OUTLINE – WEEK VII   **LECTURE 7**

A. **Introduction**
   1. Sound and the other arts
   2. Sound's neglect in film
   3. Importance of sound in film
B. **Components of the soundtrack**
   1. Verbal: dialogue; off-screen voice; singing
   2. Music: source music and underscoring
   3. Sound effects/natural sounds
   4. Silence
   5. The concept of sound design
C. **Uses of Sound**
   1. Synchronous sound
   2. Asynchronous sound
   3. Sound montage
      a. Between sounds
      b. Between image and sound
   4. Sound mix
   5. Size of sounds
   6. Angle of sounds
   7. Color of sounds
   8. Movement of sounds
   9. Transition between sounds
   10. Editing principles
   11. The choreographed image
   12. Melodeclamation
D. **Aesthetic effects**
   1. Revealer of reality
   2. Intensifier of image
   3. Interpreter of image
   4. Director of spectator attention within frame
   5. Subject, source, mover of action
   6. Setting and characterization: objective/subjective sound
   7. Mood and atmosphere
   8. Metaphor, symbol
   9. Motif
   10. Overture and lyrical interlude
   11. Spatial correlative
   12. Carrier of pace
   Sound Analysis
E. **Introduction and Screening**

Notes

Notes

CRITICAL FILM ANALYSES

CAPTAIN BLOOD (1935)

Chia-chi Wu

Warner Bros. Pictures. Producers: Harry Joe Brown, Gordon Hollingshead. Executive producers: Jack L. Warner, Hal B. Wallis. Director: Michael Curtiz. Screenwriter: Casey Robinson. Photography: Hal Mohr, Ernest Haller. Special photography effects: Fred Jackman. Art: Anton Grot. Editor: George Amy. Gowns: Milo Anderson. Music Leo F. Forbstein. Music arrangement: Erich Wolfgang Korngold. Orchestral arrangement: Hugo Friedhofer, Ray Heindorf. Sound: C.A. Riggs. Sound Recording: Nathan Levinson. Based on the novel of the same title by Rafael Sabatini. Running time: 119 mins.

CAST: Errol Flynn (Peter Blood); Olivia de Havilland (Arabella Bishop); Lionel Atwill (Colonel Bishop); Basil Rathbone (Levasseur); Ross Alexander (Jeremy Pitt); Guy Kibbee (Hagthorpe); Henry Stephenson (Lord Willoughby); Robett Barratt (Wolverstone); Hobart Cavanaugh (Dr. Bronson); Donald Meek (Dr. Whacker); J. Carrol Naish (Cahusac); Pedro de Cordoba (Don Diego); George Hassell (Governor Steed); Harry Cording (Kent); Leonard Mudie (Baron Jeffreys); Vernon Steele (King James).

(Erich Wolfgang) Korngold reveals further evidence of an innate ability to appraise the real function of music in film—which is to give impetus to action, and drama to motion, while reinforcing, via musical ideas, character and situation.

Joseph O'Sullivan[125]

---

[125] "The Sea Hawk: The Classic Film Scores of Erich Wolfgang Korngold," see the microfiche included in the production file of *Captain Blood*, the Research Library of Academy of Motion Picture, Arts and Sciences.

Listen to *Captain Blood* from the very beginning. The overture accompanying the title sequence is a well-recorded fanfare of orchestral music. As the music smoothes over the changes of title cards (among which is a credit card devoted exclusively to the Austrian-born composer Erich Wolfgang Korngold), different melodies pour out, providing us a preview of the major musical themes which will recur throughout the film. The story opens, with a title suggesting the historical backdrop of the film (England in 1685, the tumultuous reign of King James II). At the same time, the string and woodwind melody changes to a whirling tempo and an ominous tone to accompany Jeremy Pitt's frantic ride to Blood's home. Sound effects begin to come in, with hoofbeats and thunders serving as the accents of the unsettling melody. Jeremy arrives. Contemporaneous with the stopping of his horse, the music reaches a brief climax that is augmented by timpani and swiftly drops in volume. Jeremy dismounts from his horse and strides towards Blood's place. The music immediately escalates in volume but comes to a sudden stop when its loudness intensifies/is intensified by the banging on the door. Follows Jeremy's call of urgency: "Dr. Blood! Dr. Blood!" When Dr. Blood enters the scene, musical motives resume as dialogue ensues, yet in a minimal volume and at a steady pace, subtly subordinating itself to the flow of Errol Flynn's voice.

And keep your ears open even after the music subsides in this sequence. Consider how sounds that might go unnoticed are contrived and selected, their acoustic properties carefully adjusted or altered, to give an impression of an "appropriate," "natural noise" produced by the visuals. Listen to the noises of the saddle, the footsteps, the banging, opening or closing of the doors. These are foley, sound effects carefully produced and recorded in synchronization with the projected image. Prompted by the request to treat a friend wounded in a rebellion against King James II, Blood returns to his chamber to get himself prepared. His opening of the door is cued on the soundtrack by the creaking noise of a window being opened. Almost simultaneously the image is cut to a neighbor pushing the window open, a woman with a baby in her arms. The woman inquires the condition of the battle, and we hear the baby cry loudly. In the reverse shot in which Jeremy replies to her, the baby's crying is continued yet shifted to a lower volume. The whimper sinks to the background (ambient sound: surrounding or background noise), denoting Jeremy's distance from the woman (use of sound perspective: the more subdued the sound, the farther we take it to be; or vice versa) as well as cueing the off-screen space occupied by her. Then the visual track cuts to Blood's chamber, of which the sonic world comes alive with Blood and the maid's witty dialogue exchange, interwoven again with foley: their footsteps, the fluffing of his layered attire, the placing of the kettle on the table, etc.

Yet the fact we may find our ears "strained" in trying to register such meticulous auditory information bespeaks our experiences of film "viewing", in which watching or spectatorship is usually privileged over hearing and listening. It also points to the paradoxical role of sound, particularly in classical Hollywood cinema, in that its intricate "design" is felt to be most effective only when it is "perceived and appreciated by the audience in visual terms—the better the sound, the better the image."[126] Sound always plays second fiddle to the image, supporting, clarifying and enhancing the visual events. As the sound effects in the first sequence of *Captain Blood* demonstrate, sound adds to an aural dimension to the self-effacement and transparency finessed by classical Hollywood cinema, the tenets of which dictate that the use of filmic techniques be subsumed to the presentation of the story, and the viewers' attention be directed to the flow of events rather than the constructed-ness of visual or aural operation. In other words, the audio work, more often than not, remains a handmaiden to the image, striving for a crystal, causal relation to the visuals.

The use of classical music in *Captain Blood* seems to be in accord with such principles of image-sound correlation as well. Formulated in the Puccinni-Mahler-Strauss-Wagner idiom, the

---

[126] Walter Murch, "Foreward," in Michel Chion, *Audio-Vision: Sound on Screen*, edited and translated by Claudia Gorbman (New York: Columbia University Press, 1994), viii.

score is orchestrated to either elucidate or intensify the atmosphere or the mood intended by visuals, rather than undermining or contradicting the image track. Certain musical conventions carried over from opera or symphonic poems into film music also help strengthen such sound-image ties. For instance, as mentioned above, the overture of the title sequence presents to us a preview of major musical passages, which the composer Erich Wolfgang Korngold would employ recurrently and thematically throughout the film. The progress of the overture might be simplistically transcribed as follows,

Passage A: the short and lively sounding of trumpets and brass
Passage B: a sweeping string passage characterized by repeated, ascending arpeggio of sevenths
Passage A: on woodwind instruments
Passage B: on string instruments again
Passage C: chromatic modulations to mark the transition from the title sequence to the opening of the story.

For the rest of the film, passage A will be repeated, with variations in tempo, harmony or musical instruments, to underlie Captain Peter Blood's free-spirited and anti-authoritarian heroism in scenes of rebellion or triumphant battles. Passage B is to underscore his delicate, tender romanticism, constantly elaborated or modulated in scenes with Arabella Bishop. Making a particular melody synonymous with a particular character is a use of leitmotif, a technique best known as perfected in the work of the German romantic composer Richard Wagner. Moreover, although there is no distinct melody attributed to the evil characters, to mark their menace Korngold deployed instruments with a dark timber, such as snare drum, viola, and cello, and deliberately conducted them in a low pitch.

A seamless integration of sound and image is also illustrated in the scene depicting the horror of the slaves' existence at the sugar plantation and stockade. The seemingly endless circular movement of the water wheels and stone mills on the visual track is translated aurally into brief, endlessly repeated musical motives of "interval second" (i.e., the musical interval embracing two neighboring keys, say, on the piano). Following the pace of the slaves' plodding steps, the progress of the musical motives sounds to be ascending or rising, but at the same time conveys a strong sense of entrapment or "being mired" due to its repetition and monotonous, heavy beats. Meanwhile, the fiendish score highlights the sharp cracks of the overseer's whipping as each whip lands on a slave's body right on the beat (mostly the second beat of 4/4 metrical measure). Later in the sequence, a black slave strikes a gong, calling the others to witness the punishment of a runaway slave. Each strike of the gong puts the accent on the first beat, with the gong's timber blended into music orchestrated between tuba, strings, brass, and cymbal. As the runaway is to be branded, listen to the flute that sneaks into the close-up of the fire tongs. In digressing from a clarified tonality and a distinct integral musical phrase, the few notes played on the flute produce an effect that is unnerving and unsettling, anticipating the pain to be afflicted on the slave's flesh.

The aural effect articulates a trademark in Korngold's film music: instrumental musical effects are explored to such an extent that the seemingly well-defined line between the two major categories of sound in cinema—music and sound effects—is subtly subverted and blurred. Do we consider the (a)tonal or musical fragments produced by the flute as music or sound effects? Are the thundering climaxes in other scenes conceived as a result of music, of sound effects, or a mixture of both? Moreover, how does the filmmaker accomplish a transposition of music into speech (the third major element in sound design) through the editing device? Note here how the disquieting music of the branding scene is cleverly reinforced by and transformed to the speech that initiates the next sequence, as we see and hear the governor lament, "What a cruel shame that any man is made to suffer so!" This utterance, ironically, is a comment upon his gouty foot.

   Captain Blood was nominated for Academy Award as Best Picture but lost to *Mutiny on the Bounty*. Korngold was nominated for best score, and Nathan Levinson for best sound recording. The film was a boxoffice success. Domestic boxoffice receipts registered a profit of 1,087,000 dollars, and the total earnings veered toward 2,475,000 dollars with foreign takings included.[127] The success of *Captain Blood* launched Errol Flynn, completely unknown before this film, and Olivia de Havilland into stardom. The swashbuckling genre had enjoyed tremendous popularity in the silent era but almost died out for half a decade after the coming of sound in 1927. Until 1934, it is presumed that early recording equipment handicapped the production in that it confined action to the range of the microphones.[128] The successful dubbing and sound recording in *Captain Blood* thus confirmed the resurrection of this genre, and ushered in five years of Warner swashbuckling films. It also marked the beginning of Erich Wolfgang Korngold's distinguished career in film music. Korngold was the first composer of international reputation that went to Hollywood. He would go on to score five more films in this genre starring Errol Flynn.

(The writer wishes to thank Szu-hsien Li and Mirai Konishi, for their comments on musical theory and sound recording, respectively.)

THE EXORCIST (1973)
William Whittington

Warner Bros., December 1973. MPAA Rating R. Running Time: 121 MINS. Director: William Friedkin, Written for the Screen and Produced by: William Peter Blatty, based on his novel, Executive Producer: Noel Marshall, Director of Photography: Owen Roizman, Makeup Artist: Dick Smith, Special Effects: Marcel Vercoutere, Production Design: Bill Malley, Music: Krzysztof Penderecki, Hans Werner Henze, George Crumb, Aton Webern, Beginnings, Mike Oldfield, David Borden, Additional Music Composed by: Jack Nitzsche, Editors: Jordan Leondopoulos, Evan Lottman, Norman Gay, Sound: Chris Newman, Dubbing mixer, Buzz Knudson, Sound Effects Editors: Fred Brown, Ross Taylor. Special Sound Effects: Ron Nagle, Gonzalo Gavira, Doc Siegel, Bob Fine, Sound Consultant: Hal Landaker, Music Editor: Gene Marks.

CAST: Ellen Burstyn (Chris MacNeil), Max von Sydow (Father Merrin), Lee J. Cobb (Lt. Kinderman), Kitty Winn (Sharon), Jack MacGowran (Burke Dennings), Jason Miller (Father Karras), Linda Blair (Regan), The Devil (as Himself).

---

[127] See the file of *Captain Blood* in the Warner Bros. Archive, the Cinema-TV library, the University of Southern California.
[128] Robert E. Morsberger, "Captain Blood," *Magill's Survey of Cinema* (series 11, volume 1), pp. 400-404.

Georgetown. A fog descended on the street early that evening, and a stark light streamed from the second story window, where she was—where it was. He arrived at the curbside by taxi, his attaché in hand, ready for battle with a familiar opponent, yet not realizing how grave the outcome would be.

The arrival of the Exorcist Father Merrin (played by Max von Sydow) to the home of Chris MacNeil (Ellen Burstyn), an actress and mother to Regan MacNeil (Linda Blare), a young girl possessed by the devil, is one of the most resonant scenes in horror film history. It is the haunting lull before the terrifying ritual of exorcism that is performed to purge the demon from Regan's body and save her soul, yet woven into this struggle is the battle for another soul, that of Father Karras (Jason Miller), a priest and psychologist, who fears a loss of faith brought on by a family crisis and personal doubts. In the end, Father Karras finds that his ultimate redemption may lie in the fate of this young girl.

Novelist William Peter Blatty drew inspiration for *The Exorcist* from a real-life account of the possession of a fourteen-year-old boy. The novel remained on the *New York Times*' Best Seller list for 55 weeks and influenced a generation of horror writers such as Stephen King (*Carrie*) and Peter Straub (*Ghost Story*). In 1973, director William Friedkin (*The French Connection*) adapted the book to the screen and energized the horror of the demonic, a genre trend which included films such as *Rosemary's Baby*, *The Omen* and *The Sentinel*.

In terms of box office receipts, *The Exorcist*, along with films like *The Godfather*, *The Sting* and *American Graffiti*, brought the Hollywood film industry out of the economic downturn of the early 1970s and essentially defined the notion of the "blockbuster." The film cost 13 million dollars, took 10 months to complete and earned 82 million dollars domestically, placing it among the top grossing films of that decade. The film was re-released in 1976 and 1979—the latter featured a re-mixed Dolby Stereo soundtrack, a fact which punctuates the importance of sound in the film. The film won Academy Awards for Best Screenplay and Best Sound.

Like most films, the sound design of *The Exorcist* is a complex weave of dialogue, music, ambience (presence or background noises), Foley (footsteps, glass breaks, and other effects produced in synchronization with the projected image) and sound effects. Yet in the horror genre, sound often rivals the image in function, style and impact. The narrative of *The Exorcist* (which may at first seem fragmented) is carefully constructed through repeated motifs and themes, such as good vs. evil, control vs. lack of control, the domestic vs. the fantastic. The sound design reflects and reinforces these narrative themes in expressive ways.

The opening sequence set in Northern Iraq uses sound to establish conflicts and plot points that will later recur in the film. As Father Merrin makes his way through the streets, the sounds from a foundry pound like a heartbeat. The motif of heart sounds tells us something about the character of Merrin. Specifically, we discover that he has a heart condition as we see him take nitroglycerin pills at a cafe. The chanting and music within the sequence offer a variation on this idea, using heart-like rhythms. The motif builds to a frightening crescendo moments later inside the study of a fellow archeologist. In the scene, Merrin examines relics from the dig and the ticking clock in the room inexplicably stops. Silence. This sound (or in this case the lack of it) foreshadows Merrin's death from a heart attack at the end of the film.

The Iraq sequence ends with another important narrative and sonic metaphor established. This sound spectacle occurs when Merrin goes to face the statue of the laughing demon. Suddenly, we hear the sound of two dogs fighting. The sound effect is amplified, processed, and thus privileged, revealing the endless battle between good and evil. This sonic movement finds echoes throughout the film: for example, Carl, the butler, and the film director Burke Dennings (played by Jack MacGowran) fight and snarl at one another during the

MacNeil dinner party; and more importantly, the possessed Regan growls and attacks the two priests during the exorcism. The film narrative and the sound track depend on these variations and echoes. They are sometimes subtle, sometimes obvious, yet they function skillfully to structure the story. It is here that the unity of the film is found.

As the film shifts location to Georgetown, the sounds become domestic, familiar in their nature. Commuter trains roar by on tracks and bridges, children's voices reverberate from playgrounds, and church bells chime and toll. Yet there is something ominous in the cutting and mixing of these sounds. Expressive effect is created through an alternation of loud and soft or rise and fall. Sounds rise and are cut off as the picture cuts from scene to scene or at times within scenes. The candle sequence is an excellent example of rise and fall within a scene. The soundtrack sonically establishes the attic space (with Foley) as Chris MacNeil bumps into old furniture, her footsteps creak on the floor boards, then whoosh her candle loudly flares up and out. The effect is a jolt to our ears. This scare technique is an attribute of the genre. Horror films work to create a tension and release. Tension is established also in our expectation of the fantastic and elements of the fantastic creep into the sound design as the demon penetrates the MacNeil house. Unfamiliar scrapes come from the attic, beds thump without cause, and the demon groans and screams names and profanities. These are the staples of the genre and its sound design.

The sound design of the Georgetown sequence explores the primary theme of control, which proves a major factor in the narrative. Young Regan is losing control of her mind, body and soul. Her mother Chris MacNeil seeks the advice of doctors, who endless examine Regan's condition. In terms of sound design, Regan is strapped into X-ray devices, while machines whirl and click around her. The sound effects imply torture and control. The attempts are ineffective and a spiritual solution is explored. In the MacNeil home, Regan's environment is filled with the same loss of control—beds thump, objects shatter, and walls crack. The demon possesses the sonic environment. Ultimately, Regan loses control of her body and voice. She spews vulgarities (as well as pea soup), she speaks in tongues, and she takes on other personalities. Father Karras uses a tape recorder to capture these sounds and analyze the voices, which seem to capture a sonic hell of pain and suffering.

The notion of loss of control of the voice is essential to the film. The loss of voice is a loss of personality. It also implies a more sinister purpose—a shift in authority. The demon uses voices to confuse and taunt the priests. During the famous head rotation scene, the voice of the murdered Director Burke Dennings asks: "Do you know what she did?" The choice of Dennings' voice refers to his murder as well as the vulgar nature of Regan's self mutilation. During the exorcism, the demon also uses the voice of Father Karras's mother. The voice pleads to "Demie" for help. The range of voices attacks Karras's faith and provides us with echoes of previous events and characters in the narrative, so the sound cutting acts as an important structuring device. The priests in turn attack the demon with the words of the ritual and the faith in their own voice of authority.

Reinforcing the sound effects, Foley, ambience and dialogue of *The Exorcist* is a careful use of music. The original score of the film was abandoned by the director; instead, Friedkin chose to use existing classical and contemporary music. The most famous piece was Tubular Bells by Mike Oldfield, which because of the film received extensive air-play on popular radio in 1973-1974. Bells uses tones and rhythm to create a dream like mood as Chris MacNeil walks through Georgetown on Halloween. Like Merrin in the beginning of the film, Chris MacNeil is walking into a battle with the unknown. This particular musical work has influenced the scores of films by John Carpenter (*Halloween*).

Through careful repetition and variation, the impact of the sound design of *The Exorcist* is amplified to a frenzied and terrifying status, which threatens the notion of image over sound. Clearly within the horror genre, nothing is as it seems, and sometimes it is more frightening to hear what is in the dark than to see it.

ALL THAT JAZZ (1979)
Shannon Mader

Executive Producer: Daniel Melnick. Associate Producers: Kenneth Utt, Wolfgang Glattes. Producer: Robert Alan Aurthur. Director: Bob Fosse. Screenplay: Robert Alan Aurthur, Bob Fosse. Cinematography: Giuseppe Rotunno. Editor: Alan Heim. Music Arranged and Conducted by: Ralph Burns. Choreography: Bob Fosse. Production Design: Philip Rosenberg. Fantasy Designer: Tony Walton. Set Decoration: Gary Brink, Edward Stewart. Costume Design: Albert Wolsky. Columbia Pictures and Twentieth Century-Fox. 123 min.

CAST: Roy Scheider (Joe Gideon), Jessica Lange (Angelique), Ann Reinking (Kate Jagger), Leland Palmer (Audrey Paris), Cliff Gorman (Davis Newman), Ben Vereen (O'Connor Flood), Erzebert Foldi (Michelle Gideon), Deborah Geffner (Victoria), Keith Gordon (Young Joe), John Lithgow (Lucas Sergeant), Michael Tolin (Dr. Ballinger), William La Massena (Jonesy Hecht), Chris Chase (Leslie Perry), Kathryn Doby (Kathryn).

The year was 1974. With *Lenny*, his bio-pic about the comedian Lenny Bruce, near completion, Bob Fosse began working on his next project, the Broadway musical *Chicago*. One day during rehearsals Fosse got up, walked out and grabbed a cab to New York Hospital. He knew something was wrong, but it was only later that he learned he was having a heart attack. After undergoing bypass surgery several weeks later, Fosse suffered another heart attack.

While recuperating from his multiple heart attacks, Fosse came across Hilma Wolitzer's *Ending*, a novel about a woman whose husband is dying of cancer. Stuart Ostrow, the Broadway producer behind such hits as *1776* and the Fosse-directed *Pippin*, bought the rights to the novel and hired Robert Alan Aurthur, a friend of Fosse's who had written the screenplays to such films as *For Love of Ivy* (Daniel Mann, 1968), *Grand Prix* (John Frankenheimer, 1966), *Warlock* (Edward Dmytryk, 1959), and *Edge of the City* (Martin Ritt, 1957) but who had lately been down on his luck, to adapt it. But as the project progressed (Paramount Pictures even hired Robert Carradine to star in it), Fosse grew increasingly disenchanted with the prospect of doing a serious drama about death. "I wanted music and dancing in it," he later claimed.[129] So *Ending* was called off, and Fosse announced that he was going to make *All That Jazz*, a film musical about his own near-death experience, instead.[130]

In preparation for the film, Fosse and Aurthur interviewed almost everyone who had known or worked with Fosse at the time of his heart attacks. From the resulting mass of interviews, Fosse and Aurthur put together a screenplay, the first draft of which used real names. The names were subsequently changed, but the real-life counterparts are obvious

---

[129] Martin Gottfried, *All His Jazz: The Life and Death of Bob Fosse* (New York: Da Capo Press, 1998) 350.
[130] *All That Jazz* was *Chicago*'s original title.

enough.[131] However, the dialogue, much of which came directly from life, remained. But despite this basis in reality, *All That Jazz* is anything but a realistic film. In a nod to *8 1/2* (Federico Fellini, 1963), Fosse uses real-life experiences and individuals merely as the springboard for a surrealistic flight of fancy that freely mixes autobiographical fact with moments of sheer fantasy. In the end, the film is less about Fosse's life than about Fosse's hallucinations, daydreams, and memories. Subjective reality, not objective reality, is Fosse's real focus.

And being the formalist that he is, Fosse relies primarily on the formal elements of film (e.g., visual design, editing, sound design) to communicate this subjective reality. Especially noteworthy is Fosse's manipulation of two formal elements in particular: editing and sound design. Though best known for his unique editing style, Fosse was no less a master of film sound. In fact, his use of sound is probably even more sophisticated than his editing. But because sound has never received the attention that editing has, the sophistication of Fosse's sound tracks has been overshadowed by the sophistication of his editing. So as you're watching *All That Jazz*, make sure that you listen to it, too, or you're going to miss a lot.

Take, for example, the montage that opens the film. This montage will be repeated several times during the course of the film (what do we call something that's repeated?), so it's important. What makes it seem unimportant is that fact it consists of nothing more than Joe Gideon's morning ritual—listening to Vivaldi's "Concerto for Strings and Continuo", putting his contacts in, downing a couple Dexedrine, and smoking in the shower. If you listen closely, however, you will notice that this montage consists of sounds as well as images. The most obvious sounds are the Vivaldi and the line of dialogue that comes from Gideon's mouth at the end of the montage: "It's showtime, folks." The Vivaldi and the line dialogue are not the only sounds, however. In fact, the montage is—at first—composed of a dizzying array of sounds: the sound of someone coughing, the clack of a cassette being inserted into a cassette player, the click of the play button being pushed, the Vivaldi, the plop of an Alka Selzter tablet as it hits the water, the fizz as it dissolves, and the shhhhhh of a shower. A more cacophonous combination of sounds can hardly be imagined. Far from matching, the sounds clash: the Vivaldi, for instance, is preceded by the sounds of the cassette being inserted and the cassette player being turned on. This is a kind of collision montage, albeit one produced aurally: the abrasive sounds of a mechanical contraption are juxtaposed with the mellifluous sounds of the Vivaldi. It is worth pointing out in this regard that Fosse did not have to combine these sounds; he could have simply removed the sounds of the cassette player and started with the Vivaldi. Instead, Fosse uses this discordant combination of sounds to convey Gideon's chaotic and disordered life. (Notice that the sounds clash with the images, too: the Vivaldi is heard over top of such grotesque images as a bloodshot eye and a man smoking in the shower. This only adds to the sense of discordance.) This brief but recurring montage thus functions as a more than just a musical interlude; it's an objective correlative for the state of Gideon's life.

In addition to its sound montages, *All That Jazz* impresses with its use of subjective sound. Though rarely used in most mainstream film, subjective sound is used repeatedly in the film. Take, for instance, the scene in which Gideon suffers his first attack. The attack occurs during a reading of the show he is directing. As the cast and crew listen, each cast member reads his or her lines. Audrey has the first line: it's a joke—and it draws uproarious laughter.

---

[131] Joe Gideon was of course based on Bob Fosse. Audrey Paris, played by Leland Palmer, was based on Fosse's real-life wife, Gwen Verdon. And the character of Kate Jagger, played by Ann Reinking, was based on, well, Ann Reinking. Reinking had been one of Fosse's many flames. Jessica Lange, who plays Angelique, the angel of death, had been Fosse's girlfriend at the time she was cast, but the couple had subsequently broken up when Fosse discovered that Lange was seeing Mikhail Baryshnikov. (Fosse couldn't tolerate infidelity on the part of his girlfriends.) The real-life parallels go beyond Fosse's love life, however. They extend to his professional life as well. For instance, Gideon's dance assistant, Kathy, was played by Kathryn Doby, Fosse's real-life dance assistant, and Davis Newman, the comedian in the film Gideon is editing, was played by Cliff Gorman, the actor who had originally played Lenny Bruce on Broadway. (Dustin Hoffman played Bruce in the film version.) And Leslie Perry, the reviewer who trashes Gideon's film, was played by Chris Chase, a real-life entertainment reporter and critic.

But as the cast and crew are laughing, the sound of their laughter drops off the sound track. We still see them laughing; we just don't hear them laughing. The effect is distancing—and suffocating: it feels as if we're encased in a glass booth, cut off from everyone else but still able to see them. The scene is not totally silent, however. We hear what Joe is hearing, and he's only hearing the sounds which he makes. So instead of hearing the lines being read and the cast and crew reacting to them, we hear Joe as he taps his fingers, as he grinds his fingernails on a metal pipe, as he snuffs out a cigarette, as he takes out another cigarette and lights it, as he crushes that cigarette with his shoe, and as he breaks a pencil in half and drops it on the ground. It is thus almost entirely through sound that Fosse conveys to us Gideon's angina attack. Notice, too, that this array of sounds is followed by a moment of complete silence: the insert of Angelique, the angel of death, lifting her veil is totally silent. The silence is then shattered by Audrey bursting through a door, rushing out of the building to the hospital.

Even more remarkable than the film's use of subjective sound, however, is its use of asynchronous sound. Take, for example, the scene in which Gideon escapes from his hospital bed and aimlessly wanders the hospital. Despite the absence of any realistic motivation, the comedian's monologue on death begins playing on the sound track again. As the comedian recounts the five stages of death (anger, denial, bargaining, depression, acceptance) outlined by Dr. Kubler-Ross in *On Death and Dying*, Fosse shows us Gideon going through these stages. For instance, as the comedian does his bit on anger ("Jesus Christ! Goddamn sonofabitch! It ain't fair!"), we hear Gideon moan, "No, no, not now." And as the comedian does his bit on denial, we see Gideon dance in the puddles of water that cover the floor of the hospital's boiler room. For depression we see Gideon bashing his head into a wall, and for acceptance we see Gideon embrace and then kiss on the lips a sickly old woman writhing in pain. A more audacious use of sound (note that this is a sound/image montage as well as an example of asynchronous sound) would be hard to find in recent American film.

Needless to say, this brief overview does not begin to exhaust the film's rich use of sound. Dozens of other examples could be cited (e.g., Ethel Merman singing "There's No Business Like Show Business" over top of the film's final image—wait till you see what it is). The film's use of sound is far less obtrusive or obvious than its editing, however, so it may be necessary to watch film more than once to fully grasp the sophistication and complexity of its sound track. For the sake of your grade as well as your own personal enrichment, it is advised that you do so.

Despite (or perhaps because of) the film's formal sophistication, critical reaction was mixed. While a few critics lauded it (e.g., Vincent Canby), many found it derivative and self-indulgent. Still, the film was nominated for nine Academy Awards, including Best Actor (Roy Scheider), Best Cinematography (Giuseppe Rotunno), Best Director (Fosse), Best Picture, and Best Screenplay Written Directly for the Screen. But because this was the year that *Kramer vs. Kramer* (Robert Benton, 1979) swept the Oscars, *All That Jazz* was left with the technical awards, winning for Best Editing, Best Costume Design, Best Art Direction/Set Decoration, and Best Music. Fosse did not go entirely unrecognized, however. He and Akira Kurosawa shared the Golden Palm at Cannes.

Though not a hit, the film made back its costs. This is surprising given how much it cost. Originally budget at $6 million, the film's rocky production history (e.g., Richard Dreyfus was replaced by Roy Scheider) and Fosse's own tendency to overshoot resulted in an extra $4 million being spent before Columbia finally pulled the plug. With the picture only halfway done, Daniel Melnick, the film's executive producer, turned to Twentieth Century-Fox. With their backing, the film was finally finished, costing somewhere between $12 and $20 million, an astronomical sum for a film of this kind.

FARGO (1997)

William Whittington

Credits: A Polygram Release. Gramercy Pictures. Working Title Films. A Joel and Ethan Coen film. Executive Producers Tim Bevan and Eric Fellner. Producer Ethan Coen. Directed by Joel Coen. Screenplay by Joel and Ethan Coen. Cinematography Roger Deakins.

Cast: William H. Macy, Steve Buscemi, Peter Stormage, Kristin Rudrud, Harve Presnell, Frances McDormand, John Carroll Lynch. MPAA Rating: R. Running Time: 1 hour 37 min.

Ya. Fargo. That's where all this happened or so they say. In this "true story," the Coen Brothers (Ethan and Joel) have returned to their minimalist, darkly humorous roots, not seen since their first film *Blood Simple*. The story entwines the lives of Jerry Lundegaard (William H. Macy), a car salesman, and Marge Gunderson (Frances McDormand), a female police chief, who is 7 months pregnant. It is a grim tale of emotional and physical isolation and the madness, a kind of cabin fever, which results. Early on in the film, Jerry Lundergaard hatches a scheme to secure funds for new car lot. He hires two thugs played by Steve Buscemi and Peter Stormare to kidnap his wife, Jean, played by Kristin Rudrid. A ransom is set to be paid by Jean's wealthy father, Wade Gustafson, played by Harve Presnell (who was a 1960s musical star in films such as *The Unsinkable Molly Brown* and *Paint Your Wagon* and is cast against type here). But plans go terribly wrong when a routine traffic stop after the abduction turns deadly, and the thugs kill an innocent State Trooper and two witnesses. Chief Marge Gunderson is left to follow up the leads and unravel the "malfeasance."

The sound design of the film is elegant, simple and understated as it carefully matches the emotional and thematic core of the narrative, turning simple ordinary sounds into metaphoric constructions. This is a film about isolation, both physical and emotional, and this theme permeates the soundtrack on all levels—dialogue, music and effects. The most noticeable manifestation is on the dialogue track. It is hard to miss the thick, midwest accents, which are exaggerated and comical. In particular, the vowel "a" is pulled out rather than enunciated, while other linguistic constructions are abbreviated or clipped. Some of the key variants include: "Ya", "You betcha!", "You don't say?", and "He was kind a funny look'en." Almost akin to linguist inbreeding, a complete dialect has formulated from the isolation of the folks within the region. These are simple people yet an angry reserve can often be detected beneath the surface. Wade grumbles, and Scotty curses with his parents. Within the narrative, the regional dialect clashes with Steve Buscemi's fast, linguistically crude city-speak. While his linguistic turns are humorous, they present such an unending stream of verbiage that it ultimately leads to his demise at the hands of his partner. His partner, in contrast, rarely speaks, preferring to remain silent in his madness. He becomes a perverse rift on the Paul Bunyon icon seen as a visual motif throughout the film.

The one character, who is our anchor within the film, is Marge Gunderson, the police chief. She is sharply drawn, intelligent, methodical, and she combats the isolation through her compassion and unwavering support of her husband as well as her professionalism on the job. In the production notes for the film, Francis McDormand explains: "I think Marge is representative of those Midwesterners who accept their lives at face value. With that as her point of view, she is a happy woman, a content wife and expectant mother, and a confident, competent cop." In short, Marge overcomes the barren landscapes with resolve and acceptance.

The sound effects within the film are exceptionally recorded. Gone is the pristine clarity you would expect from sound effects in a similar police drama; rather, many of the effects are recorded through dividers or barriers, primarily windows. For example, the insular feel of the environment is emphasized as we hear Marge tread out to her cruiser, through the outer doors of her home, the storm doors, and finally, the car door. The irony of this is her cruiser won't start so she retraces her steps, thus repeating all the sounds. The insular recordings match the insularity of these character's lives and their environment.

Another very important sound effect comes from the cars within the film. On many occasions, we hear the beeping tone of the car as keys are left in ignitions or headlights are left on. The sound effect ties into the narrative, which is about cars, creating a metaphor for American social mobility. The car motif spans the entire film. Events occur in cars, in car lots, and at a car dealership. The idea is that the automobile is somehow tied to upward mobility as well as financial independence. It is an icon of the American dream, albeit turned perverse and humorous, and the sound track bears this out.

The most striking use of sound design comes at the end of the film, when Marge approaches the cabin where the thugs have been hiding out. As the bleach blond Peter Stormare stuffs his partner into the wood chipper, the grater whines and jams cruelly on the deadman's leg. Subsequently, Marge's voice can't be heard over the noise. The sound of the wood chipper is a metaphor for madness. It is the modern day ax, the weapon of death for the isolated. The buzz of the chipper is the madness in the characters mind, deafening him to Marge's approach. The moment is humorous, gruesome and telling. The intertextual reference to the Bunyon myth is part of the irony.

The music of the film is difficult to define. It rolls along like wind, in fact taking the place of wind effects at some points. The orchestrations feel as if they are folk songs from the old country played on an accordion. The arrangements are simple variants of the same theme over and over, emphasizing the barren landscapes and the unending nature of these characters existence. The Muzak within car dealership picks up on this idea and strips the environment of its humanity. It is the sonic equivalent to florescent lights. Music does occur within the diegesis of the film, which again emphasizes the themes of the film. As Jerry enters the bar at the beginning of the film, a country song plays on the juke box. The lyrics talk about "so called social security" and an escape to "the big city." Once again, this is about emotional and financial security and upward mobility, moving to the big city away from the farm and country life.

The critical reception for the film was exceptional. Detour Magazine said: "*Fargo* is as clear and bracing as the North Dakota sunlight that it illuminates it, and finds the Coen brothers at the top of their form, with new confidence and maturity." The National Board of Review of Motion Pictures named *Fargo* one of the best films of 1996, and it was voted best film of the year by the New York Film Critics Circle. It also received Academy Awards for Best Actress and Best Original Screenplay. According to *Daily Variety*, the film has grossed $24 million domestically as of April 1997.

8
Modes of Representation: Realism and Formalism

The shot, considered as material for the purpose of composition, is more resistant than granite. This resistance is specific to it. The shot's tendency toward complete factual immutability is rooted in its nature. This resistance has largely determined the richness and variety of montage forms and styles—for montage becomes the mightiest means for a really important creative remolding of nature.

—*Sergei Eisenstein,* Film Form

In achieving the aims of baroque art, photography has freed the plastic arts from their obsession with likeness. Painting was forced, as it turned out, to offer us illusion and this illusion was reckoned sufficient unto art. Photography and the cinema on the other hand are discoveries that satisfy, once and for all and in its very essence, our obsession with realism.

—*André Bazin,* What is Cinema?

CTCS 190 LECTURE OUTLINE – WEEK VIII   **LECTURE 8**

A. **Mode of Representation**
   1. Definition
   2. Types
B. **Realism**
   1. Nature of the film medium and objective renderings
   2. Realism as a method
   3. Realism as an attitude of mind
   4. Some types of realist filmmaking include:
      a. Primitive Realism/Photojournalism
      b. Naturalism
      c. Hollywood's Classical Realism/Romantic-Idealist Realism
      d. Social Realism
      e. French Poetic Realism
      f. Italian Neo-Realism
      g. English Free Cinema/Proletarian Realism
      h. Psychological-Sociological Realism
      i. Documentary Realism in the Non-Fiction Film and in the Fiction Film (*Film Noir*)
      j. Dogme '95
C. **Formalism**
   1. Nature of the film medium and subjective renderings
   2. Formalism as a method
   3. Formalism as an attitude of mind
   4. Some types of formalist filmmaking include:
      a. Early "trick" films
      b. Expressionism (German Expressionism and *Film Noir*)
      c. Soviet Expressive Realism
      d. Expressive Stylization
      e. High-Tech Style
      f. Avant-garde film
      g. Animation
D. **Introduction and Screening**

Notes

Notes

TYPES OF REALIST/FORMALIST FILMMAKING

CTCS 190 Document

Realist Filmmaking

I. *Primitive Realism/Photojournalism*

- first school of realism in film, influenced by photography and the stage, resulting is such characteristics as:
- the camera placed in such a way (approximately fifth row center in theater) to record the reality of movement as a spatial-temporal whole.
  - e.g., the Lumiére Brothers' series of "arrival films" (*The Arrival of a Train at the Station*, 1895).

II. *Naturalism*

- derived from the literary school of the Goncourt Brothers, Emile Zola (France), George Eliot, Thomas Hardy (England), and Frank Norris, Theodore Dreiser, Jack London (United States), arising from the influences of Darwin (heredity as determinant), Freud (instinct as determinant), and Marx (environment as determinant), encouraged by post-World-War I mood of cynicism and amorality (roughly, 1900-1930 in America), resulting in such characteristics as:
- image of man as determined by heredity, instinct, and environment.
- a corresponding style which records surface details as well as below-the-surface details (i.e., root causes).
  - e.g., Erich von Stroheim's erotic comedies of manners (*Blind Husbands*, 1918, *The Wedding March*, 1925, and especially *Greed*, 1924); King Vidor's *The Big Parade* (1924).

III. *Hollywood's Classical Realism*

- Hollywood fiction film's predominant style (1929-1945), but should be qualified as a "romantic/idealist" type of realism, resulting in such characteristics as:
- transparency: technique erasing itself as it creates itself, immersing the spectator in the characters and their situations and thus accepting them as real.
- world as homogenous, larger-than-life, and idealized: in general, young/beautiful/handsome people who are morally good as protagonists; morally evil/unheroic people as antagonists; therefore, differentiating and describing good and evil behavior while using the hero/villian dichotomy; poetic justice (triumph of good) operative; God is alive, world is meaningful ("can-do" ideology subscribed to); therefore, tensions/ contradictions/disruptions in society or between people are

embodied throughout the film but in the end are smoothed out/erased/transcended; re-affirmation of the status quo and predominant social order (patriarchal capitalism) in spite of some probing; closure and ending which is usually upbeat/happy; heterosexual romance, leading to marriage is seen as part of the good and as part of plot; at end: espousal of conservative values but centrist ideology predominates; patriotism invoked.

IV. Hollywood Social Realism

- within Hollywood's Classical "Romantic-Idealist" Realism, a Social Realism surfaced from time to time, especially at Warner Brothers, 1929-1945, resulting from such determinants as:
    - the awakening of social consciousness in America during the Depression, eliciting a social realism in journalism (serious political commentary, documentary reporting, oral histories of the Depression, and political cartoons in leftist publications), photography, painting, the novel, popular music, and even film.
- sound-on-film contributed to this type of realism as well as the Warner Brothers' house style, though the New Deal and Hays Office moralism removed much of the hard edge, resulting in such characteristics as the following:
    - a proletarian, nitty-gritty quality.
    - focus on interaction of the individual within social institutions.
    - a highly cynical attitude towards social institutions.
    - the common man as protagonist, especially the worker or society's loser.
    - smart, tough, almost hard-boiled dialogue.
    - casting of players with by and large average, ordinary "man-in-the-street" looks.
    - e.g., Warner Brothers' products, such as Mervyn LeRoy's *I Am a Fugitive from a Chain Gang* (1932); and elsewhere, such films as Lewis Milestone's *All Quiet on the Western Front* (Universal, 1930) and *Of Mice and Men* (United Artists, 1939).

V. French Poetic Realism

- a blend of realism and lyricism in the French cinema, 1934-1940.
- emanates from the realist-naturalist fiction of Emile Zola and Guy de Maupassant, the hard-boiled writers of the 1930s, Louis Delluc and "photogenie," the semi-documentaries of Jean Grémillon and the stress and sadness of France during the Depression and encroaching fascism and subsequent occupation during World War II, resulting in such characteristics as:
    - focus on working-class, urban protagonist who is severely alienated and disaffected, up against class politics and modern industrialization.
    - symbolic/allegorical dimension to story which is organized around a single consciousness; character, setting, poetic dialogue, all built from highly realistic details.
    - e.g., Jean Vigo's *L'Atalante* (1934); Julien Duvivier's *Pépé le Moko* (1937); Marcel Carné's *Port of Shadows* (1938).

VI. Italian Neo-Realism

- post-World War II renaissance in Italian filmmaking, influenced by hardships of World War II and its aftermath and French poetic realism, resulting in such characteristics as:

- a concern for the people of Italy, particularly the working and unemployed classes, the innocent children, the outcasts, bandits, and prostitutes, as they tried to rise again out of the ashes of the war.
- the reality of the streets, peopled with actors and non-professionals, wherein an occurrence's actual duration and spatialization were respected with lighting playing a minor expressive role, dictated by camerawork.
- exposing problems, while urging that something be done about them.
- Robert Rossellini (*Open City*, 1945; *Paisan*, 1946; *Germany Year Zero*, 1948), Vittorio de Sica (*Shoeshine*, 1946; *The Bicycle Thief*, 1948; *Umberto D*, 19540, Aldo Vergano (*The Sun Rises Again*, 1946), Alberto Lattuada (*The Bandits*, 1946; *Without Pity*, 1948), Luigi Zampa (*To Live in Peace*, 1947; *The Difficult Year*, 1948).

VII. English Free Cinema/Proletarian Realism

- Commercial filmmaking in England (the work of British directors Michael Anderson, Roy Boulting, David Lean, Peter Glenville, Alexander MacKendrick, Carol Reed) embraced the social realist strain laid out by thirties documentarist John Grierson's theory and practice.
- World War II deepened this strain when the commercial and documentary film units united in an effort to fight the war.
- Around 1955, England's social realism was compounded by a movement called "Free Cinema" or "proletarian realism." A cry of dissatisfaction at the way things were, which first was heard in the magazine *Sequence* in 1947 (which became *Sight and Sound* in 1952), "Free Cinema" strengthened the British cinema's moorings. Financed by the British Film Institute and supported by the equally anti-establishment Angry Young Man School of novelists and playwrights, practitioners of this style started with short films and graduated to features, resulting is such characteristics as:
  - a focus on the common man that shivered with a topicality reflecting the whole British isle, not just the metropolitan and southern English culture, while brazenly scoffing at the status quo.
  - e.g., Jack Clayton's *Room at the Top*, 1958; Richardson's *Look Back in Anger*, 1958; Reisz's *Saturday Night and Sunday Morning*, 1960; John Schlesinger's *A Kind of Loving*, 1962; and Anderson's *This Sporting Life*, 1963).

VIII. Psychological Realism

- influence of the New York stage upon Hollywood fiction film, 1946-1965, where psychological-sociological playwrights (Tennessee Williams, Arthur Miller, William Inge, Paddy Chayefsky, etc.) and method directors (Elia Kazan, Martin Ritt, etc.) and method actors/actresses (Marlon Brando, Paul Newman, Joanne Woodward, Julie Harris) creates a stylized realism, resulting in such characteristics as:
  - emphasis on character (rather than plot) and its delineation in terms of age, looks, gender, ethnicity, religion, race, class, regionality, dream life, the past, sexuality, work, recreation, and especially family resulting in a character complexity and bringing to the fore the anti-hero/heroine.
  - dialogue manifested diction and rhythms of speech approximating a respective class and region.
  - regional setting becomes distinctive.
  - method acting: reasoned, intelligent wherein characters become internalized.
  - studio shot verisimilitude or location work.
  - deglamorizing costume, hairstyle and makeup.

– e.g., Elia Kazan's *A Streetcar Named Desire* (1951); Martin Ritt's *Hud* (1963).

IX. Documentary Realism in the Non-Fiction Film and in the Fiction Film (Film Noir)

– documentary realism is often allied with the non-fiction film (film with a believable recording of people's behavior, social institutions, social problems, processes of nature), but it can be allied with the fiction film (for examples, Hollywood war films during and after World War II and the spate of Hollywood fiction films that dealt with the underside of American life and rendered in the film noir film style, 1940-1960). Note: film noir begins steeped in an expressionist style—e.g., Boris Ingster's *Stranger on the Third Floor*, 1940—but film noir also travels the avenues of documentary realism—Henry Hathaways' *The House on 92nd Street*, 1945—and the combination expressionism/ documentary realism—Raoul Walsh's *White Heat*, 1949.
– Characteristics of documentary realism include:
  – the depiction of events that have actually happened: selection and ordering of these events are in evidence though not as severe as in other styles of realism.
  – when the subject is human behavior, the film usually uses the people endemic to the time and space of the subject matter (not professional actors and stars).
– usually shot on location.
– presentations of supporting documents, such as photographs, objects a person has made or owned, and earlier newsreels or clips from movies, home movies or TV shows.
– often includes voice-over narrator, title cards, interviews, and appearance of film paraphernalia.
– filmmaking technique can be polished or can lack polish (use of handheld camera work, direct sound recording, available light, etc.).
– attempt to teach, not just enlighten; persuade, not just communicate.
  – e.g., documentary realism in non-fiction film: Irving Saraf/Allie Light's *In the Shadow of the Stars* (1991); or in the fiction film: John Farrow's *Wake Island* (1942).

X. Dogme '95 (Dogma '95)

– Dogme '95 began as idea by Lars Von Trier as an attempt to create "simpler films, with less equipment, and a set of self imposed restraints." Along with Thomas Vinterberg, he "conceived a new set of school rules." As Vinterberg states: "It was easy...We asked ourselves what we most hated about film today and then drew up a list banning it all." (See Richard Kelly, *The Name of this Book is Dogme95*, Faber and Faber, 2000, p. 5-6)
– Beginning as a Danish film movement, Dogme '95 is also the name of a manifesto, written by Von Trier and Vinterberg, that seeks to challenge 'certain tendencies' in the cinema today by having directors and filmmakers adhere to the "Vows of Chastity"
  – The Vows of Chastity:
    1. Shooting must be done on location. Props and set must not be brought in (if a particular prop is necessary for the story, a location must be chosen where the prop is to be found).
    2. The sound must never be produced apart from the images or vice versa (music must not be used unless it occurs where the scene is being shot).
    3. The camera must be hand-held. Any movement or immobility attainable in the hand is permitted (the film must not take place where the camera is standing; shooting must take place where the film takes place).

4. The film must be in colour. Special lighting is not acceptable (if there is too little light for exposure, the scene must be cut or a single lamp attached to the front of the camera).
5. Optical work and filters are forbidden.
6. The film must not contain superficial action (murders, weapons, etc. must not occur).
7. Temporal and geographical alienation are forbidden. (That is to say that the film takes place here and now).
8. Genre movies are not acceptable.
9. The film format must be Academy 35 mm.
10. The director must not be credited.

– Originally, the only way for a film to receive certification as a "Dogme film" was for the four founding filmmakers of Dogme '95 "brotherhood" (Von Trier, Vinterberg, Levring, and Kragh-Jacobsen) to view the film and approve it. Increasingly, since 2000, directors just have to sign a piece of paper stating "To my conscience, I did this film following Dogme rules" to receive a certificate.

– Thomas Vinterberg's *Dogme#1: Festen [The Celebration]*; Lars Von Trier's *Dogme#2: Idioterne [The Idiots]*; Soren Kragh-Jacobsen's *Mifune*; Harmony Korine's *Julien Donkey-Boy*; Kristian Levring's *The King is Alive*.

Formalist Filmmaking

I. *The early "trick" films*

– a style of filmmaking that countered photojournalism and primitive realism at the dawn of film history.

– associated with stage magician-turned-filmmaker George Méliès (Paris, 1895-1913).

– through happenstance, Méliès discovered that motion picture photography, editing, and the printing process all can be magical instruments.

– by means of reverse motion, fast motion, dissolves, and superimpositions, jump cuts, negative images, double exposures, etc., he made movies about appearances, changes, transformations, probabilities and improbabilities, nether worlds and other terrestrial worlds.

– furthermore, he placed these "tricks" of the cinema in a story form (which came down to a series of theatrical scenes strung together—remember he came from the stage).

– e.g., Méliès' *A Trip to the Moon* (1902).

II. *Expressionism*

– a formalist style that, since the beginning of the century, was felt in most all of the arts (i.e., music, literature, painting, theater, and film).

– there have been many periods of expressionism in film.

– for one, the Golden Age of the German Cinema, 1919-1933, was a period when Expressionism became the favored style.

– e.g., Robert Wiene's *The Cabinet of Dr. Caligari* (1919); Fritz Lang's *Metropolis* (1931).

– for another, *film noir*, a style that infiltrated Hollywood between 1940 and 1960, a transgeneric style, but epicentered in the genre of the suspense thriller and its various

subcategories, was inflected with a heavy dose of Expressionism in its initial stage (1940-1945).
  – e.g., Billy Wilder's *Double Indemnity* (1944).
  – film noir's expressionism was diluted, as mentioned already, by documentary realism; film noir, after 1945, was either pure Expressionism (e.g., Joseph H. Lewis's *The Big Combo*, 1955), pure documentary realism (Jules Dassin's *The Naked City*, 1948), or a combination of the two (Billy Wilder's *Ace in the Hole*, 1951).
  – no matter the period, these various modes of Expressionism have the following characteristics in common:
    – the desire to express essential/basic reality of film's subject; not reproduce the mere appearance or surface reality of the subject.
    – the subject was inner feelings, subjective states, interiority and personal reality as opposed to outer feelings and impersonality.
    – angular, hallucinatory, violently emotional formal strategies that relied on exaggeration, exclamation, hyperbole, and distortion; for examples, the play of light and shadow in the frame, canted angles.

III. Soviet Expressive Realism

  – Russian cinema during its Golden Age (1925-1933) combined realism and expressionism, resulting in such characteristics as:
    – the collective masses as hero; individuals depicted as part/representative of a group.
    – collective masses who, through human will, rationality, and the application of Marxist-Leninist theories, transforms human and non-human environments to an idealist state in which everyone is the same and equal.
    – composition (framing/staging/photographing) was ennobling, mythic (e.g., people on heights, low camera angle against the sky), backlighting—natural but low key at times and soft focus to idealize.
    – image put together in terms of dynamic editing or montage (additive or collision) to instill in viewers a revolutionary spirit, to make them act in the way the group on screen was acting, to manipulate them; the use of film as a weapon, as propaganda.
    – e.g., Eisenstein's *Strike* (1925), *The Battleship Potemkin* (1925), *October* (1928), Pudovkin's *Mother* (1926), *End of St. Petersburg* (1927), *Storm over Asia* (1928); Dovzchenko's *Arsenal* (1929) and *Earth* (1930).

IV. Expressive Stylization

  – Due to the counter-culture sensibility, the influences of Modernism, documentary filmmaking, the avant-garde, and TV programming and TV commercials, as well as the director-as-auteur tenet imported from France, there occurs in Hollywood fiction film during the years 1963-1976 a salient trend toward experimentation of all formal strategies, resulting in such characteristics as:
    – different ways of telling or ordering the story, with a preference for episodic and contextual structures (literary design).
    – extravagant title design; thematic use of color, plus use of color as a structuring device and as an editing principle; use of overlight, underlight, available light, candlelight; playing around with different film stocks and filters; extensive use of location (visual design).

- awry/split/decentered framing; energization of off-screen space; lenses of varying focal lengths that experiment with motion and perspectives; handheld camera; steadicam in conjunction with subjective shots; daringly conspicuous camera moves and use of angulation; distortion of movement (composition).
- in general, diminishment of shot's length (getting rid of entrances and exits, for one thing); jump and shock cutting; montage type of visual structuring of scene is preferred to long-take composition in-depth; playing with modes of transition (editing).
- eclectic use of various types of music; source music and/or song slapped over image rather than directed into image; foregrounding of music; use of music to create choreographed passages; use of music as an editing principle; use of asynchronous sound (sound design).
– This formal experimentation brought about the awareness of film technique while watching a movie, the awareness of the construction of a movie, awareness of how a movie is made, awareness of film medium as medium, as well as awareness on the part of the spectator of the director's function and significance in making a film.
– e.g., Mike Nichols's *The Graduate* (1967); Arthur Penn's *Bonnie and Clyde* (1967).

V. High-Tech Style

– a dominant style in Hollywood fiction film from 1977, brought on by postmodernism and film as sensation-aesthetic, resulting in such characteristics as:
– an employment of the latest technology in production and consumption of a film, especially in quantity and quality of special effects and stunt work, as well as the employment of the latest exhibition technology in the presentation of a film.
- use of high concept in literary design.
- emphasis on star who plays personae rather than character itself.
- visually slick images designed like TV commercials or MTV music-videos.
- fast-paced montage as a visual structuring mode.
- use of rock score recorded and presented in high-decibel system.
– e.g., James Cameron's *Terminator 2: Judgment Day* (1991); Kevin Reynold's *Waterworld* (1995).

VI. Avant-garde Film

– the term avant-garde comes from a military term which means the vanguard which surveys the strategic situation before the main ranks enter the battle. In this sense, the artistic avant-garde generally has been viewed as those who initiate artistic change through innovation as well as a rejection of traditional means.
– the term was first applied to art and culture at the turn-of-the-century in referring to modernist practices in painting and sculpture such as cubism, futurism, dada, Constructivism, and surrealism. In film, the term was first used in 1920s France by a group of filmmakers who wanted to break with tradition as established by the French film industry and in so doing to politicize their work. These filmmakers included Louis Delluc, Germaine Dulac, and Jean Epstein.
– These filmmakers were interested in exploring many issues similar to the ones being explored by the avant-garde in painting and sculpture, including: issues of high art versus popular art, spectator-screen relations, simultaneity, subjectivity, the unconscious and psychoanalysis, and rhythm (e.g., Germaine Dulac's *The Smiling Madame Beaudet* (1928), Rene Clair's *Entr'acte* (1924) and Luis Buñuel's *Un Chien Andalou* (1928)).

- There were many ramifications of early avant-garde experimentation, including: the reworking of genres, exploring the limits of film language (e.g. breaking with conventional narrative forms and processes), and redefining the representation of subjectivity. Much avant-garde filmmaking attacks concepts of traditional filmic narrative, often encouraging the audience to give up its passive role and become active in the construction of meaning in the text. This is done through formal innovations, including experimentation with subjective camera and editing styles which can create nonrepresentational rhythmic visual poems and dream-like images, disrupting clear narrative flow.
- From this historic avant-garde which is largely associated with dada and surrealism, the later avant-garde developed. One branch is the American avant-garde closely allied with the modernist painters experimenting with abstraction, created dream-like imagery as seen in the works of Maya Deren (*Meshes of the Afternoon* (1943)) and Kenneth Anger (*Fireworks* (1947)). Another branch is the European Structural Materialists who are interested in exploring the artifice of cinema by exploiting Brechtian techniques of distanciation and playing with montage. Another branch, usually associated with a feminist avant-garde, experiments with narrative by attempting to denaturalize in and lay bare the role of cinema in the construction of subjectivity. These filmmakers include Chantal Ackerman, Agnes Varda, Sally Potter, and Jane Campion.

VII. Animation

- a form of filmmaking in which inanimate objects, individual drawings, or computer-generated images are filmed frame by frame, each frame differing only minutely from the next. When these frame are projected sequentially, they create the illusion of motion through the phenomenon of persistence of vision.
- animation allows the possibility of creating completely fantastic worlds, characters, and ways of seeing the world.
- the beginnings of animation correspond with the beginnings of cinema. Many of the 19th century toys based on the principle of persistence of vision, such as the Praxinoscope, used drawn images to create the illusion of movement.
- Walt Disney studios, perhaps the most recognized animators, in the beginning focused solely on making animated films. They were the first American studio to produce a feature length animated film with *Snow White and the Seven Dwarves* (1937).
- with technological advances, computer animation has become a significant feature in Hollywood filmmaking. Not only used for creating fantastic creatures and situations as in Steven Spielberg's *Jurassic Park* (1993) and James Cameron's *True Lies* (1994), computer animation has been used to create a completely fabricated world in Disney/Pixar's feature-length film *Toy Story* (1995).

A DIALECTIC APPROACH TO FILM FORM

From *Film Form* (1929) by Sergei Eisenstein, Translated by Jay Leyda

> In nature we never see anything isolated, but everything in connection with something else which is before it, beside it, under it, and over it.
>
> Goethe[132]

According to Marx and Engels the dialectic system is only the conscious reproduction of the dialectic course (substance) of the external events of the world.[133]

Thus:

The projection of the dialectic system of things
into the brain
into creating abstractly
into the process of thinking
yields: dialectic methods of thinking;
dialectic materialism—   PHILOSOPHY.

And also:

The projection of the same system of things
while creating concretely
while giving form
yields: ART.

The foundation for this philosophy is a dynamic concept of things:
Being—as a constant evolution from the interaction of two contradictory opposites.
Synthesis—arising from the opposition between thesis and antithesis.

A dynamic comprehension of things is also basic to the same degree, for a correct understanding of art and of all art-forms. In the realm of art this dialectic principle of dynamics is embodied in
CONFLICT
as the fundamental principle for the existence of every artwork and every art-form.

For art is always conflict:

[132] In *Conversations with Eckerman* (5 June 1825), translated by John Oxenford.
[133] Razumovsky, Theory of Historical Materialism, Moscow, 1928.

(1) according to its social mission,
(2) according to its nature,
(3) according to its methodology.

According to its social mission because: It is art's task to make manifest the contradictions of Being. To form equitable views by stirring up contradictions within the spectator's mind, and to forge accurate intellectual concepts from the dynamic clash of opposing passions.

According to its nature because: Its nature is a conflict between natural existence and creative tendency. Between organic inertia and purposeful initiative. Hypertrophy of the purposive initiative—the principles of rational logic—ossifies art into mathematical technicalism. (A painted landscape becomes a topographical map, a painted Saint Sebastian becomes an anatomical chart.) Hypertrophy of organic naturalness—of organic logic—dilutes art into formlessness. (A Malevich becomes a Kaulbach, an Archipenko becomes a waxworks side-show.)

Because the limit of organic form (the passive principle of being) is Nature. The limit of rational form (the active principle of production) is Industry. At the intersection of Nature and Industry stands Art.

The logic of organic form vs. the logic of rational form yields, in collision,

the dialectic of the art-form.

The interaction of the two produces and determines Dynamism. (Not only in the sense of a space-time continuum, but also in the field of absolute thinking. I also regard the inception of new concepts and viewpoints in the conflict between customary conception and particular representation as dynamic—as a dynamization of the inertia of perception—as a dynamization of the "traditional view" into a new one.)

The quantity of interval determines the pressure of the tension. (See in music, for example, the concept of intervals. There can be cases where the distance of separation is so wide that it leads to a break—to a collapse of the homogeneous concept of art. For instance, the "inaudibility" of certain intervals.)

The spatial form of this dynamism is expression.
The phases of its tension: rhythm.

This is true for every art-form, and, indeed, for every kind of expression.

Similarly, human expression is a conflict between conditioned and unconditioned reflexes. (In this I cannot agree with Klages, who, a) does not consider human expression dynamically as a process, but statically as a result, and who, b) attributes everything in motion to the field of the "soul," and only the hindering element to "reason."[134] ["Reason" and "Soul" of the idealistic concept here correspond remotely with the ideas of conditioned and unconditioned reflexes.])

This is true in every field that can be understood as an art. For example, logical thought, considered as an art, shows the same dynamic mechanism:

> . . . the intellectual lives of Plato or Dante or Spinoza or Newton were largely guided and sustained by their delight in the sheer beauty of the rhythmic relation between law and instance, species and individual, or cause and effect.[135]

[134] Ludwig Klages, *The Science of Character*, translated by W. H. Johnston, London, George Allen & Unwin Ltd., 1929.
[135] Graham Wallas, *The Great Society, A Psychological Analysis.* Macmillan, 1928, p. 101.

This holds in other fields, as well, e.g., in speech, where all its sap, vitality, and dynamism arise from the irregularity of the part in relation to the laws of the system as a whole.

In contrast we can observe the sterility of expression in such artificial, totally regulated languages as Esperanto.

It is from this principle that the whole charm of poetry derives. Its rhythm arises as a conflict between the metric measure employed and the distribution of accents, over-riding this measure.

The concept of a formally static phenomenon as a dynamic function is dialectically imaged in the wise words of Goethe:

> *Die Baukunst ist eine ertarrte Musik.*
> (Architecture is frozen music.)[136]

Just as in the case of a homogeneous ideology (a monistic viewpoint), the whole, as well as the least detail, must be penetrated by a sole principle. So, ranged alongside the conflict of social conditionality, and the conflict of existing nature, the methodology of an art reveals this same principle of conflict. As the basic principle of the rhythm to be created and the inception of the art-form.

Art is always conflict, according to its methodology.

Here we shall consider the general problem of art in the specific example of its highest form—film.

Shot and montage are the basic elements of cinema.

Montage has been established by the Soviet film as the nerve of cinema.

To determine the nature of montage is to solve the specific problem of cinema. The earliest conscious film-makers, and our first film theoreticians, regarded montage as a means of description by placing single shots one after the other like building-blocks. The movement within these building-block shots, and the consequent length of the component pieces, was then considered as rhythm.

A completely false concept!

This would mean the defining of a given object solely in relation to the nature of its external course. The mechanical process of splicing would be made a principle. We cannot describe such a relationship of lengths as rhythm. From this comes metric rather than rhythmic relationships, as opposed to one another as the mechanical-metric system of Mensen-dieck is to the organic-rhythmic school of Bode in matters of body exercise.

According to this definition, shared even by Pudovkin as a theoretician, montage is the means of unrolling an idea with the help of single shots: the "epic" principle.

In my opinion, however, montage is an idea that arises from the collision of independent shots—shots even opposite to one another: the "dramatic" principle.[137]

A sophism? Certainly not. For we are seeking a definition of the whole nature, the principal style and spirit of cinema from its technical (optical) basis.

We know that the phenomenon of movement in film resides in the fact that two motionless images of a moving body, following one another, blend into an appearance of motion by showing them sequentially at a required speed.

This popularized description of what happens as a blending has its share of responsibility for the popular miscomprehension of the nature of montage that we have quoted above.

---

[136] In *Conversations with Eckerman* (23 March 1829).
[137] "Epic" and "dramatic" are used here in regard to methodology of form—not to *content* or *plot!*

Let us examine more exactly the course of the phenomenon we are discussing—how it really occurs—and draw our conclusion from this. Placed next to each other, two photographed immobile images result in the appearance of movement. Is this accurate? Pictorially—and phraseologically, yes.

But mechanically, it is not. For, in fact, each sequential element is perceived not next to the other, but on top of the other. For the idea (or sensation) of movement arises from the process of superimposing on the retained impression of the object's first position, a newly visible further position of the object. This is, by the way, the reason for the phenomenon of spatial depth, in the optical superimposition of two planes in stereoscopy. From the superimposition of two elements of the same dimension always arises a new, higher dimension. In the case of stereoscopy the superimposition of two nonidentical two-dimensionalities results in stereoscopic three-dimensionality.

In another field: a concrete word (a denotation) set beside a concrete word yields an abstract concept—as in the Chinese and Japanese languages, where a material ideogram can indicate a transcendental (conceptual) result.

The incongruence in contour of the first picture—already impressed on the mind—with the subsequently perceived second picture engenders, in conflict, the feeling of motion Degree of incongruence determines intensity of impression; and determines that tension which becomes the real element of authentic rhythm.

Here we have, temporally, what we see arising spatially on a graphic or painted plane.

What comprises the dynamic effect of a painting? The eye follows the direction of an element in the painting. It retains a visual impression, which then collides with the impression derived from following the direction of a second element. The conflict of these directions forms the dynamic effect in apprehending the whole.

I. It may be purely linear: Fernand Léger, or Suprematism.

II. It may be "anecdotal." The secret of the marvelous mobility of Daumier's and Lautrec's figures dwells in the fact that the various anatomical parts of a body are represented in spatial circumstances (positions) that are temporally various, disjunctive. For example, in Toulouse-Lautrec's lithograph of Miss Cissy Loftus, if one logically develops position A of the foot, one builds a body in position A corresponding to it. But the body is represented from knee up already in position A + a. The cinematic effect of joined motionless pictures is already established here! From hips to shoulders we can see A + a + a. The figure comes alive and kicking!

III. Between I and II lies primitive Italian futurism—such as in Balla's "Man with Six Legs in Six Positions"—for II obtains its effect by retaining natural unity and anatomical correctness, while I, on the other hand, does this with purely elementary elements. III, although destroying naturalness, has not yet pressed forward to abstraction.

IV. The conflict of directions may also be of an ideographic kind. It was in this way that we have gained the pregnant characterizations of a Sharaku, for example. The secret of his extremely perfected strength of expression lies in the anatomical and spatial disproportion of the parts—in comparison with which, our I might be termed temporal disproportion.

Generally termed "irregularity," this spatial disproportion has been a constant attraction and instrument for artists. In writing of Rodin's drawings, Camille Mauclair indicated one explanation for this search:

> The greatest artists, Michelangelo, Rembrandt, Delacroix, all, at a certain
> moment of the upthrusting of their genius, threw aside, as it were, the ballast
> of exactitude as conceived by our simplifying reason and our ordinary eyes, in
> order to attain the fixation of ideas, the synthesis, the *pictorial handwriting*

of their dreams.[138]

Two experimental artists of the nineteenth century—a painter and a poet—attempted esthetic formulations of this "irregularity." Renoir advanced this thesis:

> Beauty of every description finds its charm in variety. Nature abhors both vacuum and regularity. For the same reason, no work of art can really be called such if it has not been created by an artist who believes in irregularity and rejects any set form. Regularity, order, desire for perfection (which is always a false perfection) destroy art. The only possibility of maintaining taste in art is to impress on artists and the public the importance of irregularity. Irregularity is the basis of all art.[139]

And Baudelaire wrote in his journal:

> That which is not slightly distorted lacks sensible appeal; from which it follows that irregularity—that is to say, the unexpected, surprise and astonishment, are an essential part and characteristic of beauty.[140]

Upon closer examination of the particular beauty of irregularity as employed in painting, whether by Grünewald or by Renoir, it will be seen that it is a disproportion in the relation of a detail in one dimension to another detail in a different dimension.

The spatial development of the relative size of one detail in correspondence with another, and the consequent collision between the proportions designed by the artist for that purpose, result in a characterization—a definition of the represented matter.

Finally, color. Any shade of a color imparts to our vision a given rhythm of vibration. This is not said figuratively, but purely physiologically, for colors are distinguished from one another by their number of light vibrations.

The adjacent shade or tone of color is in another rate of vibration. The counterpoint (conflict) of the two—the retained rate of vibration against the newly perceived one—yields the dynamism of our apprehension of the interplay of color.

Hence, with only one step from visual vibrations to acoustic vibrations, we find ourselves in the field of music. From the domain of the spatial-pictorial—to the domain of the temporal-pictorial—where the same law rules. For counterpoint is to music not only a form of composition, but is altogether the basic factor for the possibility of tone perception and tone differentiation.

It may almost be said that in every case we have cited we have seen in operation the same Principle of Comparison that makes possible for us perception and definition in every field.

In the moving image (cinema) we have, so to speak, a synthesis of two counterpoints—the spatial counterpoint of graphic art, and the temporal counterpoint of music.

Within cinema, and characterizing it, occurs what may be described as:

visual counterpoint

In applying this concept to the film, we gain several leads to the problem of film grammar. As well as a syntax of film manifestations, in which visual counterpoint may determine a whole new system of forms of manifestation. (Experiments in this direction are illustrated in the preceding pages by fragments from my films.)

---

[138] In the preface to Baudelaire's *Les fleurs du mal*, illustrated by Auguste Rodin, Paris, Limited Editions Club, 1940.

[139] Renoir's manifesto for *La Société des Irrégularistes* (1884) is thus synopsized by Lionello Venturi in his *Painting and Painters*, New York, Scribners, 1945; the original text can be consulted in *Les archives de l'Impressionisme*, edited by Lionello Venturi, Paris, Durand-Ruel, 1939, I. pp. 127–129.

[140] Charles Baudelaire, *Intimate Journals* (13 May 1856), translated by Christopher Isherwood. New York, Random House, 1930.

For all this, the basic premise is:

The shot is by no means an element of montage.
The shot is a montage cell (or molecule).

In this formulation the dualistic division of

Sub-title and shot
and
Shot and montage

leaps forward in analysis to a dialectic consideration as three different phases of one homogeneous task of expression, its homogeneous characteristics determining the homogeneity of their structural laws.

Inter-relation of the three phases:

Conflict within a thesis (an abstract idea)—formulates itself in the dialectics of the sub-title—forms itself spatially in the conflict within the shot—and explodes with increasing intensity in montage-conflict among the separate shots.

This is fully analogous to human, psychological expression. This is a conflict of motives, which can also be comprehended in three phases:

1. Purely verbal utterance. Without intonation—expression in speech.

2. Gesticulatory (mimic-intonational) expression. Projection of the conflict onto the whole expressive bodily system of man. Gesture of bodily movement and gesture of intonation.

3. Projection of the conflict into space. With an intensification of motives, the zigzag of mimic expression is propelled into the surrounding space following the same formula of distortion. A zigzag of expression arising from the spatial division caused by man moving in space. Mise-en-scène.

This gives us the basis for an entirely new understanding of the problem of film form.

We can list, as examples of types of conflicts within the form—characteristic for the conflict within the shoe, as well as for the conflict between colliding shots, or, montage:

1.   Graphic conflict.
2.   Conflict of planes.
3.   Conflict of volumes.
4.   Spatial conflict.
5.   Light conflict.
6.   Tempo conflict, and so on.

Nota bene: This list is of principal features, of dominants. It is naturally understood that they occur chiefly as complexes.

For a transition to montage, it will be sufficient to divide any example into two independent primary pieces, as in the case of graphic conflict, although all other cases can be similarly divided:

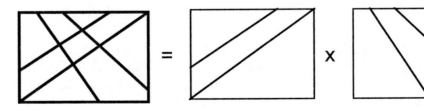

Some further examples:

7. Conflict between matter and viewpoint (achieved by spatial distortion through camera-angle).

8. Conflict between matter and its spatial nature (achieved by *optical distortion* by the lens).

9. Conflict between an event and its temporal nature (achieved by *slow-motion* and *stop-motion*)

and finally

10. Conflict between the whole *optical* complex and a quite different sphere.

Thus does conflict between optical and acoustical experience produce:

sound-film,

which is capable of being realized as

audio-visual counterpoint.

Formulation and investigation of the phenomenon of cinema as forms of conflict yield the first possibility of devising a homogeneous system of visual dramaturgy for all general and particular cases of the film problem.

Of devising a dramaturgy of the visual film-form as regulated and precise as the existing dramaturgy of the film-story.

From this viewpoint on the film medium, the following forms and potentialities of style may be summed up as a film syntax, or it may be more exact to describe the following as:

a tentative film-syntax.

We shall list here a number of potentialities of dialectical development to be derived from this proposition: The concept of the moving (time-consuming) image arises from the superimposition—or counterpoint—of two differing immobile images.

I. Each moving fragment of montage. Each photographed piece. Technical definition of the phenomenon of movement. No composition as yet. (A running man. A rifle fired. A splash of water.)

II. An artificially produced image of motion. The basic optical element is used for deliberate compositions:

A. *Logical*

Example 1 (from *October*): a montage rendition of a machine-gun being fired, by cross-cutting details of the firing.

Combination A: a brightly lit machine-gun. A different shot in a low key. Double burst: graphic burst + light burst. Close-up of machine-gunner.

Combination B: Effect almost of double exposure achieved by *clatter* montage effect. Length of montage pieces—two frames each.

Example 2 (from *Potemkin*): an illustration of instantaneous action. Woman with pince-nez. Followed immediately—without transition—by the same woman with shattered pince-nez and bleeding eye: impression of a shot hitting the eye.

B. *Illogical*

Example 3 (from *Potemkin*): the same device used for pictorial symbolism. In the thunder of the *Potemkin*'s guns, a marble lion leaps up, in protest against the bloodshed on the Odessa steps. Composed of three shots of three stationary marble lions at the Alupka Palace in the Crimea: a sleeping lion, an awakening lion, a rising lion. The effect is achieved by a correct calculation of the length of the second shot. Its superimposition on the first shot produces the first action. This establishes time to impress the second position on the mind. Superimposition of the third position on the second produces the second action: the lion finally rises.

Example 4 (from *October*): Example 1 showed how the firing was manufactured symbolically from elements outside the process of firing itself. In illustrating the monarchist *putsch* attempted by General Kornilov, it occurred to me that his militarist *tendency* could be shown in a montage that would employ religious details for its material. For Kornilov had revealed his intention in the guise of a peculiar "Crusade" of Moslems (!), his Caucasian "Wild Division," together with some Christians, against the Bolsheviki. So we intercut shots of a Baroque Christ (apparently exploding in the radiant beams of his halo) with shots of an egg-shaped mask of Uzume, Goddess of Mirth, completely self-contained. The temporal conflict between the closed egg-form and the graphic star-form produced the effect of an instantaneous *burst*—of a bomb, or shrapnel.

Thus far the examples have shown primitive-physiological cases—employing superimposition of optical motion exclusively.

III. Emotional combinations, not only with the visible elements of the shots, but chiefly with chains of psychological associations. Association montage. As a means for pointing up a situation emotionally.

In Example 1, we had two successive shots A and B, identical in subject. However, they were not identical in respect to the position of the subject within the frame:

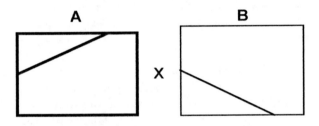

producing dynamization in space—an impression of spatial dynamics:

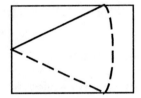

The degree of difference between the positions A and B determines the tension of the movement.

For a new case, let us suppose that the subjects of Shots A and B are not identical. Although the associations of the two shots are identical, that is, associatively identical.

This dynamization of the subject, not in the field of space but of psychology, i.e., emotion, thus produces:

emotional dynamization.

Example 1 (in *Strike*): the montage of the killing of the workers is actually a cross montage of this carnage with the butchering of a bull in an abattoir. Though the subjects are different, "butchering" is the associative link. This made for a powerful emotional intensification of the scene. As a matter of fact, homogeneity of gesture plays an important part in this case in achieving the effect—both the movement of the dynamic gesture within the frame, and the static gesture dividing the frame graphically.

This is a principle subsequently used by Pudovkin in The End of St. Petersburg, in his powerful sequence intercutting shots of stock exchange and battlefield. His previous film Mother, had a similar sequence: the ice-break on the river paralleled with the workers' demonstration.

Such a means may decay pathologically if the essential viewpoint—emotional dynamization of the subject—is lost. As soon as the film-maker loses sight of this essence the means ossifies into lifeless literary symbolism and stylistic mannerism. Two examples of such hollow use of this means occur to me:

Example 2 (in *October*): the sugary chants of compromise by the Mensheviki at the Second Congress of Soviets—during the storming of the Winter Palace—are intercut with hands playing harps. This was a purely literary parallelism that by no means dynamized the subject matter. Similarly in Otzep's *Living Corpse*, church spires (in imitation of those in *October*) and lyrical landscapes are intercut with the courtroom speeches of the prosecutor and defense lawyer. This error was the same as in the "harp" sequence.

On the other hand, a majority of purely dynamic effects can produce positive results:

Example 3 (in *October*): the dramatic moment of the union of the Motorcycle Battalion with the Congress of Soviets was dynamized by shots of abstractly spinning bicycle wheels, in association with the entrance of the new delegates. In this way the large-scale emotional content of the event was transformed into actual dynamics.

This same principle—giving birth to concepts, to emotions, by juxtaposing two disparate events—led to:

IV. Liberation of the whole action from the definition of time and space. My first attempts at this were in October.

Example 1: a trench crowded with soldiers appears to be crushed by an enormous gun-base that comes down inexorably. As an anti-militarist symbol seen from the viewpoint of subject alone, the effect is achieved by an apparent bringing together of an independently existing trench and an overwhelming military product, just as physically independent.

Example 2: in the scene of Kornilov's *putsch*, which puts an end to Kerensky's Bonapartist dreams. Here one of Kornilov's tanks climbs up and crushes a plaster-of-Paris Napoleon standing on Kerensky's desk in the Winter Palace, a juxtaposition of purely symbolic significance.

This method has now been used by Dovzhenko in *Arsenal* to shape whole sequences, as well as by Esther Schub in her use of library footage in *The Russia of Nikolai II and Lev Tolstoy*.

I wish to offer another example of this method, to upset the traditional ways of handling plot—although it has not yet been put into practice.

In 1924-1925 I was mulling over the idea of a filmic portrait of actual man. At that time, there prevailed a tendency to show actual man in films only in long uncut dramatic scenes. It was believed that cutting (montage) would destroy the idea of actual man. Abram Room established something of a record in this respect when he used in The Death Ship uncut dramatic shots as long as 40 meters or 135 feet. I considered (and still do) such a concept to be utterly unfilmic.

Very well—what would be a linguistically accurate characterization of a man?

> His raven-black hair...
> The waves of his hair...
> His eyes radiating azure beams...
> His steely muscles...

Even in a less exaggerated description, any verbal account of a person is bound to find itself employing an assortment of waterfalls, lightning-rods, landscapes, birds, etc.

Now why should the cinema follow the forms of theater (and painting rather than the methodology of language, which allows wholly new concepts of ideas to arise from the combination of two concrete denotations of two concrete objects? Language is much closer to film than painting is. For example, in painting the form arises from abstract elements of line and color, while in cinema the material concreteness of the image within the frame presents—as an element—the greatest difficulty in manipulation. So why not rather lean towards the system of language, which is forced to use the same mechanics in inventing words and word-complexes?

On the other hand, why is it that montage cannot be dispensed with in orthodox films?

The differentiation in montage-pieces lies in their lack of existence as single units. Each piece can evoke no more than a certain association. The accumulation of such associations can achieve the same effect as is provided for the spectator by purely physiological means in the plot of a realistically produced play.

For instance, murder on the stage has a purely physiological effect. Photographed in one montage-piece, it can function simply as information, as a sub-title. Emotional effect begins only with the reconstruction of the event in montage fragments, each of which will summon a certain association—the sum of which will be an all-embracing complex of emotional feeling. Traditionally:

1. A hand lifts a knife.
2. The eyes of the victim open suddenly.
3. His hands clutch the table.
4. The knife is jerked up.
5. The eyes blink involuntarily.
6. Blood gushes.
7. A mouth shrieks.
8. Something drips onto a shoe...

and similar film clichés. Nevertheless, in regard to the action as a whole, each fragment-piece is almost abstract. The more differentiated they are the more abstract they become, provoking no more than a certain association.

Quite logically the thought occurs: could not the same thing be accomplished more productively by not following the plot so slavishly, but by materializing the idea, the impression, of Murder through a free accumulation of associative matter? For the most important task is still to establish the idea of murder—the feeling of murder, as such. The plot is no more than a device without which one isn't yet capable of telling something to the spectator! In any case, effort in this direction would certainly produce the most interesting variety of forms.

Someone should try, at least! Since this thought occurred to me, I have not had time to make this experiment. And today I am more concerned with quite different problems. But, returning to the main line of our syntax, something there may bring us closer to these tasks.

While, with I, II, and III, tension was calculated for purely physiological effect—from the purely optical to the emotional, we must mention here also the case of the same conflict-tension serving the ends of new concepts—of new attitudes, that is, of purely intellectual aims.

Example 1 (in *October*): Kerensky's rise to power and dictatorship after the July uprising of 1917. A comic effect was gained by sub-titles indicating regular ascending ranks ("*Dictator*"—"*Generalissimo*"—"*Minister of Navy—and of Army*"—etc.) climbing higher and higher—cut into five or six shots of Kerensky, climbing the stairs of the Winter Palace, all with exactly the *same* pace. Here a conflict between the flummery of the ascending ranks and the "hero's" trotting up the same unchanging flight of stairs yields an intellectual result: Kerensky's essential nonentity is shown satirically. We have the counterpoint of a literally expressed conventional idea with the *pictured* action of a particular person who is unequal to his swiftly increasing duties. The incongruence of these two factors results in the spectator's purely *intellectual* decision at the expense of this particular person. Intellectual dynamization.

Example 2 (in *October*): Kornilov's march on Petrograd was under the banner of "In the Name of God and Country." Here we attempted to reveal the religious significance of this episode in a rationalistic way. A number of religious images, from a magnificent Baroque Christ to an Eskimo idol, were cut together. The conflict in this case was between the concept and the symbolization of God. While idea and image appear to accord completely in the first statue shown, the two elements move further from each other with each successive image (see Figure 10). Maintaining the denotation of "God," the images increasingly disagree with our concept of God, inevitably leading to individual conclusions about the true nature of all deities. In this case, too, a chain of images attempted to achieve a purely intellectual resolution, resulting from a conflict between a preconception and a *gradual discrediting of it in purposeful steps.*

Step by step, by a process of comparing each new image with the common denotation, power is accumulated behind a process that can be formally identified with that of logical deduction. The decision to release these ideas, as well as the method used, is already intellectually conceived.

The conventional descriptive form for film leads to the formal possibility of a kind of filmic reasoning. While the conventional film directs the emotions, this suggests an opportunity to encourage and direct the whole thought process, as well.

These two particular sequences of experiment were very much opposed by the majority of critics. Because they were understood as purely political. I would not attempt to deny that this form is most suitable for the expression of ideologically pointed theses, but it is a pity that the critics completely overlooked the purely filmic potentialities of this approach.

In these two experiments we have taken the first embryonic step towards a totally new form of film expression. Towards a purely intellectual film, freed from traditional limitations, achieving direct forms for ideas, systems, and concepts, without any need for transitions and paraphrases. We may yet have a

synthesis of art and science.

This would be the proper name for our new epoch in the field of art. This would be the final justification for Lenin's words, that "the cinema is the most important of all the arts."

THE ONTOLOGY OF THE PHOTOGRAPHIC IMAGE

From *What Is Cinema?* (1967) by André Bazin

If the plastic arts were put under psychoanalysis, the practice of embalming the dead might turn out to be a fundamental factor in their creation. The process might reveal that at the origin of painting and sculpture there lies a mummy complex. The religion of ancient Egypt, aimed against death, saw survival as depending on the continued existence of the corporeal body. Thus, by providing a defense against the passage of time it satisfied a basic psychological need in man, for death is but the victory of time. To preserve, artificially, his bodily appearance is to snatch it from the flow of time, to stow it away neatly, so to speak, in the hold of life. It was natural, therefore, to keep up appearances in the face of the reality of death by preserving flesh and bone. The first Egyptian statue, then, was a mummy, tanned and petrified in sodium. But pyramids and labyrinthine corridors offered no certain guarantee against ultimate pillage.

Other forms of insurance were therefore sought. So, near the sarcophagus, alongside the corn that was to feed the dead, the Egyptians placed terra cotta statuettes, as substitute mummies which might replace the bodies if these were destroyed. It is this religious use, then, that lays bare the primordial function of statuary, namely, the preservation of life by a representation of life. Another manifestation of the same kind of thing is the arrow-pierced clay bear to be found in prehistoric caves, a magic identity-substitute for the living animal, that will ensure a successful hunt. The evolution, side by side, of art and civilization has relieved the plastic arts of their magic role. Louis XIV did not have himself embalmed. He was content to survive in his portrait by Le Brun. Civilization cannot, however, entirely cast out the bogy of time. It can only sublimate our concern with it to the level of rational thinking. No one believes any longer in the ontological identity of model and image, but all are agreed that the image helps us to remember the subject and to preserve him from a second spiritual death. Today the making of images no longer shares an anthropocentric, utilitarian purpose. It is no longer a question of survival after death, but of a larger concept, the creation of an ideal world in the likeness of the real, with its own temporal destiny. "How vain a thing is painting" if underneath our fond admiration for its works we do not discern man's primitive need to have the last word in the argument with death by means of the form that endures. If the history of the plastic arts is less a matter of their aesthetic than of their psychology then it will be seen to be essentially the story of resemblance, or, if you will, of realism.

Seen in this sociological perspective photography and cinema would provide a natural explanation for the great spiritual and technical crisis that overtook modern painting around the middle of the last century. André Malraux has described the cinema as the furthermost evolution to date of plastic realism, the beginnings of which were first manifest at the Renaissance and which found its completest expression in baroque painting.

It is true that painting, the world over, has struck a varied balance between the symbolic and realism. However, in the fifteenth century Western painting began to turn from its age-old concern with spiritual realities expressed in the form proper to it, towards an effort to combine this spiritual expression with as complete an imitation as possible of the outside world.

The decisive moment undoubtedly came with the discovery of the first scientific and already, in a sense, mechanical system of reproduction, namely, perspective: the camera obscure of Da Vinci foreshadowed the camera of Niepce. The artist was now in a position to create the illusion of three-dimensional space within which things appeared to exist as our eyes in reality see them.

Thenceforth painting was torn between two ambitions: one, primarily aesthetic, namely the expression of spiritual reality wherein the symbol transcended its model; the other, purely psychological, namely the duplication of the world outside. The satisfaction of this appetite for illusion merely served to increase it till, bit by bit, it consumed the plastic arts. However, since perspective had only solved the problem of form and not of movement, realism was forced to continue the search for some way of giving dramatic expression to the moment, a kind of psychic fourth dimension that could suggest life in the tortured immobility of baroque art.[141]

The great artists, of course, have always been able to combine the two tendencies. They have allotted to each its proper place in the hierarchy of things, holding reality at their command and molding it at will into the fabric of their art. Nevertheless, the fact remains that we are faced with two essentially different phenomena and these any objective critic must view separately if he is to understand the evolution of the pictorial. The need for illusion has not ceased to trouble the heart of painting since the sixteenth century. It is a purely mental need, of itself nonaesthetic, the origins of which must be sought in the proclivity of the mind towards magic. However, it is a need the pull of which has been strong enough to have seriously upset the equilibrium of the plastic arts.

The quarrel over realism in art stems from a misunderstanding, from a confusion between the aesthetic and the psychological; between true realism, the need that is to give significant expression to the world both concretely and its essence, and the pseudorealism of a deception aimed at fooling the eye (or for that matter the mind); a pseudorealism content in other words with illusory appearances.[142] That is why medieval art never passed through this crisis; simultaneously vividly realistic and highly spiritual, it knew nothing of the drama that came to light as a consequence of technical developments. Perspective was the original sin of Western painting.

It was redeemed from sin by Niepce and Lumière. In achieving the aims of baroque art, photography has freed the plastic arts from their obsession with likeness. Painting was forced, as it turned out, to offer us illusion and this illusion was reckoned sufficient unto art. Photography and the cinema on the other hand are discoveries that satisfy, once and for all and in its very essence, our obsession with realism.

No matter how skillful the painter, his work was always in fee to an inescapable subjectivity. The fact that a human hand intervened cast a shadow of doubt over the image. Again, the essential factor in the transition from the baroque to photography is not the perfecting of a physical process (photography will long remain the inferior of painting in the reproduction of color); rather does it lie in a psychological fact, to wit, in completely satisfying our appetite for illusion by a mechanical reproduction in the making of which man plays no part. The solution is not to be found in the result achieved but in the way of achieving it.[143]

This is why the conflict between style and likeness is a relatively modern phenomenon of which there is no trace before the invention of the sensitized plate. Clearly the fascinating

---

[141] It would be interesting from this point of view to study, in the illustrated magazines of 1890-1910, the rivalry between photographic reporting and the use of drawings. The latter, in particular, satisfied the baroque need for the dramatic. A feeling for the photographic document developed only gradually.

[142] Perhaps the Communists, before they attach too much importance to expressionist realism, should stop talking about it in a way more suitable to the eighteenth century, before there were such things as photography or cinema. Maybe it does not really matter if Russian painting is second-rate provided Russia gives us first-rate cinema. Eisenstein is her Tintoretto.

[143] There is room, nevertheless, for a study of the psychology of the lesser plastic arts, the molding of death masks for example, which likewise involves a certain automatic process. One might consider photography in this sense as a molding, the taking of an impression, by the manipulation of light.

objectivity of Chardin is in no sense that of the photographer. The nineteenth century saw the real beginnings of the crisis of realism of which Picasso is now the mythical central figure and which put to the test at one and the same time the conditions determining the formal existence of the plastic arts and their sociological roots. Freed from the "resemblance complex," the modern painter abandons it to the masses who, henceforth, identify resemblance on the one hand with photography and on the other with the kind of painting which is related to photography.

Originality in photography as distinct from originality in painting lies in the essentially objective character of photography. [Bazin here makes a point of the fact that the lens, the basis of photography, is in French called the "objectif," a nuance that is lost in English.—TR.] For the first time, between the originating object and its reproduction there intervenes only the instrumentality of a nonliving agent. For the first time an image of the world is formed automatically, without the creative intervention of man. The personality of the photographer enters into the proceedings only in his selection of the object to be photographed and by way of the purpose he has in mind. Although the final result may reflect something of his personality, this does not play the same role as is played by that of the painter. All the arts are based on the presence of man, only photography derives an advantage from his absence. Photography affects us like a phenomenon in nature, like a flower or a snowflake whose vegetable or earthly origins are an inseparable part of their beauty.

This production by automatic means has radically affected our psychology of the image. The objective nature of photography confers on it a quality of credibility absent from all other picture-making. In spite of any objections our critical spirit may offer, we are forced to accept as real the existence of the object reproduced, actually re-presented, set before us, that is to say, in time and space. Photography enjoys a certain advantage in virtue of this transference of reality from the thing to its reproduction.[144]

A very faithful drawing may actually tell us more about the model but despite the promptings of our critical intelligence it will never have the irrational power of the photograph to bear away our faith.

Besides, painting is, after all, an inferior way of making likenesses, an ersatz of the processes of reproduction. Only a photographic lens can give us the kind of image of the object that is capable of satisfying the deep need man has to substitute for it something more than a mere approximation, a kind of decal or transfer. The photographic image is the object itself, the object freed from the conditions of time and space that govern it. No matter how fuzzy, distorted, or discolored, no matter how lacking in documentary value the image may be, it shares, by virtue of the very process of its becoming, the being of the model of which it is the reproduction; it is the model.

Hence the charm of family albums. Those grey or sepia shadows, phantomlike and almost undecipherable, are no longer traditional family portraits but rather the disturbing presence of lives halted at a set moment in their duration, freed from their destiny; not, however, by the prestige of art but by the power of an impassive mechanical process: for photography does not create eternity, as art does, it embalms time, rescuing it simply from its proper corruption.

Viewed in this perspective, the cinema is objectivity in time. The film is no longer content to preserve the object, enshrouded as it were in an instant, as the bodies of insects are preserved intact, out of the distant past, in amber. The film delivers baroque art from its convulsive catalepsy. Now, for the first time, the image of things is likewise the image of their duration, change mummified as it were. Those categories of resemblance which determine the

---

[144] Here one should really examine the psychology of relics and souvenirs which likewise enjoy the advantages of a transfer of reality stemming from the "mummy-complex." Let us merely note in passing that the Holy Shroud of Turin combines the features alike of relic and photograph.

species photographic image likewise, then, determine the character of its aesthetic as distinct from that of painting.[145]

The aesthetic qualities of photography are to be sought in its power to lay bare the realities. It is not for me to separate off, in the complex fabric of the objective world, here a reflection on a damp sidewalk, there the gesture of a child. Only the impassive lens, stripping its object of all those ways of seeing it, those piled-up preconceptions, that spiritual dust and grime with which my eyes have covered it, is able to present it in all its virginal purity to my attention and consequently to my love. By the power of photography, the natural image of a world that we neither know nor can see, nature at last does more than imitate art: she imitates the artist.

Photography can even surpass art in creative power. The aesthetic world of the painter is of a different kind from that of the world about him. Its boundaries enclose a substantially and essentially different microcosm. The photograph as such and the object in itself share a common being, after the fashion of a fingerprint. Wherefore, photography actually contributes something to the order of natural creation instead of providing a substitute for it. The surrealists had an inkling of this when they looked to the photographic plate to provide them with their monstrosities and for this reason: the surrealist does not consider his aesthetic purpose and the mechanical effect of the image on our imaginations as things apart. For him, the logical distinction between what is imaginary and what is real tends to disappear. Every image is to be seen as an object and every object as an image. Hence photography ranks high in the order of surrealist creativity because it produces an image that is a reality of nature, namely, an hallucination that is also a fact. The fact that surrealist painting combines tricks of visual deception with meticulous attention to detail substantiates this.

So, photography is clearly the most important event in the history of plastic arts. Simultaneously a liberation and a fulfillment, it has freed Western painting, once and for all, from its obsession with realism and allowed it to recover its aesthetic autonomy. Impressionist realism, offering science as an alibi, is at the opposite extreme from eye-deceiving trickery. Only when form ceases to have any imitative value can it be swallowed up in color. So, when form, in the person of Cézanne, once more regains possession of the canvas there is no longer any question of the illusions of the geometry of perspective. The painting, being confronted in the mechanically produced image with a competitor able to reach out beyond baroque resemblance to the very identity of the model, was compelled into the category of object. Henceforth Pascal's condemnation of painting is itself rendered vain since the photograph allows us on the one hand to admire in reproduction something that our eyes alone could not have taught us to love, and on the other, to admire the painting as a thing in itself whose relation to something in nature has ceased to be the justification for its existence.

On the other hand, of course, cinema is also a language.

---

[145] I use the term *category* here in the sense attached to it by M. Gouhier in his book on the theater in which he distinguishes between the dramatic and the aesthetic categories. Just as dramatic tension has no artistic value, the perfection of a reproduction is not to be identified with beauty. It constitutes rather the prime matter, so to speak, on which the artistic fact is recorded.

CRITICAL FILM ANALYSES

Oil for the Lamps of China (1935) and *Chariots of Fire* (1981)

Paul N. Reinsch

OIL FOR THE LAMPS OF CHINA

Credits: Warner Bros. Pictures, Inc. / A Cosmopolitan Production. Directed by Mervyn LeRoy. Written by Laird Doyle. Based on the novel of the same name by Alice Tisdale Hobart. Photographed by Tony Gaudio. Art direction by Robert M. Haas. Edited by William Clemens. Gowns by Orry-Kelly. Music by Leo F. Forbstein. 110 mins.

Cast: Pat O'Brien (Stephen Chase), Josephine Hutchinson (Hester Adams), Jean Muir (Alice), Lyle Talbot (Jim), Arthur Byron (The boss), John Eldredge (Don), Donald Crisp (McCargar), Willie Fung (Kin), Tetsu Komai (Ho), Henry O'Neill (Hartford), Ronnie Cosby (Bunsy), William Davidson (Swaley), George Meeker (Bill Kendall).

CHARIOTS OF FIRE

Credits: Produced by David Puttnam for Allied Stars and Enigma Productions / released by Warner Brothers. Directed by Hugh Hudson. Written by Colin Welland. Photographed by David Watkin. Edited by Terry Rawlings. Original music by Vangelis. Art Direction by Len Huntingford, Anne Ridley, and Andrew Sanders. Costume Design by Milena Canonero. 123 mins. MPAA rating: PG.

Cast: Ben Cross (Harold M. Abrahams), Ian Charleson (Eric Liddell), Nigel Havers (Lord Andrew Lindsay), Nicholas Farrell (Aubrey Montague), Ian Holm (Sam Mussabini), John Gielgud (Master of Trinity), Lindsay Anderson (Master of Caius), Nigel Davenport (Lord Birkenhead), Cheryl Campbell (Jennie Liddell), Alice Krige (Sybil Gordon), Dennis Christopher (Charles

Paddock), Brad Davis (Jackson Scholz), Patrick Magee (Lord Cadogan), Peter Egan (Duke of Sutherland).

A recent top ten list of "Business Movies" includes well-known films such as Billy Wilder's *The Apartment* (1960), *Save the Tiger* (1973), and even Werner Herzog's *Fitzcarraldo* (1982).[146] The list does not include Mervyn LeRoy's *Oil for the Lamps of China*. But this is hardly surprising. LeRoy's film is nearly forgotten as an early and still biting depiction of big business, and is overshadowed by famous films he helmed for Warner Brothers in the same period: *Little Caesar* (1930) and *I Am a Fugitive from a Chain Gang* (1932). One of four LeRoy-directed films released in 1933, *Oil for the Lamps of China*, like these earlier films, is a fine example or realism, or more specifically, of Hollywood Social Realism.

Today's second feature, *Chariots of Fire*, was a surprise Best Picture Winner in 1981. This film met with more critical, and public, success than first time director Hugh Hudson could have imagined (and more of each than LeRoy's). That the film won Best Picture over the likes of Warren Beatty's *Reds*, Spielberg/Lucas's *Raiders of the Lost Ark*, and the star driven *On Golden Pond* surprised more than just Hudson. At the Academy Awards ceremony in 1982 the triumphant producers proclaimed "The British are coming!" While the film did not ultimately represent the continuing triumph of English product in the United States, the film did significantly aid the film industry in England and made audiences aware of English films and filmmakers. This film is demonstrates the opposing stylistic tendency of films: formalism.

This pair of film is connected by their exploration of the male in turmoil (*Chariots* actually gives us two men to follow). The protagonists must negotiate a relationship with work, family, and historical forces well beyond his control. Each film participates with this subject matter in its own way and the films' similarities and differences in their aesthetics choices in depicting the subject reveals the determinations of technology and history.

Ordinary (yet uniquely driven), *Oil for the Lamps of China*'s Stephen Chase attempts to serve two mistresses — work and a woman — while making the world a better place. At the film's beginning he is shipped to China as an employee of Atlantis Oil in order to "extend the frontiers of civilization." For the remainder of the film Stephen struggles to be a model employee (and therefore, also a model citizen) and a devoted husband to his wife Hester. The camera records the Chase family's activities over the course of several years and in various parts of China as their relationship and Chinese culture undergo profound change. The film conveys this information cleanly and objectively, and the accumulation of details — Asian actors, music coded as "oriental," set, props, and costumes — provide a realistic presentation of China as only the Classical period could.

Alice Tisdale Hobart's book (1933) was a best-seller and its adaptation into a film was a foregone conclusion. Warner Brothers was uniquely suited to filming this work. More than other studios (read MGM), Warner Brothers' films directly addressed social issues of the moment. They were not alone in this engagement however. The stock market crash of 1929 and subsequent Great Depression resulted in a concern for documentation and reportage, and films followed this general cultural trend in depicting working-class characters cornered by institutions. As Robert Sklar states: "In the first half decade of the Great Depression, Hollywood's moviemakers perpetrated one of the most remarkable challenges to traditional values in the history of mass commercial entertainment."[147]

The studios also wanted to make money. In the so-called "Pre-Code period"[148] studios presented increased amounts of sex and violence to convince audiences to part with their hard-

---

[146] The list can be found in the November 2002 issue of *MBA Jungle*. This is not an endorsement.
[147] Sklar, Robert, *Movie-Made America: A Cultural History of American Movies*, Rev. Ed. New York: Vintage, 1994, 175.
[148] The Production Code did, in fact, exist from 1930-34 but the lack of enforcement allowed studios to behave as though it did not. Hence, the name. See Thomas Doherty's *Pre-Code Hollywood*, and Lea Jacobs' *The Wages of Sin*.

earned and increasingly scarce income. Like all good things, this too ended. From 1934 forward the movies softened their social critiques and toned down the sexual and violent content as a result of new Production Code Administrator Joseph Breen's enforcement activities. Breen's office thoroughly evaluated films before the beginning of principal photography. It is at this moment, or just after, that LeRoy filmed *Oil for the Lamps of China*.

The most obvious adjustment on the part of the studio is in changing the company Hobart directly names – Standard Oil – into the fictional "Atlantis Oil" for the film. Warner Brothers was strongly encouraged by the Production Code office to make this change and actually consulted with Standard Oil during the making of the film.[149] The possible threat of litigation or even offense to a major company is enough to make any studio rethink any aspect of a film. *Oil for the Lamps of China* serves as a clear example of how films can critique business but this criticism is tempered in myriad ways by the status of films themselves as the products of an industry. Hobart's indictment of Standard Oil becomes something else when transmitted to celluloid.

Like other films of the 30s, *China* begins with a text message. This one reads: "The characters and the institution portrayed in this story are not actual but the production of fiction. The oil business was chosen because light has ever been symbolic of progress." This comment is not attributed to anyone onscreen, and certainly does not appear in Hobart's text. It is merely the first indication that Hobart's negative portrayal of a particular company – Standard Oil, which also represents all other companies who treat people in the same way – has been softened, and transformed in some ways into an endorsement of the role business has to play in "civilizing" the world, seemingly by any means necessary. Most of the film depicts Stephen Chase's disappointments as he waits for the day when Atlantis will truly 'take care of its own,' but the final appearance of this phrase indicates its ultimate truth.

If the tone of the film is tempered by the industry's unwillingness to attack big business and the increased pressure from the Breen Office, the Warner Brother house style is still in evidence and presents the Chase family's plight with the clean cutting and expertly placed static camera which are some of its hallmarks. Sets constructed on the studio lot interact with footage shot in the Mojave Desert and footage of China to create an objective portrait of the country (with a side trip to Japan thrown in for good measure). Sources indicate that Robert Florey and two cameramen shot some 20,000 ft. of film in China secretly but the footage was not used since it was deemed "too realistic."[150] LeRoy's film offers the viewer access to a faraway land, which while exotic and other, the camera can capture and explain as well as any other.

Chariots of Fire is based on true events and encountered none of the production difficulties of its companion film of today. It is the story of the 1924 English Olympic team, with a particular focus on two men: Harold M. Abrahams and Eric Liddell. Both men are extraordinary talented and wholly different. Abrahams is a Jew who runs to be the best, to be considered worthy of being an Englishman, and "run . . . off their feet" all who oppose him. Liddell is a Scottish Christian torn between his father's advice to run as a "muscular Christian," and his sister's insistence that he work as a missionary. The faith of both men has made them who they are and motivates their actions.

Though much of the film follows the facts of the training for, and participation in, the Olympics by Abrahams, Liddell and other members of the team, *Chariots of Fire* can not be mistaken for a documentary, or a realistic portrayal of the time. The production design situates the viewer in Cambridge, England, Scotland, and Paris but is not concerned a recreation of the past but rather an impression of it. The film's approach to the story is established immediately. Abrahams' funeral in 1978 opens the film. As Lord Andrew Lindsay (Nigel Havers) speaks at

---

[149] Leonard J. Leff and Jerold L. Simmons, *The Dame in the Kimono: Hollywood, Censorship, and the Production Code*, Rev. Ed. Lexington, Kentucky: UP of Kentucky, 2001.
[150] See the American Film Institute Catalog entry on the film.

the funeral, he implores his audience (and the viewers) to "close your eyes and remember those few young men with hope in our hearts and wings on our heels." As he makes this statement the camera moves in on Aubrey Montague (Nicholas Farrell) who looks up....

And the film fades to a group of young men joyfully running on a beach. Vangelis' synthesizer score (non-diegetic, anachronistic), fills the soundtrack. The scene is not so much a presentation of a particular moment (the men are part of the Olympic team so we can narrow the "when" down) or a particular place (the beach is finally identified as adjoining the Carlton Hotel in Kent where the team trains). It is, rather, a visual memory, Montague's most directly but not his alone. Lindsay and others (potentially) share in this image of men and the "wings on [their] heels." The scene, and music, have been imitated and parodied, but the beauty of these bodies in motion and their evident joy – seen in facial expressions and in the (unique) way they move – demonstrate the transformative power of film; the scene shows how sound and image can create a persuasive impression.[151] The shot is repeated as an end credits sequence, and therefore bookends visually and thematically nearly all the viewer knows about these men.

Pauline Kael calls the film a "piece of technological lyricism."[152] Though this is not wholly a compliment in her review, the phrase does highlight the way the filmmakers use available technology to present an impression of bodies in motion. Powerful zoom lenses allow a focus on a single runner in the midst of a sea of rapidly moving bodies. When Abrahams and Liddell race, the action is seen head-on, and the use of a long lens flattens space. The amount of distance covered by Abrahams is obscured and his sense of running too slow and failing to cover ground fast enough, is conveyed visually. As he sits in the stands afterwards, the defeat is repeated in slow motion which draws out the moment of his disappointment, and accentuates his feeling of failure. Races throughout the film are seen in slow motion to heighten the emotion of the competition and to aestheticize the participants. When Abrahams sees Liddell run in the Scotland v. France meet, the race begins in "normal" speed but when Liddell is thrown to the ground and rises up with ferocious determination to win the race, the film shifts to slow motion. This shift makes Liddell's heroic act all the more otherworldly.

We should also note that Hudson's use of slow motion for athletic events is certainly not his invention. Leni Riefenstahl's *Olympiad* (1938) recorded at the 1936 games is an ode not so much to competition as to the human form. Diving competitions are presented as montages not of triumph and loss but of nearly abstract forms in motion. Slow motion permits and encourages the viewer to marvel at the young men and women so completely in control of their movements.

Chariots of Fire ties together subjective renderings of real lives. There are occasional titles onscreen to situate the viewer, and there is text at the conclusion of the film stating how Abrahams and Liddell spent the remainder of their lives. But notice how the film presents Abrahams' loss in the 200 meters to the dreaded Americans. Abrahams has a newspaper clipping hanging in the room as he talks to Montague which shows that he came in third. There is talk of Abrahams' disappointment but the viewer must attentively follow the film to understand the narrative. And prior to this scene the film depicts Montague falling in midst of his race. At no point is the viewer given a table of medal wins (as contemporary television coverage demands).

Compare how this film presents movement in time and space to today's other feature, *Oil for the Lamps of China*. One film devotes considerably more attention to the specifics of time and place through the use of onscreen titles and dialogue whose primary purpose is to

---

[151] This scene was shown at the 1986 Academy Awards to demonstrate the role that sound plays in one's impression of the film. The scene was shown once with only the sound of feet running and then again with the famous music. With the score included, one writer says "the runners gained the grace of dancers and the action became special, more than life." (William H. Phillips, *Film: An Introduction*, New York: Bedford, 1999).

[152] Kael, Pauline, *5001 Nights at the Movies*, New York: Holt, 1991, 131.

indicate how much time has passed. The other film flows from moment to moment, and place to place in order to enhance the feeling of the story and its themes.

A few more notes about *Oil for the Lamps of China*. In the second half of this course we have focused on genre. LeRoy himself labels this film an "adventure."[153] If *Treasure of the Sierra Madre* is an adventure, think of the ways these two films are similar, and different. *Oil for the Lamps of China* also represents the continuity editing / classical cutting system in full bloom. The movies have adjusted to the presence of sound both in the movie and on the celluloid itself, and are telling stories in what can best be seen as a Classical manner. Note the precise cutting as Stephen and Hester meet in the hotel in Yokohama. Eyeline matches, the shot / reverse shot pattern, and other features situate the characters and viewer in space and foreshadow the relationship between the two which will develop as the film progresses. Notice too the way the film moves the characters and audience through time and space.[154] The fan (and accompanying "gong" sound) which move Stephen Chase and Hester from the hotel to the teahouse is inventive, mood-setting, and thoroughly "oriental." The smooth dissolve from the Chases' black vase in their filthy house in King Nang to the vase in the comfortable home which Hester has created in a month's time (while pregnant no less) shows both continuity and change. Here too we see pages turning in a book superimposed over the shots of the vase. This motif visually moves the story forward (pages turning = narrative progress) and proclaims the film's fidelity to the (then) well-known literary work. Yet it is the film's "fidelity" which some critics dispute.

The film met with a mixed reception. Some reviewers praised the work of LeRoy, O'Brien, and Hutchinson. Others, such as English author Graham Greene see the film as a missed opportunity. He remarks: "It is a pity that so interesting a theme should have been passed first through the mind of a good, sincere and sentimental woman and then through the mind of a perhaps less sincere but certainly not less sentimental Hollywood scenario-writer."[155] *The New York Times* reviewer bemoans the conclusion of the film, noting that "in its closing scenes the drama makes a curious effort to endow the Atlantis Oil Company with nobility, apparently in a last-minute attempt to correct any impression it may have given that the company is not a completely noble institution."[156]

Chariots of Fire, on the other hand, won numerous awards in the year, including the aforementioned Oscars for Best Picture and Original Score. It also won the Oscars for Best Original Screenplay and Best Costume Design. Ian Holm was awarded the Best Supporting Actor at the Cannes Film Festival. In the United States the film grossed nearly 55 million and received praise from the majority of critics.

---

[153] *Mervyn LeRoy: Take One*, New York: Hawthorn, 1974, 180. LeRoy also relates how during the production of *China* his first child was born. He reveals that he left a crowd of 300 extras with no warning in order to attend to the birth. LeRoy draws no connection between this and the events of the film's narrative. We can of course. Though some would argue that he was necessarily exploited by the studio and the economic system of the United States generally, one can perhaps take comfort in the fact that unlike the fictional Stephen Chase, LeRoy was both willing and able to put his family in a position of greater importance than his work.
[154] The film did have some 30 minutes cut after a preview, so the film's overall narrative flow was almost certainly more impressive in the original cut. See Nick Roddick, *A New Deal in Entertainment*, London: BFI, 1983, 217.
[155] David Parkinson, Ed. The *Graham Greene Film Reader*, New York: Applause, 1995, 47.
[156] Andre Sennwald, "The Strand Theatre Presents a Film Version of Mrs. Hobart's '*Oil for the Lamps of China*,'" June 6, 1935, 25:2.

Sunset Boulevard (1950) and Adaptation (2002)
Robert Buerkle

Sunset Boulevard

Credits: Produced by: Charles Brackett; Directed by: Billy Wilder Screenplay: Charles Brackett, D.M. Marshman, Jr., & Billy Wilder Cinematography: John F Seitz; Editing: Doane Harrison & Arthur Schmidt Art Direction: Hans Dreier & John Meehan; Set Decoration: Sam Comer & Ray Moyer; Music: Franz Waxman. Paramount Pictures, 110 minutes.

Cast: Joe C. Gillis: William Holden; Norma Desmond: Gloria Swanson Max Von Mayerling: Erich von Stroheim; Betty Schaefer: Nancy Olson Sheldrake: Fred Clark; Morino: Lloyd Gough; Artie Green: Jack Webb Undertaker: Franklyn Farnum; 1st finance man: Larry Blake; 2nd finance man: Charles Dayton And as themselves: Cecil B. DeMille, Hedda Hopper, Buster Keaton, Anna Q. Nilsson, H. B. Warner, Ray Evans, Jay Livingston, Sidney Skolsky.

Adaptation

Credits: Produced by: Edward Saxon, Jonathan Demme, Vincent Landay Directed by: Spike Jonze; Screenplay: Charlie Kaufman & Donald Kaufman; Cinematography: Lance Acord; Music: Carter Burwell; Sound: Drew Kunin; Editing: Eric Zumbrunne; Art Direction: Peter Andrus Costumes: Casey Storm; Production Design: K.K. Barrett. Columbia Pictures, 114 minutes).

Cast: Charlie/Donald Kaufman: Nicolas Cage; Susan Orlean: Meryl Streep John Laroche: Chris Cooper; Valerie: Tilda Swinton; Amelia: Cara Seymour Robert McKee: Brian Cox; Alice the waitress: Judy Greer; Caroline: Maggie Gyllenhaal; Marty: Ron Livingston; Ranger Steve Neely: Stephen Tobolowsky; Matthew Osceola: Jay Tavare; Russell: Litefoot; Buster Baxley: Gary Farmer;Defense attorney: Peter Jason; Orlean's husband: Curtis Hanson And as themselves: John Malkovich, Catherine Keener, John Cusack, & Spike Jonze.

I have to go right home. I know how to finish the script now. It ends with Kaufman driving home after his lunch with Amelia, thinking he knows how to finish the script.

—Charlie Kaufman (driving home after his lunch with Amelia, thinking of how to finish his script)

Discussing realism and formalism within movies about Hollywood, particularly this pair of *Sunset Boulevard* and *Adaptation*, can prove somewhat tricky. Here's the conundrum: the realist style strives for transparency; by using formal aesthetics in a natural manner and seeking a one-to-one correspondence with the real world, realism purports to draw attention away from the form in order to display the content as objective truth. Yet Hollywood films confound this intent. By depicting the film industry and the filmmaking process, Hollywood films inherently draw attention to the film's form, to the very artifice of the film being viewed, by revealing the inner-workings of the medium and revealing that this is all a subjective rendering, regardless of what style the filmmaker may employ. It's for this reason that this pair is so apt for today's topic; for while formalism may be obvious in its subjectivity, these films make it clear that even realism still filters through the artist, and is thus also a subjective mode.

Both *Sunset Boulevard* and *Adaptation* take great strides to use the real Hollywood as a claim to realist legitimacy—by using the actual Paramount and Columbia lots, by going behind-the-scenes of the actual Hollywood productions of *Samson and Delilah* and *Being John Malkovich*, and by having real Hollywood stars play themselves, from Cecil B. DeMille and Buster Keaton to John Cusack and Catherine Keener, these films' claim to realism serves to repeatedly reveal the very film we are watching to be a product of that same system. The numerous in-jokes on the film industry and the writing process only serve to strengthen that self-consciousness. We can link this method to Documentary Realism, in that each film is using events that have actually happened, people endemic to the time and space of the subject matter, and shooting on location—that such people and places are actually stars and soundstages, due to the context, is incidental. And with both films, the blend of fact and fiction goes even deeper. *Sunset Boulevard*'s Norma Desmond is startlingly similar to actress Gloria Swanson; Swanson herself had been absent from the screen for nine years when she appeared in *Sunset Boulevard*, and despite attempting a few sound films, she never regained the popularity she achieved in the silent era, when she was the epitome of Hollywood glamour. Further, when Erich von Stroheim's Max says that there were three great directors of the silent era: "Cecil B. DeMille, D.W. Griffith, and me," he's not far off—Erich von Stroheim was indeed one of the great directors of the silent era, and had himself directed Swanson in the unreleased Queen Kelly, the very film Norma screens for Joe in *Sunset Boulevard*. And Swanson had indeed made films with Cecil B. DeMille, who plays himself while directing the actual production of his own *Samson and Delilah* on the Paramount lot. The melding of fantasy and reality is even more mind-bending in *Adaptation*; not only are we given the similar sequence of the real Spike Jonze directing the actual production of *Being John Malkovich* on the Columbia lot (incidentally shot in a documentary realist style with handheld video footage and subtitled names), but we supposedly witness the writing of the very film we are watching, in the film we are watching. When Charlie says, "Start when life begins on the planet…" we remember that the film did in fact begin with this sequence, and as Charlie gives into the formulaic, genre-driven, cliché-filled style of Robert McKee and his brother Donald, the film itself takes that same turn, becoming a mystery/suspense thriller filled with drugs, guns, sex, car chases, life lessons, and tragic deaths—the very things Charlie had insisted against in the first act.

Yet we shouldn't get too caught up in the self-reflexivity of these films due to their content—after all, realism and formalism are about the form, and how the formal qualities are being utilized. In this regard, we can make a more significant comparison, as both films make a very deliberate distinction between which scenes and sequences are depicted in a realist manner, and which are shown more formally. Further, both make this distinction based on what we are to perceive as the "real world," and what we are to recognize as filtered through some character's subjective view of that world.

In *Sunset Boulevard*, the separation lies between Joe's world—which is essentially the real world—and Norma's, a fantasy dreamscape of her silent era stardom extending into the present-day Hollywood which has all but forgotten her. Outside Norma's mansion, the film exhibits a blend of realist styles, particularly Hollywood Social Realism and Documentary Realism. In addition to the documentary aspects already mentioned, we can note such Social Realist qualities as the gritty, common-man element of focusing on a down-and-out, unemployed writer; the cynical attitude Joe (and resultantly the film) takes toward the Hollywood institution, as well as the focus on his interaction with that institution; and the tough, hard-boiled dialogue which characterizes Joe's voiceovers. But most indicative of the film's realist style is the relative lack of formal traits—or at least, of noticeable formal traits. The world outside the mansion is grim, matter-of-fact, and essentially plain. Aesthetics such as lighting, set and costume design, composition, editing, and sound are all used in a natural, transparent manner. Yet from the moment Joe pulls into Norma's driveway, a more formalist world is introduced, one which centers not only on the mansion, but on Norma herself.

Early on, Joe makes the astute observation that Norma "was still sleepwalking among the giddy heights of a lost career." Indeed, sleepwalking seems an apt metaphor for Norma's interaction with the world, as she seems to keep one foot in reality and one foot in a dream of Hollywood yesteryear, a time when she was adored by millions and demanded great awe and respect in the movie business. This delusional slant on the world manifests itself aesthetically in a subjective, formalized version of reality, most immediately evident in the gothic stylings of her mansion and the expressionistic depiction of this setting. The set design is unavoidable—tall, looming columns; intricate detail in every wall, every curtain, and every piece of furniture; and vast, spacious rooms overflowing with mementos, objet d'arts, excessive ornamentation, and all of Norma's reminders of her lost fame (particularly the plentiful glamour photos of her youth). Norma's costuming is equally heavy-handed, with elaborate costumes by Edith Head accentuated by an abundance of jewelry, sunglasses, and headwear (including that leopard print babushka that perfectly matches her leopard-print car seats). But most notable is the heavily expressionistic lighting—angular shadows drape every room and deep wells of light and darkness fragment each shot, creating an exaggerated, almost hallucinatory distortion of the world, as well as an uncanny ambience that intensifies the film's foreshadowing of doom. In visual design alone, we can see Billy Wilder painting Norma's world in a deliberately formalist manner. The sound design is equally important; note the deep, eerie tones that emanate from the organ as wind howls through its pipes, tones which are perfectly incorporated into the soundtrack, creating a haunting atonality with the film's score. The compositions in Norma's world are strikingly different from those outside as well, with plenty of deep-angle shots, split frames, and arresting compositions in depth, as opposed to the more traditional framings which occur in other scenes. Not surprisingly, subjectivity, interiority, and personal reality are common traits of expressionism, and *Sunset Boulevard* has all of these in spades.

However there's another drastically formalist aesthetic at work here that many tend to overlook—the performance of Gloria Swanson. Not only has Norma's career in silent pictures skewed her view of reality, but the pantomimic style of silent screen performance seems to have seeped into her own personality. Every action and gesture is marked by dramatic, exaggerated motions, every utterance by drawn out enunciation, and her wide-eyed stares and deliberate, over-the-top expressions are made all the more flamboyant by her too-perfect makeup and ridiculous eyelashes. Norma Desmond seems to be playing to the audience with every line and movement (whether her fictional audience or we, the literal audience, is uncertain) and Swanson demands attention to such an extent that she seems to drive the story even in her absence. This overt acting and the gothic, expressionistic visual scheme allows the character of Norma and the mansion setting to compliment one another, as the two seem inter-reliant. Certainly, the mansion is Norma's sanctuary from reality, as Joe explains: "The plain fact was she was afraid of that world outside, afraid it would remind her that time had passed"—a realization Norma refuses, eventually choosing full-on delusion over accepting the truth.

We should note that the formalism centered on Norma does not exist only in the mansion, but seems to follow her outside as well. This is especially noticeable on the Paramount soundstage, where Norma's subjectivity creeps in on the real world. As a celestial spotlight is turned on Norma and the score takes a whimsical turn, the cast and crew of DeMille's current epic are suddenly consumed by Norma's fantasy, all amassing around the former star in a temporary return to her heyday, and all framed in a steep bird's-eye view. For a moment, even we the audience are pulled into this subjective mindset—yet DeMille quickly breaks the façade by dispersing the crowd, while Wilder simultaneously returns the light, the camera, and the soundtrack to their rightful, realist positions. Here, the formalist subjectivity that characterizes Norma's world interrupts the realist mode at work outside, even if only briefly.[157]

Just as *Sunset Boulevard* uses realism and formalism to delineate reality from subjectivity, *Adaptation* equally separates the real world from interior sequences using this stylistic binary. Here, the passages linked to the dreams and writing of both Charlie and Susan are displayed in expressive stylization, while the rest of the film remains surprisingly realist. Despite Spike Jonze's background in music videos and commercials, he shows unexpected formal restraint in much of the film. Scenes of dialogue use standard shot/reverse shots, with compositions and camera angles fitting of the spatial relationships within the scene. The visual design remains realist throughout; sets, lighting, and color schemes never become overt or excessive, but rather remain practical and natural. The editing is rarely intrusive (aside from a few cuts meant to jar Charlie out of his dreams or voiceovers), and the sound design is essentially unnoticeable, with sound effects appropriate but not overdone, and the score remaining subtle if at all present.

The realist mode of filmmaking can often be used to great effect, and becomes most notable in sequences when we may expect a more formalist perspective—specifically the film's two car crashes. In both cases, the overwhelming effect of the crash comes directly from Jonze's refusal to give in to formalism, choosing instead to depict the event as a person in the car would experience it—in real time, remaining inside the vehicle, rather than the slow-motion, overlapping takes, or wide shot exteriors that typically characterize Hollywood crashes. The first crash, for instance, is precluded by a series of shot/reverse shot sightline matches inside the car Laroche is driving; our first view of the oncoming vehicle is actually from Laroche's viewpoint, looking over his shoulder toward his mother in the backseat, with the truck approaching outside of her window. A series of quick cuts simulates the jarring confusion in that second of impact (perhaps a very minor formal touch), and the only view outside the car is a brief shot at the tail end of the sequence, used mostly to establish what has just happened (since the entire crash lasts less than three seconds). Compare this with the subjectiveness of the ensuing scene, where close-ups of Laroche's face on a stretcher are intercut with frenetic handheld shots of ambulances and emergency crews, sped up slightly faster than real-time and chopped into near jump-cuts in order to provide an interiorized sense of Laroche's disoriented mindset.

This scene is actually the only formalist passage not linked directly to Charlie or Susan's subjectivity; every other aesthetically-deliberate scene is depicted as flowing from the mind of these two protagonists, justifying the formalism as a peek into the character's mind. The first such instance occurs in the opening scene on the Columbia lot, as the camera slowly tracks into a closeup of Charlie (the slow track-in is a common trope to indicate interiority) as Charlie

---

[157] We should note that *Sunset Boulevard*'s combination of realism and formalism also comes from its engagement with film noir. As the 190 Reader explains, noir uses elements of both documentary realism and expressionism, and in *Sunset Boulevard* we see many of the noir tropes at work—the chiaroscuro lighting, decentered framing, fatalistic tone, hard-boiled dialogue, and voiceover narration (here, extending from beyond the grave) are just a few.

wonders, "Why am I here? How did I get here?" The screen immediately goes to a time-lapse montage of the planet's evolution from the dawn of time, through the extinction of the dinosaurs, the Ice Age, the rise of urban civilization, to Charlie's own birth. The sequence is astonishingly heavy-handed; the time-lapses are both peculiar and beautiful, and the severe cross-fading at times leaves three different images on the screen at once. Further, the sudden cut to the dawn of time is a punchline of sorts—we expect the question of "How did I get here?" to relate to something in Charlie's own past, so the unexpected answer to that question obviously makes us aware of the humorous juxtaposition. If there's any doubt that this is linked to Charlie's own subjectivity, that doubt is later removed when Charlie starts his own screenplay with that very sequence.

Formalist passages typically occur this way, linked to Charlie or Susan's writing. When Susan begins typing about the history of orchid hunting, the film gives way to a stylized montage of notable orchid hunters over the past one hundred years. As Laroche expounds on the relationship between orchids and insects to Susan (who's taking notes on his oration), the film similarly turns to a formalist sequence of bees and flowers; although Laroche narrates the scene, the close-ups of Susan which bracket it indicate that she is actually the one imagining these events.

Yet ultimately, everything is filtered through Charlie's subjectivity, as he is the one who is actually writing the film itself. Passages linked to Susan's consciousness are often subsequently connected with Charlie reading her book, suggesting that these formal sequences are traveling from her writing of *The Orchid Thief*, through Charlie's own adaptation of that book, and into the film we are watching. When Susan initiates an abstract dream sequence comprised solely of orchid close-ups, we hear her voiceover: "The reason was not that I love orchids...What I wanted was to see this thing that people were drawn to in such a singular and powerful way." Susan seems to be controlling this series of images. Yet this voiceover and montage of orchids then crossfades to Charlie reading her book, and we realize the visuals are coming not from Susan, but from Charlie reading her words.

As Charlie tries to connect all the sprawling strands of both his life and *The Orchid Thief*, he begins hypothesizing on Darwin, evolution, and adaptation. Time-lapse shots of Charles Darwin, Charlie, Laroche, Susan, and the ghost orchid itself are all linked through one continuous pan right, methodically indicating Charlie's desperate attempts to combine all these elements into one screenplay. Charlie has a revelation: "That's what I need to do—tie all of history together," upon which this ponderous sequence is broken, replaced by a different formalist passage. Charlie begins a stream-of-consciousness rant into his tape recorder, and though we remain in the real world space of his room, the scene is fragmented by a series of jump-cuts as he babbles. Here, we're not in a fantasy sequence, yet we're still given the subjectivity of his free association through the formal choice of jump-cutting, indicating the scattered, broken thoughts of Charlie's freestyle rambling. Even though we stay in the "real world" (rather than a dream sequence), the formalism is still attached to Charlie's mindset.

There is, however, one formalist sequence of the film which is not motivated by Charlie or Susan's subjectivity—the film's final shot. After Charlie drives off in his car, musing in voiceover about how he's going to finish the film, the camera follows his car as it turns into the street and lets it trail away, lingering on the street and panning down to a flowerbox in the foreground rather than following Charlie. Though the scene has up to this point remained realist, the film subtly shifts to expressive stylization as time gradually speeds up, shifting into another rapid time-lapse shot, similar to those which have characterized many of Charlie's fantasy sequences. But why do we get this here, when Charlie has left the scene and thus is not directly connected to this formal intrusion? Because by this point, we realize that everything in the film is coming from Charlie, as the film itself is the brainchild of the character. Even the literary design becomes formalized—the self-reflexive voiceover, the jumbling of timeframes, and the continual references to the film's own design all draw attention to the film's writing, constantly reminding us that even when Charlie is absent from a scene, he still controls it. Thus the final time-lapse shot is still logical, as the entire film is presented through Charlie.

So we end where we began, realizing that even realist filmmaking remains subjective to some extent, as this pair of Hollywood-on-Hollywood movies deliberately indicates. Certainly, these films use both realism and formalism to great extents. But in the self-reflexivity inherent to these movies-about-movies, they show that while formalist filmmaking may be obvious in its subjective view of the content, realist filmmaking remains subjective as well, as the content still must pass through the director, stars, cinematographer, editor, numerous designers, and, as particularly evident here, the writer.

9
THE PRODUCTION PROCESS

Collaboration is the core of cinematic creativity. From the most independent filmmaker to the largest studio production, people work together, divide the labor, contribute their particular expertise. There may be one single, guiding intelligence that integrates or orchestrates all the collaborations, or there may be many. There may even be an external, abstract force that is doing the orchestration on the economic level: the force of the box office, which is the representative of the audience and its willingness to pay. We must understand, once again, that the Hollywood imagination is an economic system, an economics of the imagination.

—Robert Kolker, *Film, Form and Culture*, 1999

Production Personnel and Their Functions in
The Sixth Sense (1999)

These **production companies** provide financial backing and other resources, usually through all phases of production.

The person whose name is shown first in the credits is said to have received "top billing". Alternately, if more than one name appears at the same time or at the same height, they are said to have "equal billing", with the importance of the people concerned decreasing from left to right.

This credit signifies the **casting director**, who auditions and helps to select the actors in a film. The producer and/or director typically selects the leads and possibly the main supporting actors, however the casting director is responsible for all other speaking parts (both supporting and bit parts), and typically works in conjunction with a casting agency.

In collaboration with the production designer, director of photography, and director, the **costume designer** plans and executes the film's wardrobe, designing or selecting clothing appropriate to the character, setting, and, most especially, the performer.

The **production designer** visualizes the film's setting by orchestrating set and costume design, art direction, etc.; by determining and coordinating such factors as architecture, costume, makeup, props, and color schemes, the production designer is vital to establishing the world of the film.

The **director of photography** (aka the cinematographer or DP) works with the director to set up shots and choose lenses, camera movements and lighting schemes.

The **screenwriter**'s chief task is to develop the screenplay or script. This may be his or her own original story, an existing property which the writer adapts, or an idea which the producer hires the writer to develop; writers may also be brought into to revise or rewrite an existing screenplay.

The **director** is the primary artistic force responsible for overseeing production and assembly of the film, however he/she may also be involved earlier in the project; the director confers with key creative people and orchestrates the other teams involved in the production, as well as communicates with the actors to develop each scene in accordance

OPENING CREDITS:

Hollywood Pictures and
Spyglass Entertainment present

A Kennedy/Marshall/
Barry Mendel production

Bruce Willis

The Sixth Sense

Toni Collette

Olivia Williams

Haley Joel Osment

Donnie Wahlberg

Glenn Fitzgerald
Mischa Barton

Trevor Morgan
Bruce Norris

Casting by
Avy Kaufman

Costume Design
Joanna Johnston

Music by
James Newton Howard

Edited by
Andrew Mondshein

Production Designer
Larry Fulton

Director of Photography
Tak Fujimoto, A.S.C.

Executive Producer
Sam Mercer

Produced by
Frank Marshall, Kathleen Kennedy
and Barry Mendel

Written and Directed by
M. Night Shyamalan

These names refer to the producers who see the film through from start to finish; see producer credits below.

Billing: the relative sizes, positions, and order of names in the opening credits. A great deal of importance is placed on billing, with higher positions generally designating higher importance, and additional significance given to names which appear before the actual title of the movie (there's also additional significance given to "special billing," where a major star takes a supporting role and is given the final cast credit of "and," "with," or "featuring").

Typically, only principal and supporting players receive billing in the opening credits. See other cast distinctions on next page.

This credit goes to the film's **composer**, the individual who writes the musical score for the film. He or she usually starts work when the production stage is completed and, at the start, confers with the director and/or producer.

The **editor** gathers together and catalogues all of the film's footage, then orders and trims both the image and sound tracks into a final cut. Working with the director, he/she makes creative decisions about how the footage should be cut together, combining the best takes into an "assembly cut," which will become a "rough cut," and ultimately, a "fine cut." Today, footage is often transferred onto video and edited via computer.

The **executive producer** often arranges financing for the project, obtains the literary property, or brings some sort of clout or esteem with his or her name.

The **producer**'s responsibilities are chiefly financial and organizational. There are three general types of producers: (1) independent producers who shop a property to studios and production companies to gain financing; (2) those hired by a studio or production company to put together a specific project; or (3) those who work full-time for a company generating ideas and developing potential films. The producer usually remains through all five stages of the film: development, preproduction, principal photography, postproduction, and distribution.

CLOSING CREDITS:

an M. Night Shyamalan film ◄

This **"possessory credit"** is given to the director of the film, and indicates the general belief that the director is the individual most responsible for the look and sound of the finished film. This credit has become rather controversial in recent years, as it neglects the other creative contributors to the film, particularly the writer (however in this case, Shyamalan is actually both the writer and the director of the film, making it less problematic).

Principal players are the lead roles in the film; these actors generally have the most lines, and the story revolves directly around their characters.

Supporting players are secondary to the leads, but still vitally significant to the story. These characters usually appear in more than one scene and effect important plot points. There are exceptions, of course—Donnie Walberg's character appears in one brief scene, however his part is of great importance to the story, thus his is still a supporting role.

Bit players have relatively minor roles; they usually appear in only one scene.

In addition to principal, supporting, and bit parts, there is also a fourth category of performer—the **extra**. Extras appear in non-specific, non-speaking parts, usually as part of a crowd or as background to a scene. As such, these players are not listed in the credits.

Other types of doubles are also performers chosen to replace the actor for some reason or another (such as **body doubles** or **photo doubles**). In this case, an actor was needed to appear as a younger Cole in photographs.

Stunt performers are actors who specialize in performing stunts.

(Cast)

Character	Actor
Malcolm Crowe	Bruce Willis
Cole Sear	Haley Joel Osment
Lynn Sear	Toni Collette
Anna Crowe	Olivia Williams
Tommy Tammisimo	Trevor Morgan
Vincent Grey	Donnie Wahlberg
Darren	Peter Tambakis
Bobby	Jeffrey Zubernis
Stanley Cunningham	Bruce Norris
Sean	Glenn Fitzgerald
Mr. Collins	Greg Wood
Kyra Collins	Mischa Barton
Mrs. Collins	Angelica Torn
Bridesmaid	Lisa Summerour
Young Man Buying Ring	Firdous Bamji
Young Woman Buying Ring	Samia Shoaib
Darren's Mom	Hayden Saunier
Kitchen Woman	Janis Dardaris
Visitor #2	Neill Hartley
Visitor #3	Sarah Ripard
Visitor #4	Heidi Fischer
Visitor #5	Kadee Strickland
Visitor #6	Michael J. Lyons
Kyra's Sister	Samantha Fitzpatrick
Society Lady #1	Holly Rudkin
Society Lady #2	Kate Kearney-Patch
Woman at Accident	Marilyn Shanok
Dr. Hill	M. Night Shyamalan
Commercial Narrator	Wes Heywood
Hanged Child	Nico Woulard
Hanged Female	Carol Nielson
Hanged Male	Keith Woulard
Burnt Teacher	Jodi Dawson
Gunshot Boy	Tony Donnelly
Secretary	Ronnie Lea
Spanish Ghost on Tape	Carlos X. López
Young Vincent	Gino Inverso
Mrs. Sloan	Ellen Sheppard
Anna's Father	Tom McLaughlin
Anna's Mother	Candy Aston Dennis
Shaken Driver	Patrick F. McDade
Husband	Jose L. Rodriguez

Mr. Willis' Stunt Double	Terry Jackson
Cole Photo Double	Peter Dinich
Stunt Coordinator	Jeff Habberstad
Stunt Performers	Steve Mack
	Mick O'Rourke

Unit Production Manager
Sam Mercer ◄

Here, the director performs a **cameo** role. A cameo is a brief, minor role, one normally considered a bit part (or even an extra part), which is played by a well-known celebrity or some other such significant person.

A **stunt double** is a performer who specifically takes the part of another actor for a stunt. Stunt doubles rarely (if ever) speak, and are typically chosen to resemble the actor that they are replacing as much as

The **stunt coordinator** plans and arranges all the film's stunts.

The **unit production manager** (aka the line producer or UPM) is an executive responsible for the day-to-day administration of the production unit, dealing with call sheets and production logs,

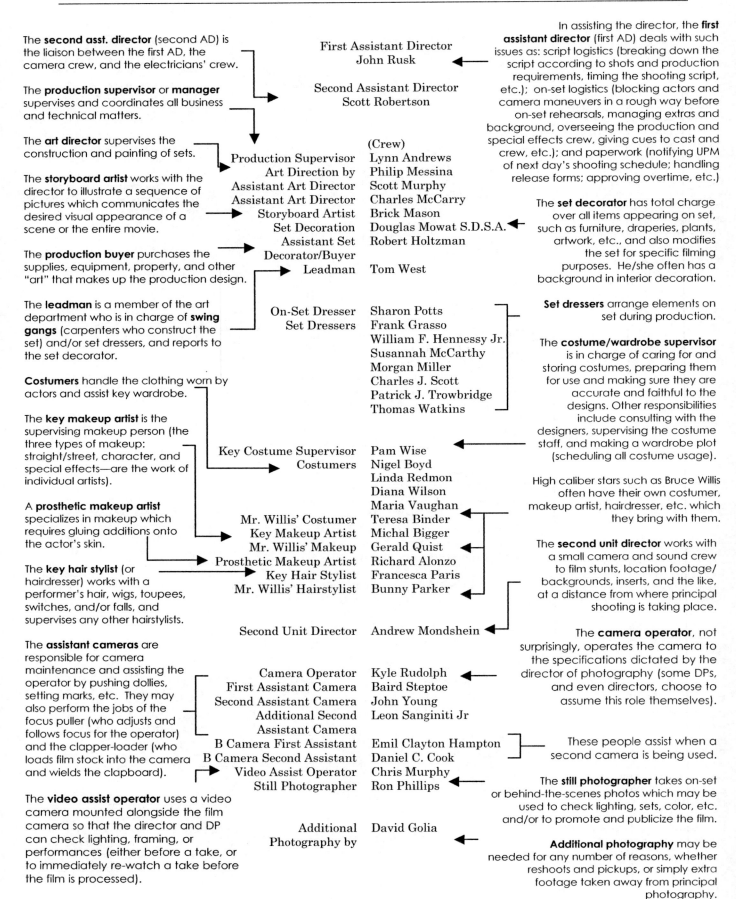

The **second asst. director** (second AD) is the liaison between the first AD, the camera crew, and the electricians' crew.

The **production supervisor** or **manager** supervises and coordinates all business and technical matters.

The **art director** supervises the construction and painting of sets.

The **storyboard artist** works with the director to illustrate a sequence of pictures which communicates the desired visual appearance of a scene or the entire movie.

The **production buyer** purchases the supplies, equipment, property, and other "art" that makes up the production design.

The **leadman** is a member of the art department who is in charge of **swing gangs** (carpenters who construct the set) and/or set dressers, and reports to the set decorator.

Costumers handle the clothing worn by actors and assist key wardrobe.

The **key makeup artist** is the supervising makeup person (the three types of makeup: straight/street, character, and special effects—are the work of individual artists).

A **prosthetic makeup artist** specializes in makeup which requires gluing additions onto the actor's skin.

The **key hair stylist** (or hairdresser) works with a performer's hair, wigs, toupees, switches, and/or falls, and supervises any other hairstylists.

The **assistant cameras** are responsible for camera maintenance and assisting the operator by pushing dollies, setting marks, etc. They may also perform the jobs of the focus puller (who adjusts and follows focus for the operator) and the clapper-loader (who loads film stock into the camera and wields the clapboard).

The **video assist operator** uses a video camera mounted alongside the film camera so that the director and DP can check lighting, framing, or performances (either before a take, or to immediately re-watch a take before the film is processed).

First Assistant Director
John Rusk

Second Assistant Director
Scott Robertson

(Crew)
Production Supervisor   Lynn Andrews
Art Direction by   Philip Messina
Assistant Art Director   Scott Murphy
Assistant Art Director   Charles McCarry
Storyboard Artist   Brick Mason
Set Decoration   Douglas Mowat S.D.S.A.
Assistant Set   Robert Holtzman
Decorator/Buyer
Leadman   Tom West

On-Set Dresser   Sharon Potts
Set Dressers   Frank Grasso
                             William F. Hennessy Jr.
                             Susannah McCarthy
                             Morgan Miller
                             Charles J. Scott
                             Patrick J. Trowbridge
                             Thomas Watkins

Key Costume Supervisor   Pam Wise
Costumers   Nigel Boyd
                             Linda Redmon
                             Diana Wilson
                             Maria Vaughan
Mr. Willis' Costumer   Teresa Binder
Key Makeup Artist   Michal Bigger
Mr. Willis' Makeup   Gerald Quist
Prosthetic Makeup Artist   Richard Alonzo
Key Hair Stylist   Francesca Paris
Mr. Willis' Hairstylist   Bunny Parker

Second Unit Director   Andrew Mondshein

Camera Operator   Kyle Rudolph
First Assistant Camera   Baird Steptoe
Second Assistant Camera   John Young
Additional Second   Leon Sanginiti Jr
Assistant Camera
B Camera First Assistant   Emil Clayton Hampton
B Camera Second Assistant   Daniel C. Cook
Video Assist Operator   Chris Murphy
Still Photographer   Ron Phillips

Additional   David Golia
Photography by

In assisting the director, the **first assistant director** (first AD) deals with such issues as: script logistics (breaking down the script according to shots and production requirements, timing the shooting script, etc.); on-set logistics (blocking actors and camera maneuvers in a rough way before on-set rehearsals, managing extras and background, overseeing the production and special effects crew, giving cues to cast and crew, etc.); and paperwork (notifying UPM of next day's shooting schedule; handling release forms; approving overtime, etc.)

The **set decorator** has total charge over all items appearing on set, such as furniture, draperies, plants, artwork, etc., and also modifies the set for specific filming purposes. He/she often has a background in interior decoration.

Set dressers arrange elements on set during production.

The **costume/wardrobe supervisor** is in charge of caring for and storing costumes, preparing them for use and making sure they are accurate and faithful to the designs. Other responsibilities include consulting with the designers, supervising the costume staff, and making a wardrobe plot (scheduling all costume usage).

High caliber stars such as Bruce Willis often have their own costumer, makeup artist, hairdresser, etc. which they bring with them.

The **second unit director** works with a small camera and sound crew to film stunts, location footage/backgrounds, inserts, and the like, at a distance from where principal shooting is taking place.

The **camera operator**, not surprisingly, operates the camera to the specifications dictated by the director of photography (some DPs, and even directors, choose to assume this role themselves).

These people assist when a second camera is being used.

The **still photographer** takes on-set or behind-the-scenes photos which may be used to check lighting, sets, color, etc. and/or to promote and publicize the film.

Additional photography may be needed for any number of reasons, whether reshoots and pickups, or simply extra footage taken away from principal photography.

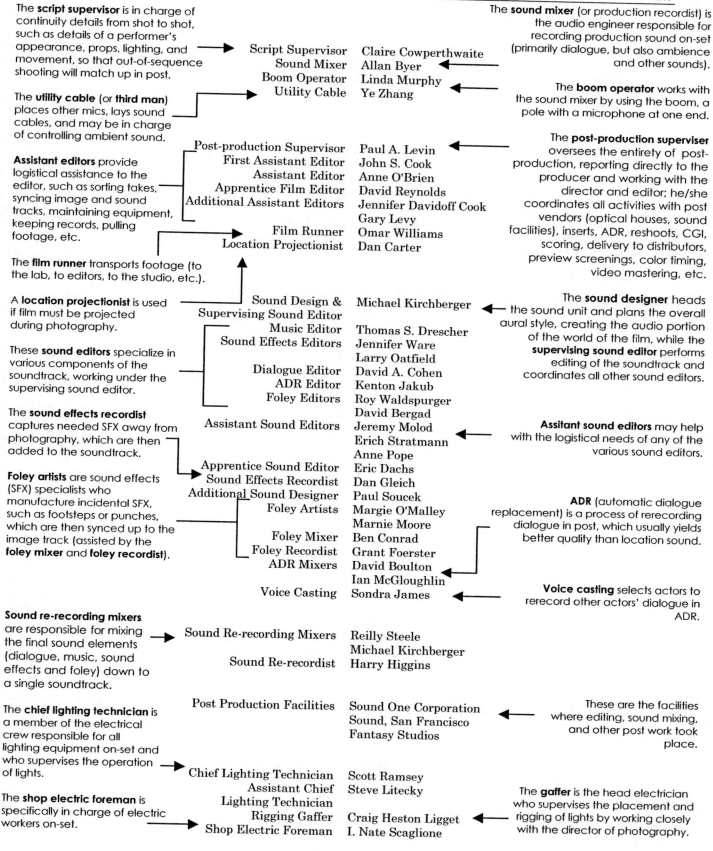

The **script supervisor** is in charge of continuity details from shot to shot, such as details of a performer's appearance, props, lighting, and movement, so that out-of-sequence shooting will match up in post.

The **utility cable** (or **third man**) places other mics, lays sound cables, and may be in charge of controlling ambient sound.

Assistant editors provide logistical assistance to the editor, such as sorting takes, syncing image and sound tracks, maintaining equipment, keeping records, pulling footage, etc.

The **film runner** transports footage (to the lab, to editors, to the studio, etc.).

A **location projectionist** is used if film must be projected during photography.

These **sound editors** specialize in various components of the soundtrack, working under the supervising sound editor.

The **sound effects recordist** captures needed SFX away from photography, which are then added to the soundtrack.

Foley artists are sound effects (SFX) specialists who manufacture incidental SFX, such as footsteps or punches, which are then synced up to the image track (assisted by the **foley mixer** and **foley recordist**).

Sound re-recording mixers are responsible for mixing the final sound elements (dialogue, music, sound effects and foley) down to a single soundtrack.

The **chief lighting technician** is a member of the electrical crew responsible for all lighting equipment on-set and who supervises the operation of lights.

The **shop electric foreman** is specifically in charge of electric workers on-set.

Script Supervisor — Claire Cowperthwaite
Sound Mixer — Allan Byer
Boom Operator — Linda Murphy
Utility Cable — Ye Zhang

Post-production Supervisor — Paul A. Levin
First Assistant Editor — John S. Cook
Assistant Editor — Anne O'Brien
Apprentice Film Editor — David Reynolds
Additional Assistant Editors — Jennifer Davidoff Cook
— Gary Levy
Film Runner — Omar Williams
Location Projectionist — Dan Carter

Sound Design & Supervising Sound Editor — Michael Kirchberger
Music Editor — Thomas S. Drescher
Sound Effects Editors — Jennifer Ware
— Larry Oatfield
Dialogue Editor — David A. Cohen
ADR Editor — Kenton Jakub
Foley Editors — Roy Waldspurger
— David Bergad
Assistant Sound Editors — Jeremy Molod
— Erich Stratmann
— Anne Pope
Apprentice Sound Editor — Eric Dachs
Sound Effects Recordist — Dan Gleich
Additional Sound Designer — Paul Soucek
Foley Artists — Margie O'Malley
— Marnie Moore
Foley Mixer — Ben Conrad
Foley Recordist — Grant Foerster
ADR Mixers — David Boulton
— Ian McGloughlin
Voice Casting — Sondra James

Sound Re-recording Mixers — Reilly Steele
— Michael Kirchberger
Sound Re-recordist — Harry Higgins

Post Production Facilities — Sound One Corporation
Sound, San Francisco
Fantasy Studios

Chief Lighting Technician — Scott Ramsey
Assistant Chief Lighting Technician — Steve Litecky
Rigging Gaffer — Craig Heston Ligget
Shop Electric Foreman — I. Nate Scaglione

The **sound mixer** (or production recordist) is the audio engineer responsible for recording production sound on-set (primarily dialogue, but also ambience and other sounds).

The **boom operator** works with the sound mixer by using the boom, a pole with a microphone at one end.

The **post-production superviser** oversees the entirety of post-production, reporting directly to the producer and working with the director and editor; he/she coordinates all activities with post vendors (optical houses, sound facilities), inserts, ADR, reshoots, CGI, scoring, delivery to distributors, preview screenings, color timing, video mastering, etc.

The **sound designer** heads the sound unit and plans the overall aural style, creating the audio portion of the world of the film, while the **supervising sound editor** performs editing of the soundtrack and coordinates all other sound editors.

Assitant sound editors may help with the logistical needs of any of the various sound editors.

ADR (automatic dialogue replacement) is a process of rerecording dialogue in post, which usually yields better quality than location sound.

Voice casting selects actors to rerecord other actors' dialogue in ADR.

These are the facilities where editing, sound mixing, and other post work took place.

The **gaffer** is the head electrician who supervises the placement and rigging of lights by working closely with the director of photography.

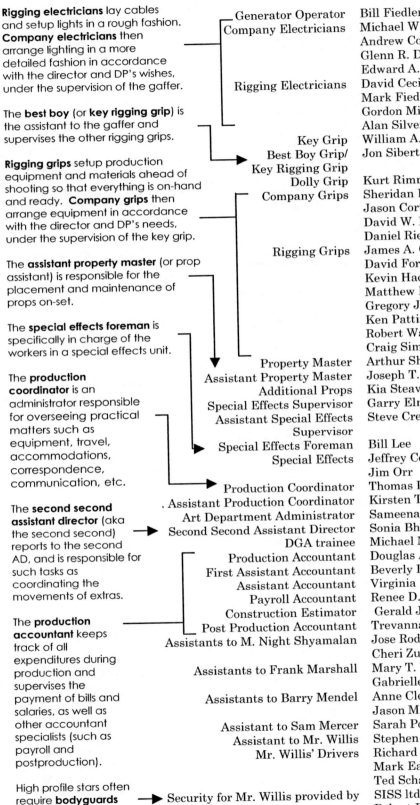

Rigging electricians lay cables and setup lights in a rough fashion. **Company electricians** then arrange lighting in a more detailed fashion in accordance with the director and DP's wishes, under the supervision of the gaffer.

The **best boy** (or **key rigging grip**) is the assistant to the gaffer and supervises the other rigging grips.

Rigging grips setup production equipment and materials ahead of shooting so that everything is on-hand and ready. **Company grips** then arrange equipment in accordance with the director and DP's needs, under the supervision of the key grip.

The **assistant property master** (or prop assistant) is responsible for the placement and maintenance of props on-set.

The **special effects foreman** is specifically in charge of the workers in a special effects unit.

The **production coordinator** is an administrator responsible for overseeing practical matters such as equipment, travel, accommodations, correspondence, communication, etc.

The **second second assistant director** (aka the second second) reports to the second AD, and is responsible for such tasks as coordinating the movements of extras.

The **production accountant** keeps track of all expenditures during production and supervises the payment of bills and salaries, as well as other accountant specialists (such as payroll and postproduction).

High profile stars often require **bodyguards** during production.

Generator Operator
Company Electricians

Rigging Electricians

Key Grip
Best Boy Grip/
Key Rigging Grip
Dolly Grip
Company Grips

Rigging Grips

Property Master
Assistant Property Master
Additional Props
Special Effects Supervisor
Assistant Special Effects
Supervisor
Special Effects Foreman
Special Effects

Production Coordinator
. Assistant Production Coordinator
Art Department Administrator
Second Second Assistant Director
DGA trainee
Production Accountant
First Assistant Accountant
Assistant Accountant
Payroll Accountant
Construction Estimator
Post Production Accountant
Assistants to M. Night Shyamalan

Assistants to Frank Marshall

Assistants to Barry Mendel

Assistant to Sam Mercer
Assistant to Mr. Willis
Mr. Willis' Drivers

Security for Mr. Willis provided by

Bill Fiedler
Michael W. Brennan
Andrew Conner
Glenn R. Davis
Edward A. Smith
David Cecil
Mark Fiedler
Gordon Minard
Alan Silverstein
William A. Miller
Jon Sibert

Kurt Rimmel
Sheridan Braxton
Jason Cortazzo
David W. Lowe
Daniel Rieser
James A. Casey
David Fortino
Kevin Hackenberg
Matthew Hanlon
Gregory Johnson
Ken Pattison
Robert Wayne See
Craig Simpson
Arthur Shippee
Joseph T. Conway
Kia Steave-Dickerson
Garry Elmendorf
Steve Cremin

Bill Lee
Jeffrey Cox
Jim Orr
Thomas Doc Boguski
Kirsten Turner
Sameena Usmani
Sonia Bhalla
Michael Meader
Douglas A. Moreno
Beverly L. Mink
Virginia E. Beard
Renee D. Czarapata
Gerald James Scaife
Trevanna Post
Jose Rodriguez
Cheri Zucca
Mary T. Radford
Gabrielle Mahler
Anne Clements
Jason Miller
Sarah Poindexter
Stephen Eads
Richard Curry
Mark Eads
Ted Schambers
SISS ltd.
Robert Biddle

The **key grip** supervises the other grips (workers who carry and arrange equipment, props, and elements of the setting and lighting). The key grip works closely with the gaffer, and often doubles as a construction coordinator and a backup for the camera crew.

A **dolly grip** assists the camera crew by pushing a dolly that carries the camera, either from one set-up to another or during a moving camera shot.

The **property master** supervises the use of all props (movable objects relevant to the story; not to be confused with set dressing), and often responsible for buying, acquiring, and/or manufacturing needed props; also works in conjunction with the script supervisor in maintaining continuity.

The **special effects supervisor** oversees the preparing and executing of process shots, miniatures, matte work, FX makeup, and other technical shots produced on-set, consulting with the director and DP on an ongoing basis (note that this does not include CGI and other visual effects done in postproduction). Though special effects work was relatively minor in this film, FX units in modern films can include hundreds of workers specializing in a vast range of disciplines.

The **art department administrator** runs the art department, the people concerned with the film's visual artistry and the overall "look" of the film. He/she handles practical and logistical matters as dictated by the production designer and/or art director.

A **DGA trainee** is an applicant placed on the production by the Director's Guild to gain experience as part of a training program.

These are all **personal assistants** to the director, producers, and star.

These **drivers'** sole purpose is to transport the star from place to place.

The **construction coordinator** manages such logistical necessities as budgeting, tracking costs, generating reports, etc., as well as coordinating the building of sets; he is responsible for the physical integrity of all structures on-set.

The **key greensman** takes care of all foliage (plants, flowers, trees, shrubs, grass, etc.) on set or on location.

Scenic artists are members of the set crew responsible for painting sets and backgrounds.

As the name implies, **sculptors** model or carve figures from clay, stone, metal, wood, etc. to create set pieces or three-dimensional models.

A **facilities coordinator** manages the operation of specific equipment.

Studio teachers provide instruction for child performers for three hours every school day during the shoot.

Dialect consultants work with actors to provide accents appropriate to the characters and setting of the film.

A **unit publicist** is a member of the producer's crew who creates and distributes promotional material regarding the production, as well as arranging press and TV interviews and other mass media coverage.

An **animal handler** (aka a **wrangler**) is responsible for animals used during filming; wranglers may work with animals in genral or may be specific to a particular type of animal.

Set medics provide for the medical needs of the entire cast and crew, as well as emergency medical logistics when required. These person may be EMTs, paramedics, nurses, or physicians.

The **score recorder and mixer** is responsible for the technical aspects of recording the score.

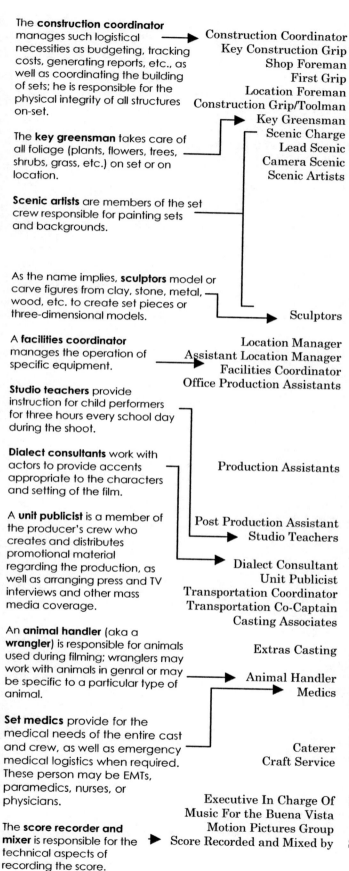

Construction Coordinator — Paul Williams
Key Construction Grip — Duncan M. Spencer
Shop Foreman — Carmen S. Santoro
First Grip — James D. Doherty
Location Foreman — Paul Maiello
Construction Grip/Toolman — Christopher F. Graneto
Key Greensman — James Breen
Scenic Charge — Ricky Riggs
Lead Scenic — Lewis Bowen
Camera Scenic — Stephen Siersema
Scenic Artists — Greta Alexander
Margaret Boritz
Thom Bumblauskas
Jennifer Desnove
Erika Katz
Nancy Stroud
John Thomas
Penny Thomas
Matthew Turner
Karen Wainwright
Sculptors — Dave Barnes
Kate Bartoldus
Location Manager — Andrew Ullman
Assistant Location Manager — Patricia Taggart
Facilities Coordinator — Missy Moyer
Office Production Assistants — Carl J. Davis
Stacie M. Ziegenfuss
Jefferson Chaney
Francis X. Doerr Jr
Dan Rosenfelt
David Cutler
Production Assistants — Megan Fenerty
Cory M. McCall
Raymond Morgan
Virle Reid
Post Production Assistant — Jae Stein-Grainger
Studio Teachers — Carolyn Grimley
Pamela Thompson
Dialect Consultant — Lilene Mansell
Unit Publicist — Joseph L. Everett
Transportation Coordinator — John F. Morrone III
Transportation Co-Captain — John Tarlini Sr
Casting Associates — Julie Lichter
Beth Bowling
Mike Lemon Casting
Extras Casting — Diane Heery
Barbara Muehleib
Animal Handler — Kathleen Kelly
Medics — Mary Berkelbach
Denise DePalma
Barbara Young
Caterer — Home on the Range
Craft Service — Vince Digiacomo

Executive In Charge Of Music For the Buena Vista Motion Pictures Group — Kathy Nelson
Score Recorded and Mixed by — Shawn Murphy

The **key construction grip** supervises the work of all the other various builders (carpenters, plasterers, upholsterers, painters, tillers, etc.)

The **shop foreman** is in charge of the workers in the studio's shop, while the location foreman is responsible for builders on location.

The **location manager** finds locations based on the director's needs, negotiates their use, acquires filming permits, and manages other needs while filming on location.

Production assistants (or PAs) run errands, make copies, get coffee, and perform other menial tasks. They are typically newcomers to the film industry (or recent film school graduates...) just starting out and looking for experience. Office PAs are specific to the production office and Post-PAs work with the editors, while general PAs usually work on-set.

The **transportation coordinator** is responsible for managing drivers and coordinating the transportation of cast, crew, and equipment to and from the various sets and locations as needed.

Casting associates assist the casting director in auditioning and selecting supporting actors and bit players.

Extras casting are concerned solely with providing extras for background and crowd scenes.

The **caterer** provides meals to the cast and crew, while **craft services** provides snacks and beverages between meals.

The **executive in charge of music** researches, obtains rights to, and provides songs for a production. Alternately, this may be done by a **music supervisor**, who would also coordinate the work of the composer, editor, and sound mixers.

Orchestrators adapt and arrange the score for all the instruments in the orchestra.

These are the facilities at which the orchestral score and choral components of the score were recorded.

The **auricle operator** handles the equipment used for recording the orchestra on the scoring stage.

This **optical** company does the actual printing of the title designer's work (and possibly other work needed to be produced by an optical printer)

The **color timer** adjusts the final print so that the colors match from shot to shot.

An **effects supervisor** may be hired to supervise a particular aspect of the effects—in this case, specifically the makeup effects.

Mechanical effects involve some machine-oriented effects on-set, such as animatronics, explosions, or any other effect produced by mechanical devices.

The **mold department** designs and produces molds from which multiple props, prosthetics, etc. can be produced.

This **key fabricator** supervised the mold department.

The **digital effects supervisor** is the chief of the visual effects crew.

Visual effects companies operate separately from the production company producing the film; as such, a separate **visual effects producer** manages financial and organizational responsibilities in regard to visual effects production.

Orchestrations by

Electronic Score Produced by
Orchestra Conducted by
Orchestra Recorded at
Orchestra Contractor
Choir Recorded at
Choir Contractor
Auricle Operator
Music Preparation

Titles Designed & Produced by
Opticals
Negative Cutter
Color Timer

Makeup Effects Design and Created by
Stan Winston Studio

Effects Supervisor
Key Artists

Mechanical Designer
Key Hair Stylist
Mold Department Supervisor
Mold Department

Key Fabricator
Production Coordinator

Visual Effects by
Dream Quest Images

Digital Effects Supervisor
Visual Effects Producer

Jeff Atmajian
Brad Dechter
Robert Elhai
James Newton Howard
J.T. Hill
Pete Anthony
The Newman Scoring Stage
Sandy De Crescent
Signet Soundelux Studios
Sally Stevens
Richard Grant
Jo Ann Kane

The Picture Mill
Cineric, INC.
Mo Henry
Dan Valliere

John Rosengrant
Richie Alonzo
Lindsay Macgowan
Scott Stoddard
Trevor Hensley
Joey Orosco
Al Sousa
Michael Ornelaz
Anthony McCray
Darin Bouyssou
Grady Holder
Carey Jones
Alon Dori
Connie Cadwell
Stiles White

Tim Landry
David McCullough

(Special Thanks)
City of Philadelphia
Philadelphia Authority for Industrial Development
Greater Philadelphia Film Office and
Sharon Pinkenson, Executive Director
Peco Energy Company
Southeastern Pennsylvania Transportation Authority
Striped Bass Restaurant
Shadow Broadcast Services
Radio clip courtesy of KYW – AM
Marc H. Glick
Stephen Breimer
Peter Benedek
Jeremy Zimmer
Sherwin Das

The **conductor** directs the orchestra's performance of the score. This is often done by the composer himself, but not always (as seen here).

The **music preparer** organizes the sheet music for each member of the orchestra and choir.

The **title designer** is responsible for any words which appear on screen, particularly the credits.

The **negative cutter** cuts and splices the negative so that it conforms to the final edited version of the film. This is the actual film recorded by the camera, and every print of the film produced will be made from this negative.

Special effects makeup involves effects which are applied directly to an actor's skin (thus combining both effects and makeup), such as squibs.

"**Key artists**" simply signifies artists of some importance; these individuals most likely were the primary creative forces on projects involving a greater number of workers.

Another key hair stylist; this one was specifically responsible for hairdressing involving special effects makeup.

Another production coordinator; this one was specifically responsible for special effects concerns.

Visual effects are those completed in postproduction, such as CGI (computer-generated imagery) or digital alterations to the image.

Special thanks are usually given to people or companies which donate products or services, allow the filmmakers to use certain locations, provide product placement fees, or offer other considerations to the production.

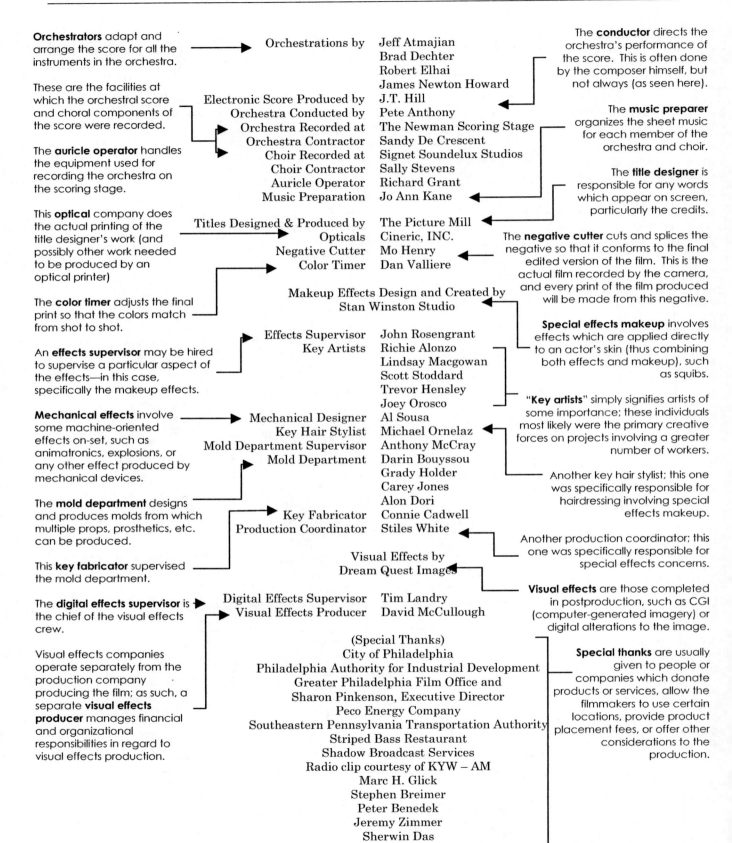

These are the appropriate credits and copyright acknowledgements for the various songs and musical pieces used outside of the film's score.

(Songs)

"Crazy Girl"
written and performed by Jamie Dunlap and Scott Nickoley
courtesy of Masterource

"Come See About Me"
written by Brian Holland, Edward Holland, Jr. and Lamont Dozier
performed by The Supremes
courtesy of Motown Record Company, L.P.
under license from Universal Music Special Markets

"Space Cocktail"
written by Laurent Lombard and Syd Dale
performed by Laurent Lombard
courtesy of Opus 1

Schubert: "Piano Quintet in A Major D667, 'Trout'Andante (Tema Con Variazioni)"
performed by The Colorado String Quartet
courtesy of Laserlight
by arrangement with Souce/Q

"I Fall in Love Too Easily"
written by Sammy Cahn and Kule Styne
performed by Chet Baker
courtesy of Blue Note Records,
a division of Capitol Records, Inc.
Under license from EMI-Capitol Music Special Markets

"Head"
written by Timothy Bircheno, David Tomlinson and Tim Gordine
performed by Tin Star
courtesy of V2 Records

"Unknown Rider"
written by Thomas Bracht and Dudley Taft
performed by Second Coming
courtesy of Capitol Records
under license from EMI-Capitol Music Special Markets

American Humane Association was on set to monitor the animal action. No animal was harmed in the making of this film. AHA90624-1

This indicates that any use of animals was in accordance with the AHA's regulations.

These credits acknowledge the various companies used for equipment and supplies, film stock and printing, and sound.

Lighting and Grip Equipment by Xeno Lights, Inc.

Prints by
Technicolor

Filmed with
Panavision
Cameras and Lens

Produced & Distributed
on Eastman Film

 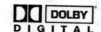

This indicates that the film has been approved by the Motion Picture Association of America.

This seal indicates this film was made in accordance with union regulations of the AFL-CIO-CLC

Copyright ©MCMXCIX Spyglass Entertainment Group, LP
All Rights Reserved

This is the year and possessor of the film's copyright according to US law.

This is a copyright disclaimer for the UK.

This motion picture was created by Sixth Sense Productions, Inc. for purposes of copyright law in the United Kingdom

Distributed by
Buena Vista Pictures Distribution

This is the company which distributed the film.

The credits end with the logos of the three production companies which produced the film.

Kennedy/Marshall Company

Spyglass Entertainment

Hollywood Pictures

Credit Breakdown by Robert Buerkle & Paul N. Reinsch

Production Personnel By Teams:

The Development Team:
• Executive Producer
• Producers
• Screenwriter

The Producer's Team:
• Unit Production Manager/Line Producer
• Associate Producers
• Production Supervisor
• Production Coordinator
• Production Accountants
• Location Manager
• Transportation Supervisor & Drivers
• Craft Services & Caterers
• Security & Bodyguards
• Casting Director, Associates, & Assistants
• Extras Casting
• Unit Publicist
• Office Production Assistants

The Director's Team:
• Director
• First Assistant Director
• Second Assistant Director
• Second Second Assistant Director
• Third Assistant Director
• Production Assistants
• Script Supervisor
• Dialogue Coach & Dialect Consultants
• Stunt Coordinator
• Choreographer
• Animal Wrangler
• Storyboard Artist
• Second Unit Director

The Cast:
• Principal Players
• Supporting Players
• Bit Players
• Extras
• Cameo Players
• Stunt Performers
• Stunt Doubles, Body Doubles, etc.

The Camera Crew:
• Director of Photography/Cinematographer
• Camera Operator
• First Assistant Camera/Focus Puller
• Second Assistant Camera/Clapper-Loader
• Key Grip
• Dolly Grip
• Rigging Grips & Company Grips
• Additional Camera or Photography

The Electrical/Lighting Crew:
• Gaffer
• Best Boy/Key Rigging Grip
• Chief Lighting Technician
• Key Grip
• Rigging Grips & Company Grips
• Rigging Electricians & Company Electricians
• Shop Electric Foreman

The Production Design Team:
• Production Designer
• Art Director
• Set Decorator
• Set Dressers
• Leadman
• Swing Gangs
• Construction Coordinator
• Key Construction Grip
• Shop & Location Foremen
• Art Department Administrator
• Key Greensman
• Scenic Artists, Model-makers, Scuptors, etc.
• Property Master
• Production Buyer
• Costume Designer
• Key Wardrobe/Costume Supervisor
• Costumers
• Key Hairdresser
• Key Makeup Artist

The Sound Crew:
• Sound Designer
• Sound Mixer
• Boom Operator
• Utility Cable/Third Man
• Playback Operator

The Editing Team:
• Editor
• Postproduction Supervisor
• Assistant Editors
• Supervising Sound Editor
• Music, Sound FX, Dialogue, ADR, & Foley Editors
• Assistant Sound Editors
• Postproduction Assistants

The Music Team:
• Composer
• Music Editor
• Orchestrator
• Conductor
• Music Supervisor
• Score Recorder and Mixer

Effects Personnel:
• Special Effects Units, Companies, & Personnel
• Special Effects Supervisor
• Special Effects Makeup Artists
• Mechanical Effects Personnel
• Visual Effects Units, Companies, & Personnel
• Digital Effects Supervisor
• Sound Effects Personnel
• Foley Artists, Recordist, & Mixer

Various Lab Personnel:
• Negative Cutter
• Color Timer
• Key Re-recording Mixer
• Optical Artist or Company
• Title Designer
• Lab Technician

CRITICAL FILM ANALYSES

Papillon (1973)

Robert Buerkle

CAST: Steve McQueen (Papillon) Dustin Hoffman (Dega) Victor Jory (Indian Chief) Don Gordon (Julot) Anthony Zerbe (Leper Colony Chief) Robert Deman (Maturette) Woodrow Parfrey (Clusiot) Bill Mumy (Lariot) George Coulouris (Dr. Chatal) Ratna Assan (Zoriama) William Smithers (Warden Barrot) Gregory Sierra (Antonio) Barbara Morrison (Mother Superior) Ellen Moss (Nun) Dalton Trumbo (Commandant).

CREW: Directed by Franklin J. Schaffner. Screenplay by Dalton Trumbo and Lorenzo Semple Jr. Based on the novel by Henri Charrière. Produced by Ted Richmond (executive producer), Franklin J. Schaffner, Robert Dorfmann, and Robert Laffont (associate producer). Original music by Jerry Goldsmith. Cinematography by Fred Koenekamp. Editing by Robert Swink. Casting by Jack Baur. Production design by Anthony Masters. Art direction by Jack Maxstead. Costume design by Anthony Powell. Makeup by Charles H. Schram. Sound by Richard Portman. Assistant directors Jose Lopez Rodero and Juan Lopez Rodero. Allied Artists, 1973, in Technicolor and Panavision. Running time: 150 minutes.

The production chronicle of Papillon is such a saga of bad luck, dissention, and difficulty that it seems remarkable that a motion picture came out of it at all—much less the reasonably successful one it turned out to be.[158]

Bruce Cook, Dalton Trumbo biographer

---

[158] Bruce Cook, *Dalton Trumbo* (New York: Charles Scribner's Sons, 1977), p. 3.

I was astounded...to hear of the rumors circulated about *Papillon*. The financial difficulties, the artistic differences, and the production problems. Some day perhaps I will have a forum from which to put the rumors to rest by declaring all of them to have been true.[159]

— Franklin J. Schaffner, director of *Papillon*

Selling 2.5 million copies in America and a total of 10 million worldwide, Henri Charriere's autobiographical novel *Papillon* blends elements of "Alexandre Dumas, Victor Hugo, and Daniel Defoe, [with] a hardboiled style not unlike Mickey Spillane's"[160] in the true story of Charriere's imprisonment on Devil's Island, his nine escape attempts, and his eventual freedom. An undeniable crowd-pleaser, it's no wonder that the book's publisher, Robert Laffont, guarded the film rights zealously. Included in the bill any would-be producer had to pay was Laffont's own involvement in the film—though once Robert Dorfmann bought the property, Laffont settled for a meager associate producer credit on the project (note the credits above). The French Dorfmann soon joined forces with American producer Ted Richmond, and the project was underway.

Upon obtaining the rights to the novel, the first order of business was to fill the two requisite posts of director and leading man. A French lead (like the real-life Papillon) would bring fine business in Europe, but not abroad; an American, on the other hand, would rake in the American dollars, as well as box office receipts in Europe and Asia. Steve McQueen, who broke into Hollywood with *The Blob* (1958), hit true stardom in *The Great Escape* (1963), and continued his success with such films as *The Thomas Crown Affair* and *Bullitt* (both 1968), was not only an American mega-star, but the top box office draw in France—and reputedly the first choice of Charriere himself. And while McQueen had built his success on action vehicles, he was ready to test his acting chops with a more challenging role; with Franklin J. Schaffner, director of *Planet of the Apes* (1968) and *Patton* (1970) onboard, McQueen would get just that opportunity. Schaffner later noted, somewhat cynically referencing the broad appeal of Hollywood product, "The only people who make international pictures are the Americans. That is why, obviously, they came first to McQueen and then they came to me."[161] But it would still be an international production of sorts—with French and American producers, the film would utilize the British and Spanish, as well as Americans, in comprising its crew.

Next up was getting a screenplay together. An early treatment had already been tried and discarded; once Schaffner was attached, he turned to scribe William Goldman, having had a good working relationship with his older brother, James. It was Goldman who established what would become the essential structure of the script: the nine escape attempts of the novel would be far too unwieldy; instead, three would suffice. Further, it was Goldman's idea to conclude the story midway through the novel, ending with Papillon's final escape (though the novel continues on with his life in Venezuela). Yet the story would soon go through another significant mutation.

Goldman recollected, "I was present at the meeting at which some guys said, 'Dustin Hoffman is getting hot. If we only had a part for Dustin Hoffman, that would be terrific.' And we scoffed because there *was* no part."[162] There was but one solution: to combine all the secondary roles, a drastic change to the screenplay's current version, though a notion which Schaffner would approve so long as Hoffman could be had.

---

[159] Franklin J. Schaffner, Letter to Sidney Wise, July 16, 1974. Franklin J. Schaffner Film Library, Franklin and Marshall College. Cited in Erwin Kim, *Franklin J. Schaffner* (London: The Scarecrow Press, Inc., 1985) p. 285.

[160] Kim, p. 286.

[161] "The American Film Institute Seminar with Franklin Schaffner," February 21, 1974, pp. 33-4. Transcript 192, Louis B. Meyer Library, American Film Institute, as referenced in Kim, p. 288.

[162] John Brady, *The Craft of the Screenwriter* (New York: Simon and Schuster, 1981), p. 120, as referenced in Kim, p. 290.

In truth, the choice to acquire Hoffman was also motivated by more practical reasons. Plagued with financial problems from the start, the production was quickly abandoned by its original company, paving the way for Allied Artists to take it over. Allied Artists was a small operation by this time, virtually out of production altogether, and as the budget for *Papillon* climbed from an original $4 million to an estimated $14 million—roughly *six times* Allied Artists' net worth—an extremely complicated financing deal had to be conceived. The dealings were conditional on McQueen's involvement, leading to his salary being upped to from $1.75 million to an even $2 million in order to guarantee his participation, a record in its time for a leading actor's salary.[163] Yet with a budget quickly spiraling out of control, McQueen's clout alone didn't calm the financiers. Were it to back the extremely expensive project, Allied wanted the sort of box office assurance that could only be provided by two name-brand stars. Thus Hoffman was pursued—and pursued relentlessly. Producers had quite a time attracting the actor, ultimately having to pay up $1.25 million for the rising star.[164] As Schaffner put it, "Dustin was bought—not brought—into the film."[165]

The new revamp meant a drastic change to the source material; *Papillon* is an undeniable loner in the novel, with no relationship lasting more than a handful of pages; yet by combining the secondary roles into the singular personage of Louis Dega, the script would inevitably lean into buddy film territory—undoubtedly the very thing that Allied Artists was hoping for. Such a shift, however, might not seem a bad idea with William Goldman onboard—after all, he single-handedly refined the genre with *Butch Cassidy and the Sundance Kid* (1969). Yet at this point, Goldman's participation had run it's course, and he stepped aside for the film's next writer, whose responsibility it would be to rework the Dega character and restructure the rest of the script accordingly.

That writer was Dalton Trumbo, who surely had no idea what he was getting into when signing on to the project. For Allied Artists still had one final condition for Schaffner and company: *Papillon* had to be ready for a Christmas 1973 release, meaning that filming had to begin immediately—a problem considering that as of yet, there was no finished script. What resulted was a pair of highly unlikely and unorthodox circumstances in film production: first, Trumbo would have to accompany the crew on location, writing the screenplay while it was being shot in order to keep the script ahead of filming;[166] second, due to this unusual necessity, the film would need to be shot virtually in sequence.

It was already February of '73, leaving a mere nine months to scout locations, shoot, score, and edit the film before getting it into theaters. And so the crew packed up and left for Spain to shoot the bulk of the picture, where more trouble awaited. Five days were lost while Schaffner refused to leave America—the Spanish crew had yet to be compensated for the work they had done, and Schaffner would not depart until his crew was paid. Dorfmann insisted that payment had been settled, but upon his arrival, Schaffner learned it was still not the case. Ultimately, the company spent a full month in Spain; the actual shooting took merely a week of that time. This situation was to repeat itself soon after, while filming the boat scenes in transport to French Guiana. Schaffner and McQueen learned that yet again, the crew was waiting to be paid—including above-the-line personnel such as the director of photography. The director again refused to work—this time, with his star in support—and more than another week was lost while payments were settled.

---

[163] With those of Hoffman and Schaffner at $1.25 million each, the film would also break the previous record for the combined total salary of a director and his two stars.

[164] Hoffman would also become the source for the sort of on-set "primadonna" tantrums one might expect more from an actor of McQueen's stature. For example, Hoffman reportedly became indignant upon learning of McQueen's salary, having been led to believe that he and McQueen would share equal billing on the film as well as enjoy equal salaries. Discovering that McQueen was getting $750,000 more left the actor quite incensed. Noted in Cook, p. 5.

[165] Marshall Terrill, *Steve McQueen: Portrait of an American Rebel* (New York: Donald I. Fine, Inc., 1993), p. 259.

[166] Trumbo would end up having only 60 pages of the script finished upon leaving for Spain.

Problems remained rampant, some large, some small, but all causing unneeded hassles and delays. The actual locations in French Guiana had gone to ruin and could not be used, so the search was on for suitable alternatives. After considering Guatemala, Honduras, the Grand Cayman Islands, and Barbados, Jamaica was finally chosen for the jungle locations, largely for the nation's socio-political and economic stability, allowing the crew to operate without becoming embroiled in any local turmoil (French Guiana would, however, be used in the closing sequence). Yet another sort of problem arose with the local population—larceny. Theft and pilferage was a constant problem while in Jamaica, with the prop and costuming departments being methodically raided and sets being stripped bare. By the end, a total of $30,000 was lost to thieves alone.[167]

All the while, Dalton Trumbo was hustling to stay a few pages ahead of filming. Every morning, Schaffner would meet with Trumbo in the wee-hours of dawn to make a final run through the pages that would be shot that day, then again that night to see what Trumbo had written during the day. This continued throughout production until they came to the Guajira Indian village sequence, which had been postponed until the end of the shooting schedule, as neither writer nor director could come up with the proper conceptualization that would fit the rest of the film. Said Schaffner: "It was an awkward inclusion in the movie because it was one sequence which every macho male remembers out of the book—go among the heathens…and fuck your way to glory, and you're fed at the same time…Grand!"[168] Furthering the problem is that Papillon cannot speak the native language, and the natives cannot speak his. Trumbo, unfortunately, never got the chance to tackle the dilemma; with about 30 pages left to write, he became ill and had to be transported back to the U.S., where x-rays would reveal cancer in his left lung.

Though a tragedy in itself, this was a particularly bad time to replace a screenwriter, as a Writers Guild strike was on in America. Yet Trumbo was immensely popular and revered among his peers, and many a writer offered their services upon learning of his illness, regardless of the strike. Trumbo had another idea, however, and asked that his son Christopher take over; Christopher Trumbo soon arrived with Schaffner's approval, working uncredited while polishing up a few scenes and taking on the problematic village sequence. The solution was to address the sequence as the fantasy it is: while running through the jungle, Papillon is hit by a poisoned dart, allowing for events to progress in a quasi-hallucinatory sequence without dialogue. "As he has stumbled into paradise, there is no reason why Papillon would want to leave…rather than Papillon leaving the village, the village leaves him."[169] The sequence was also moved from its initial position in the Goldman script in order to balance the film's momentum, making better dramatic sense.

Regardless of complications—many, many complications—the production was far from a disaster. In fact, despite the numerous delays, Schaffner still wrapped a full week ahead of schedule. And every extra day was a blessing, as editor Robert Swink had to get all the footage assembled for the approaching December deadline. But of course, there had to be one last hitch. With Jamaica lacking of any remotely impressive cliffs, the final scene—Papillon's dramatic plunge of escape—was yet to be shot. A search of northern California's shores proved fruitless, and it was now October—time was becoming scant. Finally, an answer came by way of the stuntman hired for the jump, who claimed he knew of an appropriate cliff off the island of Maui. With Schaffner due in Rome in only five days for post-production, a skeleton crew hopped a plane for Hawaii. Bad weather hit the first day there; the winds blew in the wrong direction on the second. Out of time, the leap was finally shot on the third day in less than ideal conditions. Regardless, filming was finally over.

---

[167] Cook, p. 5-6.
[168] Kim, p. 296.
[169] Kim, p. 297.

Papillon was indeed ready for its Christmas release, though the material is hardly the stuff for holidays. Critical reaction at the time of the film's release was considerably harsh, mostly due to the film's somber tone. Stuart Byron called the film "emotionally draining," while Andrew Sarris, in as positive a spin as he could muster, called it "an exhilarating movie [made] out of the most dangerously depressing material." Pauline Kael referred to the film as "a monument to the eternal desire of movie-makers to impress people and win awards."[170] Yet in this case, the audience may have been ahead of the critics. People flocked to see the film, and the picture grossed over $53 million with $22.5 million in rentals in America alone, making it Allied Artists' most successful film ever. And in time, critics warmed up to the picture, ultimately coming to revere *Papillon* as a classic.

TERMINATOR 2: JUDGMENT DAY (1991)
William Whittington

1991 Tri-Star/Carolco Release. A Pacific Western Production in Association with Lightstorm Entertainment. A James Cameron Film. Executive Producers Gale Anne Hurd and Mario Kassar, Co-Producers: B.J. Rack, Stephanie Austin. Written by James Cameron and William Wisher. Produced and Directed by James Cameron. Cinematography Adam Greenberg, A.S.C. Sound Designer Gary Rydstrom. Editors Conrad Buff, Mark Goldblatt, A.C.E., Richard A. Harris. Computer Graphics Images by Industrial Light & Magic. Special Makeup and Terminator Effects Created at Stan Winston Studio.

CAST: Arnold Schwarzenegger, Linda Hamilton, Edward Furlong, Robert Patrick, Joe Morton. MPAA Rating: R. Running time: 137 minutes.

The future is not set. In *Terminator 2: Judgment Day*, Sarah Conner (played by Linda Hamilton) reminds us once again that the battle for the future will be fought in the present. The story of T2 again pits Sarah Conner against the forces of the Cyberdyne Company and its militaristic off-spring the Terminators. This time, however, one Terminator is received as an assassin, the other as a savior. The target is no longer Sarah Conner, but her young son John Conner (played by Edward Furlong), who is destined to become the future leader of the resistance army. The question remains: "Who will reach him first?"

Released in 1991, *T2* was the most expensive film made that year, costing approximately $80 million dollars. In contrast, the original *Terminator*, released by the Hemdale Corporation in 1984, cost a mere $6 million dollars and advanced Arnold Schwarzenegger to another level of world-wide stardom. This original story was written and directed by James Cameron, a former truck driver turned writer-director, whose only other film was *Piranha 2*. Cameron later penned such films as *Rambo*, *Aliens* and *The Abyss* and would go on to direct *Titanic*. Following the

---

[170] Critical reactions taken from Terrill, p. 267.

success of the original *Terminator* (over $80 million in box office receipts), the sequel rights became entangled in a complex web of legal wrangling that took years to resolve. Finally, Carolco bought the rights for over $10 million dollars and financed the sequel.

In terms of casting, the sequel necessitated the return of the original stars. The strength of the first film had relied heavily on the tender love story between Sarah Conner and Kyle Reese (played by Michael Bien); however, the Reese character was killed at the end of the first installment. Obviously, the sequel had to take a different tact. (The Reese character, however, does have a place in the "Special Edition" of the film, returning in a dream sequence.) The two most important casting choices in the production process were of course Arnold Schwarzenegger and Linda Hamilton.

While the first film made Schwarzenegger a media icon, the sequel would make him a rich one. His paycheck was upwards of $15 million dollars, not including his participation in box office receipts and ancillary products (clothing, sunglasses, video games, videos/DVDs/Laser discs). Hamilton would return as well, but her character would transform both physically and emotionally. Prior to the sequel, Hamilton had stared in a highly successful television series *Beauty and the Beast*. For *T2*, she would pump iron for months, preparing for her return as freedom fighter and terminator hunter. Through her physical transformation, the film questions if she has become what she most despises—a Terminator. Joining the cast of the sequel was Joe Morton (as computer genius Miles Dison). Morton is a veteran of many John Sayles films, including a feature role in another well regarded science fiction film *Brother from Another Planet*. Lastly, Edward Furlong in his first film appearance plays the young John Conner, who comes to embody the humanity that his mother has lost.

The costly settling of the sequel rights in 1990 necessitated a quick production turn around and release in the Summer of 1991. The writing of the script by James Cameron and William Wisher lasted less than 8 weeks, an incredibly short period for a major feature. Wisher had done an uncredited re-write on the first film so he knew the material as well as Cameron. Script revisions were also made during the production, which is not uncommon for most Hollywood films. The largest revisions, however, came in the editing process, when large chunks of the film would be paired away for time considerations. There are two special editions of the film which are available on laser disc, which restore this excised material.

Principle photography took place primarily on location and in studios in Southern California and took approximately six months to complete. For one of the key action set pieces, the filmmakers utilized the Renco Investment Company building to double as the high tech Cyberdyne Systems. This glass building would become "a war zone" as Sarah and her companions attempt to alter the future by destroying the research data inside. The explosions and gun fire within this sequence are primarily mechanical effects. However, the helicopter sequence in which a motorcycle crashes through a second story window and propels the T1000 onto the helicopter was achieved through a mix of computer and mechanical effects.

T2 is a seminal film in terms of special effects. It incorporated mechanical effects, computer generated images (CGI) and morphing effects originally developed for the Cameron film *The Abyss*. CGI involves compositing, manipulating and/or creating images within the digital realm without any appreciable loss in quality that is customary with other optical effects processes. Some of the more mundane uses of the technology included removing stunt cables and changing road signs. Morphing technology involves a computer rendering process which allows a seamless transformation between two highly disparate images. This software allows the T-1000 Terminator to mimic another character like Sarah Conner or a prison guard. *T2* clearly ushered Hollywood cinema into the digital era. On close analysis, however, the film utilizes less than 5 minutes of actual computer effects. The remaining effects are constituted through mechanical means, puppets and/or makeup. Examples of these puppet effects include the splitting head sequence and the sequence in which the Schwarzenegger Terminator is riddled with bullets by the police. These mechanical effects were developed by Stan Winston and his team of artists and sculptors.

Post production editing continued up until the final release of the film, primarily to accommodate the special effects shots which required additional time to create. The initial screen time of the film was well over 2 3/4 hours, which was paired down drastically. Key scenes of character development were removed for pace considerations, though these scenes can be seen on special laser disc releases. The longer versions significantly reconfigure the narrative structure, character motivations, and intent of the film.

The sound design of the film took over eight months to prepare. Gary Rydstrom and his team at Skywalker Sound used everything from canned dog food to Burger King shakes to create the complex weave of sounds in the film. Because of the clarity of recording and attention to detail, the sound track is considered one of the best sound mixes in contemporary cinema. Essential to this mix is the music. The mostly rhythmic music score was produced by Brad Fidel, and the primary motifs involves wood and metal percussion. These motifs create a metaphoric contrast between the Terminators and the humans. The film also includes music from Heavy Metal group Guns N' Roses ("You Could be Mine") and also an ironic use of George Thurogood's "Bad to the Bone."

The critical reception of the film was mixed. Many critics felt it was simply a glossy remake of the original without the human element. Still others saw it as exceptional summer movie fare. David Ansen of *Newsweek* wrote: "Thunderously visceral...Some of the most spectacular special effects in eons...Schwarzenegger is impressive, hilarious, almost touching." Not surprisingly, the film did garner Academy Awards for Best Special Effects and Best Sound. The film has grossed $204 million dollars as of January 1997 in domestic sales according to *Daily Variety*. A short 3D sequel to the film was done for the Disney Corporation and is now running at Disney World in Florida and Universal Studios in Los Angeles. Recently, the Hollywood trades noted that half of the sequel rights for *T3* were sold to a producer for approximately $4 million dollars, but James Cameron has said he is not interested in returning to helm the project but will produce. But as Sarah Conner has noted: "The future is not set."

References

Don Shay and Jody Duncan. *T2: The Making of Terminator 2—Judgment Day.* NY: Bantam Books, 1991.

THE SHAWSHANK REDEMPTION (1994)

Chris Cooling

A Columbia Pictures release. Castle Rock Entertainment presents The Shawshank Redemption. *Directed by Frank Darabont. Produced by Niki Marvin. Screenplay by Frank Darabont. Based on the Short Novel "Rita Hayworth and Shawshank Redemption" by Stephen King. Executive Producers Liz Gloster and David Lester. Director of Photography Roger Deakins BSC. Edited by Richard Francis-Bruce. Production Design by Terence Marsh. Costume Design by Elizabeth McBride. Music by Thomas Newman.*

CAST: Tim Robbins (Andy Dufresne), Morgan Freeman (Ellis Boyd "Red" Redding), Bob Gunton (Warden Norton), William Sadler (Heywood), Clancy Brown (Captain Hadley), Gil Bellows (Tommy), James Whitmore (Brooks Hatlen). 142 mins.

When one considers that in the past such films as *Terminator 2: Judgment Day* (1991) and *Waterworld* (1995) have been screened in this class to highlight the complexities of the production process the comparatively quiet, low-budgeted, special-effect and explosion free *The Shawshank Redemption* may appear to be an odd choice. In a way, however, this skepticism is a perfect testament to the film's accomplishments: though it's hard to miss noticing the assured performances and elegant storytelling when watching the film, a number of other elements, both on- and off-screen, are successful precisely because they are meant to go unnoticed. As writer-director Frank Darabont has suggested, for example, *Shawshank*'s production designer, Terence Marsh (a two-time Oscar winner for the far showier *Doctor Zhivago* and *Oliver!*), failed to receive even a nomination for his work here because the Motion Picture Academy assumed he merely found the right prison to shoot in. This is far from the case.

But we're getting a bit ahead of ourselves. Any consideration of *The Shawshank Redemption*'s production process has to begin with Stephen King. Though the words "Stephen King" are by now synonymous with "horror novel," thanks to best-sellers such as "Carrie," "The Dead Zone," and "The Shining," many are unaware of his considerable skills with more character-driven stories. This week's film is adapted from King's "Rita Hayworth and Shawshank Redemption," part of a four-novella collection entitled "Different Seasons." Before *The Shawshank Redemption*, this book was perhaps best known for its inclusion of "The Body," the basis for Rob Reiner's film *Stand By Me* (1986). Given that the unexpected success of that film allowed Reiner to found his own production company, Castle Rock Entertainment (fans of King will recognize the name as a fictional town in Maine where many of his stories are set), it makes perfect serendipitous sense that Frank Darabont ultimately got the chance to direct his first feature film, adapted from the same collection, through the same company.

A self-described "lover of the movies," King's early and rapid success as a novelist made him immensely wealthy, both from the novels themselves and the lucrative movie deals that inevitably followed. As a result he chose to be more casual towards those who wished to adapt his shorter pieces. Student filmmakers pay heed, as he continues this policy today: his asking price for the right to film one of his short stories is one dollar. Frank Darabont was one such student filmmaker; his short version of King's "The Woman in the Room," which aired on PBS in 1983, impressed the author so much that when Darabont expressed interest in "Rita Hayworth and Shawshank Redemption," a similar deal was set in place. Though Darabont had attained some success as a screenwriter in the late 1980s scripting such films as *The Fly II* (1989) and *A Nightmare on Elm Street 3: Dream Warriors* (1987), he sought to break out of the horror genre. And break out he did: in May 1992, he submitted his screenplay for *The Shawshank Redemption* to Castle Rock. Two weeks later he had received a green light and a $25 million budget.

Consider that Rob Reiner's critical and financial success with *Stand By Me* was soon followed by *Misery* (1990), also from a King novel, and for which Kathy Bates won an Academy Award as Best Actress. Further Castle Rock hits such as *When Harry Met Sally...* (1989) and Wolfgang Petersen's *In the Line of Fire* (1993) led to an industry-wide perception of the company as a high-quality 'boutique,' an independent firm that functioned amongst the big studios. At the time, Castle Rock was a division of Columbia Pictures (a subsequent deal with Ted Turner married it into the Time-Warner family), much in the same way that the "indie"-seeming Miramax is ultimately owned by the Disney Corp.

The association of Castle Rock with quality led to *The Shawshank Redemption* becoming a lightning rod for A-list talent during its pre-production phase. Behind the camera were hired such acclaimed professionals as the aforementioned Marsh, costume designer Elizabeth McBride (Oscar nominated in 1989 for *Driving Miss Daisy*), sound mixer Willie Burton (Oscar winner in 1988 for *Bird*), make-up artist Kevin Haney (Oscar winner for *Driving Miss Daisy*), director of photography Roger Deakins, BSC (who won a special award from the American Society of Cinematographers for his work on *The Shawshank Redemption*), and composer Thomas Newman (*Scent of a Woman*). In addition to stars Morgan Freeman and Tim Robbins, Brad Pitt was cast in the role of Tommy Williams until scheduling problems caused him to be replaced. The rest of the cast was fleshed out with dependable character actors such as Clancy Brown (*Shoot to Kill*), William Sadler (*Die Hard 2*) and screen veteran James Whitmore (Oscar nominated for his one-man film, *Give'em Hell, Harry!*).

While the cast was assembled by Casting Director Deborah Aquila, Terence Marsh embarked on a five-month search to find an appropriately gloomy gothic setting to serve as the eponymous site of redemption. The abandoned Ohio State Reformatory was ultimately chosen, and nearby Mansfield became the town in which the remainder of the film was shot (except for a brief trip to the U.S. Virgin Islands). In use from 1896 to 1990, the state of disrepair into which the Mansfield Reformatory had fallen presented a considerable challenge to Marsh and his team, who quickly set about restoring and modifying the complex to suit their needs. In effect, the Reformatory became a fully functioning studio devoted to a single movie, as Marsh had to "convert several spaces inside the institution into working set pieces for the film." Sets built inside the prison include: the library; the infirmary, for which the prison's original hospital was restored; the mess hall, originally a visiting room; the Warden's office, and the Brewster Hotel interior, both of which were built in the original administrative wing.

Surprisingly, a key feature of the building not used in the film were its cells, as their implacable solidity made them impractical for filming. Noted Marsh, "they are stone and steel, five-by-seven feet. You cannot pull out walls and get cameras and microphones in, so we basically had to build them to tell our story." The cellblock as it appears on-screen was created in a warehouse about a mile from the actual prison; though steel was used for the doors and staircases, the rest was little more than plywood and fiberglass. The original cells were not completely useless, however: their toilets, sinks, cots and tables were used as set dressing in each new cell. In the words of Construction Coordinator Sebastian Milito, "a lot of detail was used to make [the set] not look like what it is—a pile of wood."

A similarly mammoth undertaking designed to achieve unnoticeable authenticity was met by the costume department, which produced over 900 convict uniforms. Each pair of hand-cut jeans was put through a stone-wash cycle, to fade them. In other cases, members of McBride's team would rub the costumes with sandpaper in order to break them in.

Diligent 190 students, who stay to the end of a film's credit sequence, are probably familiar with the ubiquitous declaration of the American Humane Association, "No Animal Was Harmed In The Making Of This Film." Even the earning of this statement proved to be a challenge for the Shawshank production team. A representative was on hand to closely observe all scenes involving Brooks' pet crow, Jake. Though the crow was handled with the utmost care, the AHA was unwilling to condone its being fed a live maggot on film: to kill even a single maggot would prevent the filmmakers from displaying the association's endorsement. To avoid potential bad press, the production was delayed while crew members found a maggot that had died of natural causes.

Much of the post-production process for *The Shawshank Redemption* consisted of reducing it to a manageable length, often by excising scenes that had read well in both the novella and the script, but simply did not translate to film. A lengthy comic sequence involving a guard's investigation of a tunnel, and subsequent fall into a pool of human filth, was dropped for reasons of dramatic pacing. The compelling opening credit sequence, in which Andy flashes back to his wife's death while on trial for her murder, was devised in the editing room: Darabont's original opening presented the two moments as separate, lengthier scenes.

Upon its release in September 1994, even the film's most passionate defenders, of which there were many, cited the film's length as one of its only flaws. One must naturally take this criticism with a grain of salt, as the film cannot succeed without convincingly portraying the despair and seeming endlessness of prison life. Aside from this question of length, *The Shawshank Redemption* was almost universally praised by critics, with special attention given to the lead performances and Darabont's work as a writer-director.

Surprisingly, however, the film was something of a box office disappointment, making only $28.3 million in North America and a dismal $4.8 million upon its worldwide release. Nevertheless, the film's critical success resulted in an impressive seven Oscar nominations: Best Actor - Morgan Freeman, Best Cinematography, Best Original Score, Best Sound, Best Adapted Screenplay, Best Editing, and Best Picture. The film was re-released in February 1995 to capitalize on this attention with a new poster campaign. The original image of Robbins facing up into the rain was now dwarfed by a massive list of the film's achievements, such as award nominations, appearances on top ten lists, quotes from rave reviews, and so on. Again, few turned out.

Crushed at the box office upon its release by the huge opening of *Pulp Fiction*, *The Shawshank Redemption* was doomed to be caught between Tarantino's film and *Forrest Gump* in the subsequent Oscar race, winning in none of its categories. All of this is not to say, however, that the film had no impact on the industry. Thomas Newman's stirring score led to his joining the A-list of film composers, and the film's theme often appears in trailers for other movies. After winning the USC Scripter Award in 1995, Frank Darabont became a highly-paid script doctor, working on such films as *Eraser* (1996), *The Fan* (1996), and *Saving Private Ryan* (1998). His second feature film, *The Green Mile* (1999), is one of the most highly anticipated films of the upcoming winter season. Once again, the film is a Castle Rock production based on a Stephen King story; indeed, it is even set in a prison. Starring Tom Hanks, the new film will likely prove to be more of a financial success than Darabont's first. Perhaps it will inspire people to continue discovering *The Shawshank Redemption* on videotape. After all, to paraphrase Andy Dufresne, like hope, the film is a good thing, amongst the best of things, and no good thing ever dies.

Sources:

Darabont, Frank. *The Shawshank Redemption: The Shooting Script*. New York: Newmarket Press, 1996.

Hruska, Bronwen. "Two Pros and Countless Cons." *Entertainment Weekly* (Sep. 30, 1994): 34.

10
GENRE: CLASSICAL PHASE

Thus genre can be seen as a form of social ritual. Implicit in this viewpoint is the notion that these ritual forms contribute to what might be called a contemporary American mythology. In a genuine 'national cinema' like that developed in Hollywood, with its mass appeal and distribution, with its efforts to project an idealized cultural self-image, and with its reworking of popular stories, it seems not only reasonable but necessary that we seriously consider the status of commercial filmmaking as a form of contemporary mythmaking.

—Thomas Schatz, 1981

CTCS 190 LECTURE OUTLINE – WEEK X   **LECTURE 9**

PART 1: THE CLASSICAL PERIOD: 1929-1945

   A. Definition of Genre
      1. Content/form distinction
      2. Myths, conventions, and iconography as constituents of a genre
   B. Film Genres
      1. Tragedy
      2. Comedy
      3. Melodrama
      4. Boundaries between genres
      5. Genre as aesthetically neutral
      6. Review of films screened in class as examples of genre
   C. Historical Overview of Genre in American Film
      1. 1895-1928 – The Silent Period: the codification of genres
      2. 1929-1945 – The Classical Period: the crystallization of genres
      3. 1946-1962 – The Postclassical Period: the breaking up of genres
      4. 1963-1976 – The Modernist Period: the explosion of genres
      5. 1977-present – The Postmodernist Period: the revision of genres
   D. Conditions and Causes for Genre in American Film
      1. Financial
      2. Aesthetic
      3. Global sensibility
   E. Implications of Genre
      1. Genre as comforter, confirmer, and instiller of hope/optimism
      2. Genre as "sugar-coating the pill"
      3. Genre as cultural myth
      4. Genre as ritual
      5. Genre as formative influence on the production and consumption of a film text
   F. Genre as a Dynamic System
   G. Case Study of a Genre Film in its Classical Phase: myths, conventions, iconography
   H. Relationship of genre and mode of representation
   I. Introduction and Screening of a Genre Film in its Classical Phase

Notes

Notes

HOLLYWOOD GENRES (excerpts)

Thomas Schatz, 1981

THE GENIUS OF THE SYSTEM

> *Whenever a motion picture becomes a work of art it is unquestionably due to men. But the moving pictures have been born and bred not of men but of corporations. Corporations have set up the easels, bought the pigments, arranged the views, and hired the potential artists. Until the artists emerge, at least, the corporation is bigger than the sum of its parts. Somehow, although our poets have not yet defined it for us, a corporation lives a life and fads a fate outside the lives and fates of its human constituents.*

> —Fortune magazine, December 1932[171]

> *Paradoxically, the supporters of the politique des auteurs[172] admire the American cinema, where the restrictions of production are heavier than anywhere else. It is also true that it is the country where the greatest technical possibilities are offered to the director. But the one does not cancel out the other. I do, however, admit that freedom is greater in Hollywood than it is said to be, as long as one knows how to detect its manifestations, and I will go so far as to say that the tradition of genres is a base of operations for creative freedom. The American cinema is a classical art, but why not then admire in it what is most admirable, i.e. not only the talent of this or that filmmaker, but the genius of the system.*

> —André Bazin[173]

The studio system

François Truffaut, French critic turned filmmaker, recently suggested that "when a film achieves a certain success, it becomes a sociological event, and the question of its quality

---

[171] The *Fortune* magazine excerpt is from a report on the Metro-Goldwyn-Mayer studio. Reprinted in Tino Balio, *The American Film Industry* (Madison: University of Wisconsin Press, 1976), p. 263.
[172] The "auteur policy," which held that certain film directors should be considered the "authors" of their films.
[173] André Bazin's "La politique des auteurs" essay appeared originally as an editorial in *Cahiers du Cinema* in 1957, and is reprinted in Peter Graham's anthology, *The New Wave* (London: Secker and Warburg, 1968), p. 154.

becomes secondary"[174] (Truffaut, 1972). The success of a film may or may not depend upon its artistic quality—and this is a bone of critical contention which forever will separate elitists like John Simon from populists like Pauline Kael. But in the final analysis any film's quality, itself based upon subjective critical consensus, is incidental to the *fact* of its social and economic impact. Truffaut's observation would seem to coincide, interestingly enough, with the U.S. Supreme Court's 1915 decision that "the exhibition of motion pictures is a business pure and simple, originated and conducted for profit." Both Truffaut and the Supreme Court have recognized a fundamental tenet of commercial filmmaking: producers may not know much about art, but they know what sells and how to systematically deliver more of the same. If what the producer delivers happens to be evaluated critically as art, so much the better.

Essentially, the function of the Hollywood production companies always has been to create what Truffaut termed sociological events. In their continual efforts to reach as massive an audience as possible, early filmmakers investigated areas of potential audience appeal and, at the same time, standardized those areas whose appeal already had been verified by audience response. In the gradual development of the business of movie production, experimentation steadily gave way to standardization as a matter of fundamental economics. Between 1915 and 1930 the studios had standardized, hence economized, virtually every aspect of film production[175] (Balio, 1976). Because of this heavy regimentation, the studios of Hollywood's "classic" era (roughly 1930 to 1960) have been referred to as factory production systems. The analogy is not without basis in actual industry practice: the "studio system" functioned to mass produce and mass distribute movies. This is considerably different from the "New Hollywood," where the studios function primarily as distribution companies—that is, they distribute films which, for the most part, are produced independently.

Until the '50s, the major studios (MGM, Twentieth Century-Fox, Warner Brothers, Paramount, RKO) not only made motion pictures, but they also leased them through their own distribution companies to theaters which they themselves controlled. Although the "majors"—along with significant "minors" like Columbia, Universal-International, Republic, and Monogram—never controlled more than one sixth of all movie theaters in the United States, they did control most of the important "first-run" houses. In the mid-'40s, when Hollywood's audience was at its peak, the five majors owned or controlled the operations of 126 of the 163 first-run theaters in the nation's twenty-five largest cities. Not only did the audiences attending these theaters provide the bulk of revenue for the studios, but they also determined the general trends of studio production and cinematic expression. The U.S. Supreme Court dismantled this monopolistic "vertical structure" in 1948, after ten years of court battles with Paramount. This was one of the key factors, along with the advent of television and other cultural developments, in the eventual "death" of the studio system. By this time, however, Hollywood had read the pulse of its popular audience in developing an engaging and profitable means of narrative cinematic expression—the conventions of feature filmmaking were firmly established.

Thus the artist and the industrialist were cast into a necessary and highly productive relationship—each one struggling with but also depending upon the other for the success of their commercial art. While filmmakers learned to adapt their own and their audience's narrative impulse to the demands of the medium, businessmen learned to exploit the medium's capacity for widespread dissemination and consumption. While filmmakers advanced narrative traditions developed in drama and literature, producers and exhibitors advanced the commercial potential anticipated by previous forms of mass entertainment. So by the time the movie industry had standardized the feature-length narrative film by the late 'teens, the medium's mixed heritage was fairly obvious. The movies had their roots in both classic

---

[174] François Truffaut, "A Kind Word for Critics," *Harpers* (October 1972), p. 100
[175] Descriptions and histories of the Hollywood studios' birth, development, and eventual death can be found in various sources, the most comprehensive being Balio, *The American Film Industry*.

literature and bestselling pulp romances, in legitimate theater as well as vaudeville and music halls, in traditions of both "serious art" and American "popular entertainment."[176]

The contemporary mass audience, ultimately, is in good part responsible for the development of the studio system—the same audience whose leisure time and spending money became, in social historian Arnold Hauser's words, "a decisive factor in the history of art"[177] (Hauser, 1951, p. 250). By its attraction to the cinema, this audience encouraged mass distribution of movies, as well as an adherence to filmmaking conventions. Feature filmmaking, like most mass media production, is an expensive enterprise. Those who invest their capital, from the major studio to the struggling independent, are in a curious bind: on the one hand, their product must be sufficiently inventive to attract attention and satisfy the audience's demand for novelty, and on the other hand, they must protect their initial investment by relying to some extent upon established conventions that have been proven through previous exposure and repetition.

We should note here that in film production—and in virtually any popular art form—a successful product is bound up in convention because its success inspires repetition. The built-in "feedback" circuits of the Hollywood system ensured this repetition of successful stories and techniques, because the studios' production-distribution-exhibition system enabled filmmakers to gauge their work against audience response. It is as if with each commercial effort, the studios suggested another variation on cinematic conventions, and the audience indicated whether the inventive variations would themselves be conventionalized through their repeated usage.

We should also note that this is a *reciprocal* relationship between artist and audience. The filmmaker's inventive impulse is tempered by his or her practical recognition of certain conventions and audience expectations; the audience demands creativity or variation but only within the context of a familiar narrative experience. As with any such experience it is difficult for either artist or audience to specify precisely what elements of an artistic event they are responding to. Consequently, filmic conventions have been refined through considerable variation and repetition. In this context, it is important to remember that roughly 400 to 700 movies were released *per year* during Hollywood's classic era, and that the studios depended increasingly upon established story formulas and techniques. Thus any theory of Hollywood filmmaking must take into account this essential process of production, feedback, and conventionalization.

The studio system's role in the evolution of narrative filmmaking was considerable, in terms of its national and international popularity and, more importantly, in its systematic honing of filmic expression into effective narrative conventions. The international film market fluctuated throughout the studio era due to the Depression and the war, but conservative estimates indicate that Hollywood products occupied anywhere from 70 to 90 percent of the available screen time in most European and Latin American countries. In addition, the Motion Picture Association of America's "classification of subject matter" for the year 1950 indicates that over 60 percent of all Hollywood productions that year were either Westerns (27%), crime/detective

---

[176] Distinctions among various levels of cultural expression (elite, popular, mass, folk, and so on) are treated most effectively in: Russell Nye, *The Unembarrassed Muse* (New York: Dial Press, 1970); George H. Lewis, *Side-Saddle on the Golden Calf* (Pacific Palisades, Cal.: Goodyear Publishing Co., Inc., 1972); and Stuart Hall and Paddy Whennel, *The Popular Arts* (Boston: Beacon Press, 1964). See also Dwight MacDonald's seminal essay, "A Theory of Mass Culture," in Bernard Rosenberg and David Manning White's anthology, *Mass Culture: The Popular Arts in America* (New York: The Free Press, 1964). See also Walter Benjamin's "Art in the Age of Mechanical Reproduction," in Gerald Mast and Marshall Cohen's anthology, *Film Theory and Criticism* (New York: Oxford University Press, 1974).
[177] Arnold Hauser, *The Social History of Art*, Vol. IV: *Naturalism, Impressionism, and the Film Age* (New York: Vintage Books, 1951), p. 250.

films (20%), romantic comedies (11%), or musicals (4%), and that roughly 90 percent fell into some preestablished classification—mystery/spy, war, etc.[178] (Sterling and Haight, 1978).

The implications of these data are twofold. First, Hollywood's domination of not only national but international production and distribution suggests that its influence extended well beyond the United States. Second, and even more significantly, the Hollywood imprint generally involved not only isolated production techniques and narrative devices, but established story types or "genres" like the Western or the musical. And these genres have in turn traveled well—think of what Italy's "spaghetti Westerns," Japan's samurai films, or the French New Wave's hardboiled detective films owe to genres developed by the Hollywood studio system.

The genre film and the genre director

Simply stated, a genre film—whether a Western or a musical, a screwball comedy or a gangster film—involves familiar, essentially one-dimensional characters acting out a predictable story pattern within a familiar setting. During the reign of the studio system, genre films comprised the vast majority of the most popular and profitable productions, and this trend has continued even after its death. In contrast, non-genre films tended to attract greater critical attention during the studio era—films like John Ford's *The Grapes of Wrath*, Charlie Chaplin's *Monsieur Verdoux*, Billy Wilder's *The Lost Weekend*, and Jean Renoir's *Diary of a Chambermaid*.

These and other non-genre films generally traced the personal and psychological development of a "central character" or protagonist. The central characters are not familiar types whom we've seen before in movies (like the gangster, the music man, the Westerner). Rather, they are unique individuals whom we relate to less in terms of previous filmic experience than in terms of our own "real-world" experiences. The plot in non-genre films does not progress through conventional conflicts toward a predictable resolution (as with the gangster dead in the gutter, the climactic musical show). Instead it develops a *linear* plot in which the various events are linked in a chronological chain and organized by the central character's own perceptual viewpoint. The plot resolution generally occurs when the significance of the protagonist's experiences—of the "plot line"—becomes apparent to that character or to the audience, or to both.

Non-genre films represent a limited portion of Hollywood's productions, and as we might expect, many were directed by foreign-born filmmakers like Wilder and Renoir. But equally significant are those foreign directors who adapted so effectively to Hollywood's genre-based system, as shown, for example, in Fritz Lang's Westerns and crime films, Ernst Lubitsch's musicals and romantic comedies, and Douglas Sirk's and Max Ophuls' social melodramas.

Actually, the dependence of certain premiere American directors upon established film genres is equally significant and just as often overlooked. Whether we discuss Griffith's melodramas, Keaton's slapstick comedy, Ford's Westerns, or Minnelli's musicals, we are treating Hollywood directors whose reputations as artists, as creative filmmakers, are based upon their work within popular genres. As the studio era recedes into American film history, it becomes increasingly evident that most of the recognized American *auteur* directors did their most expressive and significant work within highly conventionalized forms.

The auteur *policy*

Even with this reservation, we certainly cannot dismiss the *"auteur* policy," the single most productive concept in film study over the past quarter century, although we should be aware of

---

[178] Statistics on motion picture production, distribution, exhibition, and consumption are available in Christopher H. Sterling and Timothy R. Haight's invaluable source work, *The Mass Media: Aspen Institute Guide to Communication Industry Trends* (New York: Praeger Publishers, 1978).

its limitations as well as its assets.[179] The notion of directorial authorship—that the director is the controlling creative force and hence *potentially* the "author" of his films—is a necessary and logical critical approach. Anyone who discussed "the Lubitsch touch" in the '30s or anticipated the next "Hitchcock thriller" in the '40s was, in fact, practicing this critical approach.

Originally, the *auteur* approach was formalized by a group of critics—among them François Truffaut, Eric Rohmer, and Jean-Luc Godard—writing for the French film journal *Cahiers du Cinema*. Working throughout the 1950s under editor André Bazin, the *Cahiers* critics fashioned the "*auteur* policy" (*la politique des auteurs*) as an alternative to content-oriented, plot-theme analyses of movies. Significantly, the *auteur* policy was developed not to treat foreign filmmakers who had a great deal of control over their productions. Rather, the policy was designed to reconsider those Hollywood directors who, despite the constraints of the studio system, were able to instill a *personal style* into their work.

In order to understand the artistry of commercial filmmaking, argued the *auteur* critics, we must complement the dominant critical concern for a film's "subject matter" with more subtle consideration of visual style, camerawork, editing, and the various other factors which make up the director's "narrative voice." Alfred Hitchcock once said that he is "less interested in stories than in the manner of telling them"[180] (Sadoul, 1972, p. 117). *Auteur* analysis is, in effect, a formalized critical response to this particular conception of filmmaking.

As the *auteur* policy was refined and eventually introduced to English and American critics by Andrew Sarris and others, the Hollywood film industry underwent a steady revaluation. The reputations of directors like Hitchcock and Minnelli, who had been dismissed by many American critics because they worked in such lowbrow forms, were substantially reconsidered. In addition, a number of directors, who somehow had escaped the attention of American critics (Howard Hawks is a prime example), now were recognized as major filmmakers, along with many other exceptional stylists who had directed low-budget "B" productions (Sam Fuller, Anthony Mann, and others). Even the esteem of a widely heralded director like John Ford, whose popular and critical reputation had long been established, underwent a critical revaluation that reflected a basic reconsideration of Hollywood filmmaking. *Auteur* critics argued persuasively that Ford's genre films—war movies like *They Were Expendable* and Westerns like *The Searchers* and *The Man Who Shot Liberty Valance*—demonstrated a stylistic richness and thematic ambiguity that made them artistically superior to the calculated artistry and social consciousness of "serious" Ford films like *The Informer* and *The Grapes of Wrath*.

Experience had taught the *auteur* critics that, because of the popular and industrial nature of commercial filmmaking, the serious film artist often comes in through the back door. Too often "serious social drama" in the cinema is less serious, less genuinely social, and certainly less dramatic than the supposed "escapist entertainment" fare of a Ford Western or a Minnelli musical or a Hitchcock thriller. *Auteur* critics, in acknowledging the popular and industrial demands placed upon filmmakers, rejected the artificial distinctions between art and enter-

---

[179] A reasonably comprehensive survey of the *auteur* policy can be gleaned from the following sources:
—Alexandre Astruc, "La camera stylo," and André Basin, "La politique des auteurs," both of which are reprinted in Graham, *The New Wave*.
—special sections devoted to film authorship generally and the *auteur* theory specifically in three anthologies: Mast and Cohen's *Film Theory and Criticism* (op. cit.); *Movies and Methods*, Bill Nichols, ed. (Berkeley: University of California Press, 1976); *Awake in the Dark*, David Denby, ed. (New York: Vintage Books, 1977).
—of the countless studies devoted to individual directors, I find these particularly useful: Andrew Sarris, *The American Cinema* (New York: E. P. Dutton and Co., 1968); Georges Sadoul, *Dictionary of Film Makers* (Berkeley: University of California Press, 1972); several monographs in the "Cinema One" series published by the British Film Institute and *Sight and Sound* in conjunction with either Viking or the Indiana University Press, including Robin Wood's *Howard Hawks* (1968), Geoffrey Nowell-Smith's *Visconti* (1967), Jim Kitses' *Horizons West* (1969), Jon Halliday's *Sirk on Sirk* (1971), Joseph McBride's *Orson Welles* (1972). See also Robin Wood, *Hitchcock's Films* (New York: Castle Books, 1965); Joseph McBride and Michael Wilmington, *John Ford* (New York: De Capo Press, Inc., 1974), which nicely complements Peter Bogdonovich's analysis-cum-interview, also titled *John Ford* (Berkeley: University of California Press, 1968).
[180] Sadoul, *Dictionary of Film Makers*, p. 117.

tainment, and thus they signaled a substantial evolution in the way people—filmmakers, viewers, and critics alike—thought about movies.

In retrospect, it seems quite logical that *auteur* and genre criticism would dominate Hollywood film study. These two critical methods do complement and counterbalance one another in that genre criticism treats established cinematic forms, whereas *auteur* criticism celebrates certain filmmakers who worked effectively within those forms. Both approaches reflect an increased critical sensitivity to the penchant for conventionalization in commercial filmmaking. In fact the *auteur* approach, in asserting a director's consistency of form and expression, effectively translates an *auteur* into a virtual genre unto himself, into a system of conventions which identify his work. And further, the director's consistency, like the genre's, is basic to the economic and material demands of the medium and to his popularity with a mass audience. As John Ford, who himself considered film directing "always a job of work," once suggested: "For a director there are commercial rules that it is necessary to obey. In our profession, an artistic failure is nothing; a commercial failure is a sentence. The secret is to make films that please the public and also allow the director to reveal his personality"[181] (Sadoul, 1972, p. 89).

One of the essential attributes of *auteur* analysis is its structural approach: Its method is to uncover the "deep structure" (the directorial personality) in order to interpret and evaluate the "surface structure" (his or her movies). The socioeconomic imperatives of Hollywood filmmaking, however, indicate that there are a number of deep structures—industrial, political, technical, stylistic, narrative, and so on—which inform the production process. Further, when we consider a director working within an established genre we are faced with another, even "deeper," structure than that of the director's personality. The genre's preestablished cultural significance in effect determines the range and substance of any one director's expressive treatment of that genre.

That one director's treatment is more effective than another's motivates the film critic, who examines the filmmaker's manipulation and variation of formal, narrative, and thematic conventions. Generally, and especially regarding a director working within a well-developed genre, the knowledgeable critic must distinguish between the director's and the genre's contribution to a film's expressive quality. In examining Sam Peckinpah's *The Wild Bunch*, for example, one must be familiar with the history of the Western and with Peckinpah's career in order to determine how he has reinvented the genre's conventions.

Analyzing a genre director's work, which has grown along with a genre, represents an even more difficult critical challenge. Consider John Ford, who began directing silent, two-reel Westerns in 1917 and continued to produce the most popular and significant films within the genre until the early 1960s. And what of a director like Alfred Hitchcock, who in a sense "invented" the psychological thriller and who completely dominated that genre from the late 1920s through the 1960s? We will discuss these issues in later chapters, but for now they can stand as open questions that indicate the complexity involved in criticizing Hollywood genre films.

The studio production system itself, designed for the variations-on-a-theme approach characteristic of genre filmmaking, is at the very heart of this critical dilemma. Because of the practical budgetary problems of set design, scriptwriting, and so forth, the studios encouraged the development of film genres. Obviously, costs could be minimized by repeating successful formulas. Box-office returns alone provided sufficient criteria for continued genre production; the studios clearly need not understand *why* certain narratives appealed to viewers. They only required assurance that the appeal indeed existed and could be exploited financially. Thus, many aspects of studio production were refined to accommodate genre filmmaking: the "stables" of writers and technical crews whose work was limited to certain types of films; the studio sets

---

[181] *Ibid.*, p. 89.

and sound stages designed for specific genres; even the "star system," which capitalized upon the familiar, easily categorized qualities of individual performers. (Try to imagine, for instance, a passionate kiss between John Wayne and Ginger Rogers. It just doesn't work, essentially because of the close connections between a star's screen persona and his or her status as a generic convention.)

Genre and narrative conventions

As this example indicates, any genre's *narrative context* imbues its conventions with meaning. This meaning in turn determines their use in individual films. In general, the commercial cinema is identifiable by formal and narrative elements common to virtually all its products: the Hollywood movie is a story of a certain length focusing upon a protagonist (a hero, a central character); and it involves certain standards of production, a style of ("invisible") editing, the use of musical score, and so on. The genre film, however, is identified not only by its use of these general filmic devices to create an imaginary world; it is also significant that this world is predetermined and essentially intact. The narrative components of a non-genre film—the characters, setting, plot, techniques, etc.—assume their significance as they are integrated into the individual film itself. In a genre film, however, these components have prior significance as elements of some generic formula, and the viewer's negotiation of a genre film thus involves weighing the film's variations against the genre's preordained, value-laden narrative system.

An example of this process may be seen in a conventional gunfight in a Western film. Everything—from the characters' dress, demeanor, and weapons to their standing in the dirt street of an American frontier community—assumes a significance beyond the film's immediate narrative concerns. This significance is based on the viewer's familiarity with the "world" of the genre itself rather than on his or her own world. As Robert Warshow observed in his analysis of the gangster genre, "it is only in the ultimate sense that the type appeals to the audience's experience of reality; much more immediately, it appeals to the previous experience of the type itself; it creates its own field of reference"[182] (Warshow, 1962, p. 130). It is not their mere repetition which endows generic elements with a prior significance, but their repetition within a conventionalized formal, narrative, and thematic context. If it is initially a popular success, a film story is reworked in later movies and repeated until it reaches its equilibrium profile—until it becomes a spatial, sequential, and thematic pattern of familiar actions and relationships. Such a repetition is generated by the interaction of the studios and the mass audience, and it will be sustained so long as it satisfies the needs and expectations of the audience and remains financially viable for the studios.

Genre as a social force

Any viewer's familiarity with a genre is the result of a *cumulative process*, of course. The first viewing of a Western or musical actually might be more difficult and demanding than the viewing of a non-genre film, due to the peculiar logic and narrative conventions of the genre. With repeated viewings, however, the genre's narrative pattern comes into focus and the viewer's *expectations* take shape. And when we consider that the generic pattern involves not only narrative elements (character, plot, setting) but thematic issues as well, the genre's *socializing* influence becomes apparent.

Moreover, in examining film genres, these popular narratives whose plots, characters, and themes are refined through usage in a mass medium, we are considering a form of artistic expression which involves the audience more directly than any traditional art form had ever done before. There are earlier forms that anticipated this development, especially performative arts such as Greek or Renaissance drama. However, not until the invention of the printing press and then the popularization of dime novels, pulp literature, and Beadle books (named for their

---

[182] Robert Warshow, *The Immediate Experience* (Garden City, N.Y.: Doubleday and Co., Inc., 1962), p. 130.

publisher, Erastus Beadle) did the social and economic implications of popular narrative formulas begin to take shape. Henry Nash Smith considered these implications in his evocative study of America's "Western myth," entitled *The Virgin Land*. Smith is especially interested in the creative posture assumed by individual pulp writers who produced and reproduced popular Western tales for an eager, impressionable audience. Smith's fundamental thesis is that these authors participated, with their publishers and audience, in the creative celebration of the values and ideals associated with westward expansion, thereby engendering and sustaining the Western myth. He contends that the pulp writer is not pandering to his market by lowering himself to the level of the mass audience, but rather that he or she is cooperating with it in formulating and reinforcing collective values and ideals. "Fiction produced under these circumstances virtually takes on the character of automatic writing," Smith suggests. "Such work tends to become an objectified mass dream, like the moving pictures, soap operas, or comic books that are the present-day equivalents of the Beadle stories. The individual writer abandons his own personality and identifies himself with his readers"[183] (Smith, 1950, p. 91).

There have, of course, been pulp novelists like James Fenimore Cooper and Zane Grey, just as there have been genre directors like John Ford and Sam Peckinpah, who used exceptional formal and expressive artistry in Western storytelling and whose writing seems anything but automatic. In underscoring the relationship of pulp Western novels to a mass audience and hence to American folklore, however, Smith's study adds an important dimension to our discussion. He suggests that these novels were written not only for the mass audience, but *by* them as well. Produced by depersonalized representatives of the collective, anonymous public and functioning to celebrate basic beliefs and values, their formulas might be regarded not only as popular or even elite art but also as *cultural ritual*—as a form of collective expression seemingly obsolete in an age of mass technology and a genuinely "silent majority."

This view of the nature and function of popular narrative artistry has been extended, predictably enough, into the realm of commercial filmmaking, where many of the same principles apply. In fact, André Bazin's "La politique des *auteurs*" essay was conceived as a warning to *auteur* critics that they look at the many other aspects of filmmaking besides directing that contribute to the authorship of any individual movie. Bazin suggests:

> *What makes Hollywood so much better than anything else in the world is not only the quality of certain directors, but also the vitality and, in a certain sense, the excellence of a tradition. Hollywood's superiority is only incidentally technical; it lies much more in what one might call the American cinematic genius, something which should be analyzed, then defined, by a sociological approach to its production. The American cinema has been able, in an extraordinarily competent way, to show American society just as it wanted to see itself. (1968, pp. 142-143)*[184]

The basis for this viewpoint is the level of *active but indirect audience participation* in the formulation of any popular commercial form. And that participation is itself a function of the studio system's repeating and handing down, with slight variation, those stories that the audience has isolated through its collective response.

It should be mentioned that because of the narrow range of distribution and the limited audience feedback involved in the nineteenth century, the pulp author's degree of cooperation with his or her audience was quite different from that of the Hollywood filmmaker.[185] Furthermore, the dime pulp or bestselling novel is the product of an individual consciousness and is communicated through a personal medium of expression. The Hollywood genre film,

[183] Henry Nash Smith, *The Virgin Land* (Cambridge, Mass.: Harvard University Press, 1950), p. 91.
[184] Bazin, in Graham, *The New Wave*, pp. 142–143.
[185] Smith mentions this fact.

conversely, is both produced and consumed collectively. We are dealing here with the studio system over a period of sustained and widespread popular success, from the early years of the sound film through the gradual relinquishing, after some four decades, of the studios and their production system to the commercial television industry. These are the years before American filmmakers began to appeal, as they have tended to more recently, to a specialized market or age group. The Hollywood studios and the genre film had their heyday simultaneously—and this is no coincidence—when films were seen as mass entertainment by a general public who regularly (one might even say religiously) went "to the movies" in numbers peaking in the mid- to late-40's at 90 million viewers per week.

Before examining genre filmmaking as a form of collective cultural expression, however, we should acknowledge that certain commercial and technological aspects of the cinema qualify this approach. Dwight MacDonald in his "Theory of Mass Culture" posits "the essential quality of Mass, as against High or Folk, Culture: it is manufactured for mass consumption by technicians employed by the ruling class and is not an expression of the individual artist or the common people themselves"[186] (MacDonald, in Rosenberg and White, 1964). From this viewpoint, even Shakespeare is more a technician than an individual artist. Nevertheless, MacDonald's observations do encourage us to avoid any simplistic association of commercial filmmaking with either elite or folk expression.

Just as we must temper our view of the cinematic *auteur* by acknowledging the depersonalizing production system in which he or she works, so too must we temper our view of the genre film as a kind of secular, contemporary cultural ritual. The cinema's commercial feedback system rarely affords the audience any direct or immediate creative input. Rather it allows it to affect future variations by voicing collective approval or disapproval of a current film. Such a response has a cumulative effect, first isolating and then progressively refining a film story into a familiar narrative pattern. As Robert Warshow observes in his study of the gangster genre: "For such a type to be successful means that its conventions have imposed themselves upon the general consciousness and become accepted vehicles of a particular set of attitudes and a particular aesthetic effect. One goes to any individual example of the type with very definite expectations, and originality is accepted only in the degree that it intensified the expected experience without fundamentally altering it"[187] (Warshow, 1962, p. 130).

In a limited sense, any genre film is the original creation of an individual writer or director, but the nature and range of that originality are determined by the conventions and expectations involved in the genre filmmaking process. Thus, any critical analysis of that originality must be based firmly on an understanding of both the genre and the production system in which any individual genre film is generated. Ultimately, we need to complement elitist critical attitudes with a broader, more culturally and industrially responsive approach. In a certain sense, this approach could be dismissed as simply a formulation of a populist "low art" bias to offset elitist "high art" biases in film study. I hope, however, that the value of the ideas developed in this book will be realized in their application, and not in the context of critical debate. Whatever one's objections to *auteurism*, the fact remains that close analysis of certain directors' movies, along with detailed study of their directing methods, does validate the *auteur* policy as something more than merely a critical bias—it does reveal some fundamental truth about filmmaking and film art. So too should a genre approach, when applied sensibly and with care, reveal some essential truths about commercial filmmaking that will enrich our understanding and appreciation of cinematic art.

---

[186] Dwight MacDonald, *op. cit.*, p. 60.
[187] Warshow, *op. cit.*, p. 130.

FILM GENRES AND THE GENRE FILM

> I really want to go back to film school.... Or maybe I'll get my masters in anthropology. That's what movies are about anyway. Cultural imprints.
>
> —Writer-director George Lucas, discussing *Star Wars*[188]

Thus far, we have been considering those qualities of Hollywood filmmaking which determine its status as a commercial art form. Our consideration of those qualities led us to the hypothesis that popular cinematic story formulas—or film genres express the social and aesthetic sensibilities not only of Hollywood filmmakers but of the mass audience as well.

In many ways, this view of contemporary commercial art resists the elitist critical assumption that the artwork carries an asocial, terminal value—that the artwork is an end in itself, somehow disengaged from the mundane trappings of its initial sociocultural environment. The academic or scholarly context in which we generally are exposed to the high arts tends to support this bias, simply because we do study traditional artworks with little concern for the social imperatives involved in their creation. We presume that aesthetic objects do in fact "transcend" the culture in which they were produced, primarily because of their significance for us as members of a modern technocratic society. Our appreciation of Homer's epic poetry, Shakespeare's drama, or Dickens' novels is only marginally related, if at all, to the traditions of oral history, of the Elizabethan popular theater, or of the serialized pulp romances in which those works participated. The historical "gatekeeping" function of aesthetic tradition has singled out great works of art for posterity, and thus we have been less sensitive to their sociological qualities than to their formal and aesthetic qualities. We should avoid, however, assuming that we can study and evaluate the products of our own culture from a similar critical and historical distance.

Film critic Robin Wood, in an essay entitled "Ideology, Genre, Auteur," expresses misgivings about these critical oversights in genre study:

> *The work that has been done so far on genres has tended to take the various genres as "given" and discrete, and seeks to explicate them, define them in terms of motifs, etc.; what we need to ask, if genre theory is ever to be productive, is less What? than Why? We are so used to the genres that the peculiarity of the phenomenon itself has been too little noted. (Wood, 1977, p. 47)*[189]

As Wood suggests, genre study has tended to disengage the genre from the conditions of its production and to treat it as an isolated, autonomous system of conventions. As a result, genre

---

[188] Paul Rosenfield, "Lucas: Film-maker with the Force," *Los Angeles Times* (June 5, 1977), "Calendar" section, p. 43.

[189] Robin Wood, "Ideology, Genre, Auteur," *Film Comment* (Jan–Feb 1977), p. 47.

study tends to give only marginal attention to the role of the audience and the production system in formulating conventions and participating in their evolutionary development.

Genre study may be more "productive" if we complement the narrow critical focus of traditional genre analysis with a broader sociocultural perspective. Thus, we may consider a genre film not only as some filmmaker's artistic expression, but further as the cooperation between artists and audience in celebrating their collective values and ideals. In fact, many qualities traditionally viewed as artistic shortcomings—the psychologically static hero, for instance, or the predictability of the plot—assume a significantly different value when examined as components of a genre's ritualistic narrative system. If indeed we are to explain the *why* of Hollywood genres, we must look to their shared social function and to their formal conventions. Once we examine these shared features, we then can address a particular genre and its films.

Genre as system

Perhaps we should begin by noting a basic distinction between film genre study and its predecessor, literary genre study. In the study of literature, generic categories have been virtually imposed on works of fiction (or poetry or drama), representing the efforts of critics or historians to organize the subject matter according to their own subjective criteria. Literary analysts thus have tended to treat their subject in terms that may be irrelevant to those who produce and consume them. Not so with the commercial cinema, however. Because of the nature of film production and consumption, identifying film genres scarcely involves the subjective, interpretive effort that it does in literature. Film genres are not organized or discovered by analysts but are the result of the material conditions of commercial filmmaking itself, whereby popular stories are varied and repeated as long as they satisfy audience demand and turn a profit for the studios.

We are most aware of a generic "contract" when it is violated. The violation may involve casting an established performer "against type," as when musical star Dick Powell portrayed private eye Philip Marlowe in *Murder My Sweet* (even the title was changed from *Farewell My Lovely* so that audiences wouldn't mistake the film for a musical). Or the violation may simply be a matter of a vehicle (as a car on a western set) from one genre turning up on the set of another. (Wisconsin Center for Film and Theater Research); (Private Collection)

The significance of this distinction is twofold. First, it indicates that a film genre is a "privileged" cinematic story form—that is, only a limited number of film stories have been refined into formulas because of their unique social and/or aesthetic qualities. Second, as the product of audience and studio interaction, a film genre gradually impresses itself upon the culture until it becomes a familiar, meaningful system that can be *named* as such. Viewers, filmmakers, and critics know what it means to call this film a Western or that one a musical, and this knowledge is based on interaction with the medium itself—it is not the result of some arbitrary critical or historical organization.

To identify a popular cinematic story formula, then, is to recognize its status as a coherent, value-laden narrative system. Its significance is immediately evident to those who produce and consume it. Through repeated exposure to individual genre films we come to recognize certain *types* of characters, locales, and events. In effect, we come to understand the system and its significance. We steadily accumulate a kind of narrative-cinematic *gestalt* or "mind set" that is a structured mental image of the genre's typical activities and attitudes. Thus all of our experiences with Western films give us an immediate notion, a complete impression, of a certain type of behavioral and attitudinal system.

Because it is essentially a narrative system, a film genre can be examined in terms of its fundamental structural components: plot, character, setting, thematics, style, and so on. We should be careful, though, to maintain a distinction between the *film genre* and the *genre film* Whereas the genre exists as a sort of tacit "contract" between filmmakers and audience, the genre film is an actual event that honors such a contract. To discuss the Western genre is to address neither a single Western film nor even all Westerns, but rather that system of conventions which identifies Western films as such.

There is a sense, then, in which a film genre is both a *static* and a *dynamic* system. On the one hand, it is a familiar formula of interrelated narrative and cinematic components that serves to continually reexamine some basic cultural conflict: one could argue, for example, that all Westerns confront the same fundamental issues (the taming of the frontier, the celebration of the hero's rugged individualism, the hero's conflicts with the frontier community, etc.) in elaborating America's foundation ritual and that slight formal variations do not alter those static thematic characteristics. On the other hand, changes in cultural attitudes, new influential genre films, the economics of the industry, and so forth, continually refine any film genre. As such, its nature is continually evolving. For example, the evolution of Western heroes from agents of law and order to renegade outlaws or professional killers reflects a genuine change in the genre. One could even argue that the term "Western" means something different today from what it did two or three decades ago.

Thus genre experience, like all human experience, is organized according to certain fundamental perceptual processes. As we repeatedly undergo the same type of experience we develop expectations which, as they are continually reinforced, tend to harden into "rules." The clearest example of this process in any culture is in its games. A game is a system of immutable rules (three strikes in baseball) and components determining the nature of play. Yet no two games in a sport are alike, and a theoretically infinite number of variations can be played within the "arena" that the rules provide. Similarly, certain styles of traditional or popular music involve a variations-on-a-theme approach both within and among individual pieces. In folk and blues traditions, for example, most compositions are generated from a very few chord progressions.

The analogies between film genres and other cultural systems are virtually endless. What such examples seem to highlight is the dual nature of any "species" (or "genus," the root for the word *genre*), that is, it can be identified either by its rules, components, and function (by its static deep structure) or conversely by the individual members which comprise the species (by its dynamic surface structure).

Think of a Western movie, or a musical, or a gangster film. Probably you won't think of any individual Western or musical or gangster film, but rather of a vaguely defined amalgam of actions and attitudes, of characters and locales. For as one sees more genre films, one tends to negotiate the genre less by its individual films than by its deep structure, those rules and conventions which render this film a Western and that film a musical. This distinction between deep and surface structures—between a genre and its films—provides the conceptual basis for any genre study. Of all the analogies we might use to better understand this distinction, the most illuminating involves the "deepest" of human structures: language.

The language analogy

> What is natural to mankind is not oral speech but the faculty of constructing a language, i.e. a system of distinct signs corresponding to distinct ideas.
>
> —Ferdinand de Saussure[190]

Among other things, the commercial cinema is a communication system—it structures and delivers meaning. Throughout its history, evocative phrases like "the grammar of film" and "the cinematic language system" have suggested that filmic communication is comparable to verbal communication, although the extent and usefulness of that comparison are limited. Most recently, the film-language analogy has undergone renewed interest within the growing field of *semiology* (or semiotics), a science that proposes to study human interaction as a vast network of social and interpersonal communication systems. Semiology is itself the brain child of Swiss linguist Ferdinand de Saussure, who suggested that language provides the "master pattern" for the study of cultural signification. According to de Saussure, verbal language is the one sign system shared by all cultures; its basic structure informs every system of social communication.

That language study and its jargon are a metaphor for genre study should be obvious. Through the "circuit of exchange" involving box-office "feedback," the studios and the mass audience hold a virtual "conversation" whereby they gradually refine the "grammar" of cinematic "discourse." Thus a genre can be studied, like a language, as a formalized sign system whose rules have been assimilated, consciously or otherwise, through cultural consensus. Our shared knowledge of the rules of any film genre enables us to understand and evaluate individual genre films, just as our shared knowledge of English grammar enables me to write this sentence and you to interpret it. The distinction between grammar and usage, closely akin to that between deep structure and surface structure, originates in de Saussure's distinction between *langue* and *parole* in verbal language. For de Saussure, the speaker's and listener's shared knowledge of the grammatical rules that make up the language system (*la langue*) enables them to develop and understand a virtually unlimited range of individual utterances (*la parole*). American linguist Noam Chomsky has described this distinction in terms of *competency* and *performance*; he suggests that we should differentiate between our inherent capacity to speak and interpret on the one hand and our actually doing so on the other[191] (Chomsky, 1964).

If we extend these ideas into genre study, we might think of the *film genre* as a specific grammar or system of rules of expression and construction and the individual genre film as a manifestation of these rules. Of course, film differs from language in that our verbal competence

---

[190] The portion of Ferdinand de Saussure's Course in *General Linguistics*, first published in Paris in 1916, in which Saussure proposes the study of semiology, "a science that studies the life of signs within a society," and also outlines the general principles of semiology (langue/parole, signifier/signified, etc.), is reprinted in *The Structuralists: From Marx to Lévi-Strauss*, Richard and Fernande DeGeorge, editors (Garden City, N.Y.: Doubleday and Co., Inc., 1972), pp. 58–79. The reference in the text appears on page 62 of DeGeorge.

[191] For Chomsky's clearest description of this distinction, see *Current Issues in Linguistic Theory* (The Hague: Mouton Publishers, 1964).

is relatively consistent from speaker to speaker, whereas our generic competence varies widely. If each of us had the same exposure to Hollywood's thousands of genre films, a critical theory would probably be easier to construct. But obviously not everyone has a minimal understanding of even the most popular and widespread genres, let alone the obscure structural delights of such "subgenres" as the beach-blanket movies of the '60s or the car-chase movies of the '70s.

Moreover, although verbal language systems are essentially neutral and meaningless, film genres are not. As a system, English grammar is not meaningful either historically or in socially specific terms. It is manipulated by a speaker to *make* meaning. A film genre, conversely, has come into being precisely because of its cultural significance as a meaningful narrative system. Whereas a verbal statement represents a speaker's organization of neutral components into a meaningful pattern, a genre film represents an effort to reorganize a familiar, meaningful system in an original way.

Another interesting aspect of the language analogy concerns the tension between grammar and usage. Grammar in language is absolute and static, essentially unchanged by the range and abuses of everyday usage. In the cinema, however, individual genre films seem to have the capacity to affect the genre—an utterance has the potential to change the grammar that governs it. Even in film technology (the impact of widescreen on the Western, for example, or of technicolor on the musical), we can see that individual usage influences both viewers and other filmmakers, and hence encourages them in effect to renegotiate the generic contract. Whether or not some static nuclear deep structure exists, which defines the genre and somehow eludes the effects of time and variation, we cannot overlook the gradual changes (as revealed in individual genre films) in form and substance on the genre's surface. Genres evolve, and they tend to evolve quite rapidly due to the demands of the commercial popular media. But whether this evolution represents mere cosmetic changes in the surface structure (equivalent to fashionable clichés or idioms in verbal language) or whether it reflects substantial changes in the deep structure (the generic system itself) will remain, at least for now, an open question.

Perhaps the ultimate value of the film-language analogy is as a sort of method or methodological model. That is, the similarities between a language and a genre as communication systems should encourage the analyst to approach individual genre films in much the same way that the linguist approaches individual utterances. Like all signifying systems, languages and genres exist essentially within the minds of their users: No single study of English grammar or of a film genre could possibly describe the system completely. In this sense, studying film genre is not unlike going to school as competent six-year-old speakers of English and then being taught English grammar. In each case, we study the system that is the basis for our existing competence.

In all of this, we should not lose sight of the critical, evaluative factor that motivates the genre critic, while it is virtually irrelevant to the linguist. The linguist's concern is the process whereby we verbally communicate meaning; any concern for the quality of that communication falls under the domain of rhetoric. As such, the film genre critic must be both linguist and "rhetor"—that is, he or she is concerned with both the process and the quality of any generic communication. The critic develops competence, a familiarity with the system, by watching and interpreting movies and noting similarities. Ultimately, he or she is concerned with recognizing, appreciating, and articulating *differences* among these movies. As critics, we understand genre films because of their similarity with other films, but we appreciate them because of their difference. Therefore an outline of a basic grammar of genre filmmaking should precede any critical analysis of individual films within a genre.

Toward a grammar of film genre

At this stage, we are somewhere "between" the point of departure (watching movies) and the point of arrival (appreciating and articulating difference—i.e., being critical). We can appreciate difference only when we begin to examine films systematically, when we consider the systems whereby an individual film "makes meaning." Thus far, we have considered the commercial and formal systems involved in Hollywood filmmaking from a rather superficial perspective. In narrowing our focus to examine the workings of Hollywood genres, we will begin to understand how commercial and formal systems are realized in actual production. Genre production itself should be addressed on three distinct levels of inquiry: those characteristics shared by virtually all genre films (and thus by all genres), those characteristics shared by all the films within any individual genre, and those characteristics that set one genre film off from all other films.

Our ultimate goal is to discern a genre film's quality, its social and aesthetic value. To do this, we will attempt to see its relation to the various systems that inform it. For example, in examining a film like *The Searchers*, it is not enough simply to isolate the formal characteristics that identify it as belonging to a particular genre. Nor is it enough to isolate the elements that make it superior. Initially we have to discern those traits that make the film—and indeed the Western form itself—generic. To repeat Wood's observation: we are so accustomed to dealing with genres, with familiar filmic narrative types, that we tend to isolate these types from one another, thus overlooking many of their shared social and aesthetic features. Before considering the Western, gangster, musical, and other Hollywood genres as individual narrative systems, then, we will discuss the qualities that identify these forms as genres.

A genre film, like virtually any story, can be examined in terms of its fundamental narrative components: plot, setting, and character. These components have a privileged status for the popular audience, due to their existence within a familiar formula that addresses and reaffirms the audience's values and attitudes. Thus the genre film's narrative components assume a preordained thematic significance that is quite different from non-generic narratives. Each genre film incorporates a specific cultural context—what Warshow termed its "field of reference"—in the guise of a familiar *social community*. This generic context is more than the physical setting, which some genre critics have argued defines the genre as such. The American frontier or the urban underworld is more than a physical locale which identifies the Western or the gangster film; it is a cultural milieu where inherent thematic conflicts are animated, intensified, and resolved by familiar characters and patterns of action. Although all drama establishes a community that is disturbed by conflict, in the genre film both the community and the conflict have been conventionalized. Ultimately, our familiarity with any genre seems to depend less on recognizing a specific setting than on recognizing certain dramatic conflicts that we associate with specific patterns of action and character relationships. There are some genres, in fact, like the musical and the screwball comedy, that we identify primarily through conventions of action and attitude, and whose settings vary widely from one film to the next.

From this observation emerges a preliminary working hypothesis: the determining, identifying feature of a film genre is its cultural context, its community of interrelated character types whose attitudes, values, and actions flesh out dramatic conflicts inherent within that community. The generic community is less a specific place (although it may be, as with the Western and gangster genres) than a network of characters, actions, values, and attitudes. Each genre's status as a distinct cultural community is enhanced by Hollywood's studio production system, in that each generic context is orchestrated by specialized groups of directors, writers, producers, performers, sets, studio lots, and even studios themselves. (Consider Warner Brothers' heavy production of gangster films in the early '30s and MGM's musicals in the late '40s.)

A genre, then, represents a *range of expression* for filmmakers and a *range of experience* for viewers. Both filmmakers and viewers are sensitive to a genre's range of expression because of previous experiences with the genre that have coalesced into a system of value-laden narrative conventions. It is this system of conventions—familiar characters performing familiar actions which celebrate familiar values—that represents the genre's narrative context, its meaningful cultural community.

Iconography: Imagery and meaning

The various generic communities—from the Old West to the urban underworld to outer space—provide both a visual arena in which the drama unfolds and also an intrinsically significant realm in which specific actions and values are celebrated. In addressing the inherent meaning or intrinsic significance of objects and characters within any generic community, we are considering that genre's *iconography*. Iconography involves the process of *narrative and visual coding* that results from the

Most genre films provide us with iconographic cues even before the opening credit sequences have finished, as shown here with *The Band Wagon*. (Private Collection)

repetition of a popular film story. A white hat in a Western or a top hat in a musical, for instance, is significant because it has come to serve a specific symbolic function within the narrative system.

This coding process occurs in all movies, since the nature of filmic storytelling is to assign meaning to "bare images" as the story develops. In the final sequence of *Citizen Kane*, for example, the symbolic reverberations of the burning sled and the "No Trespassing" sign result from the cumulative effects of the film's narrative process. These effects in *Kane* accumulate within that single film, though, and had no significance prior to our viewing of that film.

A *generic icon*, in contrast, assumes significance not only through its usage within individual genre films but also as that usage relates to the generic system itself. The Westerner's white horse and hat identify a character before he speaks or acts because of our previous experiences with men who wear white hats and ride white horses. The more interesting and engaging genre films, of course, do more than merely deliver the codes intact—as did many of those "B" Westerns of the '30s that almost literally "all look alike"—but instead manipulate the codes to enhance their thematic effect.

Consider the dress code of the principal characters in *The Man Who Shot Liberty Valance* (John Ford, 1962). In this film, Jimmy Stewart portrays Ransom Stoddard, an Eastern-bred lawyer bent upon civilizing the Western community of Shinbone. Early in the film, Stoddard takes work as a dishwasher (Shinbone then had little need for lawyers) and continually wears a white apron—even during his climactic gunfight with Liberty Valance. Lee Marvin, portraying the archetypal Western antagonist, Liberty Valance, hired by local cattlemen to prevent statehood and the fencing in of their rangeland, wears black leather and carries a black, silver-knobbed whip. Mediating these two opposing figures is Tom Doniphon (John Wayne), a charismatic local rancher who sympathizes with the cause of statehood. Doniphon eventually murders Valance to save Stoddard, thus enabling Stoddard to gain political prominence and to assume the role of community leader. Throughout the film, Doniphon is dressed in various combinations of black and white. His clothing reflects his ambiguous role as murderous purveyor of eventual social order. Of course, director Ford develops Doniphon's tragic role by manipulating a good deal more than the iconography of Western dress, but this example suggests how filmmakers use a genre's established visual codes to create complex narrative and thematic situations.

A genre's iconography involves not only the visual coding of the narrative, but indicates *thematic value* as well (white civilization good versus black anarchy evil, with black-and-white as thematically ambiguous). We distinguish between characters who wear white and characters who wear black in Westerns, or those who sing and dance and those who do not in musicals, and these distinctions reflect the thematic conflicts inherent within these communities. Because visual coding involves narrative and social values, it also extends to certain nonvisual aspects of genre filmmaking. Such elements as dialogue, music, and even casting may become key components of a genre's iconography.

Think, for example, of the appropriateness of the casting in the film just described (Stewart as naive idealist, Marvin as maniacal anarchist, Wayne as stoic middleman), or think of the way certain movie stars are generally associated with specific genres. Katharine Hepburn, Fred Astaire, Joan Crawford, and Humphrey Bogart have become significant components of a genre's meaning-making system. When we think of Bogart as the typical hardboiled detective or of Astaire as the ultimate, spontaneous, self-assured music man, we are thinking not of the particular human being or of any single screen role but rather of a *screen persona*—i.e., an attitudinal posture that effectively transcends its role in any individual film.

A genre's iconography reflects the value system that defines its particular cultural community and informs the objects, events, and character types composing it. Each genre's implicit system of values and beliefs—its *ideology* or world view—determines its cast of characters, its problems (dramatic conflicts), and the solutions to those problems. In fact, we might define film genres, particularly at the earlier stages of their development, as social problem-solving operations: They repeatedly confront the ideological conflicts (opposing value systems) within a certain cultural community, suggesting various solutions through the actions of the main characters. Thus, each genre's problem-solving function affects its distinct formal and conceptual identity.

Character and setting: Communities in conflict

In discussing the grammar (or system of conventions) of any Hollywood film genre, it is important to note that the *material economy*, which motivated the studios to refine story formulas, translates into *narrative economy* for filmmakers and viewers. Each genre incorporates a sort of narrative shorthand whereby significant dramatic conflicts can intensify and then be resolved through established patterns of action and by familiar character types. These dramatic conflicts are themselves the identifying feature of any genre; they represent the transformation of some social, historical, or even geographical (as in the Western) aspect of American culture into one locus of events and characters. Although the dramatic conflicts are basic to the generic "community," we cannot identify that community solely by its physical setting. If film genres were identified by setting alone, then we would have to deal with an "urban" genre that includes such disparate forms as gangster films, backstage musicals, and detective films. Because the setting provides an arena for conflicts, which are themselves determined by the actions and attitudes of the *participants*, we must look to the generic character types and the conflicts they generate in identifying any genre. And we might consider a generic community and its characters in relation to the system of values which both define the problem and eventually are appealed to in solving it.

What emerges as a social problem (or dramatic conflict) in one genre is not necessarily a problem in another. Law and order is a problem in the gangster and detective genres, but not in the musical. Conversely, courtship and marriage are problems in the musical but not in the gangster and detective genres. Individualism is celebrated in the detective genre (through the hero's occupation and world view) and in the gangster film (through the hero's career and eventual death), while the principal characters in the musical compromise their individuality in their eventual romantic embrace and thus demonstrate their willingness to be integrated into the social community. In each of these genres, the characters' identities and narrative roles (or "functions") are determined by their relationship with the community and its value structure. As such, the generic character is psychologically static—he or she is the physical embodiment of an attitude, a style, a world view, of a predetermined and essentially unchanging cultural posture. Cowboy or Indian, gangster or cop, guy or doll, the generic character is identified by his or her function and status within the community.

The static vision of the generic hero—indeed of the entire constellation of familiar character types—helps to define the community and to animate its cultural conflicts. For example, the Western hero, regardless of his social or legal standing, is necessarily an agent of civilization in the savage frontier. He represents both the social order and the threatening savagery that typify the Western milieu. Thus he animates the inherent dynamic qualities of the community, providing a dramatic vehicle through which the audience can confront generic conflicts.

This approach also enables us to distinguish between such seemingly similar "urban crime" formulas as the gangster and detective genres. Usually, both genres are set in a contemporary urban milieu and address conflicts principally between social order and anarchy and between individual morality and the common good. But because of the characteristic attitudes and values of the genre's principal characters, these conflicts assume a different status in each genre and are resolved accordingly. The detective, like the Westerner, represents the man-in-the-middle, mediating the forces of order and anarchy, yet somehow remaining separate from each. He has opted to construct his own value system and behavioral code, which happens (often, almost accidentally) to coincide with the forces of social order. But the detective's predictable return to his office retreat at film's end and his refusal to assimilate the values and lifestyle of the very society he serves ultimately reaffirm his and the genre's—ambiguous social stance. The gangster film, conversely, displays little thematic ambiguity. The gangster has aligned himself with the forces of crime and social disorder, so both his societal role and his

Consider the complex of imagery at work in each of these stills. The dress, demeanor, tools, setting, and of course the performers themselves all provide specific generic information to the viewer. (Private Collection); (Wisconsin Center for Film and Theater Research)

conflict with the community welfare demand his eventual destruction.

All film genres treat some form of threat—violent or otherwise—to the social order. However, it is the attitudes of the principal characters and the resolutions precipitated by their actions which finally distinguish the various genres from one another. Nevertheless, there is a vital distinction between kinds of generic settings and conflicts. Certain genres (Western, detective, gangster, war, et al.) have conflicts that, indigenous to the environment, reflect the physical and ideological struggle for its control. These conflicts are animated and resolved either by an individual male hero or by a collective (war, science fiction, cavalry, certain recent Westerns). Other genres have conflicts that are not indigenous to the locale but are the result of the conflict between the values, attitudes, and actions of its principal characters and the "civilized" setting they inhabit. Conflicts in these genres (musical, screwball comedy, family melodrama) generally are animated by a "doubled" hero—usually a romantic couple whose courtship is complicated and eventually ideologically resolved. A musical's setting may be a South Pacific island or the backstage of a Broadway theater, but we relate to the film immediately by its treatment of certain sexual and occupational conflicts and also by our familiarity with the type of characters played by its "stars."

Thus, it is *not* the musical numbers themselves which identify these films as musicals. Many Westerns and gangster films, for example, contain musical numbers and still aren't confused with musicals (Westerns like *Dodge City* and *Rio Bravo*, for instance, or gangster films like *The Roaring Twenties* and *The Rise and Fall of Legs Diamond*). The frontier saloon and the gangster's speakeasy may be conventional locales within their respective communities, but their entertainment function clearly is peripheral to the central issue. However, in "musical Westerns" like *Annie Get Your Gun*, *The Harvey Girls*, and *Oklahoma!*, the nature and resolution of the dramatic conflicts as well as the characterization clearly are expressed via the musical formula. In *The Harvey Girls*, for instance, the narrative centers around the exploits of several dozen women—including Judy Garland and Cyd Charisse, which should provide us with a generic cue—who migrate West to work in a restaurant. Certain Western conventions are nodded to initially: the girls are told aboard the train headed West that "You're bringing civilization.... You girls are bringing order to the West"; later, there is a comic brawl between these "Harvey Girls" and the local saloon girls. But the Western genre's fundamental traits (the individual male hero responding to the threat of savagery and physical violence within an ideologically unstable milieu) are not basic to the film. Once the characters and conflicts are established, the setting might as well be Paris or New York City or even Oz.

As I hope these examples indicate, the various Hollywood genres manipulate character and social setting quite differently in developing dramatic conflicts. We might consider a broad distinction between genres of *determinate space* and those of *indeterminate space*, between genres of an ideologically contested setting and an ideologically stable setting. In a genre of determinate space (Western, gangster, detective, et al.), we have a symbolic arena of action. It represents a cultural realm in which fundamental values are in a state of sustained conflict. In these genres, then, the contest itself and its necessary arena are "determinate"—a specific social conflict is violently enacted within a familiar locale according to a prescribed system of rules and behavioral codes.

The iconographic arena in determinate genres is entered by an individual or collective hero, at the outset, who acts upon it, and finally leaves. This entrance-exit motif recurs most in genres characterized by an individual hero: for example, the Westerner enters a frontier community, eliminates (or perhaps causes) a threat to its survival, and eventually rides "into the sunset"; the detective takes the case, investigates it, and returns to his office; the gangster, introduced to urban crime, rises to power, and finally is killed or jailed. In these genres, the individual hero incorporates a rigid, essentially static attitude in dealing with his very dynamic, contested world.

Similarity and difference: the distinctive narrative contexts of the screwball comedy (*It Happened One Night*, above) and the gangster film (*The Public Enemy*, below) clearly overwhelm the apparent similarities between these two scenes. (Culver Pictures); (Culver Pictures)

In contrast, genres of indeterminate space generally involve a doubled (and thus dynamic) hero in the guise of a romantic couple who inhabit a "civilized" setting, as in the musical, screwball comedy, and social melodrama. The physical and ideological "contest" which determines the arena of action in the Western, gangster, and detective genres is not an issue here. Instead, genres of indeterminate space incorporate a civilized, ideologically stable milieu, which depends less upon a heavily coded place than on a highly conventionalized value system. Here conflicts derive not from a struggle over control of the environment, but rather from the struggle of the principal characters to bring their own views in line either with one another's or, more often, in line with that of the larger community.

Unlike genres of determinate space, these genres rely upon a progression from romantic antagonism to eventual embrace. The kiss or embrace signals the integration of the couple into the larger cultural community. In addition, these genres use iconographic conventions to establish a social setting—the proscenium or theater stage with its familiar performers in some musicals, for example, or the repressive small-town community and the family home in the melodrama. But because the generic conflicts arise from attitudinal (generally male-female) oppositions rather than from a physical conflict, the coding in these films tends to be less visual and more ideological and abstract. This may account for the sparse attention they have received from genre analysts, despite their widespread popularity.

Ultimately, genres of indeterminate, civilized space (musical, screwball comedy, social melodrama) and genres of determinate, contested space (Western, gangster, detective) might be distinguished according to their differing ritual functions. The former tend to celebrate the values of *social integration*, whereas the latter uphold the values of *social order*. The former tend to cast an attitudinally unstable couple or family unit into some representative microcosm of American society, so that their emotional and/or romantic "coupling" reflects their integration into a stable environment. The latter tend to cast an individual, violent, attitudinally static male into a familiar, predetermined milieu to examine the opposing forces vying for control. In making this distinction, though, we should not lose sight of these genres' shared social function. In addressing basic cultural conflicts and celebrating the values and attitudes whereby these conflicts might be resolved, all film genres represent the filmmakers' and audience's cooperative efforts to "tame" those beasts, both actual and imaginary, which threaten the stability of our everyday lives.

Plot structure: From conflict to resolution

As a popular film audience, our shared needs and expectations draw us into the movie theater. If we are drawn there by a genre film, we are familiar with the ritual. In its animation and resolution of basic cultural conflicts, the genre film celebrates our collective sensibilities, providing an array of ideological strategies for negotiating social conflicts. The conflicts themselves are significant (and dramatic) enough to ensure our repeated attendance. The films within a genre, representing variations on a cultural theme, will employ different means of reaching narrative resolution, but that closure is generally as familiar as the community and its characters. (Think of the general discomfort felt upon realizing, even quite early in seeing a genre film, that Cagney's heroic gangster would "get his" or that Tracy and Hepburn would cease their delightful hostilities and embrace in time for the closing credits.)

Actually, the most significant feature of any generic narrative may be its resolution—that is, its efforts to solve, even if only temporarily, the conflicts that have disturbed the community welfare. The Western, for example, despite its historical and geographical distance from most viewers, confronts real and immediate social conflicts: individual versus community, town versus wilderness, order versus anarchy, and so on. If there is anything escapist about these narratives, it is their repeated assertion that these conflicts can be solved, that seemingly timeless cultural oppositions can be resolved favorably for the larger community.

In a Hollywood Western, as in virtually any Hollywood genre film, plot development is effectively displaced by setting and character: once we recognize the familiar cultural arena and the players, we can be fairly certain how the game will be played and how it will end. Because the characters, conflicts, and resolution of the non-generic narrative are unfamiliar and unpredictable, we negotiate them less by previous filmic experiences than by previous "real-world" (personal and social) experiences. Clearly, both generic and non-generic narratives must rely to some degree upon real-world and also upon previous narrative-filmic experiences in order to make sense. In the genre film, however, the predictability of conflict and resolution tends to turn our attention away from the linear, cause-and-effect plot, redirecting it to the conflict itself and the opposed value systems it represents. Instead of a linear chain of events, which are organized by the changing perceptions of an individual protagonist, the genre film's plot traces the intensification of some cultural opposition which is eventually resolved in a predictable fashion.

Thus, we might describe the plot structure of a genre film in the following way:

establishment (via various narrative and iconographic cues) of the generic community with its inherent dramatic conflicts;

animation of those conflicts through the actions and attitudes of the genre's constellation of characters;

intensification of the conflict by means of conventional situations and dramatic confrontations until the conflict reaches crisis proportions;

resolution of the crisis in a fashion which eliminates the physical and/or ideological threat and thereby celebrates the (temporarily) well-ordered community.

In this plot structure, linear development is subordinate to and qualified by the *oppositional* narrative strategy. Opposing value systems are either mediated by an individual or a collective, which eliminates one of the opposing systems. Or else these oppositions are actually embodied by a doubled hero whose (usually romantic) coupling signals their synthesis. In either instance, resolution occurs, even if only temporarily, in a way that strokes the collective sensibilities of the mass audience. It is in this context that the genre film's function as cultural ritual is most evident.

In their formulaic narrative process, genre films celebrate the most fundamental ideological precepts—they examine and affirm "Americanism" with all its rampant conflicts, contradictions, and ambiguities. Not only do genre films establish a sense of continuity between our cultural past and present (or between present and future, as with science fiction), but they also attempt to eliminate the distinctions between them. As social ritual, genre films function to stop time, to portray our culture in a stable and invariable ideological position. This attitude is embodied in the generic hero—and in the Hollywood star system itself—and is ritualized in the resolution precipitated by the hero's actions. Whether it is a historical Western or a futuristic fantasy, the genre film celebrates certain inviolate cultural attributes.

Ultimately, the sustained success of any genre depends upon at least two factors: the thematic appeal and significance of the conflicts it repeatedly addresses and its flexibility in adjusting to the audience's and filmmakers' charging attitudes toward those conflicts. These can be seen, for example, in the Western hero's status as both rugged individualist and also as agent of a civilization that continually resists his individualism. The degree to which that opposition has evolved over the past seventy-five years has accommodated changes in our cultural sensibilities. Or consider science fiction, a literary and cinematic genre that realized widespread popularity in the late '40s and early '50s. This genre articulated the conflicts and anxieties that accompanied the development of atomic power and the prospect of interplanetary travel. Because science fiction deals with so specialized a cultural conflict—essentially with the limits and value of human knowledge and scientific experimentation—it is considerably less flexible, but no less topical, than the Western. Nevertheless, each genre has a static nucleus that manifests its thematic oppositions or recurring cultural conflicts. And each genre has, through the years, dynamically evolved as shown by the ways its individual films manipulate those oppositions. If we see genre as a problem-solving strategy, then, the static nucleus could be conceived as the problem and the variety of solutions (narrative resolutions) as its dynamic surface structure.

In this sense, a genre's basic cultural oppositions or inherent dramatic conflicts represent its most basic determining feature. Also the sustained popularity of any genre indicates the essentially unresolvable, irreconcilable nature of those oppositions. Resolution involves a point of dramatic closure in which a compromise or temporary solution to the conflict is projected into a sort of cultural and historical timelessness. The threatening external force in contested space is violently destroyed and eliminated as an ideological threat; in uncontested space the vital lover's spontaneity and lack of social inhibition are bridled by a domesticating counterpart in the name of romantic love. In each, philosophical or ideological conflicts are "translated" into emotional terms—either violent or sexual, or both—and are resolved accordingly. In the former, the emotive resolution is externalized, in the latter it is internalized. Still, he resolution does not function to *solve* the basic cultural conflict. The conflict is simply recast into an emotional context where it can be expeditiously, if not always logically, resolved.

As a rule, generic resolution operates by a process of *reduction*: the polar opposition is reduced, either through the elimination of one of the forces (in genres of determinate, contested space) or through the integration of the forces into a single unit (in genres of indeterminate, civilized space). The contest in determinate space generally is physically violent. Frequently, up until the resolution, there is more tension than action. The violent resolution usually helps the community, but only rarely does the hero assimilate its value system. In fact, his insistence that

In all genre films, there is a sense of loss. At the end of *Shane*, the initiate-hero (Brandon De Wilde) must part with the hero (Alan Ladd). (Wisconsin Center for Film and Theater Research)

he maintain his individuality emerges as a significant thematic statement. As such, these films often involve a dual celebration: the hero's industrious isolationism offsets the genre's celebration of the ideal social order.

There is a certain logic and symmetry in the gangster's death, the Westerner's fading into the sunset, the detective's return to his office to await another case. Each of these standard epilogues implicitly accepts the contradictory values of its genre, all of which seem to center around the conflict between individualism and the common good. The built-in ambiguity of this dual celebration serves, at least partially, to minimize the *narrative rupture* resulting from the effort to resolve an unresolvable cultural conflict. This violation of narrative logic is itself fundamental to all of Hollywood's story formulas, in that the demand for a "happy ending" resists the complexity and deep-seated nature of the conflict.

Because genres of social order invariably allow the individual hero his formalized flight from social integration and from the compromising of his individuality, the narrative rupture is usually less pronounced than in genres of social integration. The cultural conflicts in genres of integration are revealed through the doubling of the principal characters—that is, through their opposed relationship, usually expressed as romantic antagonism. With the integration of their opposing attitudes into a cohesive unit (the married couple, the family), the conflicts are resolved and basic communal ideals are ritualized. But the cultural contradictions that inhibit integration throughout these films—between spontaneous individual expression and social propriety, for example—cannot be resolved without severely subverting the characters' credibility and motivation.

Are we to assume that the screwball couple's madcap social behavior and mutual antagonism will magically dissolve once they are wed? Or that the conflicts, which have separated the song-anddance team throughout rehearsals, will somehow vanish after the climactic show? To avoid these questions and to minimize the sense of rupture, these genre films synthesize their oppositions through some formal celebration or social ritual: a Broadway show, a betrothal, a wedding, and so on. In this way, they don't actually resolve their conflicts; they reconstitute them by concluding the narrative at an emotive climax, at precisely the moment when the doubled principals acquiesce to each other's demands. The suggestion of living "happily ever after" tends to mask or gloss over the inevitable loss associated with each character's compromise. What is celebrated is the collective value of their integration into an idealized social unit.

This sense of loss accompanies the resolution of all genre films because of the contradictory, irreconcilable nature of their conflicts. Through violent reduction or romantic coupling, however, the loss is masked. It is, in effect, effectively redressed in the emotional climax. What is to become, we might very well ask ourselves, once the film ends, of the uninhibited music man after he weds the gold-hearted domesticator—and what's to become of her as well? What's to become of the savage frontier lawman once the social order he instills finally arrives? These are questions which, unless initiated by the films themselves, we know better than to ask. Genre films not only project an idealized cultural self-image, but they project it into a realm of historical timelessness. Typically, films produced later in a genre's development tend to challenge the tidy and seemingly naive resolutions of earlier genre films, and we will discuss this tendency in some detail when we examine generic evolution. What we should note here, though, and what is being masked by such a resolution is the fundamental appeal of both sides in a dramatic conflict. Whatever oppositions we examine in genre films—individual versus community, man versus woman, work versus play, order versus anarchy—these do not represent "positive" and "negative" cultural values. For one of the reasons for a genre's popularity is the sustained significance of the "problem" that it repeatedly addresses. Thus, generic conflict and resolution involve opposing systems of values and attitudes, *both of which* are deemed significant by contemporary American culture.

Narrative strategy and social function: Contradictions, happy endings, and the status quo

In surveying the setting, characterization, and plot structure of Hollywood film genres, we have made several general distinctions between genres of order and genres of integration. I have suggested that these two types of genres represent two dominant narrative strategies of genre filmmaking. Perhaps it would be useful to summarize these strategies.

Certain genres (Western, gangster, detective, et al.) center on an individual male protagonist, generally a redeemer figure, who is the focus of dramatic conflicts within a setting of contested space. As such, the hero mediates the cultural contradictions inherent within his milieu. Conflicts within these genres are externalized, translated into violence, and usually resolved through the elimination of some threat to the social order. The resolution in these films often is somewhat ambiguous. The hero, either through his departure or death at film's end, does not assimilate the values and lifestyle of the community but instead maintains his individuality. Genres that incorporate this narrative strategy I have termed *rites of order*.

Other genres (musical, screwball comedy, family melodrama, et al.) are set in "civilized" space and trace the integration of the central characters into the community. There is generally a doubled (romantic couple) or collective (usually a family) hero in these genres. Their personal and social conflicts are internalized, translated into emotional terms, with their interpersonal antagonism eventually yielding to the need for a well-ordered community. Integration invariably occurs through romantic love. After a period of initial hostility, the couple find themselves in a final embrace. The genres which incorporate this narrative strategy I have termed *rites of integration*.

CHARACTERISTICS OF GENRES OF ORDER AND GENRES OF INTEGRATION

	ORDER (Western, gangster, detective)	INTEGRATION (musical, screwball comedy, family melodrama)
hero	individual (male dominant)	couple/collective (female dominant)
setting	contested space (ideologically unstable)	civilized space (ideologically stable)
conflict	externalized—violent	internalized—emotional
resolution	elimination (death)	embrace (love)
thematics	mediation—redemption	integration—domestication
	macho code	maternal-familial code
	isolated self-reliance	community cooperation
	utopia-as-promise	utopia-as-reality

There is considerable overlap between the rites, of course, in that all order genres address the prospect of social integration, and all integration genres are concerned with maintaining the existing social order. But this general distinction does provide a starting point for analysis. We have a set of assumptions to develop and refine while examining individual genres and their films. For the purposes of clarity and simplicity, the following chart may be useful.

In examining both types of genres, one of our concerns must be the relationship between narrative strategy and social function. Although I have suggested that each genre represents a distinct problem-solving strategy that repeatedly addresses basic cultural contradictions, genres are not blindly supportive of the cultural status quo. The genre film's resolution may reinforce the ideology of the larger society, but the nature and articulation of the dramatic conflicts leading to that climax cannot be ignored. If genres develop and survive because they repeatedly flesh out and reexamine cultural conflicts, then we must consider the possibility that genres function as much to challenge and criticize as to reinforce the values that inform them.

As has often been said, Hollywood movies are considerably more effective in their capacity to raise questions than to answer them. This characteristic seems particularly true of genre films. And as such, the genre's fundamental impulse is to continually *renegotiate* the tenets of American ideology. And what is so fascinating and confounding about Hollywood genre films is their capacity to "play it both ways," to both criticize and reinforce the values, beliefs, and ideals of our culture within the same narrative context.

Consider Molly Haskell's description of the narrative resolution in certain melodramas of the 1930s and '40s: "The forced enthusiasm and neat evasions of so many happy endings have only increased the suspicion that darkness and despair follow marriage, a suspicion the 'women's film' confirmed by carefully pretending otherwise"[192] (Haskell, 1974, p. 124). Implicit in Haskell's statement is the assumption that the audience knew better than to believe the pat "happy end." She assumes that the audience was sensitive, consciously or otherwise, to the narrative rupture involved in a melodrama's progression from conflict to resolution. One could just as easily argue the opposite, of course, that audiences actually believed and bought wholesale, consciously or otherwise, the "neat evasions of so many happy endings."

The fact is, however, that as genres develop their conflicts are stated ever more effectively, while their resolutions become ever more ambiguous and ironic. This would seem to support Haskell's position, and further to undercut the simplistic conception of the audience as utterly naive and of the Hollywood genre film as mere escapist entertainment. Let us consider, even if only briefly, the issue of a genre's increasingly sophisticated capacity for presenting its conflicts, a capacity which seems closely related to the process of generic evolution.

Generic evolution: Patterns of increasing self-consciousness

We have already noted that genre filmmakers are in a rather curious bind: they must continually vary and reinvent the generic formula. At the same time they must exploit those qualities that made the genre popular in the first place. As Robert Warshow puts it: "Variation is absolutely necessary to keep the type from becoming sterile; we do not want to see the same movie over and over again, only the same form"[193] (Warshow, 1962, p. 147). His point is well taken: the genre's "deeper" concern for certain basic cultural issues may remain intact, but to remain vital its films must keep up with the audience's changing conception of these issues and with its growing familiarity with the genre. But how does a genre evolve, and does its evolution follow any consistent or predictable pattern? If certain formal and thematic traits distinguish a genre throughout its development, what changes as the form evolves?

First, a genre's evolution involves both internal (formal) and external (cultural, thematic) factors. The subject matter of any film story is derived from certain "real-world" characters,

---

[192] Molly Haskell, *From Reverence to Rape* (New York: Penguin Books, 1974), p. 124.
[193] Robert Warshow, *The Immediate Experience* (Garden City, N.Y.: Doubleday and Co., Inc., 1962), p. 147.

Parodies of established genres are a good indication of how we become familiar with a genre's conventions and appreciate seeing these conventions subverted. In a modern dance sequence from *The Band Wagon*, Cyd Charisse and Fred Astaire parody the hardboiled detective genre. (Hoblitzelle Theater Arts Collection)

conflicts, settings, and so on. But once the story is repeated and refined into a formula, its basis in experience gradually gives way to its own internal narrative logic. Thus, the earliest Westerns (many of which actually depicted then-current events) obviously were based on social and historical reality. But as the genre developed, it gradually took on its own reality. Even the most naive viewer seems to understand this. It comes as no surprise to learn that Western heroes didn't wear white hats and fringed buckskin, that gunfights on Main Street were an exceedingly rare occurrence, or that the towns and dress codes and other trappings of movie Westerns were far different from those of the authentic American West. In this sense, we recognize and accept the distinctive grammar—the system of storytelling conventions—that has evolved through the repeated telling of Western tales.

Simultaneously, however, we also realize that these real-world factors, basic to the genre's dramatic conflicts, are themselves changing. Consider how the changing image of Native

Americans ("Injuns") has been influenced by our culture's changing view of Manifest Destiny, the settling of the West, and the treatment of peoples whose cultures were overwhelmed by the encroachment of civilization. Or consider how the atom bomb and space travel affected the development of the science fiction genre after World War II; consider the impact of organized crime on the gangster and detective genres in the 1950s. Perhaps the effects of these external social factors are best seen case by case. A genre's formal internal evolution, however, especially when considered in terms of our growing familiarity with it over time, does seem to follow a rather consistent pattern of schematic development.

In his chapter "Textuality and Generality" (*Language and Cinema*), Christian Metz considers the internal evolution of the Western. Metz suggests that, as early as 1946 with John

Ford's *My Darling Clementine*, the "classic" Western had assumed "an accent of parody which was an integral part of the genre, and yet it remained a Western." He goes on to assert that the "superwesterns" of the 1950s "passed from parody to contestation," but that they "remained fully Westerns." He then observes that in many recent Westerns, "contestation gives way to 'deconstruction': the entire film is an explication of the [Western] code and its relation to history. One has passed from parody to critique, but the work is still a Western." Metz contends that with every "stage" of its evolutionary process, the Western sustains its essence, its generic identity. He concludes his discussion with a rather suggestive observation: "Such is the infinite text one calls a genre"[194] (Metz, 1974, pp. 148-161).

Metz views the Western genre not only as a system of individual films, but further as a composite text in itself. His point is that the Western represents a basic story, which is never completely "told," but is reexamined and reworked in a variety of ways. Within these variations, Metz discovers a pattern of historical development. His classic-parody-contestation-critique progression suggests that both filmmakers and audience grow increasingly self-conscious regarding the genre's formal qualities and its initial social function. Actually, Metz's view of the Western's formal evolution is quite similar to the views of various historians who have studied the historical development of styles and genres in other arts. Perhaps the most concise and influential study of this kind is Henri Focillon's *The Life of Forms in Art*, in which he develops a schema for the "life span" of cultural forms:

> *Forms obey their own rules—rules that are inherent in the forms themselves, or better, in the regions of the mind where they are located and centered—and there is no reason why we should not undertake an investigation of how these great ensembles . . . behave throughout the phases which we call their life. The successive states through which they pass are more or less lengthy, more or less intense, according to the style itself: the experimental age, the classic age, the age of refinement, the baroque age. (Focillon, 1942, p. 10)*[195]

Focillon's view is somewhat broader than Metz's. But he also observes that the continual reworking of a conventionalized form—whether it is an architectural style or a genre of painting—generates a growing awareness of the conventions themselves. Thus a form passes through an *experimental* stage, during which its conventions are isolated and established, a *classic* stage, in which the conventions reach their "equilibrium" and are mutually understood by artist and audience, an age of *refinement*, during which certain formal and stylistic details embellish the form, and finally a *baroque* (or "mannerist" or "self-reflexive") stage, when the form and its embellishments are accented to the point where they themselves become the "substance" or "content" of the work.

Using this strategy with film genres, we might begin with this observation: at the earliest stages of its life span, a genre tends to exploit the cinematic medium *as a medium*. If a genre is a society collectively speaking to itself, then any stylistic flourishes or formal self-consciousness will only impede the transmission of the message. At this stage, genre films transmit a certain idealized cultural self-image with as little "formal interference" as possible. Once a genre has passed through its experimental stage where its conventions have been established, it enters into its classical stage. We might consider this stage as one of *formal transparency*. Both the narrative formula and the film medium work together to transmit and reinforce that genre's social message—its ideology or problem-solving strategy—as directly as possible to the audience.

Leo Braudy describes the process of generic evolution: "Genre films essentially ask the audience, 'Do you still want to believe this?' popularity is the audience answering, 'Yes.' Change

---

[194] Christian Metz, *Language and Cinema* (The Hague: Mouton Publishers), pp. 148–161.
[195] Henri Focillon, *Life of Forms in Art* (New York: George Wittenborn, Inc., 1942), p. 10.

in genre occurs when the audience says, 'That's too infantile a form of what we believe. Show us something more complicated'[196] (Braudy, 1976, p. 179). This rather casual observation involves a number of insights, especially in its allusion to the "conversation" between filmmakers and audience and in its reference to audience "belief." The genre film reaffirms what the audience believes both on individual and on communal levels. Audience demand for variation does not indicate a change in belief, but rather that the belief should be reexamined, grow more complicated formally and thematically, and display, moreover, stylistic embellishment.

Thus, the end of a genre's classic stage can be viewed as that point at which the genre's straightforward message has "saturated" the audience. With its growing awareness of the formal and thematic structures, the genre evolves into what Focillon termed the age of refinement. As a genre's classic conventions are refined and eventually parodied and subverted, its transparency gradually gives way to *opacity*: we no longer look *through* the form (or perhaps "into the mirror") to glimpse an idealized self-image, rather we look *at* the *form itself* to examine and appreciate its structure and its cultural appeal.

A genre's progression from transparency to opacity—from straightforward storytelling to self-conscious formalism—involves its concerted effort to explain itself, to address and evaluate its very status as a popular form. A brief consideration of any Hollywood genre would support this view, particularly those with extended life spans like the musical or the Western. By the early 1950s, for example, both of these genres had begun to exhibit clear signs of formal self-consciousness. In such self-reflexive musicals as *The Barkleys of Broadway* (1949), *An American in Paris* (1951), *Singin' in the Rain* (1952), *The Band Wagon* (1953), and *It's Always Fair Weather* (1955), the narrative conflict confronts the nature and value of musical comedy as a form of popular entertainment. In accord with the genre's conventions, these conflicts are couched in a male-female opposition, but the boy-gets-girl resolution is now complicated by a tension between serious art and mere entertainment. These movies interweave motifs involving successful courtship and the success of The Show, and that success is threatened and resolved in a fashion which provides an "apology" for the musical as popular art.

In *The Barkleys of Broadway*, for instance, Ginger Rogers abandons musical comedy for "legitimate theater" but eventually returns both to the stage musical and to her former partner-spouse (Fred Astaire). Gene Kelly in *An American in Paris* must decide between a career as a painter, supported by spinster-dowager Nina Foch, and a "natural" life of dance and music with young Leslie Caron. In these and the other films, the generic conventions, which earlier were components of the genre's unspoken ideology, have now become the central thematic elements of the narrative. No longer does the genre simply celebrate the values of music, dance, and popular entertainment, it actually "critiques" and "deconstructs" them in the process[197] (Feuer, 1978).

The Western genre, which was entering its classic age in the late 1930s (*Stagecoach, Union Pacific, Dodge City, Destry Rides Again, Frontier Marshal*, all 1939), exhibits by the 1950s a similar formal and thematic self-scrutiny. Such films as *Red River* (1948), *I Shot Jesse James* (1949), *The Gunfighter* (1950), *Winchester 73* (1950), *High Noon* (1952), and *The Naked Spur* (1953) indicate that the genre had begun to question its own conventions, especially regarding the social role and psychological make-up of the hero. Consider, for example, the substantial changes in the screen persona of John Wayne or of Jimmy Stewart during this period. In such baroque Westerns as *Red River* and *The Searchers* (starring Wayne) and *Winchester 73, The Naked Spur, The Man from Laramie,* and *Two Rode Together* (Stewart), Wayne's stoic machismo and Stewart's "aw-shucks" naiveté are effectively inverted to reveal genuinely psychotic, antisocial figures.

[196] Leo Braudy, *The World in a Frame* (Garden City, N.Y.: Anchor Press/Doubleday, 1976), p. 179.
[197] For a more detailed treatment of the evolution of the musical genre, see Jane Feuer, *The Hollywood Musical: The Aesthetics of Spectator Involvement in an Entertainment Form* (Iowa City: University of Iowa, 1978), unpublished doctoral dissertation.

Naturally, we do not expect a classic Westerner like Wayne's Ringo Kid in *Stagecoach* to exhibit the psychological complexity or the "antiheroic" traits of later Western figures. Our regard for a film like *Stagecoach* has to do with its clear, straightforward articulation of the Western myth. A later film like *Red River*, which incorporates a younger figure (Montgomery Clift) to offset and qualify the classic Westerner's heroic posture, serves to refine and to call into question the genre's basic values. These values are subverted, or perhaps even rejected altogether, in later films like *The Searchers, The Wild Bunch*, and even in a comic parody like *Butch Cassidy and the Sundance Kid*. In these films, the "code of the West" with its implicit conflicts and ideology provides the dramatic focus, but our regard for that code changes as do the actions and attitudes of the principal characters.

The Western and the musical seem to represent genres in which the evolutionary "cycle" seems more or less complete. However, not all genres complete that cycle or necessarily follow such a progression. For example, in the gangster genre, various external pressures (primarily the threat of government censorship and religious boycott) disrupted the genre's internal evolution. And in the war genre, the prosocial aspects of supporting a war effort directly ruled out any subversion or even the serious questioning of the hero's attitudes. War films that did question values were made after the war and generally are considered as a subgenre. There are also genres currently in midcycle, like the "disaster" or the "occult" genres popularized during the 1970s. The disaster genre, whose classic stage was launched with *The Poseidon Adventure* and *Airport*, has evolved so rapidly that a parody of the genre, *The Big Bus* (1976), appeared within only a few years of the form's standardization. Interestingly, the audience didn't seem to know what to make of *The Big Bus*, and the film died at the box office. Apparently the genre hadn't sufficiently saturated the audience to the point where a parody could be appreciated.

Thus, it would seem that, throughout a genre's evolution from transparent social reaffirmation to opaque self-reflexivity, there is a gradual shift in narrative emphasis from social value to formal aesthetic value. Because continued variation tends to sensitize us to a genre's social message, our interests, and those of the filmmakers, gradually expand from the message itself to its articulation, from the tale to the visual and narrative artistry of its telling. It is no coincidence, then, that so many directors, who worked with a genre later in its development, are considered *auteurs*. We tend to regard early genre filmmakers as storytellers or craftsmen and later ones as artists. Naturally there are exceptions—Ford's early Westerns, Busby Berkeley's '30s musicals, all of Hitchcock's thrillers—but these involve directors whose narrative artistry and understanding of the genre's thematic complexity were apparent throughout their careers.

Generally speaking, it seems that those features most often associated with narrative artistry—ambiguity, thematic complexity, irony, formal self-consciousness—rarely are evident in films produced earlier in a genre's development. They tend to work themselves into the formula itself as it evolves. We are dealing here with the inherent artistry of the formula itself as it grows and develops. A newborn genre's status as social ritual generally resists any ironic, ambiguous, or overly complex treatment of its narrative message. But as filmmakers and audiences grow more familiar with the message as it is varied and refined, the variations themselves begin to exhibit qualities associated with narrative art.

This does not mean that early genre films have no aesthetic value or later ones no social value. There is, rather, a shift in emphasis from one cultural function (social, ritualistic) to another (formal, aesthetic). And both are evident in all genre films. A genre's initial and sustained popularity may be due primarily to its social function, but a degree of aesthetic appeal is also apparent in even the earliest, or the most transparently, prosocial genre films. Each genre seems to manifest a distinct visual and compositional identity the prospect of infinite space and limitless horizons in the Western, documentary urban realism in the gangster film, the "American Expressionism" of *film noir* and the hardboiled detective film, the musical's celebration of life through motion and song, and so on.

This aesthetic potential may have been tapped by filmmakers—writers, producers, performers, cameramen, editors, as well as directors—who quite simply made good movies. They manipulated any number of narrative and cinematic qualities that imbued their films with an artistry that may or may not have been common for the genre at that stage of its development. Whether considering artistically exceptional films early in a genre's evolution or the more self-reflexive films produced during its later stages, it is difficult not to appreciate the formal and ideological flexibility of Hollywood's genres. These story formulas have articulated and continually reexamined basic social issues, weaving a cultural tapestry whose initial design became ever more detailed and ornate, ever more beautiful.

HOLLYWOOD FILMMAKING AND AMERICAN MYTHMAKING

Throughout this study we have discussed Hollywood film genres as formal strategies for renegotiating and reinforcing American ideology. Thus genre can be seen as a form of social ritual. Implicit in this viewpoint is the notion that these ritual forms contribute to what might be called a contemporary American mythology. In a genuine "national cinema" like that developed in Hollywood, with its mass appeal and distribution, with its efforts to project an idealized cultural self-image, and with its reworking of popular stories, it seems not only reasonable but necessary that we seriously consider the status of commercial filmmaking as a form of contemporary mythmaking.

The relationship between a culture's cinema and its mythology has long been of interest to film critics and historians, particularly those genre critics who have noted the "repetition compulsion" and populist ideology of both folk tales and genre films. These notions have been applied most often to the Western, a genre whose mythic status was recognized long before its regeneration by commercial filmmakers. But studies of the Western have tended to treat the genre as an isolated phenomenon growing out of the pre-existing "myth of the West." In so doing, two significant factors usually were overlooked: the role of the commercial cinema in the development of the Western myth and also the Western's obvious kinship with other film genres. All of Hollywood's genres have been refined through the studios' cooperation with the mass audience, and all exhibit basic similarities of social function and narrative composition. As such, we should not restrict our inquiry into filmmaking and mythmaking to the Western genre alone.

But even some of the Western's most influential critics have hesitated to assign it mythic status. In the introduction to his evocative study of Western authorship entitled *Horizons West*, Jim Kitses states that, "In strict classical terms of definition myth has to do with the activity of the gods and as such the Western has no myth"[198] (Kitses, 1969, p. 13). Kitses' hesitation stems, I think, from a literary conception of myth that treats it in terms of *content* (traditional stories about the gods) rather than of *form* and *function*. Recent studies in anthropology and mythology suggest that myth should not be identified by its repetition of some classical content or "pantheistic" story. It should be perceived through its cultural function—a unique conceptual system that confronts and resolves immediate social and ideological conflicts.

This perception dates back to such pioneering anthropologists and cultural analysts as Bronislav Malinowski and Ernst Cassirer. Malinowski suggested that myth serves "an indispensible function: it expresses, enhances, and codifies belief; it safeguards and enforces morality; it vouches for the efficiency and contains practical rules for the guidance of man"[199] (Malinowski, 1926, p. 13). Although Malinowski was primarily interested in the myths of "primitive" cultures, Cassirer and others extended his ideas into a contemporary context. According to Cassirer, man's mythmaking impulse represents a distinct level of consciousness

---

[198] Jim Kitses, *Horizons West*, (Indiana University Press: Bloomington, 1969), p. 13.
[199] Bronislav Malinowski, *Myth in Primitive Psychology* (New York: W. W. Norton and Co., 1926), p. 13. See also his *Freedom and Civilization* (New York: Roy Publishers, Inc., 1944).

with its own conceptual and structural features. There is no unity of "subject matter" in myth, only a unity of function expressed in a unique mode of experience. In *Myth of the State*, Cassirer contends that this function is practical and social: it promotes a feeling of unity and harmony among the members of a society and also the whole of nature or life[200] (Bidney, 1955, pp. 379-392).

Even more significant are the more recent studies by Claude Lévi-Strauss, the proclaimed father of structural anthropology, and Roland Barthes, who has applied Lévi-Strauss' ideas to popular literature and other forms of mass-mediated culture. Lévi-Strauss' chief contribution to the study of anthropology and mythology is his insistence that any myth's cultural function is closely related to its *narrative structure*. In "The Structural Study of Myth," Lévi-Strauss states:

> A myth exhibits a "slated" structure which seeps to the surface, if one may say so, through the repetition process. However, the slates are not absolutely identical to each other. And since the purpose of myth is to provide a logical model capable of overcoming a contradiction (an impossible achievement if, as it happens, the contradiction is real), a theoretically infinite number of slates will be generated, each one slightly different from the others.[201] *(Lévi-Strauss, in DeGeorge, 1972, p. 193)*

Thus, mythmaking itself emerges as a basic human activity which structures human experience—whether social or personal, whether physical or metaphysical—in a distinct and consistent fashion. Lévi-Strauss defines mythical thought as "a whole system of reference which operates by means of a pair of cultural contrasts: between the general and the particular on the one hand and nature and culture on the other"[202] (Lévi-Strauss, 1962, p. 135). These "contrasts" are themselves reduced from the myriad ambiguities of human existence: life/death, good/evil, individual/community, and so on.

A culture's mythology, then, represents its society speaking to itself, developing a network of stories and images designed to animate and resolve the conflicts of everyday life. It is in the structure of these stories and images that we glimpse their mythic status. And as Lévi-Strauss suggests, "If there is meaning to be found in mythology, this cannot reside in the isolated elements which enter into the composition of a myth, but only in the way these elements are combined"[203] (Lévi-Strauss in DeGeorge, 1972, p. 174). Mythic elements are combined in what Lévi-Strauss terms "bundles of oppositions." Different mythologies are identified by the various ways in which these oppositions are combined, mediated, and resolved.

This "structuralist" approach to cultural storytelling provides a clear and accessible view of what might be termed man's mythmaking impulse, and one of the aims of this book has been to examine a contemporary manifestation of that impulse. In the final analysis, the relationship of genre filmmaking to cultural mythmaking seems to me to be significant and direct. Consider the basic similarities between those two activities: how the society at large participates in isolating and refining certain stories, the fact that those stories are essentially problem-solving strategies whose conflicts cannot be fully resolved (hence the infinite variations), the tendency for heroic types to mediate the opposing values inherent within the problem, and the attempt to resolve the problem in a fashion that reinforces the existing social and conceptual order. Genre films, much like the folk tales of primitive cultures, serve to defuse threats to the social order and thereby to provide some logical coherence to that order.

---

[200] See David Bidney's analysis of Cassirer's work in "Myth, Symbolism, and Truth," *Journal of American Folklore* LXVIII (October-December 1955), pp. 379-392. See also Ernst Cassirer, *An Essay on Man* (New Haven: Yale University Press, 1944), *The Myth of the State* (New Haven: Yale University Press, 1946), and The *Philosophy of Symbolic Forms* (New Haven: Yale University Press, 1955).

[201] Claude Lévi-Strauss, *The Structuralists*. (Richard and Fernande DeGeorge, eds. New York: Doubleday, 1972), p. 193.

[202] Claude Lévi-Strauss, *The Savage Mind* (Chicago: University of Chicago Press, 1962), p. 135.

[203] Lévi-Strauss, *The Structuralists*, p. 174.

Roland Barthes, in his *Mythologies*, suggests that the internal logic of any mythical system functions to *naturalize* social experience. "The very principle of myth," contends Barthes, is that "it transforms history into nature"[204] (Barthes, 1957, p. 129). Like Lévi-Strauss, Barthes views mythmaking as a fundamental human activity, and he believes it is manifested today in our ideologies, in familiar belief systems like Christianity, democracy, capitalism, monogamy, and so on. Because the values that inform these systems are woven into the fabric of our everyday lives, these ideologies do indeed seem "natural," they appear to be virtually commonsensical or self-explanatory. When the Western celebrates rugged individualism or the musical celebrates romantic love and marriage, the genre forms act as myths—they are among the various stories our culture tells itself to purify and justify the values and beliefs which sustain it. Barthes might actually be describing a film genre in this description of mythic function: "In passing from history to nature, myth acts economically: it abolishes the complexity of human acts, it gives them the simplicity of essences, it does away with all dialectics, with any going back beyond what is immediately visible, it organizes a world which is without contradiction because it is without depth"[205] (Barthes, 1957, p. 145).

It is undeniably true that many genre films—whether a Ford Western or a Minnelli musical, a Chandler-scripted detective film or one of Douglas Sirk's melodramas—do seem to foreground ideological contradictions rather than do away with them, do seem to organize a world of depth and ambiguity. Our present concerns, however, are not with the artistic manipulation of a generic formula, but rather with the social and conceptual basis for the formula itself. An understanding of where genres come from and how they work both in and on our culture must precede our efforts to differentiate or single out individual genre films for their distinctive artistry.

Examining the various connections between genre filmmaking and cultural mythmaking provides us with a number of valuable insights. This approach encourages us to reconsider and reaffirm the essential, immediate social function of the commercial cinema and especially of genre filmmaking. It demands that we adjust our critical attitude and methods to the cinema's popular and industrial nature. Like the anthropologist studying folk tales, the genre analyst necessarily studies movies in order to glean the "form of their content"—that is, to consider the ways in which popular film narratives structure experience with their formulaic treatment of basic sociocultural issues.

There are, however, two significant considerations which qualify the genre-myth analogy. The first of these involves the role of the mass audience in genre filmmaking. Hollywood movies, unlike traditional folk tales, are not the immediate, spontaneous expression of the people; they are, instead, the calculated expression of professional filmmakers. A film genre develops when the audience encourages the repetition of a film narrative, but the original narrative—the generic prototype—is the product of collaborative artistry. Professional filmmakers are cut from the same cultural cloth as the members of the audience, of course, and we can assume that their response to human existence is substantially the same as the viewers'. There have always been technological, economic, and sociopolitical constraints in Hollywood filmmaking which do affect the nature and range of film stories available. But when considering these constraints, we should also consider a basic paradox of commercial filmmaking: movies are made by filmmakers, whereas genres are "made" by the collective response of the mass audience.

The second consideration involves generic evolution. In its evolutionary process, a genre's variation tends to render both filmmakers and audience more sensitive to the form as distinct from its social function. This increasing sensitivity to a genre's formal make-up—to its rules of expression and composition—leads to a number of interesting developments as the genre evolves: self-reflexive or formally self-conscious films, genre films which parody or subvert the

---

[204] Roland Barthes, *Mythologies* (New York: Hill and Wang, 1957), p. 129.
[205] *Ibid.*, p. 145.

genre's essentially prosocial stance, the tendency for foreign filmmakers to utilize a genre's formal features as aesthetic ends in themselves with little regard for their social function, and so on. But no matter how subversive or self-reflexive a genre film might appear to be, its success—like that of the genre—is necessarily a function of popular response. As I pointed out in the last chapter, even Douglas Sirk's most stylized and outrageous melodramas were among the most popular films of their particular era.

So for a number of reasons, Sirk's *Imitation of Life* is an appropriate finishing point for this book. The film heralds the end of the "classic age" of American cinema—the effective winding down of Hollywood's mythmaking function and the ultimate death of the Hollywood studio system. By the early 1960s, Hollywood's once-massive audience had dwindled to less than half its peak postwar size, movie "palaces" were being replaced by smaller and more economical theaters catering to more specialized audiences, foreign films were imported in record numbers, and commercial television (eating up the majority of the cinema's mass audience) emerged as America's principal means of collective cultural expression.

Actually, the American cinema passed into its mannerist or baroque age by the late '50s. The decade's "subversive" melodramas, along with its psychological Westerns, self-reflexive musicals, and manic crime thrillers, collectively represent a stage of narrative, technical, and thematic evolution that was light years beyond their classic prewar predecessors. By investigating the works of the formative prewar years, we can trace the lineage which produced the baroque masterpieces of Hollywood's final years. Many viewers and most critics have overlooked their distinctive artistry—and overlooked the expressive potential of their genres as well. But Westerns like *The Searchers* and *The Naked Spur*, musicals like *The Band Wagon* and *It's Always Fair Weather*, melodramas like *The Cobweb* and *Written on the Wind*, detective films like *Touch of Evil* and *The Big Heat*—these and many others represent a period of remarkable, and I think unparalleled, artistic achievement in modern American culture. If we temper our elitist biases long enough to look closely at these films, we notice that they do indeed exhibit those qualities generally associated with narrative artistry: irony, ambiguity, thematic complexity, formal self-consciousness. But what's so amazing about the American cinema is that this artistry emerged from such an overtly formulaic and socially immediate mass medium, from an industry whose steady evolution and direct audience contact enabled it to tap the flow of our cultural juices in an accessible yet formally sophisticated means of expression.

Hollywood's tradition of genres has survived, in one form or another, the death of the studio system of film production. Commercial television has been the primary vehicle for the regeneration and continuation of these popular formulas, having co-opted Hollywood's industrial and technological base as well as its mass audience and narrative formulas. Nonetheless, there are significant aspects of commercial television production which present a substantial departure from studio filmmaking. For one, television has yielded—quite willingly, it seems—to the demands of commerce and thus has severely compromised the aesthetic integrity of its texts. In fact, both the "commercial interruptions" and the continuous "flow" of television programming render it difficult even to isolate a television text. Furthermore, although the networks have developed elaborate methods of audience analysis and feedback (Nielsen and Arbitron ratings, etc.), their essential function is not to enable the audience to participate in program development but rather to determine advertising revenues. The cinema delivers stories to an audience, whereas television delivers the audience to advertisers.

The New Hollywood also provides a potentially productive but highly complex arena for further genre study. With the death of the studio system, the American cinema has evolved from a cohesive industry to a collection of loosely related business ventures; fewer films, most of them independently produced, are competing for increasingly higher revenues despite the substantial odds nowadays against a film even being released, let alone turning a profit. Movie "blockbusters" (*The Godfather, The Exorcist, Jaws, Star Wars*, etc.) and the low-budget "exploitation" film (car-crash movies, mutilation thrillers, soft-core pornographic films) are flourishing, but that vast middle ground once dominated by the Hollywood studios is gone. And although virtually all the blockbusters of the '70s tapped directly into some established genre, their success seems to rely more on packaging, promotion, and other forms of media hype than on the movies' power as a form of collective cultural expression. Ultimately, genre analysis of current films might be best applied to the exploitation film rather than the blockbuster, mainly because the former has sustained the "formula factory" approach to film production and a certain regard for their consistent popular audience.

I am not suggesting, however, that our genre study of classic Hollywood can be applied wholesale to present-day forms. Genre study is of necessity a flexible critical method whose practice is contingent upon the system it investigates. Initial efforts to apply established literary genre theory to the cinema proved largely ineffectual, and so too, I think, would efforts to apply the critical theory developed here to the New Hollywood or to commercial television. Genre study assumes that there are certain inherent human impulses (primarily concerning narrativity and mythmaking) which are basic to humankind; it also assumes that these impulses are conditioned by—and must be studied in the context of—the specific cultural and industrial environment in which they are expressed.

It's worth suggesting that we can perceive and articulate those social conditions and any individual film's relation to them only from a considerable historical distance. It would seem that we most clearly recognize our culture's mythology in retrospect, and that at any given moment, we are in the process of formulating a mythology whose spirit and substance escape our conscious perception. In fact, our distanced viewpoint may do as much to distort as to clarify "historical reality." Hence the ambivalent conception of the term "myth" itself: a myth is both true and false, both a clarification and a distortion of real-world experience and the human condition. It is, finally, a formalized means to negotiate the present via concepts and images which are the residue of human history.

This might begin to account for the wide disparity of critical readings of '50s melodramas through time. Although we are now reading the same filmic text as viewers and critics did then, there is little question but that our historical perspective, compounded by our cultural and academic biases, renders our viewing of these films substantially different for us than it was for a '50s audience. We note now how the films anticipated certain social issues, how they accommodate our aesthetic biases regarding irony, ambiguity, and formal stylization, or how they comply with current intellectual interest in ideology and materialism. In each case, we can consider how these particular filmic narratives not only participate in but actually critique the complex workings of American mythology.

Basic to these considerations, however, both in the 1950s and today, is the immediate experience of the film itself. The ultimate value of studying cinema is a function of the depth and range of cultural insights—be they aesthetic, sociological, economic, political, mythological—which the movies afford us. The closer we examine the popular arts, the better we come to understand our culture and finally ourselves. What motivates and sustains that close study, though, is the elemental appeal of individual movies. Whatever my critical or academic investment in film study might be, I am secure in the knowledge that in the familiar darkness of a screening room or a nearby theater I once again can accompany the Westerner on his timeless search through Monument Valley, I once again might deny plausibility and the laws of gravity when Fred and Ginger turn to me and ask, "Shall we dance?"

CRITICAL FILM ANALYSES

THE ROARING TWENTIES (1939)

–Gangster Film in its Classical Phase–

Shannon Mader

Producer: Hal B. Wallis. Associate Producer: Samuel Bischoff. Director: Raoul Walsh. Story: Mark Hellinger. Screenplay: Jerry Wald, Richard Macaulay, and Robert Rossen. Art Director: Max Parker. Musical Director: Leo F. Forbstein. Orchestral Arrangements: Ray Heindorf. Cameraman: Ernest Haller. Special Effects: Byron Haskin and Edwin A. DuPar. Editor: Jack Killifer.

CAST: James Cagney (Eddie Bartlett), Priscilla Lang (Jean Sherman), Humphrey Bogart (George Halley), Gladys George (Panama Smith), Jeffrey Lynn (Lloyd Hart), Frank McHugh (Danny Green), Paul Kelly (Nick Brown). A Warner Brothers release of a Samuel Bischoff production. 104 min.

Based in part on the personal recollections of columnist Mark Hellinger, *The Roaring Twenties* is an exercise in memory as well as morality. Like all classical gangster films, *The Roaring Twenties* depicts a morally-structured universe in which good prevails and evil is punished. But unlike them, the film's condemnation of a crime-ridden era is commingled with an obvious nostalgia for it. If this seems somewhat contradictory, then I should perhaps remind you that even saints sometimes remember their sins with fondness.

Coming to fruition in 1930 with Mervyn LeRoy's *Little Caesar*, the gangster film seemed prematurely old by the time of the release of *The Roaring Twenties* nine years later. The enforcement of the Production Code in 1934 had literally exsanguinated the genre. No longer able to dwell on quasi-heroic hoodlums who, despite their brutality, elicited some sympathy, the genre had no choice but to adapt. Bloodthirsty gangsters gave way to gun-toting G-men. Bullet-ridden corpses gave way to conscience-stricken cons. And puritanical polemics on the wages of sin gave way to sociological sermons on the roots of crime. In short, the genre was bowdlerized, emasculated, and enfeebled. It continued to live on, but as a pallid reflection of what it once was.

While not all directors were conscious of the genre's decline, today's director, Raoul Walsh, seems to have been particularly so. Three of his best-known films—today's picture, *High Sierra* (1941), and the immortal *White Heat* (1949)—are self-conscious attempts to revitalized and resuscitate the genre. In the case of *The Roaring Twenties*, however, his heart seems to have been divided between a desire to revitalize it and a desire to eulogize it. Indeed, the film's nostalgic tone seems to be motivated by a nostalgia not only for the nation's past but for the genre's. Quite unlike either the early gangster films or the later *White Heat*, the mood of *The Roaring Twenties* seems at times more melancholic than maniacal, more depressing than exhilarating. While it does indeed roar, the roaring of the twenties is experienced in retrospect: we view the decade through the prism of the present. As a result, the film lacks the unrelenting immediacy of its forebears.

It differs from them in other ways as well. Torn between a desire to re-live the past and a desire to transcend it, *The Roaring Twenties* is part recapitulation, part innovation. On the one hand, it's certainly reminiscent of the early gangster films; on the other, it's decidedly different. Among its differences is the fact that it provides a sociological explanation for gangsterism.

Under the liberal leadership of President Roosevelt, the nation had taken a decisive turn to the Left. As a result, conservative attitudes towards crime were swept aside as liberal approaches gained ascendance. In the process, the responsibility for crime shifted from the criminal to society. Particularly influential were the findings of liberal sociologists who argued that poverty and the lack of economic opportunity were the primary causes of crime. Eliminate these, they said, and you will eliminate crime.

As you will see, today's film dramatizes this theory. Eddie Bartlett returns from World War I with the expectation that he'll be able to get his job back. But when he shows up at the garage at which he used to work, his old boss tells him that the position was filled years ago. Feeling betrayed, Eddie looks for work elsewhere; unfortunately, it's the same story everywhere: there are simply no jobs for the returning vets. By accident, Eddie winds up in jail, sharing a cell with another hapless veteran. It is thus through no fault of his own that Eddie becomes a criminal and is introduced to the criminal element.

According to the logic of the film, therefore, the rise of organized crime was caused by the lack of opportunity which the veterans of World War I faced on their return to America. What Prohibition did, the film seems to be arguing, was not so much create the criminal element as criminalize an element which had not been previously criminal. It provided these unemployed veterans with opportunities which they did not otherwise possess. After all, neither Eddie nor Danny are vicious by nature; they don't commit crimes for the sake of committing them. Under normal circumstances, in fact, they would have probably been law-abiding citizens. But given their situation, it was inevitable that they would turn to crime. They simply played the hand life dealt them. Or, as Eddie tells Lloyd, "Take what you can get while you can get it, cause nobody's gonna walk up to you and drop it in your lap."

In addition to a belief in the economic origins of crime, liberal sociologists believed in the corrigibility of criminals. If, after all, circumstances create the criminal, then a change in circumstances should change the criminal. Liberal sociologists therefore propounded the notion of rehabilitation. Instead of condemning the criminal, they argued, we should try to correct him.

Due perhaps to its compatibility with the Christian concept of redemption, the idea of rehabilitation gained surprisingly wide acceptance in America at the time. It even found its way—as you will see today—into a genre which had formerly seemed more attuned to the morality of the Old Testament than to that of the New. For although the gangsters who populated the genre during the 1930-33 period were irredeemable, ignominious thugs who died just as they deserved to—face down in the gutter, Eddie Bartlett dies a redeemed man. Having atoned for his sins, he dies on the steps of a church and on the stairway heaven.

HIGH SIERRA (1941)

–Gangster Film in its Classical Phase–

Chia-chi Wu

Production company: Warner Bros. Producer: Jack L. Warner and Hal B. Wallis. Director: Raoul Walsh. Screenplay: John Huston and W.R. Burnett. Based on a novel by W.R. Burnett. Photographer: Tony Gaudio. Editor: Jack Killifer. Assistant Director: Ted Smith. Music: Adolph Deutsch. Cost: Milo Anderson. Running time: 100 mins. Released: 1941.

CAST: Ida Lupino (Marie), Humphrey Bogart (Roy Earle), Alan Curtis (Babe), Arthur Kennedy (Red), Joan Leslie (Velma), Henry Travers (Pa), Elizabeth Risdon (Ma), Donald MacBride (Big Mac).

> ...the importance of the gangster film, and the nature and intensity or its emotional and aesthetic impact, cannot be measured in terms of the place of the gangster himself or the importance of the problem of crime in American life....What matters is that the experience of the gangster as *an experience of art* is universal to Americans.
>
> —Robert Warshow (original emphasis)[206]

The gangster genre seems to have thrived upon a symbiotic relation to "real" events and "real" gangsters, (e.g., Al Capone, John Dillinger, Bonnie Parker and Clyde Barrow) as exploited and circulated by sensational journalism. To examine this prolific genre, however, is to trace its own mythology and its own history on the reel rather than seeing these films simply as screen portrayals of these bandits, faithful or unfaithful. The quote by Robert Warshow suggests that the referential field, i.e., the framework of references, of any gangster film lies in other or previous gangster films instead of their real world counterparts. Therefore, the important questions to ask when we "read" a gangster film would be: in what ways it establishes or reiterates the narrative formula, constructs the gangster's mythology or solidifies a particular iconography; or, on the other hand, in what ways it consciously revises or undermines the original model, as an attempt to reinvigorate or resuscitate the genre, at the same time speaking to historically conscious film buffs.

High Sierra opens with a scene in which Roy Earle, a notorious bandit who made his name eight years earlier, is released from the prison into a world of "twerps, soda jerkers, and jitterbugs" only to find himself as "part relic and part legend" in the new world.[207] The narrative unfolds as they orchestrate the plan of a heist, reaches its climax as it goes haywire, and ends with Roy Earle's death. Parallel to the hold-up is a romantic story line between Roy and Velma

---

[206] Robert Warshow, "The Gangster as Tragic Hero," in *The Immediate Experience*, New York, Atheneum Books, 1970, p.130.
[207] Carlos Clarens, *Crime Movies: From Griffith to the Godfather and Beyond*, New York, W W Norton & Company, p. 168.

(a club-footed farm girl restored to hearth through Roy's help) and between Roy and Marie (who serves the role of the gangster's moll). With its goal-oriented protagonist, linear dramatic structure governed by a tightly chained causality, and double-plot structure, *High Sierra* stays closely to Classical Hollywood style. Yet if we see *High Sierra* in terms of the genre's history, we should underline how it enacts a dialogue with its precursors in the 30s, especially those categorized by Schatz as classic gangster films—*Little Caesar* (1930), *The Public Enemy* (1931) and *Scarface* (1932). The gangster genre briefly reached its peak in the early 30s, but was then emasculated by the dictates of Production Code Administration in the mid 1930s. Since then the genre continued but in a more subdued form. Made in the year of 1941, *High Sierra* is fully conscious of its status as a gangster film. Generically speaking, it obviously restructures the narrative formula established by the early 30s films—the gangster's rise to power and tragic fall—in that Earle is depicted as a gangster already on the decline from the beginning of the film. The introduction of Roy Earle as an *ex-convict* marks the end of the old gang's golden era, and their nostalgia is constantly conveyed by two other old gang members, Big Mac and the old doctor, whose illness and decrepitude also symbolize the demise of the good old days. At the same time, what is evoked in the characters' mourning of the old good times is indeed the film's own nostalgia for the golden era of the gangster films, in which the gangsters would cohere as a well-organized community or an ersatz family, with a strong male bond between the gangster and his sidekicks, who are always loyal, courageous and capable. In contrast, despite Roy Earle's persistence in his old gangster codes (he insists that he will work for Big Mac even after Beg Mac's death), the gangsters in the new world are portrayed as pineless, inept, and treacherous: Roy's underlings (Red and Babe) disastrously botch their first job; one of them (Mendoza) even squeals to police for his own skin.

If *High Sierra* is motivated by a nostalgia for the genre's past, it is also motivated by a nostalgia for grassroots America, a bygone era before "modern America hardened into concrete and asphalt."[208] Such nostalgia is epitomized by Earle's love of nature, his dream of rustic life style, and his background as a small town farm boy. Unlike most gangster films, which usually employ a dark urban milieu as a "surreal extension of the gangster psyche," the film replaces the iconography of an urban city with sweeping landscapes of the high sierra, lush grass and trees in the park, and other spacious, outdoor scenes. It thus represents a novelty in the gangster genre, characterized by Schatz as "rural gangster" or "rural bandit" film, as a derivative of the classic model.[209] Although the city is totally absent from the film, it is conspicuous in its absence. In its revamping of traditional gangster iconography is the replaying of several important motifs of the genre. First, the genre often equates the gangster with "nature," and inscribes the theme of nature versus culture. In classic gangster films, nature is embodied by the gangster's primitive passions and impulses, while in *High Sierra* it is associated with Earle's rural values. Second, the nature / culture opposition in the gangster film can be seen as a critique of the modern urban milieu, as a product of modern civilization. Casting the city in dark and gloomy atmosphere with walls that seem to trap the gangster, the genre demands a new and critical perspective on the ideology of social evolution and progress, especially in the context of industrialism and post-industrial capitalism. Even though *High Sierra* conjures up a mise-en-scene rich in natural landscapes, it inherits and extends the genre's critique of modern urban milieu by implying that the hostility, alienation and corruption of the urban city are responsible for Roy's passage from a farm boy to a bandit eight years earlier. Only nature can set the gangster free, if not redeem him. Meanwhile, the film presages film noir's pessimistic view of modern world, which was to become a more prominent genre in the 40s and 50s.

---

[208] *Ibid.*, p.169.
[209] Thomas Schatz, *Hollywood Genres: Formulas, Filmmaking, and the Studio System*, New York, McGraw-Hill, Inc., p. 84, pp. 102-4.

High Sierra retains the mythology of the gangster as an alienated and tragic hero, yet with subtly different overtones. The tragedy of the gangster, as Robert Warshow defines, lies in the "sense of desperation and inevitable failure," which are ironically created by the optimism of the American Dream—man as a self-made individual, as well as the belief in the pursuit of happiness conceived only in terms of material wealth and success. To Warshaw, the gangster's downfall plays out the contradictions between individualism and the ideals of equality in American capitalism, therefore representing a denial of "happier American culture."[210] Besides, the classic gangsters often elicit our sympathy by relating the crime to social causes and implying that they are created by social circumstances rather than the gangsters' inhuman brutality. *High Sierra* underlies Roy's awareness of his own existential and social alienation to intensify the sense of tragedy. In the beginning of the film, he immediately recoils from a conversation when the farmer recognizes him as the bank robber. Later in the film when he talks to the old doctor about Velma, he acknowledges the impossibility of marrying Velma, as the old timer reminisces, "Remember what Johnny Dillinger used to say about guys like you and him? That you were rushing toward death, that's it, rushing toward death."

The tragic overtone of the film is also composed through the humanization of Roy's character. Incarnated by Humphrey Bogart, the desperate loner gangster is not so much motivated by greed, envy or inhuman brutality as by his Robin Hood humanity, which is what causes his fatal fall in the end. Bogart's persona expands the criminal characterization and offsets his violence by adding contrasting elements of warmth and compassion. More importantly, one convention of the classic gangster is completely overturned in this film: the characterization of the bandit as a sexually "aberrant," "dis-oriented" psychotic, who is either overtly obsessed with mother or sister (e.g., *Scarface*, *White Heat*), mistreating woman outside the immediate family (e.g., *The Public Enemy*), or developing a homoerotic preoccupation with his sidekicks (e.g., *The Little Caesar*). In contrast, Roy Earle's new capacity for romantic love, as Schatz points out correctly, underscores the tragic irony of the hero's certain death, which is a radical reorientation of the gangster's "perverse, misdirected sexuality."[211]

High Sierra also rethematizes the death-with-dignity convention of the genre. Although the film bows to the edicts of the Production Code by having him meet a rough death at the hands of the law, the ending of the film, as the title suggests, is pregnant with moral ambiguity and can be read in a totally different light. In the final duel , the shots/reverse shots between Roy and the police are mostly built around low angle shots of Roy Earle and high angle shots of the police, which, visually, lends to the bandit a spiritual and existential superiority. The long shots of the high mountains thus become a metaphor for Roy and his superiority. It is not until he comes out of the rocks for Marie and his dog that he exposes himself to the view of the police gunman and gets shot. The myth of the gangster is re-established here: it is the gangster's own humanity and compassion rather than the law enforcers that cause his tragic downfall. The last lines delivered by Marie and the reporter are especially intriguing. As if to fulfill the film's moral obligation to give a "pro-social" message (as stipulated by Production Code), the reporter, looking down to Roy's body, grunts, "Well, well. Look at him lying here. He ain't much now, is he?" Yet this line is immediately undermined by their dialogue:

> Marie: Mister. What does it mean when a man "crashes out?"
> Reporter: Crashes out? . . . It means he is free.

What follows is a close-up of Marie's face, sad but relieved, as she murmurs, "Free." The camera tilts up and ends the film with a long shot of the high sierra, the only place Roy Earle could find refuge in.

The net cost of the film is $491,000. As the box office record of November, 1943 shows, it grossed $1,067,000 in the domestic market, and $412,000 in the foreign market.

---

[210] Robert Warshow, p. 129-131.
[211] Thomas Schatz, p. 93, p. 103.

11

GENRE: POSTCLASSICAL PHASE

The year 1946 marked the culmination of a five year "war boom" for Hollywood, with record revenues of over $1.5 billion and weekly ticket sales of 90 to 100 million. The two biggest hits in 1946 were "major independent" productions: Sam Goldwyn's The Best Years of Our Lives and David O. Selznick's Duel in the Sun. Both returned 11.3 million in rentals, a huge sum at that time, and signaled important changes in the industry—though Selznick's Duel was the more telling of the two. Like his Gone With the Wind, it was a prototype New Hollywood blockbuster: a "pre-sold" spectacle (based on a popular historical novel) with top stars, an excessive budget, a sprawling story, and state-of-the-art production values. Selznick himself termed Duel "an exercise in making a big-grossing film," gambling on a nationwide promotion-and-release campaign after a weak sneak preview. When the gamble paid off, he proclaimed it a "tremendous milestone in motion picture merchandising and exhibition."

—Thomas Schatz, "The New Hollywood"

CTCS 190 LECTURE OUTLINE - WEEK XI   **LECTURE 10**

PART 2: THE POSTCLASSICAL PERIOD: 1946-1962

    A. Conditions and Causes for Genre Experimentation in American Film
        1. The post-war years of transition in America, 1946-1962
        2. Creator and consumer sophistication
        3. Technological developments
        4. Easing of censorship
        4. The breakup of the Studio System and the Mode of Independent Production
        4. The auteur-genre dialectic
    B. Types of Genre Experimentation
        1. Topical accommodation
        2. Departure or modernization
        3. Hybrid
        4. Genre as vehicle
        5. Parody
        6. Nostalgia
        7. Remythologization
        8. Demythologization
    C. Implications of Genre Experimentation
    D. Introduction and Screening of a Genre Film in its Postclassical Phase

Notes

Notes

CHINATOWN AND GENERIC TRANSFORMATION IN RECENT AMERICAN FILMS

John G. Cawelti, 1978

One of the fascinating things about Roman Polanski's *Chinatown* is that it invokes in so many ways the American popular genre of the hard-boiled detective story. Most of us, I suppose, associate this tradition particularly with two films, both of which starred Humphrey Bogart: John Huston's *The Maltese Falcon* (1941) and Howard Hawks' *The Big Sleep* (1946). But these are only the two most-remembered and perhaps the most memorable versions of a narrative formula which has been replicated in hundreds of novels, films, and television programs. Next to the western, the hard-boiled detective story is America's most distinctive contribution to the world's stock of action-adventure stories, our contemporaneous embodiment of the drama of heroic quest which has appeared in so many different cultures in so many different guises. Unlike the western—heroic quest on the frontier—which can perhaps be traced back as far as the Indian captivity narratives of the late seventeenth century, and certainly to Cooper's Leatherstocking saga of the early nineteenth century, the hard-boiled detective story is of quite recent origin. It developed in the twenties through the medium of short action stories in pulp magazines like the famous *Black Mask*. By 1929, Dashiell Hammett had produced in *Red Harvest* the first hard-boiled detective novel. Before retiring into literary silence in the mid-thirties, Hammett had created a basic core of hard-boiled adventure in his Continental Op stories and his novels—*The Maltese Falcon* (1930), *The Dain Curse* (1929), *The Glass Key* (1931) and *The Thin Man* (1934). In very short order, the hard-boiled detective made the transition from novel to film. *The Maltese Falcon* appeared in two film versions in the early 30s, before John Huston made the definitive version in 1941. *The Glass Key* was produced in the early 30s and in the 40s; *The Thin Man* became one of the great movie successes of the later 30s, so popular that it led to a number of invented sequels. And while the hard-boiled detective flourished in film, Hammett's example was followed in novels by writers whose literary approach ranged from the subtlety and depth of Raymond Chandler and Ross Macdonald to the sensational—and bestselling—crudity of Mickey Spillane. Radio and television, too, made many series based on the figure of the hardboiled detective and his quest for justice through the ambiguous landscape of the modern American city. If a myth can be defined as a pattern of narrative known throughout the culture and presented in many different versions by many different tellers, then the hard-boiled detective story is in that sense an important American myth.

Chinatown invokes this myth in many different ways. Its setting in Los Angeles in the 1930s is very much the archetypal "hard-boiled" setting, the place and time of Hammett's and Chandler's novels. While it is true that many hard-boiled novels and films are set in different places and times—Mickey Spillane's Mike Hammer stories in New York City, John D. Macdonald's Travis McGee saga in Florida—the California city setting of Hammett and Chandler and the approximate time of their stories, memorialized in the period furnishings, visual icons, and style of the great hard-boiled films of the 1940s, have become for us the look and the temporal-spatial aura of the hard-boiled myth. It is this aura which Polanski generates, though there is something not quite right, something disturbingly off about it. In this case, it is the color. The world of the hard-boiled myth is preeminently a world of black and white. Its ambience is that compound of angular light and shadow enmeshed in webs of fog which grew out of the visual legacy of German expressionism in drama and film, transformed into what is now usually called *film noir* by its adjustment to American locales and stories. Polanski carefully controls his spectrum of hue and tone in order to give it the feel of *film noir*, but it is nonetheless color with occasional moments of rich golden light—as in the scene in the dry riverbed. These moments of warm color often relate to scenes that are outside the usual setting or thematic content—for example, scenes in the natural landscape outside the city—which are themselves generally outside the world of the hard-boiled detective story. The invocation of many other traditional elements of the hard-boiled myth, the *film noir* tone and the 1930s setting cue us to expect the traditional mythical world of the private eye hero. But the presence of color, along with increasing deviations from established patterns of plot, motive and character give us an eerie feeling of one myth colliding with and beginning to give way to others.

Let us begin by examining *Chinatown*'s relation to the traditional myth of the hard-boiled detective. The established narrative formula of the hard-boiled story has as its protagonist a private investigator who occupies a marginal position with respect to the official social institutions of criminal justice. The private eye is licensed by the state, but though he may be a former member of a police force or district attorney's staff, he is not now connected with such an organization. In the course of the story, he is very likely to come into conflict with representatives of the official machinery, though he may also have friends who are police officers. His position on the edge of the law is very important, because one of the central themes of the hard-boiled myth is the ambiguity between institutionalized law enforcement and true justice. The story shows us that the police and the courts are incapable of effectively protecting the innocent and bringing the guilty to appropriate justice. Only the individual of integrity who exists on the margins of society can solve the crime and bring about a true justice.

The marginal character of the private eye hero is thus crucial to his role in the myth. It is also central to his characterization. We see him not only as a figure outside the institutionalized process of law enforcement, but as the paradoxical combination of a man of character who is also a failure. The private eye is a relatively poor man who operates out of a seedy office and never seems to make very much money by his exploits; he is the most marginal sort of lower-middle class quasi-professional. Yet unlike the usual stereotype of this social class, he is a man of honor and integrity who cannot be made to give up his quest for true justice. He is a compelling American hero type, clearly related to the traditional western hero who manifests many of the same characteristics and conditions of marginality.

The story begins when the hard-boiled hero is given a mission by a client. It is typical that this initial mission is a deceptive one. Either the client is lying, as Brigid O'Shaughnessy lies to Sam Spade in *The Maltese Falcon*, or the client has himself been deceived and does not understand what is really at stake when he gives the detective his case, as with General Sternwood in *The Big Sleep*. Often the detective is being used as a pawn in some larger plot of the client's. Whatever his initial impetus to action, the detective soon finds himself enmeshed in a very complex conspiracy involving a number of people from different spheres of society. The ratiocinative English detective in authors like Dorothy Sayers, Agatha Christie, or Ngaio Marsh, investigates crimes by examining clues, questioning witnesses and then using his intellectual powers of insight and deduction to arrive at the solution. The hard-boiled detective investigates through movement and encounter; he collides with the web of conspiracy until he has exposed its outlines. The crime solved by the ratiocinative detective is usually that of a single individual. With this individual's means and motives for the criminal act rationally established he can be turned over to the law for prosecution. But the hard-boiled detective encounters a linked series of criminal acts and responsibilities; he discovers not a single guilty individual, but a corrupt society in which wealthy and respectable people are linked with gangsters and crooked politicians. Because it is society and not just a single individual which is corrupt, the official machinery of law enforcement is unable to bring the guilty to justice. The hard-boiled detective must decide for himself what kind of justice can be accomplished in the ambiguous urban world of modern America, and he must, in many instances, undertake to see this justice through, himself. There have always been two different tendencies within the hard-boiled myth. Some writers, like Mickey Spillane and his many current followers, place their emphasis on the hero as private vigilante avenger. Their stories climax with the hero playing the role of executioner as well as detective and judge. More complex and artistic writers, like Hammett, Chandler and Ross Macdonald, develop instead the theme of the hero's own relationship to the mythical role of lawman-outside-the-law. Their versions of the story rarely end with the detective's execution of the criminal; they prefer instead either to arrange for the criminal's self-destruction as in Chandler's *Farewell, My Lovely,* or simply to bring about the criminal's exposure and confession, as in *The Maltese Falcon.* But this latter trend, though it has produced greater literature, is perhaps best understood as a humane avoidance of the true thrust of he myth which is, I think, essentially toward the marginal hero becoming righteous judge and executioner, culture-hero for a society which has profoundly ambiguous conflicts in choosing between its commitment to legality and its belief that only individual actions are ultimately moral and just.

One further element of the hard-boiled myth needs to be particularly noted: the role of the feminine antagonist. In almost every case, the hard-boiled hero encounters a beautiful and dangerous woman in the course of his investigations and he finds himself very much drawn toward her, even to the point of falling in love. Sometimes the woman is his client, sometimes a figure in the conspiracy. In a surprising number of cases (*The Maltese Falcon, The Big Sleep, Farewell, My Lovely, I, The Jury,* and many others) the woman turns out to be the murderess, and, in Spillane at least, is killed by her detective-lover. This murky treatment of the "romance" between detective and dangerous female is occasionally resolved happily as in the Bogart-Bacall relationship at the end of the film version of *The Big Sleep* (in the novel this romantic culmination does not take place). However, such an outcome is rare. Even if the beautiful woman does not turn out to be a murderess, the detective usually separates from her at the end to return to his marginal situation, basically unchanged by what has happened to him and ready to perform more acts of justice when the occasion arises.

We can see from this brief resume of the hard-boiled formula how close a resemblance *Chinatown* bears to it. But the film deviates increasingly from the myth until, by the end of the story, the film arrives at an ending almost contrary to that of the myth. Instead of bringing justice to a corrupt society, the detective's actions leave the basic source of corruption untouched. Instead of protecting the innocent, his investigation leads to the death of one victim and the deeper moral destruction of another. Instead of surmounting the web of conspiracy with honor and integrity intact, the detective is overwhelmed by what has happened to him.

True, the action of *Chinatown* increasingly departs from the traditional hardboiled formula as the story progresses; however, there are, from the very beginning, a number of significant departures from the standard pattern. The choice of Jack Nicholson and Faye Dunaway as leading actors is a good instance of this. Nicholson and Dunaway have certain physical and stylistic resemblances to Bogart and Bacall and these are obviously played up through costume, makeup and gesture. Indeed, there is one early scene in a restaurant between them which is almost eerily reminiscent of the famous horse-racing interchange between Bogart and Bacall in *The Big Sleep.* But much as they echo the archetypal hard-boiled duo in a superficial way, Nicholson and Dunaway play characters which are very different. Dunaway has a neurotic fragility, an underlying quality of desperation which becomes even more apparent as her true situation is revealed. She never generates the sense of independence and courage that Bacall brought to her hard-boiled roles; her qualities of wit and sophistication—those characteristics which made Bacall such an appropriate romantic partner for the hard-boiled detective—are quickly seen to be a veneer covering depths of anguish and ambiguity. Nicholson also portrays, at least early on, a character who is not quite what he seems. His attempt to be the tough, cynical, and humorous private eye is undercut on all sides; he is terribly inept as a wit, as his attempt to tell his assistants the Chinese joke makes clear. Nor is he the tough, marginal man of professional honor he pretends to be at the beginning; actually, he is a successful small businessman who has made a good thing out of exploiting the more sordid needs of his fellowmen. One of the most deeply symbolic clichés of the traditional hard-boiled formula is the hero's refusal to do divorce business, in fact one of the primary functions of the private detective. By this choice the traditional private-eye of the myth established both his personal sense of honor and his transcendent vocation, distinguishing himself from the typical private investigator. However, from the beginning of *Chinatown*, it is clear that the accumulation of evidence of marital infidelity is Jake Gittes' primary business. He is, indeed, drawn into the affairs of Noah Cross, his daughter, and her husband by a commission to document a supposedly clandestine affair between the latter and a much younger woman. The name, J. J. Gittes, which Polanski and Robert Towne, the screenwriter, chose for their protagonist is a good indication of this aspect of his character. Think of the names of the traditional hard-boiled detectives: Sam Spade, with its implication of hardness and digging beneath the surface; Philip Marlowe with its aura of knightliness and chivalry; Lew Archer with its mythical overtones. Gittes, or "Gits" as Noah Cross ironically keeps pronouncing it, connotes selfishness and grasping and has, in addition, a kind of ethnic echo very different from the pure Anglo of Spade, Marlowe and Archer.

Yet, qualified and even "anti-heroic" as he is, Gittes is swept up into the traditional hard-boiled action. His initial and deceptive charge involves him in the investigation of a murder, which in turn leads him to evidence of a large-scale conspiracy involving big business, politics, crime and the whole underlying social and environmental structure of Los Angeles. Like the traditional hard-boiled detective, Gittes begins as a marginal individual, but gradually finds himself becoming a moral agent with a mission. At the same time he becomes romantically involved with a character deeply implicated in the web of conspiracy, the mysterious widow of the man who has been murdered. By the middle of the film Gittes is determined to expose the political conspiracy which he senses beneath the surface, and also to resolve the question of the guilt or innocence of the woman to whom he has been so strongly attracted. Thus far, the situation closely resembles that of *The Maltese Falcon* and *The Big Sleep*. It is at this point, however, that the action again takes a vast departure from that of the traditional hard-boiled story. Instead of demonstrating his ability to expose and punish the guilty, Gittes steadily finds himself confronting a depth of evil and chaos so great that he is unable to control it. In relation to the social and personal depravity represented by Noah Cross and the world in which he can so successfully operate, the toughness, moral concern, and professional skill of Gittes not only seem ineffectual, but lead to ends that are the very opposite of those intended. At the end of the film, Noah Cross is free to continue his rapacious depredations on the land, the city and the body of his own daughter-granddaughter; and the one person who might have effectively brought Cross to some form of justice—his daughter-mistress—has been destroyed. Gittes' confrontation with a depth of depravity beyond the capacity of the hard-boiled ethos of individualistic justice is, I think, the essential significance of the Chinatown motif in the film. Chinatown becomes a symbol of life's deeper moral enigmas, those unintended consequences of action that are past understanding and control. Gittes has been there before. In another case his attempts at individual moral action had led to the death of a woman he cared for. It is apparently this tragedy that motivated him to leave the police force and set up as a private investigator. Now he has been drawn back into moral action, and it is again, in Chinatown, that his attempt to live out the myth of individualistic justice collides with the power of evil and chance in the world. The result is not heroic confrontation and the triumph of justice, but tragic catastrophe and the destruction of the innocent.

Chinatown places the hard-boiled detective story within a view of the world that is deeper and more catastrophic, more enigmatic in its evil, more sudden and inexplicable in its outbreaks of violent chance. In the end, the image of heroic, moral action embedded in the traditional private-eye myth turns out to be totally inadequate to overcome the destructive realities revealed in the course of this story. This revelation of depths beneath depths is made increasingly evident in the film's relentless movement toward Chinatown, the symbolic locus of darkness, strangeness and catastrophe; but it also appears in the film's manipulation of action and image. The themes of water and drought, which weave through the action, not only reveal the scope of Noah Cross's conspiracy to dominate a city by manipulating its water supply, but create a texture of allusion which resonates with the mythical meanings traditionally associated with water and drought. Polanski's version of Los Angeles in the 1930s reveals the transcendent mythical world of the sterile kingdom, the dying king and the drowned man beneath it—the world, for example, of Eliot's *Wasteland* and before that of the cyclical myths of traditional cultures. Another of the film's motifs, its revelation of the rape-incest by which Noah Cross has fathered a daughter on his own daughter and is apparently intending to continue this method of establishing a progeny through the agency of his daughter-granddaughter, is another of the ways in which the hard-boiled myth is thrust into depths beyond itself. Though traditionally an erotically potent figure, the private eye's sexuality seems gentility itself when confronted with the potent perversity embodied in the figure of Noah Cross. Cross is reminiscent of the primal father imagined by Freud in *Totem and Taboo*, but against his overpowering sexual, political and economic power, our hero Oedipus in the form of J. J. Gittes proves to be tragically impotent, an impotence symbolized earlier in the film by the slashing of his nose and the large comic bandage he wears throughout much of the action.

In its manipulation of a traditional American popular myth and the revelation of the tragic inadequacy of this myth when it collides with a universe that is deeper and more enigmatic in its evil and destructive force, *Chinatown* is one of the richest and most artistically powerful instances of a type of film of which we have seen many striking instances in the last decade. It is difficult to know just what to call this type of film. On one level, it relates to the traditional literary mode of burlesque or parody in which a well-established set of conventions or a style is subjected to some form of ironic or humorous exploitation. Indeed, many of the most striking and successful films of the period have been out and out burlesques of traditional popular genres such as Mel Brooks' *Blazing Saddles* (westerns), *Young Frankenstein* (the Frankenstein horror cycle), and *High Anxiety* (Hitchcock's psychological suspense films). However, burlesque and parody embody a basically humorous thrust, and many of the most powerful generic variations of the last decade or so—films like *Bonnie and Clyde, The Wild Bunch, The Godfather* and *Nashville*—tend more toward tragedy than comedy in their overall structures. It seems odd to speak of a tragic parody or a doomed burlesque. Therefore, one is at first tempted to conclude that the connection between *Blazing Saddles* and *The Wild Bunch*, or *The Black Bird* and *The Long Goodbye* is only superficial. Yet it is clear that in many of these films the line between comedy and tragedy is not so simply drawn. What, for example, of the extraordinary combination of Keystone Cops chase scenes and tragic carnage in *Bonnie and Clyde*, or the interweaving of sophomoric high jinks and terrible violence in Altman's *MASH*? This puzzling combination of humorous burlesque and high seriousness seems to be a mode of expression characteristic of our period, not only in film, but in other literary forms. It is at the root of much that is commonly described as the literature of the absurd, or of so-called "Black humor," and is, as well, characteristic of the style of major contemporary novelists like Thomas Pynchon. By adopting this mode, American movies have, in a sense, become a more integral part of the mainstream of postmodernist literature, just as, through their frequent allusion to the narrative conventions of American film, contemporary novelists and dramatists have created a new kind of relationship between themselves and the traditions of popular culture.

The linkage between these many different kinds of contemporary literary, dramatic and cinematic expression is their use of the conventions of traditional popular genres. Basically, they do in different ways what Polanski does in *Chinatown*: set the elements of a conventional popular genre in an altered context, thereby making us perceive these traditional forms and images in a new way. It appears to me that we can classify the various relationships between traditional generic elements and altered contexts into four major modes.

First, there is the burlesque proper. In this mode, elements of a conventional formula or style are situated in contexts so incongruous or exaggerated that the result is laughter. There are many different ways in which this can be done. The formulaic elements can be acted out in so extreme a fashion that they come into conflict with our sense of reality forcing us to see these aspects of plot and character as fantastic contrivances. A good example of this is the burlesque image of the gunfighter in *Cat Ballou*. In this film we are shown how, by putting on his gunfighter costume, a process that involves strapping himself into a corset within which he can barely move, an old drunk can become the terror of the bad guys. Or, in a closely related type of altered context, a situation that we are ordinarily accustomed to seeing in rather romanticized terms can be suddenly invested with a sense of reality. This is how the famous campfire scene in *Blazing Saddles* operates. The cowboys sit around a blazing campfire at night, a scene in which we are accustomed to hearing mournful and lyrical cowboy ballads performed by such groups as the Sons of the Pioneers. Instead we are treated to an escalating barrage of flatulence. Anyone who knows the usual effect of canned wilderness fare is likely to be delighted at this sudden exposure of the sham involved in the traditional western campfire scene. Sam Peckinpah's *Ride the High Country* offers another instance of the humorous effect of a sudden penetration of reality into a fantasy when one of his aging heroes attempts to spring gracefully into the saddle and is suddenly halted by a twinge of rheumatism.

In addition to these sudden confrontations with "reality" conventional patterns can be turned into laughter by inverting them. A good example of this is the device of turning a character who shows all the marks of a hero into a coward, or vice versa. A favorite manifestation of this in recent films and novels is what might be called the hard-boiled schlemiehl, the private detective who turns out to be totally unable to solve a crime or resist villains except by accident. This type of burlesque is even more effective when the inverted presentation actually seems to bring out some latent meanings which were lurking all the time in the original convention. Mel Brooks is a particular master of this kind of burlesque. In his *Young Frankenstein*, the monster attacks Frankenstein's fiancee Elizabeth—a moment of tragic violence in the original novel—and the result is complete sexual satisfaction on both sides, something most of us had suspected all along.

These two primary techniques of burlesque, the breaking of convention by the intrusion of reality and the inversion of expected implications, have frequently appeared in the history of literature as a response to highly conventionalized genres. Just as the Greek tragedies gave rise to their burlesque counterparts in the plays of Aristophanes, the western, one of our most formally distinctive genres, has been the inspiration of parody and burlesque throughout its history from Twain and Harte's assaults on James Fenimore Cooper to Brooks' send-up of *Shane* and *High Noon*. Thus, there is nothing particularly new in the penchant toward humorous burlesque so evident in recent films. What is more striking in the films of the last decade is their use of these techniques of generic parody for ultimately serious purposes.

The second major mode of generic transformation is the cultivation of nostalgia. In this mode, traditional generic features of plot, character, setting and style are deployed to recreate the aura of a past time. The power of nostalgia lies especially in its capacity to evoke a sense of warm reassurance by bringing before our mind's eye images from a time when things seemed more secure and full of promise and possibility. Though one can, of course, evoke nostalgia simply by viewing films of the past, a contemporary nostalgia film cannot simply duplicate the past experience, but must make us aware in some fashion of the relationship between past and present. Attempts to evoke nostalgia merely by imitating past forms, as was the case with the television series *City of Angels*, do not generally work because they seem simply obsolescent. A truly successful nostalgia film—like Fred Zinneman's *True Grit*, one of the last highly popular westerns—succeeds because it set its highly traditional generic content in a slightly different context, thereby giving us both a sense of contemporaneity and of pastness. In *True Grit*, this was done in a number of ways. First of all, the central character played by Kim Darby represented an extremely contemporary image of adolescent girlhood. She was independent, aggressive and full of initiative, a shrewd horsetrader and a self-confident, insistent moralist, unlike the shy desert rose of the traditional western. John Wayne, aging and paunchy, did not attempt to cover up the ravages of the years and reaffirm without change the vigorous manhood of his earlier films. Instead, with eyepatch, unshaven face and sagging flesh, he fully enacted his aging. Similarly, the film's images of the western landscape were in many ways deromanticized. But out of this context of contemporaneity there sprang the same old story of adventure and heroism culminating in an exuberant shootout which seemed to embody everybody's best dreams of Saturday matinees. The same quality of nostalgic reinvocation of the past played an even more powerful role in Peckinpah's *Ride the High Country* in which two tired, aging and obsolescent heroes ride again, and in Dick Richard's recent version of Raymond Chandler's *Farewell, My Lovely* where a sagging Robert Mitchum moves out of the malaise of modernity and reenacts once more the ambiguous heroic quest of the hard-boiled detective of the 1930s and 1940s.

The difference between nostalgic reincarnation of an earlier genre like *Farewell, My Lovely* and the more complex ironies of *Chinatown* and Robert Altman's *The Long Goodbye* is considerable. It is a difference similar to the one between *True Grit* and neo-westerns like Altman's *McCabe and Mrs. Miller* or Arthur Penn's *Little Big Man*. In the former case, nostalgia is the end result of the film. In the latter nostalgia is often powerfully evoked, but as a means of undercutting or ironically commenting upon the generic experience itself. This brings us to the third and, in many respects, the most powerful mode of generic transformation in recent films: the use of traditional generic structures as a means of demythologization. A film like *Chinatown* deliberately invokes the basic characteristics of a traditional genre in order to bring its audience to see that genre as the embodiment of an inadequate and destructive myth. We have seen how this process of demythologization operates in *Chinatown* by seeing the traditional model of the hard-boiled detective's quest for justice and integrity over and against Polanski's sense of a universe so steeped in ambiguity, corruption and evil that such individualistic moral enterprises are doomed by their innocent naiveté to end in tragedy and self-destruction.

The work of Arthur Penn has also explored the ironic and tragic aspects of the myths implicit in traditional genres. His *Night Moves*, a transformation of the detective story, was, like *Chinatown*, the ambiguous enactment of a reluctant quest for the truth about a series of crimes. As the detective approaches a solution to the crimes, he becomes morally and emotionally involved in the quest, making it more and more difficult for him to integrate truth, feeling, and morality. In the end, like Polanski's Jake Gittes, he is more dazed than fulfilled by the catastrophe his investigation has brought about.

In other films, such as *The Left-Handed Gun, Bonnie and Clyde* and *Little Big Man*, Penn created a version of the western or the gangster film in which traditional meanings were inverted, but the effect was tragic rather than humorous. In *Little Big Man*, for example, the conventional western opposition between Indians and pioneers serves as the basis of the plot, which embodies two of the most powerful of our western myths, the Indian captivity and the massacre. However, the conventional renderings of these myths pit the humanely civilizing thrust of the pioneers against the savage ferocity and eroticism of the Indians and thereby justify the conquest of the West. Penn reverses these implications. In his film it is the Indians who are humane and civilized, while the pioneers are violent, corrupt, sexually repressed and madly ambitious. By the end, when Custer's cavalry rides forward to attack the Indian villages, our sympathies are all with the Indians. From this perspective, the conquest of the West is demythologized from the triumph of civilization into a historical tragedy of the destruction of a rich and vital human culture.

Despite its many virtues, the film version of *Little Big Man* was less artistically successful than Thomas Berger's novel on which it was based, primarily because as the film proceeds, Penn loses the ironic detachment which Berger successfully maintains throughout the novel. Penn's portrayal of Custer as a lunatic symbol of aggressive American imperialism is overstated, and toward the end the cinematic *Little Big Man* tends to fall back from the serious exploration of mythical meanings into melodramatic burlesque. This is an artistic problem common to films in the mode of demythologization of traditional genres. Penn was far more successful in *Bonnie and Clyde*, which will remain one of the major masterpieces of recent American film. Taking off from the traditional gangster film with its opposition between the outlaw and society, *Bonnie and Clyde* establishes a dialectic between conventional and inverted meanings which is far richer and more powerfully sustained throughout the film. In the traditional gangster film, a powerful individual, frustrated by the limitations of his lower-class origin, is driven to a life of crime. Initially the audience is inclined to sympathize and identify with this character, but as he becomes involved in criminal actions, he overreaches himself and becomes a vicious killer who must be tracked down and destroyed by the representatives of society. The underlying myth of this genre affirms the limits of individual aggression in a society which tolerates and even encourages a high degree of personal enterprise and violence. The gangster becomes a tragic figure not because he is inherently evil, but because he fails to recognize these limits. The myth assures us that society is not repressive or violent; instead it shows how criminal violence evokes its own inevitable doom.

It is this comforting myth of proper and improper violence that Penn demythologizes in *Bonnie and Clyde*. As in *Little Big Man*, meanings become inverted. Instead of representing a limit to aggression and violence, society is portrayed as its fountainhead, while the outlaw protagonists are seen as victims of society's bloodlust. Throughout the film, we are shown a society of depression and chaos which yearns for action, and which projects this yearning into a vicarious excitement about the robberies and murders of the Barrow gang. Penn effectively develops this theme through his representation of the newspapers which so avidly report the gang's adventures and by the reactions of witnesses to the gang's attacks on banks. Finally, its lust for the hunt aroused, society itself takes up the pursuit in packs and posses and, in a final ambush which set a new level in explicit screen violence, the doomed Bonnie and Clyde are shot to pieces. But the inversion of generic meanings is still more complex, for Penn refuses to make the opposition between gangster and society a simple reversal of traditional generic meanings as he does in *Little Big Man*. The protagonists of *Bonnie and Clyde* are not simply victims of society. They are themselves very much a part of the society they are attacking. They share its basic aspirations and confusions and they yearn above all to be reintegrated with it. In many respects, their actions reflect a desperate and misconceived attempt to achieve some measure of the status, security and belongingness which ought to be among the basic gifts of a society to its members. Instead of simply reversing the meanings conventionally ascribed to the opposing forces of criminal and society in the gangster genre, *Bonnie and Clyde* expressed a more complex and dark awareness that this basic opposition was itself a mythical simplification, and showed us the deeper and more difficult irony of the twisted and inseparable fates of individuals and their society. This was in its way a recognition of that skein of ambiguous inevitability which Polanski summed up in the symbol of *Chinatown*, and which Francis Ford Coppola developed through the fateful intertwining of individuals, "families" and society in *The Godfather*.

Though the demythologization of traditional genres has been primarily evident in the work of younger directors, it has also had some influence on the later work of some of the classic filmmakers, most noticeably perhaps in the later westerns of John Ford, particularly *The Searchers, Cheyenne Autumn* and *The Man who Shot Liberty Valance.* Indeed, in the latter film, Ford symbolized the conquest of the West through a story in which the territory's last major outlaw was killed in a shootout by a man destined to lead the territory into the blessings of civilization. In fact, the legend of Senator Stoddard's heroic deed was a myth, the actual shooting of Liberty Valance having been done by another man. Toward the end of the film, the newspaper editor to whom Senator Stoddard confesses the truth about his past makes the famous and ambiguous comment "when the legend becomes a fact, print the legend." But is this an ironic comment on the falsity of legends and newspapers alike, or is it some kind of affirmation of the significance of myth in spite of its unreality? Ford was apparently inclined to the latter interpretation, for he once told Peter Bogdanovich, "We've had a lot of people who were supposed to be great heroes and you know damn well they weren't. But it's good for the country to have heroes to look up to."[212]

This brings us to a fourth and final mode of generic transformation which might be described as the affirmation of myth for its own sake. In films in this mode, a traditional genre and its myth are probed and shown to be unreal, but then the myth itself is at least partially affirmed as a reflection of authentic human aspirations and needs. This is the element which becomes dominant in Ford's later westerns in which he seems to see the heroic ethos of the West in critical terms and becomes more and more sympathetic with the Indian victims of the Westward movement. Yet, at the same time that he became more cynical about the reality of the West, he seemed to feel even more strongly the need to affirm its heroic ideals. Thus, in his powerful late film *The Searchers,* Ford turns to the old western theme of Indian captivity, portraying the mad obsessive hatred with which a White man pursues a band of Indians who have captured and adopted his niece. Yet Ford also accepted a change in the ending of the original novel, where this mad Indian hater was finally destroyed by his obsession, in order to reaffirm at the end the heroism and self-sacrifice of this obsessive quest. *The Searchers* is a powerful and beautiful film, yet one feels uncomfortable at the end, as if the gap between Ford's sense of historical reality and his feelings about genre and myth have come into collision.

Sam Peckinpah's *The Wild Bunch,* for all its ugliness and violence, is a more coherent example of the destruction and reaffirmation of myth. Throughout the film, Peckinpah points up the gap between the conventional western's heroic struggle between pioneers and outlaws. His pioneer lawmen are despicable bounty hunters in the employ of the railroad and they kill the guilty and the innocent indiscriminately. His outlaws are not much better; they are brutal, coarse, and quite capable of leaving a wounded comrade behind. Moreover, their type of criminal operation has become absurdly obsolescent in the early twentieth-century West of the film. In the end, Peckinpah's outlaw protagonists are drawn in to a ridiculously destructive shootout with an entire Mexican village full of troops and are completely wiped out in the process. Yet the film also leaves us with a sense that through their hopeless action these coarse and vicious outlaws have somehow transcended themselves and become embodiments of a myth of heroism that men need in spite of the realities of their world.

While I have separated the four modes of generic transformation—humorous burlesque, evocation of nostalgia, demythologization of generic myth, and the affirmation of myth as myth—into separate categories in order to define them more clearly, it should be clear that most films which employ one of these modes are likely to use another at some point. Probably the best films based on generic transformation employ some combination of several of these modes in the service of one overriding artistic purpose; *Chinatown* uses both humorous burlesque and nostalgic evocation as a basis for its devastating exploration of the genre of the hard-boiled

---

[212] Quoted in Jon Tuska, *The Filming of the West.* (Garden City, N.Y.: Doubleday and Co., 1976, p. 519.)

detective and his myth. Some directors seem to have a primary predilection for one of these modes; Brooks is primarily oriented toward burlesque, Bogdanovich toward nostalgia, Penn toward demythologization and Peckinpah toward reaffirmation. Some directors—Robert Altman springs particularly to mind—have, in their best films, worked out a rich and fascinating dialectic between different modes of generic transformation. In films like *McCabe and Mrs. Miller, The Long Goodbye, Thieves Like Us*, and *Nashville* it is quite difficult to decide at the end whether Altman is attacking or reaffirming the genre on which he has based each particular work. In fact, until the last two or three years, Altman's filmography looks almost as if he had planned a systematic voyage through the major traditional film genres. That generic transformation has been so important a source of artistic energy to the most vital younger directors suggests that it is a central key to the current state of the American film.

There are probably many reasons for the importance of these modes of filmmaking in the last decade, but in conclusion, I will comment briefly on what seem to me the most important factors involved in the proliferation of this kind of film. I think it is not primarily the competition of television. Though television has been somewhat more conservative in its use of generic transformation than film, the same modes seem to be turning up with increasing frequency in television series. Instead I would point to the tendency of genres to exhaust themselves, to our growing historical awareness of modern popular culture, and finally, to the decline of the underlying mythology on which traditional genres have been based since the late nineteenth century. Generic exhaustion is a common phenomenon in the history of culture. One can almost make out a lifecycle characteristic of genres as they move from an initial period of articulation and discovery, through a phase of conscious self-awareness on the part of both creators and audiences, to a time when the generic patterns have become so well-known that people become tired of their predictability. It is at this point that parodic and satiric treatments proliferate and new genres gradually arise. Our major traditional genres—the western, the detective story, the musical, the domestic comedy—have, after all, been around for a considerable period of time and it may be they have simply reached a point of creative exhaustion.

In our time, the awareness of the persistence of genres has been intensified by an increasing historical awareness of film. A younger generation of directors has a sense of film history quite different from many of their predecessors who, like Ford and Hawks, were involved with the art of film almost from its beginnings. Similarly, audiences have a kind of sophistication about the history of genres different from earlier film publics because of the tremendous number of past films now regularly shown on television and by college film societies.

But I am inclined to think that there is more to it than that. The present significance of generic transformation as a creative mode reflects the feeling that not only the traditional genres, but the cultural myths they once embodied, are no longer fully adequate to the imaginative needs of our time. It will require another essay to explain and justify this assertion, but if I may hazard a final prediction, I think we will begin to see emerging out of this period of generic transformation a new set of generic constructs more directly related to the imaginative landscape of the second half of the twentieth century. Thus, the present period of American filmmaking will seem in retrospect an important time of artistic and cultural transition. Like many transition periods, it may also turn out to be a time of the highest artistic accomplishment.

CRITICAL FILM ANALYSES

THE KILLING (1956)
–Gangster Film in its Postclassical Phase–

Peter Britos

Distributor: United Artists. Production Company: Harris-Kubrick Pictures. Producer: James B. Harris. Writer/Director: Stanley Kubrick. Additional Dialogue by Jim Thompson. Based on the novel Clean Break by Lionel White. Photography: Lucien Ballard. Music by Gerald Fried. Editor: Betty Steinberg. Sound: Earl Snyder. Art Director: Ruth Sobotka Kubrick.

CAST: Sterling Hayden (Johnny Clay), Marie Windsor (Sherry Peatty), Coleen Gray (Fay), Jay C. Flippen (Marv Unger), Ted de Corsia (Randy Kennan), Joe Sawyer (Mike O'Reilly), James Edwards (parking lot attendant), Timothy Carey (Nikki), Vince Edwards (Val), Joseph Turkel (Tiny), Kola Wariani (Maurice). Length: 83 minutes.

> It's a bad joke without a punch-line.
>
> —Dying lines of Sherry Peatty

By 1956, when 28-year old Stanley Kubrick wrote and directed the caper film *The Killing*, the gangster genre had undergone a significant metamorphoses from its inception in the early 1930's. Ripped from the headlines of the day, the characters from the first wave of American gangster films—*Public Enemy* (1931), *Little Caesar* (1931), *Scarface* (1932)—were forged in the urban crucible of Depression era despair. An innate propensity for violence and insatiable ambition led these charismatic characters down a predictable path: a rise from hoodlum status, to kingpin initiate, to kingpin, to violent, often tragic death. The repeal of Prohibition, and the Production Code Administration crack-down on films of "moral irresponsibility," led to a phase where the gangster was subordinated to less ambiguous hero types, such as the G-Man or cop, or, they were balanced by a positive foil, a variant presaged by the hard-working, scrupulously honest Mike Powers in William Wellman's *Public Enemy.*

A more literary approach to the gangster genre was evident by the 1940's. Raoul Walsh's rural bandit film *High Sierra* (1941) and John Huston's caper *Asphalt Jungle* (1950) were both adapted from novels by W.R. Burnett. These films do not rely on the hot-headed, sexually-aberrant psychopath to justify a focus on the criminal star. Rather, like the characters played by Sterling Hayden in *Asphalt Jungle* and *The Killing*, Roy Earle (Humphrey Bogart) in *High Sierra* (1941) is a mature and pragmatic man. *High Sierra* formally signals the end of the golden era of the gangster. Eight years in the slammer has left Earle graying, world-weary and out of touch with a new set of mercenary ethics. Though he adheres to classical codes of gangster-dom, like loyalty, seniority and strong male bonds, his accomplices are back-stabbing, sniveling novices. Humanized by his romantic desires, Earle is a legend in his own time, "rushing towards death."

The Killing, Stanley Kubrick's third feature film, is based on the novel *Clean Break*, by Lionel White. The story revolves around an elaborate heist at a racetrack. The most striking feature of Kubrick's adaptation is the complex, nonlinear story structure he borrows from the novel. The film opens at the racetrack one week before the heist. The voice-over narrator introduces the action at "exactly 3:45," when Marv Unger walks into the racetrack lounge. Unger slips the bartender Mike and cashier George betting stubs with an address and time (8:00 p.m.) scribbled on the back. The very next scene, the crooked cop Kennan enters a dimly lit bar to negotiate with his loan shark. The scene is introduced by the omniscient narrator as occurring one hour earlier, thereby priming the viewer for a narrative structure with its own internal logic. The circular flashback within a flashback narrative strategy becomes a critical structuring device, as on the day of the heist, we follow the different characters through their preparations respectively, up until the moment of truth, around 4:30 p.m. and the seventh race. A succession of flashbacks bring each participant in the heist up to this crucial moment when their specific task is performed. Then the narrative picks up Johnny Clay again at 2:15, overlapping timelines of earlier actions, and follows him through to the completion of the actual hold up. The circular structure serves several functions. For one thing, it functions as a reflection on the tenuous, convoluted mechanics of strategic alliances. One weak link, one unforeseen hitch can unravel the entire fabric. Also, as an experimental narrative device, it forces the audience to continually reevaluate not only temporal and spatial relations, but the chronologic authority of cause and effect.

Stubs of paper, the radio reporter, the race track announcer, and character dialogue convey crucial time-line cues, but it's the omniscient narrator in *The Killing* who is the principle source of temporal information.

In *The Killing*, the voice-over performs several functions. Most obviously, it transmits narrative information and organizes the complicated time structure of the film. It also functions as a distancing device, putting the audience at a remove from the film's drama. It prefigures the kind of emotional distance found in Kubrick's later work.[213]

Voice-over narration was by 1956 a well-established convention of not only the hard-boiled detective genre with its ironic, often cynical tone, but the police procedural as well. The omniscient narrator of the police procedural borrowed stylistically from documentary *March of Time* newsreels with its impersonal, just-the-facts authoritarian delivery. While the pseudo-documentary technique was employed in social-problem films to depict greater "realism" and a sense of objectivity, in the police procedural it as well highlighted the impartial and scientific bent of police technology, and the cool and detached efficacy of its personnel. Kubrick's use of the omniscient narrator borrows both the impersonal, authoritative demeanor of the pseudo-documentary, and the ironic banality of the hard-boiled sleuth. Combined with the

---

[213] Falsetto, Mario. *Stanley Kubrick: A Narrative and Stylistic Analysis.* Greenwood Press, Westport, 1994. (p. 10).

documentary-like footage of the racetrack and objective, deep-focus vistas of the city streets, the apparently neutral narrator contributes to the aura of objective realism.

But at least twice the seemingly omniscient narrator gives faulty timeline information. First, when Johnny visits Unger the morning of the heist, the narrator stipulates "at seven that morning, Johnny Clay began what might be the last day of his life." However, in the next scene as Johnny checks in baggage for a night flight to Boston, again the narrator states that "it was exactly 7:00 a.m. when he got to the airport." Mario Falsetto speculates as to the possibility this was an oversight on the part of the filmmakers. However, the pairing of this time discrepancy in the Unger scene with the clearly misleading information: "Johnny began what might be the last day of his life," seems to indicate Kubrick is aware of his devices. The second error happens after the completion of the heist at the *rendez-vous* apartment. At 7:15 George Peatty complains Johnny is fifteen minutes late. But when Johnny arrives at the meeting place at 7:29, the narrator states Johnny is "still fifteen minutes late." Either George was wrong about a 7:00 *rendez-vous*, or the narrator was wrong about 7:15. The parallel timing of the errors at 7:00 a.m. and 7:00 p.m. suggests either a structural awareness on the part of the filmmakers, or a remarkable coincidence. As well, like the earlier discrepancy, the unreliable information is paired with a more obvious error: the radio announcer reports Nikki, the killer of Red Lightening, "was fatally wounded by crack police while trying to shoot his way out of the back parking lot." The audience, having witnessed an unarmed Nikki being shot while scrambling from his convertible, knows this pronouncement to be false. Surveying Kubrick's body of work, one notes his extreme distrust of those in positions of power, and the arbitrariness of their institutional pronouncements. Notice how authority is crucially flawed or unreliable in *Paths of Glory, Dr. Strangelove, Lolita, A Clockwork Orange*, the computer Hal in *2001*, the drill instructor in *Full Metal Jacket*.

The Killing can be viewed as an experimental hybrid. It borrows not only from gangster conventions, but those of the expository documentary, critical social realism and *film noir*. The film deviates from classical gangster conventions by focusing not on the gangster hero *à la* Tom Powers, Rico or Scarface, but on a group of conspirators, each with a crucial interlocking function in the overall scheme. Furthermore, with the exception of Clay, these are not professional criminals, but working class folk, most a little long in the tooth, all looking for one, quick fix. The documentary feel and realism of urban conditions is counterbalanced by the highly expressionistic use of *film noir* devices, including chiaroscuro low key lighting, transient spaces like motels, lounges and bus stops, the *femme fatale* and her loyal counterpart, baroque masks, crooked cops, dirty money, etc. Kubrick was not a stranger to *noir* aesthetics, having used it to shape his earlier film *The Killer's Kiss* (1955). Only in *The Killing, noir* does not dominate the film so much as accent it for narrative or atmospheric effect. The control the filmmaker evinces over the film extends further to a sophisticated intertextual awareness. The planning session in the apartment with the single source overhead lamp for instance, is not only an example of *noir* technique, it's a direct citation from the planning scene in *Asphalt Jungle*, where Hayden's character Dix Stanley listens to the mastermind Doc Riedenschneider lay out the logistics for the jewelry heist. In *The Killing*, Hayden has literally come of age, after five years in prison. The planning scene is an example of the film's self-reflexive commentary on its own generic and stylistic lineage. Kubrick uses the same low angle compositions and lighting scheme as the earlier film, but now Clay leads the planning session, fulfilling the potential he demonstrated in the earlier film, as the tough but smart hoodlum Dix.

The Killing ends with a final series of ironic and coincidental confrontations. An over-sized suitcase that won't lock, airport officials who insist his baggage be checked through, and an annoying poodle contribute to the gangster's downfall. His suitcase of money having popped open on the airport runway and the cash blown asunder, Faye tells Johnny to run when they can't flag down a taxi, and the airport manager points him out to the detectives. But he turns to them instead with a certain grim, fatalistic sneer, and mutters, "Eh, what's the difference."

Along with rich, detailed performances by experienced character actors, consider Kubrick's innovative use of sound (metronome, soundbridges), deep space composition, intricate blocking, frames within frames, smooth tracking shots, and the film's only subjective POV shot, after the massacre at the gang's apartment hideout.

Born in 1928, Stanley Kubrick was a photography buff as a young boy. At seventeen, *Look* magazine hired him as a staff photographer, a position he held for five years. From there, he made three short documentary films and two feature films before embarking on *The Killing*, a film Alexander Walker calls his "graduation" to big-time filmmaking.[214]   In 1998, *The Hollywood Reporter* named Kubrick one of the five most bankable directors in the world, along with Steven Spielberg, James Cameron, George Lucas and Martin Scorcese.[215.]

Filmography: *Fear and Desire* (1953), *The Killer's Kiss* (1955), *The Killing* (1956), *Paths of Glory* (1957), *Spartacus* (1960), *Lolita* (1962), *Dr. Strangelove* (1964), *2001* (1968), *A Clockwork Orange* (1971), *Barry Lyndon* (1975), *The Shining* (1980), *Full Metal Jacket* (1987), *Eyes Wide Shut* (1999).

---

[214] Falsetto, Mario. *Perspectives on Stanley Kubrick.* Simon & Schuster Macmillan, New York, 1996. (p. 6).
[215] Burman, John. *The Hollywood Reporter.* October 20-26, 1998. (pp. 15-17).

12

GENRE: MODERNIST PHASE

'Modernity' refers to the network of large-scale social, economic, technological, and philosophical changes wrought by the Enlightenment and the Industrial Revolution. 'Modernism' is usually used to denote the period of dramatic innovation in all of the arts, from around the end of the nineteenth century (Symbolism and Aestheticism) up to the Second World War, when the sense of a fundamental break with inherited modes of representation and expression became acute. Modernism is thus above all associated with a pervasive formal self-consciousness.

—Murray Smith, "Modernism and the avant-gardes"

CTCS 190 LECTURE OUTLINE – WEEK XII   **LECTURE 11**

PART 3: THE MODERNIST PERIOD: 1963-1976

- **A. Conditions and Causes for Modernism in American Film**
    1. The antiestablishmentarianism of the Age of Aquarius, 1963-1976
    1. The impact of European film
    1. The end of censorship
    1. Conglomerate takeover of the studios
    1. Director as auteur
- **B. Modernism**
    1. Modernism and the other arts; modernism and film
    2. Modernism's two basic tenets:
        a. Thematically: self-conscious engagement with social and moral values
        b. Formally: experimentation with formal strategies of the respective art form/medium
            1. New ways of telling stories
            2. Point of view
            3. Reflexivity
            4. Open texture:
                i. filmic intertextuality
                ii. non-filmic intertextuality
                iii. extra-filmic intertextuality
            5. Incorporation of different materials and styles
            6. Various other ways that break with the classical mode
    3. Classical texts versus modernist texts
        a. Transitivity vs. non-transitivity
        b. Plot vs. non-plot
        c. Omniscient POV vs. selective POV
        d. Identification vs. distance
        e. Single vs. multiple characters
        f. Closure vs. non-closure
        g. Transparency vs. self-reflexivity
        h. Containment vs. intertextuality
        i. Pleasure vs. confrontation
- **B. Implications of Modernism**
- **C. Introduction and Screening of a Genre Film in its Modernist Phase**

Notes

Notes

MODERNISM

from *Key Concepts in Cinema Studies* (1996) by Susan Hayward

Modernism is most easily understood as an art movement, although it does have socio-political resonances as explained below. You will note from the entry on postmodernism that it is difficult to pinpoint where modernism ends and postmodernism begins. It is better to think in terms of an overlap between the two—an overlap that occurs, first, because not all aspects of art became postmodern simultaneously and, second, because there is not often full agreement, among critics and theorists, on the categorizing of a particular cultural artifact. Thus a novel, say, might find itself being termed a modernist text by one critic but a postmodern text by another. This happens with the novels of Samuel Beckett. This inability to insert a dividing line points to the fact that, to a certain—if not considerable extent, postmodernism reacts less against the conventions of modernism than we might believe, even though we are aware that it must in some way be different, because it comes after (post)modernism. A useful analogy might be drawn with industry. We are acutely aware that we could not now be a post-industrial society if we had not originally possessed an industrial one. Vestiges of our industrialization remain, but they no longer carry the same meaning they once did. Take, for example, the railway systems of the United Kingdom and the United States. These were once heralded as heroic and pioneering in their engineering exploits. Now, in the interest of capital, they have been reduced to a shadow of their former self and face what appears to be permanent decline.

Modernism finds its roots in the Enlightenment period of the eighteenth century and man's (*sic*) belief in the supremacy of human reason over all other considerations. It was a period that marked the end, or rather decline, in western society of a theocratic (God-centred) interpretation of the world. As evidence of this belief in the power of human reasoning to understand the world, this age was also termed the Age of Reason. This belief in human reason meant that man (*sic*) could achieve clarity or enlightenment in scientific thought and natural philosophy (that is, natural science—maths, astronomy and physics); he would come to understand the way things really are in the universe and thereby be able to have control over nature and make the world a better place. Jeremy Bentham's enlightened prison reforms came from this spirit—including his concept of the panopticon as an alternative to cell emprisonment and the cruelty of prison treatment. The panopticon was an imagined building wherein everyone could observe everyone else—a using of the gaze as a system of total surveillance. But, as we shall see, the outcome of total surveillance is far from benign.

As such, then, the Enlightenment represented an optimistic belief in progress. Science and technology were man's tools whereby he could implement change. Science, or scientific thought, was the only valid thought, and facts the only possible objects of knowledge. In philosophy the task was to discover the general principles common to all the sciences and to use these principles as guides to human conduct and as the basis of social organization. Man controlled nature and all procedures of investigation had to be reducible to scientific method.

Not all was optimism, however. Even during that period some philosophers expressed disquiet at the totalizing effect of this positivist philosophy of science. Thus a strain of pessimism exists alongside the waves of optimism, a pessimism with which we have to concur if we look at the end of the eighteenth century in France and its bloody Revolution, particularly during the Reign of Terror. Writers of that time pointed to the ends to which man could go. The Marquis de Sade's writings are but one extreme. But consider also the 'humane' invention devised to kill off all those who fell victim to the Revolution: the guillotine. Designed by Dr. Guillotine to make death more swift and efficacious and therefore more humane, in the end it allowed for the acceleration of executions because it was so swift. In other words, it became an instrument for mass-execution.

The industrial age of the nineteenth century was a logical continuance of the Enlightenment's belief in science and technology, and represents the optimistic strain of belief in progress. Art, however, echoed the other, pessimistic, strain of the Age of Reason and signified as a counter-culture to scientific thought, producing, first, romanticism (a nostalgia for what was lost) and, second, realism (a desire to show the mostly negative effects of technological progress). The Enlightenment then produced two strains, and modernism, as its natural heir, continued in the same vein. Modernism perpetuates the belief in scientific research and the pursuit of knowledge. It believed in the positing of universal truths such as progress of which science and technology were its major proponents. However, it also expresses profound disquiet at those beliefs which it perpetuates.

As a movement we could loosely say that modernism begins at the end of the nineteenth century and 'ends' at the end of the 1960s, when post-structuralism heralded the arrival, if not the existence already, of postmodernism. Modernism was born as a reaction against realism and the tradition of romanticism. As a movement it is often also termed the avant-garde. However, it is truer to say that the avant-garde is part of the modernist aesthetic—not all modernist art is avant-garde, but avant-garde art is modernist. In its vanguardism and perception of itself as an adversary culture, modernism is 'relentless in its hostility to mass culture'.[216] It believes that only high art can sustain the role of social and aesthetic criticism. In this context, modernism's belief in progress means also a belief in modernization—including belief in the 'perpetual modernization of art'[217]—a constant renewal of that role of art as critique, therefore.

Modernism eschewed the seamless verisimilitude of realism and sought to reveal the process of meaning-construction in art. Formal concerns were, therefore, paramount. To give a couple of examples: with the realist novel, plot and character construction lead us through a narrative where the process of narration does not directly draw attention to itself—we are stitched into the narrative … [A] modernist novel, however, deliberately draws attention to its process of meaning-construction from the very first reading—compare a Jane Austen novel with one by Virginia Woolf for example. In painting, the realist aesthetic seeks to create the illusion of 'truth' before your eyes, as in a Constable painting, say. This illusion starts with the principle of perspective which gives a sense of three-dimensionality. A modernist cubist painting removes perspectival space and transposes the three dimensions 'truthfully' on to a flat two-dimensional surface. So, in a Picasso portrait, the eyes are flattened out on to the canvas and the nose is placed to the side of the face and not between the eyes. Similarly, just as the novelist draws attention to her or his own mode of meaning-production, modernist painters draw attention to the materials they use (for example Georges Braque, Jackson Pollock). In that respect, modernism is highly self-reflexive (art referring to itself).

As we know, the modernist movement and the avant-garde are closely associated with modernization and as such espoused a belief in its tools and an investment in self-reflexivity that was deliberately counter-illusionist. Nonetheless, none of its proponents were of the optimistic vein. Indeed, many expressed a mistrust of science and technology—even though, as

---

[216] Huyssen, A. (1986) *After the Great Divide: Modernism, Mass Culture and Postmodernism*, London, Macmillan Press (Language, Discourse, Society Series), p. 241.
[217] Ibid., p. 238.

we have already noted, they were inextricably part of it. This mistrust was characterized by a deep pessimism about the modern world and came about as a result of the brutal effects of science and technology on human life in the First and Second World Wars. The wanton destruction of human lives through chemical warfare, bombs of mass extinction, the using of technology and architecture to create a final solution—as in the case of the Holocaust—all these were products of man's reason. It may not be possible to see fascism purely as a formidable crisis of modernist culture.[218] However, it is not impossible to see it as a logical end to the principles of modernism taken to their extremes of anti-humanism. In this respect, then, modernism embraces the two strains evoked in the case of the Enlightenment. The tragedy, and thereby the paradox, for the modernist artist is being part of the culture and age that she or he in some regards despises: 'I am part of this age of self-reflexive formalism that can also build the technology for mass destruction'.

It is here that we can see a first set of paradoxes inherent in this movement (as we would in any movement of course). The paradox is this: in its self-reflexivity and focus on the individual, modernism seems quite anti-humanist. Yet, in its mistrust of science and technology, it has all the appearances of a relative humanism. This is further compounded when we consider that the modernist age evolved alongside, and in certain domains was part of, modern industrial technology. If we consider architecture we can make this point succinctly. Modernist architecture believed in drawing on all materials possible especially modern materials, such as reinforced concrete to construct buildings heretofore unimaginable. And yet—and here is the anti-humanist aspect of this movement—in its belief in the functionality of cheaply produced materials and their being put to use in the building of community spaces in a rationalized and standardized fashion (as with Le Corbusier's ideal concrete village) it has left many countries with a legacy of concrete jungles and towers which, though inhabited, are essentially uninhabitable. Belief in the unending potential of its materials led modernist architecture to profoundly anti-humanist practices.

Another, related and important, aspect of modernism that needs explaining is the mood of alienation and existential angst that pervades this movement and which comes about as a result of the climate of pessimism generated by the two World Wars. This mood of alienation emanates from a sense of fragmentation of the self in the social sphere and a concomitant inability to communicate effectively with others. This fragmentation of the self, in turn, raises the question of identity: 'who am I in all of this?'. In terms of its manifestation in modernist art, this tendency can best be illustrated by the novel. In the modernist novel, there is no traditional narrative of beginning, middle or end, nor is there an omniscient protagonist. Character definition is mostly, if not totally, absent. In its place, an interior monologue or stream of consciousness explores the subjective experience of an individual. The coincidence of the beginning of this movement with the emerging importance of psychoanalysis—especially in the work of Freud—cannot be sufficiently stressed. It is clear that it had a significant impact on modernism and made possible the exploration of the inner self as a way of, if not responding to, then at least describing the effects of alienation on human individuality. In this regard, then, modernism is again very self-reflexive.

Lastly, in its belief in a unified underlying reality modernism once more shows its debt to the Enlightenment. However, as we have already made clear, this leads to conceptual strategies that end up having ideological implications in that modernism can help to legitimate structures of domination and oppressions in the use of technology in war time mentioned above. In this regard, we can perceive other structures that it has served to legitimate—structures of class, binary structures around sex and race, and so on. Modernism's belief in a rationalistic interpretation of the world found its acme in the 1950s within critical theory and philosophy. The whole concept of structuralism can be seen as an attempt to provide a reassuring set of

---

[218] Ibid., p. 268.

underlying structures that are common to all: be it in the domain of the human brain, language, cultural artifacts, social organization and so on. Structuralism was to have an important impact on film theory and, albeit to a much lesser degree, on film itself. (For further details on this last point see Gidal, 1989.)[219]

If we now consider cinema's place in the modernist period we come up against a first apparent contradiction. Technologically speaking, the camera, although a modernist artifact, is seen as an instrument for reproducing reality and, as such, it is more readily associated with realism than modernism. The entire cinematic apparatus is geared towards creating the illusion of reality and it achieves this primarily through the very seamlessness of its production practices. Second, as John Orr[220] points out, the camera as a technological instrument has grown up as part of the culture of surveillance. It is also part of war technology—for example the wide-angle lens, which made cinemascope possible, is a product of First World War technology, produced as it was for tanks' periscopes to give a 180-degree view. War technology turns the weapon, the camera, into a gaze. 'Knowledge of the image becomes a form of potential capture of the symbolic, seizure of the image, and as we know the human gaze is part of this quest for knowledge, including self knowledge, a form of mirroring'.[221] The camera is also extremely self-conscious, not just because it reflects itself but also because someone (film-maker, spectator) has to watch what the camera is watching for it to have any 'meaning'. In its self-reflexivity the camera has built into it the very essence of modernism which it could exercise provided production practices do not render its operations invisible. But, of course, this is precisely what mainstream narrative cinema does.

However, as with all other art forms, cinema also has its avant-garde—although, unlike other modernist art forms, it is not explicitly hostile to mass or popular culture. In fact, many avant-garde film-makers wanted their work to reach mass audiences. Modernist cinema should be seen, therefore, as a global term that includes the work of film-makers of the avant-garde—which, depending on the period in history, can mean surrealist cinema, counter-cinema and underground cinema (to name but the most obvious). The work of these film-makers explores and exposes the formal qualities of film. Modernist cinema, in privileging formal concerns, is one that makes visible and questions its meaning-production practices. In this regard, modernist cinema questions the technology it uses, questions its power of the gaze, questions its power to represent (among other things reality, sexuality, and, just occasionally, the female body). It questions *how* it represents and *what* it represents. Modernist cinema turns the gaze into a critical weapon, turns the camera as an instrument of surveillance upon itself, starting with the fragmentation, destruction or deconstruction even of classic narrative structures.

Modernism focuses on questions of aesthetics and artistic construction. And much of modernist cinema follows that trend. Formal concerns are foregrounded over content. Certainly, the Soviet cinema of the mid- to late 1920s espoused the modernist principles of meaning being produced from style—principally from editing styles. And the montage effects, produced by fast editing, of Sergei Eisenstein's films (such as *Strike and Battleship Potemkin*, both 1925) influenced other European cinemas of the avant-garde. The avant-garde and surrealist cinema in France of the 1920s is another early manifestation of this modernist trend. Filmmakers of this generation in the early 1920s, were interested in the visual representation of the interior life of a character, that is, a formal rather than narrativized projection on to screen of the character's subjective imaginings and fantasies—dreams even (as in *Fièvre*, Louis DeRuc, 1921, about female subjectivity, hallucination and desire). This subjective cinema gave way by the mid-1920s to a concern with the plasticity of the medium and its temporal and

[219] Gidal, P. (1989) *Materialist Film*, London and New York, Routledge.
[220] Orr, J. (1993) *Cinema and Modernity*, Cambridge, Polity Press, p. 60.
[221] *Ibid.*, p. 60.

spatial qualities. The intention was to create a pure cinema where film signified in and of itself through its rhythms and plasticity (for example Jean Epstein's *Photogénies*, 1924; René Clair's *Entr'acte*, 1924). Later in the 1920s a third avant-garde was conceived out of the earlier two modes. Under the influence of surrealism, this avant-garde cinema became interested in how the temporal and spatial properties of film as well as its plasticity could be employed to reflect the workings of the unconscious especially its suppression of sexual obsessions or desires. Germaine Dulac was, arguably, the first to combine surrealist and avant-garde preoccupations in her film *La Coquille et le clergyman* (1927).

The various American avant-garde movements of the 1930s and 1940s pursued the French avant-garde tradition, particularly in its latest manifestation. Maya Deren's haunting *Meshes of the Afternoon* (1943), is an exemplary film in this respect. Deren stars in this film of paranoid dream fantasies. Her experimental play with time and space is just one way by which she achieves this sense of paranoia. By using a loop system (a single piece of film that is continuously repeated) with a sequence of a young woman fearfully coming down an anonymous street, traditional notions of time and space are eroded—instead we feel the urgency and inescapability of the woman's fear as well as the timelessness in which it is felt.

The American avant-garde of the 1960s to the mid-1970s, when it more or less died out ... tends to echo the middle period of the French avant-garde with its notion of pure cinema. It produced, among other cinemas, a minimalist cinema—where the pro-filmic event (that which the camera is aimed at) is reproduced on screen and becomes, simultaneously, the filmic event (Gidal, 1989, 16). These films were either performed events involving the film-maker or a static camera standing outside a building for hours on end. In each case, time itself is being filmed. Andy Warhol's film *Empire* (1965) is an extreme case. He left his camera running for eight hours outside the Empire State building. Generally speaking, Warhol was more contained, shooting in single takes of thirty minutes (for example *Kitchen*, 1965). The plasticity of the film was also explored by either painting on to it or scratching it and by the use of tight compositional editing (as in Carolee Schneeman's *Fuses, 1964*, which uses all three modalities to provide an intimate portrait of a couple's sexual relationship).

As we indicated above, some modernist cinema, within its formal probings and experimentation, also addressed questions of subjectivity and sexuality. However, it is not a cinema that is readily associated with politics *per se*. That being said, at certain points in history aesthetics and politics do combine to produce a political cinema, particularly in Europe. Jean-Luc Godard, in the mid- to late 1960s talked about making a political cinema politically. By that he meant making political films through a political aesthetics of film. As with the other, primarily aesthetic modernist cinema, the process of meaning-production is exposed. The difference here lies with the non-subjective intentionality of this political cinema and the greater degree of fragmentation of meaning-production. In the first instance we are privy no longer to the inner workings of the mind but, rather, as to how ideology constructs us. In the second instance, fragmentation, the gaps between signifier (the meanings produced) and the signified (the modes and means of production) are opened up and the relationship between the two is exposed. The illusion of realism and its ideological resonances are made transparent. The film as sign and as myth is deconstructed before our eyes. Godard, Agnès Varda and Margarethe von Trotta are exemplary film-makers of this second tendency of modernist cinema—a political aesthetic cinema, what is also known as counter-cinema.

A summary of episodes in Godard's film *Pierrot le fou* (1965) can serve as an illustration. Near the beginning of the film Ferdinand (alias Pierrot), who is in the advertising business, is obliged by his Italian wife to attend a cocktail party. He turns up with her, an unwilling guest. This seemingly 'innocent' beginning is in fact a reference to the state of the French film industry which, in order to compete against Hollywood products, had found itself since the mid-1950s obliged to make co-productions with Italy. At the party, the entire shooting of which is through a pink filter, women and men talk to each other in advertising-speak—but this advertising-speak is also gendered: women, therefore, talk in advertising-speak about bras and hair products, men about cars and the like. At one point Ferdinand asks an American filmmaker, Sam Fuller, 'what is cinema?' To which he gets the answer: 'film is like a battleground: love, hate, action, violence, death, in a word, emotions'. At the end of this sequence, Ferdinand picks up a huge piece of angel cake and throws it at a woman's face. He then runs out of the party and dashes home only to elope with his former lover of five years past, Marianne, who just 'happened' to be the babysitter for the evening.

Sam Fuller, then, speaks in the same clichés as the rest of the guests. Hollywood is as empty and full of air as the advertising-speak and the angel cake (a cake that is particularly American). Marianne, the symbolic name of France, might just rescue Ferdinand/Plerrot from the 'hell' in which he finds himself. In other words, the French film industry might just be able avoid going under as an indigenous industry in its own right not only by foregoing co-productions with Italy but also by refusing to follow the candy-floss practices of Hollywood (hence the pink filter) and refusing to opt for the safe classic Hollywood narrative (as exemplified by Fuller's clichés) but choosing to run with its own talent (the eloping with Marianne). Of course the ending of the film, where both protagonists die, makes it clear that this is ultimately a utopian scenario. And, as recent figures show, Hollywood is in an even more dominant position in France than it was at the time of the making of this film (in a ten-year period, 1981-91 the American share of the market in France has grown from 35 to 59 per cent).

But Godard does not confine his political statements to the celluloid war. *Pierrot le fou* is his first ostensibly political film and several international crises get similar parodic treatment, namely, the Algerian crisis and the Vietnam War. Let's take a look at the latter. Much later in the film, Ferdinand and Marianne—who have escaped Paris to some idyllic island in the sun—find themselves strapped for cash. They take a boat over to the mainland where they know they will encounter some American tourists and be able to fleece them thanks to their brilliant storytelling skills (incidentally, we have already seen that Ferdinand, at least, is not particularly successful at this). Marianne 'disguises' herself as a Vietnamese woman (she actually looks more like a geisha girl) and Ferdinand dons an American sailor's cap and blazer. Their audience is composed of two or three American sailors. Ferdinand and Marianne then act out a sketch, in a Punch and Judy style, that purports to reflect the United States/Vietnamese conflict. The actual filming of the sketch is very flat, giving the screen a comicstrip appearance and the colour is extremely hard (during his 1960s period Godard almost invariably used Eastman Kodak colour, which allows, in its processing, for the primary colours to be singled out, thus giving a harshness and violence to the image). The sketch shows Ferdinand/'Uncle Sam' dominating Marianne/'Uncle Ho' through brutal if senseless words: 'Hollywood, YAH! New York, YAH!' he yells as he swigs at a bottle of American whiskey—Marianne/'Uncle Ho' meantime crouches, cowed, mumbling in pseudo-Vietnamese. Ferdinand/'Uncle Sam' also holds a 'pretend' pistol which he continuously aims at Marianne's/'Uncle Ho's' head.

Godard's prescience is extraordinary here. It is noteworthy that in the mid-1960s, American opinion was very much behind the sending of its troops to Vietnam. By the late 1960s and early 1970s, however, opinion was wavering and was in the end radically changed thanks in part to television coverage. The then president, Richard Nixon, believed that television coverage might galvanize waning support for the war effort. It did precisely the opposite. One image in particular—the holding of a gun to a Vietnamese civilian's head and blowing his brains out—was crucial in turning public opinion against American intervention in Vietnam. The sketch in Godard's film ends with a matchbook made into an aircraft which is on fire and about to crash. Ferdinand holds the matchbook in his hand so that it also looks as if his hand is on fire—a clear allusion to the use of napalm in the war (recalling another image of a little Vietnamese girl running down a road with her back on fire). The Americans, throughout the sketch, respond with stupid, vapid comments: 'Hey, I like that!', 'It's really good'—when the sketch is patently not good but embarrassingly crude.

By placing such an internationally crucial issue within the context of evidently inappropriate cultural texts, the comic strip and Punch-and-Judy vaudeville, and filming it in elemental and violent colour while simultaneously flattening the image, Godard achieves, through visual parody and irony, a far more virulent satire than he would have done through a straightforward polemic. Nor should it be forgotten that the presence of Sam Fuller at the beginning of the film now has a further resonance: Fuller is the American film-maker most associated with the spate of Cold War movies made during the 1950s and his films, set in Korea, were notorious for their extreme violence ...Viewed in this light, Fuller's words uttered at the beginning of the film now take on different dimensions.

CRITICAL FILM ANALYSES

GOODFELLAS (1990)

–Gangster Film in its Modernist Phase–

Shannon Mader

Producer: Irwin Winkler. Director: Martin Scorsese. Executive Producer: Barbara De Fina. Screenplay: Nicholas Pileggi and Martin Scorsese, based on the book Wise Guy by Nicholas Pileggi. Cinematography: Michael Ballhaus. Production Designer: Richard Bruno. Titles: Saul and Elaine Bass.

CAST: Ray Liotta (Henry), Larraine Bracco (Karen), Robert DeNiro (James Conway), Joe Pesci (Tommy), Paul Sorvino (Paul Cicero), Frank Dileo (Tuddy), Gina Mastrogiacomo (Janice Rossi), Debi Mazar (Sandy). A Warner Brothers release. 146 min.

Consider the following two quotes:

> I don't want to film a 'slice of life' because people can get that at home, in the street, or even in front of the movie theater. They don't have to pay money to see a slice of life…. Making a film means, first of all, to tell a story. The story can be an improbable one, but it should never be banal. It must be dramatic and human. What is drama, after all, but life with the dull bits cut out.[222]

> [T]he documentary approach interested me. It doesn't focus on the overdramatic. Most gangster movies focus on the big gunfights. The book *Wise Guy* gives you a sense of the day-to-day life, the tedium—how they work, how they take over certain nightclubs, and for what reasons. It shows how it's done.[223]

---

[222] Francois Truffaut. *Hitchcock*. New York: Simon & Schuster, Inc., 1985: 103.
[223] Mary Pat Kelly. *Martin Scorsese: A Journey*. New York: Thunder's Mouth Press, 1991: 259.

The second quote, as you may have already guessed, is from Martin Scorsese. In it, he explains why the book *Wise Guy* appealed to him.

The first quote, on the other hand, is from Alfred Hitchcock. In it, he explains why he dislikes the slice-of-life approach to filmmaking. Undoubtedly, the book *Wise Guy* would *not* have appealed to him.

Encapsulated in these two quotes from these two directors are two fundamentally different views of the cinema. Whereas the one views movies as "life with the dull bits cut out," the other sees film as a medium uniquely capable of capturing the quotidian. The question is, how can film best capture the quotidian?

For Martin Scorsese at last, ordinary, everyday reality is best captured through form—more specifically, through a *deconstruction* of form. In a typically modernist approach, Scorsese remarked that his idea in *GoodFellas* was "to play around and fragment structure."[224] The question is, which structures? And why?

For one thing, Scorsese plays around with time. To take but one example, he begins the film with a scene which doesn't actually occur until much later in the film. In so doing, he restructures time. In addition, he fragments time. Large chunks of time are simply skipped over and never filled in. And by the same token, Scorsese freezes time. Indeed, the use of the freeze frame constitutes one of the film's central motifs.

The question you're probably asking is, so what? What does it matter that Scorsese fragments, freezes, and restructures time? How does that make *GoodFellas* any different from the classical gangster films?

Well, the classical gangster film was the story of a man's *rise and fall*. Hence, its story was linear: just as the protagonist first rose and then fell, so, too, did the story. It climbed and climbed until it reached a climax and then plummeted to a finish. This kind of structure is what we've been calling classical, and it's no coincidence that classical gangster films were structured in this way. The narrative structure of the classical gangster film embodied almost perfectly the moral message of the classical gangster film: everything which goes up, must come done.

In contrast, *GoodFellas* begins, not as the start of Henry's criminal ascent, but as its apex—or nadir depending on your point of view: the scene in which a still-breathing Billy Batts is repeatedly knifed. By placing this scene at the beginning of the film, Scorsese undercuts the narrative logic of the classical gangster film: instead of tying the narrative to the career path of the protagonist, Scorsese ties it to the psychological state of the protagonist. As a result, we do not experience the film chronologically but psychologically. Our experience of it is subjective, not objective: we are inside Henry's head. Everything is filtered through his consciousness.

The voice-over is obviously one way in which the film puts us inside Henry's head. Whereas the classical gangster film used an impersonal and omniscient narrator if it used one at all, *GoodFellas* has as its narrator Henry himself.[225] Rather than presenting us with an objective framework within which to evaluate the life of the protagonist, the voice-over thus enmeshes us even more in the life of Henry. Consequently, we are deprived of the independent perspective and objective morality which is necessary in order to effectively pass judgment on Henry's actions.[226] By subjectivizing narration, Scorsese thus relativizes morality. The moral universe of the classical gangster film is thereby undermined.

Henry's subjectivity is not only present on the sound track, however. It is present, albeit more obliquely, on the visual track as well. Our perceptions are filtered through his. Note, for example, the expressionistic lighting used throughout much of the film. In some scenes, the red light is nearly suffocating. Consider, for example, the above-mentioned scene in which Billy Batts is repeatedly knifed. The almost unbearably intense red conjures up images of hell. In this

---

[224] *Ibid.*, 273.
[225] Henry's wife is also heard in voice-over.
[226] Henry's wife provides us with a different perspective of course—but not a moral one. In fact, she is ultimately as amoral as Henry.

way, we are able to experience the intensity of Henry's emotions on a formal level. Notice, however, how the tone of Henry's voice-over clashes with the tone of the image. Far from being infernal, the tone of Henry's voice is actually quite elated, almost ecstatic. In counterpointing image and sound in this way, Scorsese is able to express the scene's underlying complexity: on the one hand, it represents a moral low point in Henry's life; on the other, it obviously represents an emotional high point for him as well. As a consequence, it is well nigh impossible to determine whether this scene is supposed to mark the apex or the nadir of Henry's life. Is he rising at this point, or is he falling? Again we see how Scorsese works on a formal level to undermine the moral and narrative logic of the classical gangster film.

Scorsese raises the stakes even further by placing this scene at the beginning of the film. Its ambiguity thereby infuses the entire film and conditions our experience of it.

The question you've probably been asking is, why would Scorsese want to undermine the classical gangster film? How does this relate to his objective, which is, after all, to show the daily life of the gangster?

Whether we realize it or not, genres structure our perceptions of the world. The gangster genre, for instance, structures our perceptions of gangsters: we always picture them with guns blazing. Scorsese, however, wants to open our eyes to the boring aspects of a gangster's life. He wants us to focus on the mundane, not the melodramatic—or, rather, how the melodramatic *is* mundane within the context of a gangster's life. In order to accomplish this, however, Scorsese has to break down the generic conventions which control our vision of the gangster. Fragmenting the temporal structure is simply one way of doing this. Instead of being linear, the narrative of *GoodFellas* is episodic, meandering, rambling. As a result, we do not experience the life of the gangster as a rollercoaster ride but more as a kind of bus ride with its many starts and stops.

Scorsese, in short, de-dramatizes the life of a gangster. He refuses to aggrandize the daily life of the gangster. For this reason, Scorsese's gangsters do not shoot it out with rival gangs on a daily basis. They do not hobnob with senators or foreign dignitaries. They do not drive 90 mph whenever they get behind the wheel. And perhaps most importantly, they *do* get their hands dirty. They do not sit in a darkened office as their underlings do their dirty work for them. In this respect, *GoodFellas* can be read as a critique of *The Godfather*. Scorsese strips away the Arthurian pretensions which Francis Ford Coppola brought to bear on the genre. Unlike *The Godfather* films, *GoodFellas* does not pretend to be the epic story of a family dynasty.

GoodFellas departs from the classical gangster film in many other ways. Among its many departures are the following:

1) The classical gangster was first and foremost an individualist. His individualism, in fact, accounted for both his rise *and* his fall. By contrast, Scorsese's gangsters are first and foremost company men.

2) Whereas the classical gangster was a social outcast who seemed to bear a permanent grudge against society for his pariah status, Scorsese's gangsters are by and large conformists. They feel right at home in America's materialistic culture.

3) In the classical gangster film, the gangster's greed was motivated by his desire to escape poverty. The classical gangster, after all, was either born into poverty or fell into it and turned to crime in order to get out of it. Scorsese's gangsters, on the other hand, hail from mostly working-class or lower middle-class origins. They do not turn to crime to escape a life of wrenching poverty; rather, they turn to crime almost by instinct. This is especially evident in the case of Tommy, whose thirst for blood has nothing to do with poverty.

4) In a classical gangster film, the protagonist is never a snitch. In fact, there's usually a subsidiary character who claims to be a friend of the protagonist but who rats on him. In

GoodFellas, however, it is the protagonist, the character with whom we identify most, who squeals on his friends.

5) As I have indicated already, the classical gangster film is about a gangster who rises to the top of the mob and then falls. The main character in *GoodFellas*, however, never rises to the top. In fact, he never really rises at all. Since he's part Irish, he can never join the upper echelons of the Mafia. *GoodFellas* is thus about an underling—something very unusual for a gangster film.

6) The character who bears the greatest resemblance to the classical gangster in *GoodFellas* is Tommy: he's impulsive and prone to sudden outbursts of violence; he's short and not conventionally good-looking; and he has an inferiority complex and a grudge against the world. But unlike a classical gangster film, Tommy is *not* the center of the film. Henry is. This is very different from a classical gangster film. In a classical gangster film, Henry would have been the underling or sidekick who accompanies the protagonist but who is never really the focus of our attention. In *GoodFellas*, however, it is Tommy who is pushed into the more marginal role.

7) In the classical gangster film, the gangster dies in a hail of bullets. As you will see, this is not the case with *GoodFellas*. This does not mean that Henry gets away with his crimes, but it does mean that he doesn't pay for them in the way that the classical gangster did. In fact, one *could* make the argument that Henry basically does get away with his crimes.

8) One of the more subtle ways in which *GoodFellas* departs from the classical gangster film is by having Henry cry. As you will see, he breaks down in front of Paulie when he asks him for money. This may not seem like much, but it is. Can you imagine a classical gangster crying in front of another gangster? It's inconceivable.

There are many other deviations from the classical gangster film which I could point to, but space does not permit it. *GoodFellas* is an incredibly rich film whose many layers can only be hinted at here. These notes should constitute a starting point for discussion, not an end point.

13

GENRE: POSTMODERNIST PHASE

Postmodernism...is completely indifferent to the questions of consistency and continuity. It self-consciously splices genres, attitudes, styles. It relishes the blurring or juxtaposition of forms (fiction-non-fiction), stances (straight-ironic), moods (violent-comic), cultural levels (high-low). It disdains originality and fancies copies, repetition, the recombination of hand-me-down scraps. It neither embraces nor criticizes, but beholds the world blankly with a knowingness that dissolves feeling and commitment into irony.

—Todd Gitlin, "Postmodernism defined, at last!" 1989

CTCS 190 LECTURE OUTLINE – WEEK XIII   **LECTURE 12**

PART 4: THE POSTMODERNIST PERIOD: 1977-Present

A. Conditions and Causes for Postmodernism in American Film
  1. The postmodern condition, 1977-present
  2. The emphasis on business and technology
  3. Youth culture
B. Postmodernism
  1. A periodizing concept
  2. An aesthetic sensibility
     a. Disregard and disrespect for "reality"
     b. The erasure of the distinction between popular and high culture
     c. The practice of pastiche
     d. Nostalgia for the past
     e. The mode of schizophrenic experience
     f.   The love of the cult of heterogeneity
     g. The "hip" attitude
C. Implications of Postmodernism
D. Introduction and Screening of a Genre Film in its Postmodernist Phase

Notes

Notes

POSTMODERNISM

from *Key Concepts in Cinema Studies* (1996) by Susan Hayward

This term entered into critical discourse in the late 1960s. As a concept it was seen as exemplifying a counter-position to modernism, especially modernism in its latest manifestation as total theory: structuralism. And for this reason it is a term often associated with post-structuralism, to which it is, arguably, connected. Although the two concepts do indeed co-exist, some critics feel that postmodernism—also known as the postmodern refers more to an age, particularly the 1980s and 1990s, than to a theoretical movement to which, of course, poststructuralism belongs. There appears to be no easy definition of postmodernism. Indeed there are many different ways in which it is perceived. These are never totally contradictory readings but, depending on the positioning of a particular thinker, writer or theorist, it can be given a different interpretation. This of course points to its pluralism as a concept and is something to be welcomed after the strictures of modernism and structuralism. It is also a reason why postmodernism gets aligned with post-structuralism, which is similarly pluralistic in its approach. Post-structuralism is more readily concerned with opening up the problematics in modernism and as such constitutes a critical theory of modernism. Postmodernism is perceived more as an historical condition within which are contained social, political and cultural agendas and resonances. These are interpreted, depending on the positioning of the writer or theorist, either as reflective of a mentality of 'anything goes', therefore nothing works, or of a questioning of the modernist ideals of progress, reason and science. In the first instance, theorists claim that the postmodern condition signals the death of ideology. In the second, it heralds a new scepticism about the modernist belief in the supremacy of the western world, the legitimacy of science to legislate the construction and function of gender, and the advocacy of high art over popular culture.

Ultimately, then, postmodernism is a vague term. However, in its eclecticism lies its power to be non- or anti-essentialist, it neither has nor provides a fixed meaning; in its pluralism lies its ability to be read either positively or negatively.

A first set of readings—mainstream postmodern culture and oppositional postmodern culture

Some critics see the postmodern as an effect that is a reaction against the established forms and canons of modernism. In this regard it takes issue with modernism's positive belief in progress and a unified underlying reality. Postmodernism reacts against modernism's optimistic belief in the benefits of science and technology to human kind. But, as the entry on modernism makes clear, this optimism is only part of the picture. Certain modernists did not share this optimism but mistrusted science and technology. Viewed in this light, then, postmodernism continues the pessimistic vein that already prevailed in modernism. According to Fredric Jameson (1983), postmodernism, as an effect, also represents the erosion of the distinction between high art and popular culture. The postmodern does not really refer to style but to a periodizing concept 'whose function is to correlate the emergence of new formal features in culture with the emergence of a new type of social life and a new economic order.'[227] In other words, it is a conjunctural term at the interface between artifact and the new moment of capitalism. This new moment of capitalism is varyingly called post-industrial or post-colonial society, modernization, consumer society, media society. The artifact is what is produced by and within that moment in capitalism. What is significant is that the term *post*modern is consistent with the way in which western contemporary society defines itself—that is, in relation to the past (post-colonial), but also in relation to social practice (modernization, consumer) and technology (media). In its consistency with western definitions, the postmodern looks back, is retrospective, is not defined as other, but as postmodern, as coming after. In its lack of history (defined only in relation to the past), it rejects history, and because it has none of its own—only that of others—the postmodern stands eternally fixed in a series of presents. This reading places postmodernist culture as ahistorical.

According to this view, the postmodern era has little of the optimism of post-structuralism. It is more akin to a cult than to a movement. Although Anglo-Saxon theorists refer to this concept as postmodernism or postmodernity, it is instructive to note that the country whence the term emanated, France, deliberately omits the 'ism': *le postmoderne*. This very omission warns us that this is a non-collective phenomenon and that, by implication, it focuses on the cult of the individual (a position not all critics agree with; see below). Curiously, this contemporary hedonism recalls the aesthetic culture of the symbolists at the end of the nineteenth century—particularly in France. The *fin de siècle* mood of that time—a direct reaction to the political, intellectual and moral crises taking place—manifested itself in a neoromantic nihilism wherein the individual artist became a cult figure. The death of ideology at that time left the artist in the presence of a spiritual void. How to fill the abyss of nothingness? The response was aestheticism, art for art's sake, as an end in and of itself which led to a self-sufficient formalism. In other words, only form, not content, could fill the void.

It is this pessimistic vein which finds its heritage first in the tragic modernist and later in the ahistorical postmodernist cultures. Both are traumatized by a technology that has created ideological structures of suppression and domination never seen before. Modern technology allowed images of this technology at work to be recorded (by the camera) and be brought to our attention. If there was not much footage of the First World War shown publicly, archival film shows enough of the horrors of trench warfare. More recently, images of the apocalyptic events of the Holocaust and the dropping of the atomic bomb have left modernist and postmodernist alike with seemingly unanswerable questions. How to invent, comes the cry, when invention can lead to such wholesale destruction of humanity? In answer to this daunting set of questions, modernism in its pessimistic mode presents a world as fragmented and decayed and one in which communication is a virtual impossibility. In its response to these same questions, according to theorists providing the ahistoric reading of postmodernity, postmodern culture, which can see itself only in relation to the past, bifurcates. The majority tendency is unoppositional, a unidirectional reflection towards the past, providing a conservative cultural production—that is, mainstream culture. The minority is avant-garde and oppositional.

In relation to the contemporary cultural aesthetic, then, the postmodern adopts two modes. In its mainstream mode, it manifests itself through mannerism and stylization, through pastiche—imitation of what is past. In its oppositional mode—that is, in its despair it the nothingness of the abyss—it turns to parody, an ironization of style, form and content (as in Samuel Beckett's plays and novels). Whether mainstream or oppositional, the postmodern aesthetic relies on four tightly interrelated sets of concepts: simulation, which is either parody or pastiche; prefabrication; intertextuality and bricolage. What separates the two tendencies is

---

[227] Jameson, F. (1983) "Postmodernism and Consumer Society", in: Foster, H. (ed.) *Postmodern Culture*, London, Pluto Press, p. 113.

that the oppositional postmodern aesthetic experiments with these concepts and innovates through subverting their codes, whereas the mainstream postmodern aesthetic merely replicates them. Hence the need for two distinguishing terms for the first concept, simulation: 'parody' and 'pastiche'. Parody is the domain of oppositional art. Pastiche pertains to the symptomatic in that it imitates previous genres and styles, but, unlike parody, its imitation is not ironic and is therefore not subversive. In its uninventiveness, pastiche is but a shadow of its former thing (parody). Postmodern art culls from already existing images and objects and either repeats or reinvents them as the same. To make the distinction clear, we could turn to the world of fashion and say that punk is parody, chic-punk is pastiche.

The three remaining concepts, then, are either played out in a parodic or pastiche modality. As you will see, there is considerable overlap between the concepts. In postmodern cinema, images or parts of sequences which were fabricated in earlier films are reselected. In much the same way that prefabricated houses are made up of complete units of preexisting meaning, so the visual arts see the past as a supermarket source that the artist raids for whatever she or he wants. A film could be completely constructed out of prefabricated images (and even sounds). This is particularly true for mainstream postmodern cinema. For example, a filmmaker wanting to insert a song and dance routine could select Gene Kelly's dance routine of the title song in *Singin' in the Rain* (1952), for a flashback she or he could clip in the beginning of *Sunset Boulevard* (Billy Wilder, 1950), and so on. Robert Altman's The *Player* (1992) makes reference to this pastiche culture of prefabrication (two studio scriptwriters discuss a possible script which they describe as *Out of Africa* meets *Pretty Woman*).

In this context of prefabrication, note how clever Quentin Tarantino's films are. While they appear to be a mise-en-abîme of filmic quotes, the orchestration of the quotes is so brilliantly achieved that what appears pastiche is in fact parody. He selects the quotes and then brutally overturns them. Take, for example, *Reservoir Dogs* (1991). The ten-minute torture scene in the empty warehouse, which is horrendous in its horror, is also excessively comic because the torturer, the psychopathic Mr. Blonde, dances to a 1970s song, *Stuck in the Middle with You*—a song that relates to a paranoid if not drugged perception of 'reality'. Meantime as he slices up his victim he asks, in tune with the song, 'was that as good for you as it was for me?' According to Tarantino, the filmic quotes are Abbott and Costello monster movies which combine the comic with the horror (*Sight and Sound, Vol.* 2, No. 8, 1992). They also, in their seemingly gratuitous violence, recall many a Scorsese scene of violence (for example *Taxi Driver,* 1976). This scene, as with other quotes in the film, also pulls from the B-movies. Again they are pushed to their limits. This particular torture scene derides the false bravura of cops and gangsters who 'shoot it out'—here ears are cut off, faces are slashed (before even a gun is shot!), and people torched—all to the sound of music and dancing. Not even *The Saint Valentine's Day Massacre* (1967) or The *Godfather* (Francis Ford Coppola, 1972) could match these extremes of violence-in-excess. It is precisely in scenes like this one that the film achieves the parodic. Through this use of violence, Tarantino exposes the spectator-film relationship as one of sadomasochism. We might bleed with Mr. Orange as he lies in the warehouse dying, but we also find ourselves dancing with Mr. Blonde. Compounding the parodic is Tarantino's expressed intention of making us brutally aware of the manipulative hand of the director—'he can shoot scenes like this'—and our collusion with him 'we choose to watch'. In this respect, Tarantino's work must be seen as oppositional. This makes the point that oppositional culture, postmodern or otherwise, can reach mass audiences. Tarantino is one of today's successful postmodern film-makers who can dissolve the divide between high art and low art without reducing his film to pulp, that is, to a mere series of good images.

Intertextuality, which in many respects can be seen as closely aligned with mise-en-abîme and as overlapping with prefabrication, is a term which refers to the relation between two or more texts. All texts are necessarily intertextual, that is, they refer to other texts. This relation has an effect on the way in which the present constructed text is read. All films are, to some degree, always already intertextual. Within mainstream pastiche cinema, the most obvious intertextual film is the remake. Within the parodic mode and of the more contemporary and popular filmmakers, Tarantino's films are exemplary in the way that they refer to other texts. *Pulp Fiction* (1994), for example, refers in many of its décors to the paintings of Edward Hopper—so in part the intertext is composed of painterly texts. Tarantino readily acknowledges his references to the film texts of Jean-Luc Godard. And certainly *Bande à part* (1964) with its own references to the American musical—which Godard reinscribes in a parodic mode—is a text to which *Pulp Fiction* refers. Tarantino talks about his film being based on three storylines that are the oldest chestnuts in the world, filmic narratives based on pulp fiction: a member of the gang taking out the mobster's wife whom he must not touch; the boxer who is supposed to throw the fight; gangsters on a 'mission' to kill (*Sight and Sound*, Vol. 4, No. 5, 1994, 10). Characters within film can also be intertextual of course. Again to cite Tarantino's film: Butch, the boxer, is an intertext of the character of Mike Hammer in *Kiss Me Deadly* (Robert Aldrich, 1955) and the look of the actor Aldo Ray in *Nightfall* (Jacques Tourneur, 1956).

Finally among these concepts comes bricolage. This is an assembling of different styles, textures, genres or discourses. In oppositional postmodern art this takes the form of replicating within one discourse the innovations of another. For example, the deconstruction of time and space that occurs in the *nouveau roman* is replicated in the films of Marguerite Duras, Alain Resnais and Alain Robbe-Grillet through a use of montage that disorientates. The most common replication in cinema of other textural mediums is the plasticity of video and painting which can be found in many of the 1980s film-makers' work—both mainstream and oppositional.

In mainstream postmodern cinema genres are mimicked and not renewed. In terms of subjects, themes and style, the spectator of today is reviewing either images of modernist cinema or mediatic images of its own age. With a few exceptions there are no social or political films (Stephen Frears, Neil Jordan and Dennis Potter are a few who come to mind in the British and Irish environment). Some of the major issues of the 1980s and 1990s go unheard. This dearth of subjects coincides with a cinematographic mannerism which manifests itself in at least three ways. First, by a prurient (necrophiliac?) fixation with genres and images of a bygone cinema—nostalgia at its worst. Second, by a servile simulation of television visual discourses. And, finally, by manipulating and elevating virtual reality and computer graphics to the status of real. It is in this sense that mainstream postmodern film-makers of today display a disdain for culture with a capital C. All culture, 'high' and 'low', is assimilable or quotable within their texts so that the binary divide is erased. The dissolution of the divide would be a good thing, but the result still has to have meaning. Instead, in their formalism and mannerism they aim purely and simply for the well-made image—120 minutes of good publicity clips. They invent nothing. John Orr points out that this cinema of pastiche lends itself to a double reading or, rather, contradictory readings.[228] This cinema will appeal to right and left, Black and White. *Forrest Gump* (1994) is an excellent example, since both the left and the right have found it consonant with their own ideologies. As Orr says, this cinema, while so patently empty, is also potentially dangerous—schizoid, as Orr puts it.[229]

A second set of readings—negative versus positive readings of the postmodern

(Here I am drawing on the useful and illuminating analyses to be found in Huyssen, 1990[230]; Nicholson, 1990[231]; Bruno, 1987[232]; Hawthorn, 1992[233]; Kuhn, 1990.[234]) In terms of current

---

[228] Orr, J. (1993) *Cinema and Modernity*, Cambridge, Polity Press, p. 12.
[229] *Ibid.*, p. 12.
[230] Huyssen, A. (1990) Mapping the Postmodern, in: Nicholson, L. (ed.) *Feminism/Postmodernism*, New York and London: Routledge.
[231] Nicholson, L. (ed.) (1990) *Feminism/Postmodernism*, New York and London: Routledge.

writing about postmodernism, there are at least as many positions as there are areas of concern. What follows is a summary of those positions as they affect readings of postmodern cinema. There is of course some overlapping or cross-fertilization but it is worth spelling them out if only to reiterate the pluralism of postmodernism. Postmodern discourses have been elaborated with reference to architecture, human sciences and literature, the visual arts, technology, cultural theory, social, economic and political practices, feminism and gender. As has already been mentioned, these discourses generate either positive or negative readings of the postmodern.

Negative readings tend to focus on what is perceived to be the essential schizophrenia of postmodernism: a schizophrenia which can, for example, be detected in contemporary architecture's random historical citations which have been pasted or pastiched on to so many postmodern facades.[235] Roman colonnades are mixed with Georgian windows, and so on. Jameson believes that this schizophrenia comes about as a result of a refusal to think historically.[236] Baudrillard sees this postindustrial society as the society of spectacle that lives in the ecstasy of communication.[237] This society, he believes, is dominated by electronic mass media and is characterized by simulation.[238] Baudrillard explains that this post-industrial society is one of reproduction and recycling, so rather than producing the real it reproduces the hyper-real.[239] By this he means the real is not the real, is not what can be reproduced but, rather, that which is always already reproduced which is essentially a simulation.[240] The hyper-real, then, is a simulacrum of the real. Perfect simulation is the goal of postmodernism; thereby no original is invoked as a point of comparison and no distinction between the real and the copy remains.[241] In this implicit loss of distinction between representation and the real, Baudrillard perceives the death of the individual.

In order to make this point clearer it is useful to compare the effects of the industrial machine on the individual (the subject) versus those of the post-industrial one. Whereas the industrial machine was one of production, the post-industrial one is one of reproduction.[242] In the former case, the industrial machine leads to the alienation of the subject—the subject no longer commands the modes of production. In the latter, the post-industrial machine leads to the fragmentation of the subject, to its dispersal in representation.[243] It has no history, is stuck in the ever-present. It is in effect without memory. According to Jacques Lacan, the experience of temporality and its representation are an effect of language.[244] If, therefore, the subject has no experience of temporality, has no link with the past or the future, then it is without language—that is, it lacks the means of representing the 'I'. This creates a schizophrenic condition in which the subject fails to assert its subjectivity and fails also to enter the Symbolic Order. Therefore it is stuck in the Imaginary, perhaps even in the pre-Imaginary... The question becomes 'who am I?'—even 'who made me?'. It is remarkable that the past decade or so has witnessed a spate of monster films on screen and that the question of reproduction has been central to the narrative (for example *Jurassic Park*, Steven Spielberg, 1993; *Mary Shelley's Frankenstein*, Kenneth Branagh, 1994) and identity (*Interview with the Vampire*, Neil Jordan,

[232] Bruno, G. (1987) Ramble City: Postmodernism and *Blade Runner*, October, No. 41.
[233] Hawthorn, J. (1992) *A Concise Glossary of Contemporary Literary Theory*, London, Edward Arnold.
[234] Kuhn, A. (ed) (1990) *Alien Zone*, London and New York, Verso.
[235] Huyssen, A. (1990) Mapping the Postmodern, in: Nicholson, L. (ed.) *Feminism/Postmodernism*, New York and London: Routledge, p. 237.
[236] Kuhn, A. (ed) (1990) *Alien Zone*, London and New York, Verso, p. 321.
[237] Bruno, G. (1987) Ramble City: Postmodernism and *Blade Runner*, October, No. 41, p. 67.
[238] Kuhn, A. (ed) (1990) *Alien Zone*, London and New York, Verso, p. 321.
[239] Bruno, G. (1987) Ramble City: Postmodernism and *Blade Runner*, October, No. 41, p. 67.
[240] Ibid., p. 67.
[241] Ibid., p. 68.
[242] Ibid., p. 69.
[243] Ibid., p. 69.
[244] Lacan, J. (1977) *Ecrits: A Selection*, London, Tavistock Publications (trans. A. Sheridan), p. 70.

1994). An analysis of these films would doubtless produce the missing link between past, present and future—that is, the figure of the mother who is so pre-eminently absent from these film as site of reproduction, the reproduction machine of post-industrialization 'male technology) having reproduced her (genetic engineering).

Postmodernism, as we know, refers to a general human condition in the late capitalist (post-1950s) world that impacts on society at large, including ideology, as much as it does on art and culture. Certain theorists, amongst them so-called neo-conservatives,[245] see postmodernism as a dangerous thing both aesthetically and politically. In terms of aesthetics, the danger resides in the popularization of the modernist aesthetic which, through the dissolution of the divide between high art and low art, promotes hedonism and anarchy. It promotes anarchy because it removes the function of modernist art as critique—'anything goes'—and hedonism in that it takes the subjective idealism of modernism to the point of solipsism.[246] That is, the individual subject becomes the only knowable thing. Politically speaking, because it reacts against modernism's belief in knowledge and progress, postmodernism rejects meaning in the sense of believing that the world exists as something to be understood and that there is some unified underlying reality. Ideology becomes distinctly unstable in this environment.

Postmodernism is not necessarily perceived negatively, particularly by those living in it—primarily the youth generation, but also other groupings (as I will explain). Postmodernism in its positive mode celebrates the present and is far more accepting of late capitalism and technology. It also celebrates the fact that mass communication and electronics have revolutionized the world.[247] Postmodernism delights in and is fascinated by technology. The Internet represents the height of communication in the present through mass technology. Virtual reality can 'let me be there' without moving. Late capitalism means a dispersal of the productive base: commodities are produced where it is most advantageous, the labour market has become internationalized and fragmented. But it has also produced multinational corporations, which means that capital itself is concentrated in the hands of the few. For example, the world is so small that Reebok or Nike can have their central office in New Jersey or Eugene, Oregon but not have a factory outlet anywhere in the United States. The factories are placed in parts of the world where labour is cheapest.

To the criticism that postmodernism has lost the edge of art as critique and that, in its art-for-art's-sake positioning, it resembles the *fin de siécle* mood of the nineteenth century, postmodern art appears—within its celebratory and playfully transgressive (of modernism) mode—to reject this function of art or proposes that popular culture is just as capable of offering a critique as high art. In this latter respect, the populist trend of postmodernism (as exemplified by pop art and its reference to comic-strip culture, and by pop music: rock, punk, acid)—in its deliberate counter-culture positioning challenges modernism's hostility towards mass culture.[248] It also rejects modernist belief in the 'perpetual modernisation of art'[249] and questions the exploitation of modernism for capital greed and political need. To explain: during the 1940s and the Cold War of the 1950s, modernism, in the form of abstract expressionism (as seen in the paintings of Willem de Kooning), was a school virtually 'invented' and subsequently Institutionalized as canonical high art by the United States (read: the CIA and art critics). This was done for propagandistic and political ends. The intent, successfully carried out, was to move the centre of the art world out of Europe (and the threat or taint of communism) and to make New York the world capital (in both senses of that word) of art.

---

[245] Huyssen, A. (1990) Mapping the Postmodern, in: Nicholson, L. (ed.) *Feminism/Postmodernism*, New York and London: Routledge, p. 255.

[246] Hawthorn, J. (1992) *A Concise Glossary of Contemporary Literary Theory*, London, Edward Arnold, p. 110.

[247] Ibid., p. 111.

[248] Huyssen, A. (1990) Mapping the Postmodern, in: Nicholson, L. (ed.) *Feminism/Postmodernism*, New York and London: Routledge, p. 241.

[249] Ibid., p. 238.

Postmodernism's effect of dissolving the binary divide between high and low art has, domino-style, generated others. The positive side of 'anything goes' is that dichotomies no longer function tyrannically as exclusionary. Modernism had represented a masculinization of culture, due in part to a bohemian lifestyle that excluded most women at least at first,[250] but due also to the primary areas of modernism: architecture, painting, film, theatre (the modernist novel coming, arguably, later in the 1930s). Thanks to its creative relationship between high and low art, postmodernism has made space for minority cultures, has brought about a fragmentation of culture that is positive. Thus, where gender and race are concerned, this dissolution of binary divides and deprivileging of a meritocracy within dichotomies have led, first, to a pluralism within the question of subjectivity and, second, to a questioning of defining one group in relation to the concept of 'otherness'. In its rejection of universal norms, postmodernism refutes generalizations that exclude, and advocates a plurality of individualized agency.[251] In this respect, therefore, gender and race are no longer dichotomized. Postmodernism represents, then, a cultural liberation.

Small surprise that for some groupings—particularly those who had previously been excluded by the high principles of modernism—postmodernism is seen as liberating and celebratory. Voices from the margins, minority cultures, are finding spaces within contemporary culture. In the western world this has meant hearing, among others and in differing degrees of volume, the voices of Blacks, women, women of colour, gays, lesbians, ecologists, animal rights supporters, disabled people and so on. Some of these voices are finding their way on to film. Since the 1980s, for example, there has been an emergence of Black men and women film-makers and Black stars, gay and lesbian film-makers are coming on mainstream—marking the beginnings of a pluralism therefore in this highly competitive arena.

This pluralism has extended into film theory perhaps with greater speed than into the film-making practices themselves. And this is due in part to postmodernism's impact upon or coincidence with developments in cultural studies towards a mapping of our cultures—seeing culture as pluralistic (starting in the 1960s with Raymond Williams *et al.*). It is also due to its conjuncture with feminism. Feminist criticism exposed the masculine determinations of modernist art and culture and as such, albeit through a differing optic, echoed the postmodern position. In its critique of the normalizing function of patriarchy, feminism joins up with postmodernism's critique of the modernist belief in knowledge and its use of 'master narratives' to legitimate scientific research and the pursuit of knowledge.[252] In the name of knowledge, modernism has presented a very dislocated and partisan view of the world—one that excludes more than it includes, one that belongs to a particular gender, class, race and culture.[253] Feminism rejects modernism's belief in reason and objectivity and its concomitant belief in total theory. Feminism opposes, therefore, all generalizations because they exclude.

Because feminism raises the questions of identity, identification and, ultimately, history (or lack of it where woman's place is concerned), postmodernism seems, then, a natural ally to feminism (although not all feminists agree; see Nicholson, 1990).[254] Counter to modernism's construction of the individual as a single subjectivity in relation to the 'other', postmodernism and feminism make possible the notion of a 'plurality of individual agents'.[255] For example, there is no longer a single standard norm wherein gender, identity and sexual orientation are

---

[250] Hawthorn, J. (1992) *A Concise Glossary of Contemporary Literary Theory*, London, Edward Arnold, p. 109.
[251] Nicholson, L. (ed.) (1990) *Feminism/Postmodernism*, New York and London: Routledge, p. 13.
[252] Kuhn, A. (ed) (1990) *Alien Zone*, London and New York, Verso, p. 321.
[253] Nicholson, L. (ed.) (1990) *Feminism/Postmodernism*, New York and London: Routledge, p. 5.
[254] Ibid., p. 5.
[255] Ibid., p. 13.

fixed as heterosexual.[256] Furthermore, it becomes possible to talk in terms of gender- and race-based subjectivities....[257]

The importance of this concept of pluralism for film theory is clear. The construction of subjectivity through the cinematic apparatus can be examined. This in turn generates questions around the gaze and leads to its investigation: who owns it, is it exclusively male? The whole debate around sexuality on screen gets opened up. The issue of spectator-text relations now becomes yet another way by which the filmic text can be understood as an ideological operation. Thus gender issues are no longer reduced to an 'either/or', but discussed within frameworks of gender fluidity, resistance to gender fixing, whether on screen or in connection with the spectator and the text.

[256] Ibid., p. 15.
[257] Huyssen, A. (1990) Mapping the Postmodern, in: Nicholson, L. (ed.) *Feminism/Postmodernism*, New York and London: Routledge, p. 250.

CRITICAL FILM ANALYSES

Miller's Crossing (1990)

–Gangster Film in its Postmodernist Phase–

Robert Buerkle

Crew: *Directed by Joel Coen; Produced by Ethan Coen; Written by Joel Coen and Ethan Coen; Co-produced by Mark Silverman; Line Producer: Graham Place; Executive Producer: Ben Barenholtz; Director of Photography: Barry Sonnenfeld; Production Designer: Dennis Gassner; Costume Designer: Richard Hornung; Edited by: Michael R. Miller; Music by: Carter Burwell; Supervising Sound Editor: Skip Lievsay; Casting by: Donna Isaacson and John Lyons; Twentieth Century-Fox, 1990, USA. Running time: 115 mins.*

Cast: *TOM REAGAN: Gabriel Byrne; VERNA: Marcia Gay Harden; BERNIE BERNBAUM: John Turturro; JOHNNY CASPAR: Jon Polito; EDDIE DANE: J.E. Freeman; LEO: Albert Finney; FRANKIE: Mike Starr; TIC-TAC: Al Mancini; MINK: Steve Buscemi; CLARENCE "DROP" JOHNSON: Mario Todisco; TAD: Olek Krupa; ADOLPH: Michael Jeter; TERRY: Lanny Flaherty.*

> [Miller's Crossing] now appears as part of a gangster film revival...and also in the middle of a wave of *noir*-ish adaptations from American hard-boiled fiction. ...The Coens are returning to the roots of both areas, a move which gives their film a strange air of both self-consciousness and purity, a kind of knowing classicism.[258]
> — *Monthly Film Bulletin*

We've characterized the postmodern period as "a revival of genre," noting that the period emerged from the systematic deconstruction of genres that marked the modernist era by attempting to revitalize those classic generic molds. Yet the year 1990 seemed the locus of a much more specific revival: that of the gangster film. Scorcese's *GoodFellas*, Copolla's

---

[258] Steve Jenkins, *Monthly Film Bulletin* (February, 1991) p. 49.

Godfather Part III, and Beatty's *Dick Tracy* all emerged from 1990—with Levinson's *Bugsy* immediately following in '91. And nestled among this company was the Coen brothers' *Miller's Crossing*, perhaps the most characteristically postmodern of the lot. The above quote alludes to the reasons why. As demonstrated by *Miller's Crossing*, postmodernism is indeed an <u>extension</u> of modernism, as well as a deliberate <u>break</u> from it in its attempt to return to a classical mode. Yet the end result is neither one nor the other; it is instead its own monster, with characteristics distinct to this mode of filmmaking and generic engagement.

Continuing the trend of generic experimentation that we saw begin in postclassicism, then accelerate in the modernist period, the Coens are quite self-conscious in their engagement with the genre, as demonstrated in their calculated treatment of its subtextual tropes. Gangster films have long been criticized for their over-the-top violence and their problematic treatment of women (consider James Cagney's grapefruit scene in *Public Enemy*), and many critics have taken note of the underlying homoeroticism which seems inherent to their characters. *Miller's Crossing* reveals this homoeroticism, misogyny, and sadism in varying turns, with the character of The Dane easily embodying all three. However the Coens do not veil or elide these tropes, but rather make them unavoidable. Not only is the Dane in a homosexual relationship, but his lover, Mink, beds down with Bernie Bernbaum, creating a rather unusual love triangle for a genre built on machismo and archetypes of masculinity. Further, The Dane's hate for women is blatant—after slapping around Verna, he sneers, "Go ahead and run, sweetie. I'll track down all of you whores." Yet his sadistic nature is the most evident, as he seems to relish every beating and killing he hands out, and this brutality is especially notable when strangling Tom, as he snarls "I am gonna send you to a deep, dark place, and I am gonna have fun doing it!" All these characteristics of the gangster which had classically been left muted are here brought to the surface in exaggerated form.

Miller's Crossing also engages with more primary elements of the gangster hero. According to Thomas Schatz:

> the mythology of the classic gangster film...concerns the transformation of nature into culture under the auspices of modern civilization. ...Nature in the gangster film is conspicuous primarily in its absence—or rather in the ways it is repressed in the "social animal" who is the genre's focal character.[259]

However nature is *not* absent here, but rather foregrounded in the titular location of Miller's Crossing, the patch of forest where Tom is sent to execute Bernie in a test of his loyalty to Caspar, and seemingly an equal test of his mettle as a gangster (until the point, Tom has only functioned as an advisor, keeping his hands clean of true criminality). While Tom marches Bernie deep into the woods, Bernie pleads, "Tom, you can't do this, you don't bump guys! You're not like those animals back there!" And indeed, we learn Tom is *not* like those "animals." He spares Bernie's life, despite an earlier insistence that Bernie's death was in the best interests of everyone involved, and this compassionate slip (it is the only instance when emotion gets the better of him) becomes the one mistake Tom will come to regret. The classic gangster was ruled by his emotions, a volatile, primal figure that existed on his whims and instincts; yet Tom rarely allows for emotions, suppressing them for a more level-headed, strategic approach to the criminal empire. Thus the Coens create a "head vs. heart" binary in the gangster, contrasting the classic, emotionally-unstable embodiment with this new, logically-minded figure. By the film's end, Tom amends this slip in judgment, this ill-advised indulgence of emotion. When Bernie pleads for his life a second time, again crying "Tommy, look in your heart," (repeated from the earlier scene), Tom's only response before firing is "What heart?" He's learned to eliminate that momentary lapse in judgment. Yet ironically, it would seem he's finally *become* that "animal," the primal gangster figure who acts on instinct rather than logic—as Bernie

---

[259] Thomas Schatz, *Hollywood Genres* (Boston: MacGraw-Hill, 1981) p. 82-3.

points out, "there's no angle" in it for Tom, since Caspar and The Dane are both dead by this point. He kills Bernie simply for satisfaction, giving in to the gangster mentality.

This structuring binary of head vs. heart also arises between Leo and Tom, as each occupies one side of that opposition. Leo repeatedly makes decisions based solely on his feelings for Verna, despite Tom's requests to be more rational: "Think about what protecting Bernie gets us; think about what offending Caspar loses us," Tom asks, to which Leo responds, "C'mon, Tom, you know I don't like to think." And in the end, after referencing his own "bonehead plays" versus Tom's "smart play," Leo insists, "Jesus, Tom, I'd do anything if you'd work for me again...I need you." It would seem their collaboration, Tom's head and Leo's heart, is what has maintained Leo's empire—a necessary tandem to run the gangster outfit.

The Coens indulge in the gangster genre to such an extent that an iconic component of its visual design—hats—becomes a structuring metaphor of the film. Note the countless number of times Tom loses his hat (though he doesn't chase it in his dream, he seems to be chasing it endlessly in his waking life), as well as the repeated close-ups and references to hats, from the title sequence of Tom's hat blowing away to Caspar's disdain for receiving "the high-hat." *Cineaste* interprets the hat as representative of the brains that it covers: "Losing your hat symbolizes the helplessness of your situation, whether in love or gang war, when intelligence can no longer save you."[260] *The New York Post* reads it differently: "The credit sequence...turns out to be Tom's nightmare, and what's blowing away is his control. When you're a control freak, fear of losing your hat runs deep."[261] Sabine Horst says it signifies the genre itself: "The hat...represents a semiotic system that is itself disappearing. By the end, Reagan has managed to hang on to his hat, but has lost just about everything else—and thus the film marks...the demise of the old gangster etiquette, of the genre in its classic form."[262] So what does it *really* mean? According to Tom, nothing; relating his dream, he insists, "It stayed a hat, and no, I didn't chase it. Nothing more foolish than a man chasing his hat." Yet Joel Coen disagrees with his protagonist, insisting "The hat is very significant."[263] If so, then that significance remains open to any number of interpretations.

This generic experimentation and modernist thematics readily combine in Johnny Caspar's repeated discussion of ethics, a motif which first arises in the opening lines of the film: "I'm talking about friendship. I'm talking about character. I'm talking about—hell, Leo, I ain't embarrassed to use the word—I'm talking about ethics." Here, Caspar also makes reference to the culture/nature binary and the comparison to animals, noting that without ethics, "you're back with anarchy, right back in the jungle. That's why ethics is important, what separates us from the animals." The ironic commentary is immediate: he's angry because every time he fixes a fight, Bernie sells the information, making the odds tank—"Bernie ain't satisfied with the honest dollar he can make off the fix." So while Caspar sees a fixed boxing match as an "honest dollar," he concludes Bernie to be unethical for selling out the fix—because after all, "if you can't trust a fix, what can you trust?" Leo asks if anyone else knew of the fix, to which Caspar replies, "no one who ain't got ethics." Note that those to whom he refers are corrupt boxers, bookies, and other gangsters. Caspar's continual reference to ethics is obviously ironic, satirizing the gangster figure by displacing these terms from their normal associations. Yet these notions—friendship, character, ethics, trust, and so on—are accepted by both the other characters and the audience, for these concepts are not stable in and of themselves, but rather depend on their context for meaning, shifting within their situational usage based on the consensus of the community using them. Thus the situation ethic of modernism still remains in the postmodern period, as well as the heterogeneous world in which good and evil are no longer

[260] Richard McKim, *Cineaste* (Vol. XVIII, No. 2, 1991) p. 45.
[261] David Edelstein, *The New York Post* (September 21, 1990) p. 21.
[262] Sabine Horst, "*Miller's Crossing*," *Joel & Ethan Coen*, Peter Korte and Georg Seeslen, eds. (London: Limelight Editions, 1998) p. 91.
[263] Mark Horowitz, "The A-Z of the Coen Brothers," *Film Comment* (September-October 1991) p. 26.

clear cut, but based in relativity. Here, ethics can refer to gangsters following gangster rules, following an assumed code of conduct for this community, rather than what we would consider universal standards of morality.

In addition, we see several other modernist tendencies remaining from the '63-'76 period—yet many are muddied, as the postmodern period breaks from this mode just as much as it continues it. *Miller's Crossing* doesn't provide the multiple perspectives of modernism, but does use a selective point-of-view rather than classical omniscience, as we're only privy to what Tom himself sees or knows. While we do identify with Tom, we're still kept at somewhat of a distance due to his emotionless disposition and our resultant inability to glean his motives; the exaggerated, archetypal supporting characters also help keep us detached from this world. While the film does use a fair amount of narrative causality, chance and happenstance still partially define this world. Both Tom and Leo get saved by coincidence: Tom when the police force bust Caspar's joint just in the nick of time, Leo when the cigarette of his dead bodyguard lights a newspaper aflame, the smoke alerting him of trouble. Plus, Tom's motives—the ultimate motivator of the film—are never fully rationalized. But what most irked critics was the film's convoluted plot. *Sight & Sound* declared, "The plot is of a complexity that would defy any brief synopsis,"[264] while the *L.A. Times* simply called it "a bloody thicket."[265] Rather than the simple transitivity of classicism which allowed for a passive viewing experience, here we have a story which requires the viewer's active attention, as it is comprised of a variety of transmutations and must be reconstructed retrospectively, to some degree. Yet the story *does* make logical sense; while the story may be convoluted, it still exhibits a discernable plot, and the narrative is carefully structured by repeated lines, situations, compositions, and other motifs.

With all these examples, we see *Miller's Crossing* negotiating between modernism and classicism with a push/pull dynamic of drawing the viewer in, but still holding them at arm's length, indicative of a larger dynamic at work in this period of retaining modernist characteristics while simultaneously looking toward a return to classicism, resulting in a tension between the two. Yet this does not wholly define the postmodern period, as this phase also exhibits a number of characteristics unique to itself.

In the postmodern era, the intertextuality of modernism is accelerated into pastiche, a hodgepodge of innumerable imitations meant to recall past genres, styles, and individual texts simply for the sake of invoking those past works. *Miller's Crossing* references the entire canon of gangster films by turn—the opening scene parallels the opening of *The Godfather*, both involving a balding, mustachioed Italian supplicating a crime boss for vengeance, while the closing invokes *The Godfather Part II* (the shot of the isolated protagonist), while also harkening back to final walk-away that concluded *The Third Man* (though here, it's inverted). In between, we get references to everything from *The Public Enemy* to *Once Upon a Time in America*. Outside of gangster films, several have even noted indirect echoes of Howard Hawks. What's it all mean? Nothing, really—it's just pastiche. Yet this is not to say that the film doesn't make significant intertextual references as well. The execution at Miller's Crossing is a haunting replication of a similar scene in Bertolucci's *The Conformist*, where the hero is sent to assassinate a woman in order to prove his loyalty to the fascist government; here, the parallel lends a moral heft to Tom's decision and heightens the significance of this pivotal moment. But the most significant references are to the hard-boiled novels of Dashiell Hammett, the source material for the Coens' gangster tale.

Though an original script by the Coens, *Miller's Crossing* relies heavily on the work of Hammett, just as *Blood Simple* and *The Man Who Wasn't There* are direct engagements with James M. Cain and *The Big Lebowski* revisits Raymond Chandler. The setting arises from

---

[264] Tim Pulleine, *Sight & Sound* (Winter 1990/91) p. 64.
[265] Sheila Benson, *Los Angeles Times* (October 5, 1990) Calendar/p. 10.

Hammett's 1929 novel *Red Harvest*, which painted a fictional Prohibition-era town saturated by corruption and divided between bootleggers and the political establishment. The story follows the protagonist's shifting allegiances across both sides as he plays one against the other—a plot adapted by both Kurosawa'a *Yojimbo* (1961) and Leone's *A Fistful of Dollars* (1964)—and the shootout at the Sons of Erin club is taken directly from the novel. But *Miller's Crossing* owes an even greater debt to Hammett's *The Glass Key* (1931); the plot bears a striking similarity, following a right-hand advisor to a political boss foolishly in love with a woman and in a rivalry with a fellow mobster. The hero remains loyal to his superior while manipulating events to his own advantage and taking countless beatings—all apt descriptions for Tom Reagan. Further, the thematics and world view of Hammett are all intact within *Miller's Crossing*, where there seems no world existing outside the criminal milieu and everyone is corrupt in one way or another.

Miller's Crossing takes not only from past films and hard-boiled literature, but from a variety of other discourses as well—the film exhibits a noticeable comic book stylization (consider the embellished bursts of flame spitting from Leo's Thompson machine gun and the comic book panel compositions), utilizes both Celtic and Italian folk songs (most noticeably "Danny Boy" and Frankie's jovial Italian solo), makes biblical references, uses theatrical set designs, and so on, all resulting in the postmodern collapse of high and low culture. Hard-boiled novels originated as low-class pulp, yet have since come into literary esteem, and when set against comic books and B-movies, they seem high-cult by contrast; yet the Coens seem to return such novels to their low-grade roots. The assassination attempt on Leo turns into an artful ballet of gangster film violence set against a sentimental rendition of "Danny Boy" (Terry even remarks, "The old man's still an artist with the Thompson). High and low have no meaning in the postmodern era; here, it's all melded into pop culture.

Continually taking from such a vast array of disparate spheres and discourses can have a number of effects. For one, this can often lead to a feeling of schizophrenia, where the endless number of determinations fragment the film and creates a fractured experience. More significantly, however, this leads to postmodernism being characterized by representations not of reality, but rather of other representations. Notice that the *Miller's Crossing* does not take place in any specific city, but rather an amalgam of every eastern Prohibition-era city ever portrayed on the big screen—it's not based in a real New York or Chicago, but rather in other depictions of such cities. Marcia Gay Harden has commented that she modeled her performance not on the real flappers of the '20s, but rather on performances like Jean Harlow's in *The Public Enemy*—again, on another representation. Better yet, consider this comparison to *GoodFellas*, a modernist gangster film from the same year, as explained by David Denby:

> *GoodFellas*, based on the memories of a real-life gangster, turns [the lives of gangsters] back into truth and produces a new kind of pleasure. What matters to the Coens is not what a gangster is really like, but the fabulous ways he can be represented.[266]

Based on a true story, *GoodFellas* takes great lengths to convey the real story of Henry Hill—to represent reality. *Miller's Crossing* is also based on a true story; in addition to the influence of Hammett, the film is rooted in the Capone-O'Bannion war of 1920s Chicago. Yet the Coens don't go to these historical figures for influence, but rather to James Cagney, Edward G. Robinson, Humphrey Bogart, and innumerable others. They have no interest in the historical basis for these gangsters, but rather look to their cultural representations in past films. Thus it seems fair to say that postmodern films have a rather tenuous hold on reality; whereas modernism commented on the world through a self-conscious engagement with social and moral issues, films like *Miller's Crossing* are often engaging instead with the cultural

---

[266] David Denby, *New York* (October 8, 1990) p. 59.

landscape that cinema is a part of—with other films, with other media, with other discourses—rather than the world itself.

Many reviews of *Miller's Crossing* noted the film as departing from modernism, arriving at some variation on the classical mode. David Denby claimed the Coens "give us the elements of a challenging new classicism"[267] while *Sight & Sound* described the film's manner as "not the delirious modernism of *Blood Simple*, but rather that of neo-classicism." Both recognize the film *trying* to return to classical roots—a characteristic of this period's revival of genre—yet achieving something else, as a return to pure classicism can't occur here. The quote which opened these notes is telling in its description of a "knowing classicism"—both the audience and the artists are wiser and more versed in the medium, as well as its genres, than their classical counterparts. But in addition to being more cine-literate, they're also more cynical, often criticizing the medium as readily as they embrace it. Perhaps the best description of *Miller's Crossing*, then, is to say that it plays devil's advocate to the classic gangster film; it does not wholly reject or systematically deconstruct the genre, but it does parley with its seminal texts—playfully, critically, sardonically, and yet respectfully.

---

[267] Ibid., 59.

14
FILM AS "OVERDETERMINED" ART FORM / MEDIUM

Eventually I realized that the movies not only reflected but also excluded the world, and that I needed an approach that would account for both a reflection more complicated that I had originally granted and an exclusion more systematic than I had reckoned on. In short, I needed theories of overdetermination and transformation.

—Robert Ray, 1985

CTCS 190 LECTURE OUTLINE – WEEK XIV   LECTURE 13

A. **Overdetermination and the Film Text**
B. **Cinematic Influences**
   1. Aesthetics
   2. Business practices of the industry
   3. Film technology
   4. Censorship and prior restraints
   5. Production history
   6. Critical and popular discourses
C. **Extra-Cinematic Influences**
   1. Historical events
   2. Economic situation of the country (in which the film is produced)
   3. Other forms of leisure activity
   4. Societal issues
   5. Ideology
D. **Reception as Determinant**
   1. Period in which film has been analyzed/received
   2. Gender, class, ethnicity, religious persuasion, race, sexual orientation, age
E. **Introduction and Screening**

Notes

Notes

ON OVERDETERMINATION

by Angelo Restivo

Overdetermination is a concept whose origins can be traced, first, to Marxist theory and then to psychoanalysis. According to Marx, the events of history are overdetermined: that is, they cannot be understood in a simple cause-and-effect relationship. When looking at a complex historical event such as the French Revolution, for example, we cannot say that it was simply a matter of the bourgeoisie "deciding" to create a new government. In fact, it began with the bourgeoisie asking for rather moderate reforms. How this then escalated into the storming of the Bastille, the overthrow and subsequent decapitation of the king, and so forth, can only be explained by overdetermination: not one simple cause, but a multiplicity of causes coming from all across the social classes, as each reacted to the changing circumstances.

Freud extended the notion of overdetermination to the workings of the human mind: he argues that there is never simply one cause for a neurotic symptom, but rather many, sometimes contradictory causes. Let's say, for example, that we've had a dream of flunking the cinema exam and being humiliated by our TA. Our analysis might begin by remembering the panic we felt the night before when we realized we had done none of the readings. But then, we would have to analyze our relation to the TA: perhaps in some way he reminds us of a conflict we had with our father. Ultimately, psychoanalysis would trace the determinants of the dream back to early childhood, parental rivalry, and the Oedipal conflict. It is important to note that no one of these is the "cause" of the dream; rather, it is overdetermined by all of them.

In 1968, when cinema theory was radically changing, the French introduced the notion of overdetermination to the film text. *Cahiers du cinema*—the most influential film journal in the world at the time—did an analysis of John Ford's *Young Mr. Lincoln* (1939), uncovering all the ways in which the text was overdetermined. Instead of looking for a coherent, unified meaning in the film, the authors looked for contradictions and "gaps" that marked the film as overdetermined; instead of taking the scenes at face value, they looked at the scenes as symptoms; and instead of striving for closure in their interpretation, they asserted that even the classical Hollywood text can be considered "open." Thus, the concept of overdetermination allows us to "open up" the classical, closed text of Hollywood to multiple and contradictory readings.

CRITICAL FILM ANALYSES

Red River (1948)

Robert Buerkle

CAST: John Wayne (Thomas Dunson) • Montgomery Clift (Matthew Garth) • Joanne Dru (Tess Millay) • Walter Brennan (Groot Nadine) • Colleen Gray (Fen) • Harry Carey (Mr. Melville) • John Ireland (Cherry Valance) • Noah Beery Jr. (Buster McGee) • Harry Carey, Jr. (Dan Latimer) • Chief Yowlachie (Quo) • Paul Fix (Teeler Yacey) • Hank Warden (Sims Reeves) • Mickey Kuhn (young Matt) • Ray Hyke (Walt Jergans) • Wally Wales (Old Leather)

CREW: directed by Howard Hawks • written by Borden Chase and Charles Schee, based on "The Chisholm Trail" by Borden Chase • produced by Charles K. Feldman (executive producer) and Howard Hawks • original music by Dmitri Tiomkin • cinematography by Russell Harlin • edited by Christian Nyby • art direction by John Datu • makeup by Lee Greenway • sound by Richard DeWeese • special effects by Donald Stewar Monterey Productions (distributed by RKO). Running time: 133 minutes

> Red River *is a film about cows, horses, gun play, brave women, daring men—and capitalism.*[268]

Over the course of the semester, we've witnessed an array of factors one must consider when evaluating a filmic text: aesthetic elements, historic periods, realist/formalist styles, and business and production issues to name but some. All these, along with a multitude of other considerations, both cinematic and extra-cinematic, must be paid heed when discussing how a film is ultimately determined, as we shall see with this week's example of *Red River*.

Like any film, *Red River* is the product of a specific historical moment, and we must consider that moment to understand the intricacies of the text. The film emerged from the dawn of the postwar period, a time in which America was celebrating a worldwide victory over the Axis

---

[268] Robert Sklar, "*Red River*: Empire to the West," *Cineaste*, Vol. IX, No. 1, 1978, p. 15.

forces and reveling in its position as a global superpower. Yet this time was also the dawn of a new conflict: the Cold War, an animosity between nations that centered on the divide between the U.S. and the U.S.S.R. and quickly arose in the wake of WWII (illustrative of this swiftly growing tension, the North Atlantic Treaty Organization would be formed just one year after *Red River*'s release). Many recognized the Cold War in terms of the specific political and economic binaries which divided the nations involved: democracy vs. totalitarianism, capitalism vs. communism. Thus, this is a time when the United States more than ever identifies itself as a nation of capitalists, as well as a global force.

The postwar period was also a time of economic resurgence; as veterans returned, Europeans immigrated, and families expanded with the baby boom, the population began to swell, creating higher demand for goods and services. Resultantly, this seller's market allowed for dramatic price inflation (leading to higher profits), and with wages continually rising as well, Americans could afford these increased prices. Money was available, and consumerism was quickly in vogue. Professional spheres grew, further spurring the economy, while the rise of "Madison Avenue" professions (marketing, advertising, sales, and P.R.) sparked newfound interest in the joy of spending. With the Depression safely behind and wartime rationing a thing of the past, America rediscovered the pleasure principle lost since the Jazz Age, and that principle meant dipping into those newly-filled wallets and purses. Further, these growing notions of financial success and consumerism helped solidify what was now commonly being termed "the American way of life." In short, not only did America recognize itself as capitalists like never before, but capitalism was *working*.[269] It is thus not surprising to see a film like *Red River* not only made, but meeting with critical and commercial success; it is nothing if not a celebration of capitalism.

Openly engaging with America's economic and political identity, *Red River* is about the days of the frontier, when the U.S. was moving west across the continent, acquiring land and building a nation—after all, the film begins with Tom Dunson claiming the patch of land he will develop into his ranch, essentially stealing the land from a Mexican who in turn stole the land from Native Americans. The theft is justified with the observation, "that's too much land for one man...all this land aching to be used and never has been," a line which also conveniently justifies America's own conquest of the New World, its own expansionist history. And Tom Dunson is a capitalist if ever there was one, not only building his business from the ground up but stopping at nothing to maintain it and collect his profit. Expansionism and capitalism are inherently linked here, with one the justification for the other: this land is not being used, so I will take it to build my empire. Dunson also justifies it as a common good for the nation: "Wherever they go they'll be on my land. ...I'll have enough beef to feed the whole country. Good beef for hungry people. Beef to make 'em strong—make 'em grow." The seizure of land thus becomes essential for the nation's future and for the sake of its people.

It's also significant that this was the beginning of a time where "Big Business squeezed out the little man," as growing bureaucracy, the merging of corporations, and factory automation pushed the individual out of the American workplace.[270] As such, *Red River* can be read as a celebration of the individual entrepreneur as well as capitalism. Tom Dunson builds his ranch with nothing but a cow, a bull, and the land he claims for his own, a success story of the common man—the individual American male—who rises to economic power with a business of his own (significantly, he's embodied by the very ideal of American manhood, John Wayne). Further, it is a family business, not only run by the individual American, but also supported by "son" Matthew, who we can assume will inherit the family business, and the grandfatherly Groot.

[269] Postwar overview in part condensed from Drew Casper's forthcoming book on American cinema in the postclassical period, 1946-1962.
[270] Ibid.

Certainly, *Red River* is a film about men; rugged men, active men, men who carry guns—men who fight for and defend what's theirs and what they believe in, the very sort of men newly returned from the war and now readjusting to civilian life. Yet those veterans returned with scars both physical and psychological, and while the wounds and lost limbs could be seen, the interior trauma left from combat begged to be acknowledged. As the nation was also taking interest in Freud and all things psychoanalytic, glimpses of the psychosis inevitable in that rugged, active male began to emerge throughout cinema, with *Red River* no exception. Thomas Dunson is also a man falling apart, on the verge of psychological collapse, obsessed, misguided, and full of neuroses. Though he begins the film calm and collected, diligent and focused, mentally sharp and able to do anything he sets his mind to, we witness Dunson's tragic spiral into megalomania and fixation until we, along with Matthew, see that he is no longer capable of running his business, having become a danger to both himself and others.

The male's inner conflict following the war also emerged from an uneasy tension with the female, as he returned from abroad to find women successfully holding down the industrial fort in his absence; women, it seems, were able to hold the country together without him, and his role as breadwinner now seemed threatened by Rosie the Riveter. This tension also involved the changing nature of sexual relationships during this period; not only was the female now self-sufficient, but she was becoming a different creature than the one he had left. "The male, definitely bombarded by change, options, things he never bargained for and stressed out, turned defensive."[271] Thus it is not difficult to understand this über-male fantasy which essentially pushes the female aside, allowing men to exist and carry out their business with women safely absent (the primary female role, in fact, does not appear for two-thirds of the film). "In *Red River* a nostalgia for the old order prevails as a response to the post-war gender crisis."[272] But the idea of women are not entirely missing. Robert Sklar notes Matthew as sensitive, virginal, and "soft," claiming that he "serves as bearer of the feminine principle in a society of men without women."[273] With the collapsing of gender roles in the postwar period and women entering the realm of men, Matthew, for one, seems able to cross gender positions as well—perhaps another reason he becomes a threat to Dunson, the full-fledged American male.

The family in general also ran into turmoil. In addition to growing divorce rates and troubles between mom and dad (a reality already at odds with the happy nuclear family that everyone assumed as the norm), trouble between parent and child also developed. A generation gap emerged between parents raised in an era of depression and children raised in postwar affluence, with ideas, beliefs, and a general ethos strictly at odds. As dad worked more hours, mom perhaps took her own job, and the media began to target a youth audience with its own music, fashion, and lifestyle, the divide between the ages widened. *Red River* clearly reflects this. Tom Dunson and Matthew Garth are ultimately as different as night and day, in attitude, beliefs, and even the vastly different portrayals by Wayne and Montgomery Clift. Here, the generation gap widens to the point of violence, as Matt must usurp control of the cattle drive and Dunson responds with a vow to kill him, both ironically doing what he thinks is justified.

Outside of the historical, economic, and cultural conditions of the nation, other leisure activities often play no small part in a film's production. Here, two obvious sources arise. The print media must be considered—the film is an adaptation of a *Saturday Evening Post* serial by Borden Chase, "The Chisholm Trail," and was subsequently released in book form. Chase himself cowrote the screenplay, and though the ending is drastically changed and various elements removed, he still kept a good portion of the source material intact. We also need consider the theater, particularly the New York stage, as actor Montgomery Clift (here appearing in his first screen role) was a product of the Method—a style we've previously

---

271 Ibid.
272 Sheila Ruzycki O'Brien, "Leaving Behind 'The Chisholm Trail' for *Red River*—Or Refiguring the Female in the Western Film Epic," *Literature/Film Quarterly*, Vol. 24, No. 2, 1996, p. 183.
273 Sklar, *Cineaste*, p. 17.

discussed in this class—and one of Hollywood cinema's early encounters with the school of acting which would later be embodied by Marlon Brando, James Dean, Paul Newman, and others.

We also might consider Hollywood's growing interest with a cinematic peer—the tradition of documentary filmmaking. Hollywood has often incorporated other filmic traditions, from German Expressionism in the '20s and '30s to the Hong Kong action style imported in recent years; documentary work is no exception. The postwar years saw a growing number of films which progressed along the episodic stages of a real-life process (whether past or present), much in the fashion of documentary. Notice *Red River*'s focus on the various parts and problems inherent to a large scale cattle drive from the breeding and grazing grounds of Dunson's ranch, along the Chisholm Trail, to eventual purchase in Abilene.[274] We witness practicalities like camp sites and the chuck wagon, realities such as a stampede, crossing rivers, and other obstacles which must be faced along the way, even the dealings of sale—elements which sometimes may not have dramatic merit, but remain informative to the viewer unfamiliar with such a process.

Hollywood's own history also has an influence here. "After their wartime experience making documentary and propaganda films, a number of Hollywood workers were determined to tackle fundamental human issues in their postwar movies,"[275] a few of which have already been mentioned. And what better way to comment on issues in America than by using the most uniquely American genre—the Western. Also, despite the country's economic resurgence following the war, box office receipts began slumping in 1946, as other activities vied for the population's attention. Hollywood's answer to such problems was to fall back on formulas that had worked in the past; as a result, genres remained a typical means of retaining the audience.[276]

The Western is probably most associated with its iconography: cowboys, horses, six-shooters, saloon doors, tumbleweeds, vast landscapes, shoot-outs, and a wide assortment of hats. Yet the Western is ultimately much more than this, a form with its own mythology and precise themes, set on the American frontier between about 1865 and 1890. As Will Wright notes, the classic western centered on specific thematic binaries: inside and outside society, kind and villainous, strong and weak, and most famously, wilderness and civilization.[277] The Western was thus a vehicle for solving ambiguities, as such distinctions as good and evil became clear-cut and simplistic. The classic formula centered on a villainous force (outside society, strong, associated with the wilderness) which preys upon a Western community (inside society, kind, civilized, yet weak), and a hero who is caught between the two, possessing many of the qualities and skills of the savages but fundamentally committed to the townspeople.[278] By defeating the villain/s, the hero saves and is embraced by the community, maintaining its binaric halves while providing the strength it had previously lacked. Both André Bazin and Robert Warshow agree that the very value of the Western is its capacity to handle moral ambiguity in traditionally epic terms.[279] In addition, the Western justifies violent aggression, allowing a cathartic release through appropriate means:

---

[274] Documentary influence noted by Casper.

[275] Robert Sklar, *Movie-Made America: A Social History of American Movies*, (New York: Random House, 1975), p. 280.

[276] Ibid, p. 283-5.

[277] Will Wright, *Sixguns & Society*, (Berkeley: University of California Press, 1975), p. 49-59.

[278] John G. Cawelti, *The Six-Gun Mystique*, (Bowling Green: Bowling Green State University Popular Press, 1984), p. 73.

[279] André Bazin, "The Western, or the American Film *Par Excellence*," *What is Cinema?* Vol. 2, (Berkeley: University of California Press, 1971) and Robert Warshow, "Movie Chronicle: The Westerner," *The Immediate Experience*, (New York: Antheneum Books, 1970).

> [O]ne of the major organizing principles of the Western is to so characterize the villains that the hero is both intellectually and emotionally justified in destroying them. Thus it can be argued that the Western's narrative pattern works out and resolves the tension between a strong need for aggression and a sense of ambiguity and guilt about violence.[280]

Red River, obviously, upsets this formula, and it is only through understanding the myth that we can appreciate its complexity. Binaries are no longer clear; natives still serve as a savage, antagonistic force from which society must be saved, yet the hero who combats these villains in act one ultimately becomes the antagonist himself, with Matt taking his place as hero. However even this is not clear-cut; Matt, after all, steals Tom's herd, and though Matt's intentions are honorable while Tom's are murderous, the ambiguity can never really be resolved. A paradox is created, as the violence which seems inevitable when Matt finally faces Tom *cannot* be justified here, yet remains the necessary conclusion. Hawks' revision of the original story's ending may be the result of this very problem (thus the ending, in some ways, may seem unsatisfactory).[281]

The classic Western is further invoked by the number of actors drawn from the genre's past. Harry Carey, who plays Mr. Melville at the film's end, was a star of silent Westerns, and here appears in his last screen role.[282] Paul Fix, Hank Worden, and Chief Yowlachie were also common faces within the genre.

We must also read the film as the work of an auteur, director Howard Hawks. Hawks had nearly 30 films under his belt when *Red River* was made, yet this was in fact his first Western.[283] Nonetheless, notable similarities can be observed between this film and his previous work. Peter Woolen notes that all Hawks' work, across genres, can be broken into two categories: his adventure dramas and his crazy comedies (such as *His Girl Friday*), films which are in some ways thematic inversions of one another. The former is obviously at work here.

> Hawks...seeks transcendent values beyond the individual, in solidarity with others. ...For Hawks, the highest human emotion is the camaraderie of the exclusive, self-sufficient, all-male group. Hawks' heroes are...habituated to danger and living apart from society, actually cut off from it physically...[They] pride themselves on their professionalism [and] expect no praise for doing their job well. Indeed, none is given.[284]

Further, his adventure dramas show the mastery of man over nature, over women, over the animalistic and savage. All these undercurrents can be seen at work in *Red River*, centering on a band of professional cattlemen driving their herd through the wilderness, facing dangers from both outside and within and surviving on their own abilities. We should also note the aesthetic choices of Hawks—or rather, the lack thereof. Hawks typically avoided formalism, a point he frequently mentioned,[285] and his lack of deliberate stylization also exists as an auteurist decision.

---

[280] Cawelti, p. 42.

[281] The story originally ended with Tom's death. After being shot, Matt and Tess take him back to his ranch, where he finally dies after resolving his dispute with Matthew.

[282] His son also appears in the film, playing Dan Latimer, the character trampled in the stampede.

[283] He would go on, however, to make four more, three with John Wayne.

[284] Peter Wollen, *Signs and Meaning in the Cinema*, (Bloomington: Indiana University Press, 1972, third edition), 82-3.

[285] "I try to tell my story as simply as possible, with the camera at eye level," he once noted, and indeed, this was most often the case, as was a lack of close-ups or angles. Quote from Joseph McBride, *Hawks on Hawks*, (London: Faber and Faber, 1996), p. 93.

John Wayne is practically an auteur force in his own right, and certainly a determining factor of the film. Indeed, no other actor in history has been so singularly associated with one genre,[286] and for many, Wayne was the very embodiment of the Western hero: a strong, brave, and lawful purveyor of justice whose deliberate speech and masculine swagger conveyed his straightforward nature. It is important then to consider that *Red River* marked the first time Wayne portrayed a bad character on screen (with the exception of DeMille's *Reap the Wild Wind* in 1941), dramatically subverting audience expectations for the character. This was also the first time he wore aging makeup. The youthful Wayne of the opening scenes echoes such characters as his Ringo Kid in *Stagecoach* (1939); once the film advances 14 years, we're led to realize this Western hero has grown into a darkly twisted variation on that character. Wayne is particularly influential at this point in his career, as he's now become the established actor who would rule the box office for the next 25 years; as well, Hawks was the first director to give Wayne real freedom in interpreting his role.[287] Hawks recognized the talent in Wayne, an actor much better than most realize, and many a critic agreed once the reviews came out. "The only problem with Wayne," Hawks said, "is who do you get to play with him...If you get somebody who's not pretty strong, he blows them right off the screen. He doesn't do it purposely—that's just what happens."[288] Hawks chose stage actor Clift to fit that bill, a choice Wayne was uneasy with due to his distaste for New York's Method acting. Yet Wayne quickly conceded that the boy could hold his own, and the counterbalance to Wayne's own style makes for a fantastic pairing. The subtle, interiorized performance of Clift plays perfectly against the power, conviction, and presence of Wayne.

Film technology deserves notice here. Technicolor was available at this point, and considering the film's title, color film might seem an obvious choice. Yet the color process was still in its youthful stages. Said Hawks: "When we were making *Red River*, we discussed whether to use color or not. At that time color wasn't very good. It had a kind of garish look to it. I didn't like it and we were trying to get a feeling of the period, so we made *Red River* in black-and-white."[289] As a result, the film continually suggests color, while neglecting to use it. Consider the early scene of Dunson stabbing an Indian underwater, producing a billow of black upon which the viewer must infer red. Such a shot would obviously have had a dramatically different effect had it been shot in color.

It should be noted that this film, an independent production, was actually made in 1946, yet was not released until 1948, when distributed by RKO. The film's production had its share of difficulties, with an already hefty budget of $3 million reportedly rocketing up past $4 million. The money, however, was made back. Scoring $4.5 million in North American rentals alone, the film ranked third in 1948's box office finishers, and when adjusted for inflation, *Red River* lands at ninth on the all-time list of Westerns.[290] Critics hailed the film. "One of the best cowboy pictures ever made," raved Bosley Crowther,[291] while Pauline Kael proclaimed it a magnificent horse opera.[292] Yet as Robert Sklar notes, "No one observed the most obvious fact of all: that *Red River* is rich in social significance, is as teeming with messages as it is with meat on the hoof."[293] All the better reason to enjoy *Red River* as the overdetermined film that it is.

---

[286] Though Wayne did in fact have an extensive career in other genres as well, particularly the war film.
[287] Emanuel Levy, *John Wayne: Prophet of the American Way of Life*, (Metuchen, NJ: The Scarecrow Press, Inc., 1988), p. 201.
[288] Michael Goodwin and Naomi Wise, *Take One 3*, July-August 1971, p. 21, as cited in Levy.
[289] McBride, p. 94.
[290] This figure was tabulated in the 1980s, however. Levy, p. 97.
[291] Bosley Crowther, *The New York Times*, October 1, 1948.
[292] Cited by Sklar, *Cineaste*, p. 15.
[293] Sklar, *Cineaste*, p. 15.

THE SEARCHERS (1956)

Shannon Mader

Director: John Ford. Producers: Merian C. Cooper, C.V. Whitney. Associate Producer: Patrick Ford. Screenwriter: Frank S. Nugent, based on the novel by Alan LeMay. Cinematographer: Winton C. Hoch. Art Directors: Frank Hotaling, James Basevi. Set Decorator: Victor Gangelin. Music: Max Steiner. Title Song: Stan Jones. Editor: Jack Murray. Warner Brothers. C.V. Whitney Productions. Technicolor. VistaVision. Running Time: 119 minutes.

CAST: John Wayne (Ethan Edwards), Jeffrey Hunter (Martin Pawley), Vera Miles (Lauries Jorgensen), Ward Bond (Capt. Rev. Samuel Clayton), Natalie Wood (Debbie Edwards), John Quaen (Lars Jorgensen), Olive Cary (Mrs. Jorgensen), Henry Brandon (Chief Scar), Ken Curtis (Charlie McCorry), Harry Carey, Jr. (Brad Jorgensen), Antonio Moreno (Emilio Figueroa), Hank Worden (Mose Harper), Lana Wood (Debbie as a child), Walter Coy (Aaron Edwards), Dorothy Jordan (Martha Edwards), Pippa Scott (Lucy Edwards), Pat Wayne (Lt. Greenhill), Beulah Archuletta (Look).

Together with *Citizen Kane* (Orson Welles, 1941) and *The Birth of a Nation* (D.W. Griffith, 1915), *The Searchers* is one of the most influential films ever made. Perhaps no single film has influenced the current generation of filmmakers more than *The Searchers*. Directors such as John Milius, Steven Spielberg, Paul Schrader, and Martin Scorsese rank it among their all-time favorites. Indeed, the film's effect has been so profound that its story has reappeared in film after film ever since. In fact, two of the most important films of the seventies self-consciously rework it: Martin Scorsese's *Taxi Driver* (1976) and George Lucas's *Star Wars* (1977).

Unlike *Citizen Kane* and *Birth of a Nation*, however, *The Searchers* was no initially greeted as a masterpiece. Despite positive reviews overall, the film wasn't taken very seriously by the critics. The New York *Times* film critic, Bosley Crowther, typified the dismissive attitude of the critics: he called it a "rip-snorting Western, as brashly entertaining as they come." One wonders if Crowther even saw the right film: *The Searchers* isn't exactly "rip-snorting". But at least Crowther liked the film. *Variety*'s reviewer called the film "disappointing" and confessed to "feeling that it could have been so much more."

And believe it or not, most critics agreed. *The Searchers* ranked 25th in *The Film Daily*'s poll of film critics, gathering a paltry 32 votes. A middling film like *The Eddy Duchin Story* managed to garner double that (64), while the poll's winner, *The King and I*, amassed 245. The Academy of Motion Picture Arts and Sciences was equally myopic, giving the Oscars for Best Picture to *Around the World in Eighty Days* and Best Director to George Stevens for *Giant*.

Fortunately, audience's weren't quite as stingy. *The Searchers* grossed $4,450,000 in its first run, placing it among the year's top twenty films. Nevertheless, its success paled in comparison to that of such films as *The Ten Commandments* ($34.2 million), *Around the World in Eighty Days* ($22 million), *Giant* ($12 million), and *The King and I* ($8.5 million). Even such forgettable fare as *Trapeze* ($7.3 million) and *The Teahouse of the August Moon* ($5.7 million) beat it out. Nonetheless, $4.5 million was *very* good for a film in 1956, especially a Western.

No doubt a large percentage of the gross can be directly attributed to the presence of John Wayne in the credits. For twenty-five years straight, John Wayne was one of the top ten box office draws in American movies, a record which has never been matched and probably won't be. In fact, a Harris poll recently found that Wayne remains—a little over fifteen years after his death—America's favorite star: he placed ahead of both Clint Eastwood and Tom Hanks, a fact which suggests that although America may have changed over the past few decades, its image of itself has not. And nobody personified that image more than John Wayne.

John Wayne was more than a star; he was an icon of America. Frank Sinatra called him a "star-spangled man," and actress Maureen O'Hara, Wayne's costar in *The Quiet Man* (John Ford, 1952), went even further. "John Wayne *is* the United States of America," she remarked. And following Wayne's death, President Jimmy Carter made it official: he said that Wayne "was more than a hero; he was a symbol of the many qualities that made America great."

Nearly thirty years earlier, *Time* had said much the same thing in its March 3, 1952 issue. The magazine wrote: "To millions of moviegoers and televiewers, in whose private lives good and evil often wage dreary, inconclusive little wars, John Wayne's constant re-enactment of the triumph of virtue is as reassuring as George Washington's face on a Series E bond." John Wayne thus not only embodied traditional American values—he validated them! The question, though, is, why did Americans need such reassurance in the supposedly conservative Fifties?

In the years following World War II, America changed dramatically. Economically, America was stronger than ever before, and Americans were richer than ever before. The gross national product (GNP) climbed 250 percent between 1946 and 1960. Productivity soared 200 percent between 1946 and 1957. And by the mid-1950s, nearly 60 percent of the American people had reached middle-class status. One sign of this was the fact that by 1960 three-fourths of Americans owned a car and nine-tenths owned a television. And thanks in part to the GI Bill of Rights, more Americans owned homes and were going to college than ever before in American history. Economic and technological change were so great, in fact, that in 1956 America entered a new age: the post-industrial age. For the first time, the number of white-collar workers outnumbered the number of blue-collar ones.

This economic change brought with it geographic change. Now able to own their own home, Americans flocked to the suburbs. During the 1950s, the suburbs grew at a rate six times faster than the cities. In total, 18 million Americans moved to the suburbs during that decade. And not only did people move—they kept moving. Approximately 25 percent of the population changed their home address at least once a year during the postwar period. Although many factors played a role in this miss migration, one which undoubtedly contributed to it was the fact that people were getting married and having children at unprecedented rates. By 1960, six out of ten women between the ages of 18 and 24 were married. The birth rate for third children doubled between 1940 and 1960, while the birth rate for fourth children tripled. Overall, the population grew by 19 million in the 1940s and by a whopping 30 million in the 1950s.

While the Fifties have traditionally been portrayed as an era in which the wife stayed home while the husband worked, the facts contradict this stereotype. In fact, female employment increased at a rate four times faster than men's in the 1950s, thus resulting in a situation in which by 1960 40 percent of all women over the age of sixteen held a job. And it should be noted that this phenomenon was not confided to single women: the number of working wives doubled between 1940 and 1960, while the number of working mothers increased by 400 percent.

In short, America was changing. And it was in the midst of this change that John Wayne reached his greatest popularity. To many Americans bewildered by the dizzying pace of change, Wayne represented a source of stability, a port of safety in a dangerous sea of change. Indeed, in a number of films from this period Wayne played a captain (or pilot) steering a ship (or plane) to safety against almost insurmountable odds, e.g., *Blood Alley* (William Wellman, 1955) and *The*

High and the Mighty (William Wellman, 1954). The persona of Wayne was thus fixed in the minds of Americans by the time of his performance in *The Searchers*. Hence, his persona is one of the film's determinants.

But notice what John Ford, the director of today's film, does with Wayne's persona in *The Searchers*. He casts this icon of America in the role of a bitter, unreconstructed ex-Confederate whose hatred of the Indians is pathological. In fact, he hates Native Americans so much that he's willing to kill his niece rather than see her assimilated into Native American culture. Thus, if Americans were expecting to see Wayne's usual "re-enactment of the triumph of virtue," then they were in for something of a surprise. The question you might want to ask yourself is, what exactly was Ford trying to say about America by casting this symbol of America as racist? And what, by implication, was he trying to say to those members of the audience who identified with the anachronistic Ethan Edwards and he refusal to change with the times?

The persona of John Wayne was not the only determinant which influence the production and consumption of *The Searchers*, however. The film's director, John Ford, is another cinematic determinant. The fact that the film was made on location and in VistaVision and in Technicolor are other cinematic determinants. I have already addressed some of the extra-cinematic determinants which impacted on the film (e.g., economic situation of the country), but another extra-cinematic determinant which influenced the film was the tense racial situation in America at the time. On May 17, 1954, the Supreme Court of the United States ruled unanimously in *Brown v. the Board of Education* that separate educational facilities for blacks and whites were "inherently unequal" and therefore in violation of the Equal Protection Clause of the Fourteenth Amendment. Nearly 60 years of *de jure* segregation thus came to an end. Nevertheless, *de facto* segregation persisted. Recognizing this fact, the Supreme Court revisited the issue in May 1955 and ordered that desegregation of schools proceed "with all deliberate speed." Horrified by this turn of events, state legislatures throughout the South responded by passing resolutions calling for "massive resistance" to the Court's ruling. And in the Spring of 1956, nearly 80 percent of the Southern members of Congress signed the Southern Manifesto, swearing resistance to the Court's edict. The Searchers was therefore made in the midst of political tensions which the nation had not seen since the Civil War. As a result, this is a determinant which cannot be overlooked.

THE WILD BUNCH (1969)

Mary Kearney

Warner Brothers/Seven Arts, 1969. Producer: Phil Feldman. Director: Sam Peckinpah. Associate Producer: Roy N. Sickner. Screenplay: Walon Green and Peckinpah, based on a story by Green and Sickner. Assistant Directors: Cliff Coleman and Fred Gammon. Director of Photography: Lucien Ballard. Music: Jerry Fielding. Music Supervision: Sonny Burke. Production Manager: William Faralla. Art Direction: Edward Carrere. Editor: Louis Lombardo. Special Effects: Bud Hulburd. Sound: Robert J. Miller. Wardrobe: Gordon Dawson. Makeup: Al Greenway. Second Unit Director: Buzz Henry. Panavision-70; Technicolor. Running time: 135 minutes.[294]

CAST: William Holden (Pike Bishop), Ernest Borgnine (Dutch Engstrom), Robert Ryan (Deke Thornton), Edmond O'Brien (Sykes), Warren Oates (Lyle Gorch), Jaime Sanchez (Angel), Ben Johnson (Tector Gorch), Emilio Fernandez (Mapache), Strother Martin (Coffer). L. Q. Jones (T. C.), Albert Dekker (Pat Harrington), Bo Hopkins (Crazy Lee), Dub Taylor (Mayor Wainscoat), Jorge Russek (Lt. Zomorra), Alfonso Arau (Herrera), Chano Urueta (Don Jose), Sonia Amelio (Teresa), Aurora Clavel (Aurora), Elsa Cardenas (Elsa), Fernando Wagner (German Army Officer).

Whatever it is, it isn't "Heidi."

—Charles Champlin

When *The Wild Bunch* was released in 1969, the United States was in a state of general disorientation, a condition of confusion which resulted from a decade of increasing moral and social uncertainty. Characterized by racial, gender, and generational conflict as well as student riots and large-scale urban decay, the 1960s was one of the most turbulent times in American history since the Civil War. In 1968 the American public witnessed two of the most shocking assassinations of our century, those of Robert F. Kennedy (whose older brother, John, had been assassinated five years earlier) and Martin Luther King, Jr. As violent confrontations escalated between whites and blacks, college students across the country openly revolted against U.S. involvement in the war in Vietnam which was claiming tens of thousands of American lives overseas. In such a violent and turbulent time which had seen the abrupt cessation of JFK's

---

[294] Released in 1969, the original release print of *The Wild Bunch* had more individual shots than any color film ever made—a difficult claim to substantiate today since the film was withdrawn by Warner Brothers after its debut and re-released in several different versions, none of them as long or elaborate as Peckinpah had intended. During 1969, *The Wild Bunch* was shown in alternate versions of 190, 148, 145, 143, and 135 minutes. In the spring of 1995, Warner Brothers re-released a 145-minute version of *The Wild Bunch* which has been fully restored, including color-correction and a remixed soundtrack. Originally set to be re-released with an NC-17 rating, the restored version was given a R rating.

New Frontier, perhaps the only news to celebrate was our landing on the moon ("space—the final frontier").

The film industry during this chaotic time was experiencing its own difficulties. With the gradual collapse of the studio system and the establishment of television as the major mode of entertainment, Hollywood struggled desperately to keep its central place in American popular culture. With the final scrapping of the Production Code in the 1960s and the institution of the MPAA rating system in 1968, the Hollywood film industry and its audiences began to enjoy more permissiveness in both aesthetics and subject matter (especially the display of sex and violence). As a result, the late 1960s became a period of innovative and energetic films as young directors found greater and greater artistic control over their projects.

Not surprisingly, Westerns—perhaps the only truly American genre—were also attempting to bring themselves up-to-date with the changing ways Americans perceived themselves and their past. As Thomas Schatz discusses in *Hollywood Genres*, the Western has long represented the nature of American society, using the past to represent and explore issues in the present. "The image of the Western community in Hollywood movies tends to reflect our own beliefs and preoccupations, and the Western's evolution as a genre results both from the continual reworking of its own rules of construction and expression and also from the changing beliefs and attitudes of contemporary America."[295] With a more politically savvy American public who was no longer buying the conventional mythology of the classic Western formula, the Western genre in post-war America had to struggle to maintain its popularity with audiences, revamping its portrayal of the Western community and redefining the Western hero's mission. *The Wild Bunch*, although maintaining some of the elements of the classic Western film (the landscape, the protagonist's code of honor, and the dichotomy between civilization and wilderness), is ultimately a product of the long fermentation of Western revisionism.

As a Western which focuses not on a young individualist hero but on a collective of aging outlaws, *The Wild Bunch* reveals director Sam Peckinpah's keen awareness of how the role and milieu of the classic Westerner no longer worked in the 1960s. As Schatz notes, "[Peckinpah's] men are hopelessly—and even tragically—at odds with the inexorable flow of history."[296] Disregarding the laws of nature, humanity, and God, the members of the Wild Bunch aren't looking for a cause so much as for some action as they find themselves increasingly confined by the closing of the American frontier and the onslaught of big business and technological progress. In search of greener pastures and more lucrative exploits after reeking havoc in the American Southwest, they cross into Mexico and—since the story takes place in the 1910s—directly into the Mexican Civil War. When one of the Bunch is captured and tortured by Mexican bandits, the rest of the Bunch retaliate in an act of heroism which, although revealing their allegiance to the group's mission, becomes nothing more than an end in itself.

Stunningly photographed by Lucien Ballard in widescreen Panavision-70, *The Wild Bunch* incensed the critics of the period who found the extent and detail of violence in the film outrageous, especially the depiction of cruelty in children and the slaughter of innocent bystanders.[297] Opening and closing with spectacularly shocking massacres which are constructed through rapid cuts to recreate the uncontrolled frenzy of battle and slow motion to prolong our experience of the moment of death, the violence of *The Wild Bunch* was both revolutionary and excessive for its time. While Peckinpah may be criticized for having introduced the conventions for depicting graphic violence which were later exploited in film and television, he was a director firmly committed to exposing his audiences to the dark side of human nature and the material reality of the human body. As he told *Time* magazine, "Listen, killing is no fun. I was trying to show what the hell it's like to get shot." Aware of the inherent

[295] Thomas Schatz, *Hollywood Genres: Formulas, Filmmaking, and the Studio System* (New York: McGraw-Hill, 1981) 58.
[296] Schatz, 61.
[297] According to producer Phil Feldman, it took seven visits to the Motion Picture Association of America before the film's X rating was changed to R.

appeal of violence in the Western genre, Peckinpah does not distance the audience from violence, nor does he desensitize the effect violence can have on the viewer; instead he forces us to fully realize its painful, gruesome, and destructive consequences. Released one year before the U.S. government's late disclosure of the My Lai massacre, *The Wild Bunch* remains a profound allegory of the havoc caused by American intervention in Vietnam.

Sam Peckinpah—who received his Master's degree in drama from USC and worked in television before moving onto motion pictures—also directed: *The Deadly Companions* (1961), *Ride in the High Country* (1962), *Major Dundee* (1965), *The Ballad of Cable Hogue* (1969), *Straw Dogs* (1971), *Junior Bonner* (1972), *The Getaway* (1972), *Pat Garrett and Billy the Kid* (1973), *Bring Me the Head of Alfredo Garcia* (1974), *The Killer Elite* (1975), *Cross of Iron* (1977), and *Convoy* (1978).

15
MOVIES AND MEANING / FILM CRITICISM

Film as dream, film as music. No art passes our conscience in the way film does, and goes directly to our feelings, deep down into the dark rooms of our souls.

—*Ingmar Bergman*

CTCS 190 LECTURE OUTLINE – WEEK XV   **LECTURE 14**

A. **Film Content**
B. **Film Criticism**
   1. Why criticism?
   2. Types
      a. Reviews
      b. Criticism
      c. High-end newspapers
      d. Weekly/monthly magazines
      e. Film journals
      f. Academic
         1. Auteur
         2. Genre
         3. Cultural materialist
         4. Psychoanalytic
         5. Semiotic
         6. Structuralist
         7. Star
         8. Feminist
         9. Queer
         10. Historiography/historical criticism
         11. Neoformalist
         12. Political interest criticism (race, class, gender)
   3. Discrepancy between the film experience and verbal formulation
   4. Personal taste versus critical judgment
   5. Evaluative criteria
   6. Critical suppositions
   7. Critical elements
C. **Movies in your life and of your life**
D. **Screening**

Notes

Notes

VARIOUS TYPES OF ACADEMIC CRITICISM AND THEIR RESPECTIVE METHODOLOGIES

Drew Casper, Richard L. Edwards and Mary Kearney

1) *Auteur*

From the French word meaning "author."

The auteur theory/approach/agenda/criticism assumes that films are the result of the work of a primary artist or "auteur" who uses the camera the way an author uses a pen, leaving a personal stamp on the movie.

The auteur theory is usually director-centered (at least it was in the beginning) but can privilege other film workers, for example:

> writer: Joe Eszterhas (*Basic Instinct, Showgirls, Jade*);
> actor: Charlie Chaplin and his films;
> producer: Jerry Bruckheimer and Don Simpson (*Top Gun, Bad Boy, Crimson Tide, Dangerous Minds*); and
> production house: MGM house style, RKO house style, etc.

Method: the auteur critic takes two or three films or the entire body of work of some director and traces patterns, similarities (thematic as well as formal); look at traditions and these patterns; and finally, determines the significance of these patterns.

Auteur criticism resulted in an approach to film history in terms of key directors/authors.

Francois Truffaut's essay "A Certain Tendency of the French Cinema" (*Cahiers du Cinema*, 1954) formulated the tenets, which were hardened into a theory by American critic Andrew Sarris in "Notes on the Auteur Theory" (*Film Culture*, 1962).

2) *Genre*

Genre theory/approach/agenda/criticism assumes that the narrative/story of a film is primary and that such narratives/stories can be frequently divided into separate classifications or genres.

Method: demonstrates familiar narrative patterns/myths, conventions, and iconography but with little concern for attributing individual responsibilities for these.

3) *Cultural Materialist*

Culture materialist theory/approach/agenda/criticism begins with the assumption that any film is a product of a cultural context and that filmmakers as well as spectators bring to any film exhibition a history which is beyond the control of any one person or group to change.

A film is examined largely as "symptomatic" of a given moment and evaluated on the basis of its exploitation of common knowledge and prejudices current at the time of its production as well as in terms of the way it was received by audiences.

4) *Psychoanalytic*

Psychoanalytic theory/approach/agenda/criticism takes two distinct forms: psychoanalytic content analysis or Lacanian criticism.

In psychoanalytic content analysis, narratives and images are evaluated on the basis of their psychosexual meaning, as suggested by the works of Freud and Jung.

For example, it might concentrate on family relationships discussed in terms of Oedipal conflict (the psychosexual development of typically male characters and the recurring problems this creates), or it might concentrate on "typical" images ripe with psychosexual meaning (phallic and vaginal objects and compositions).

Lacanian criticism concentrates on understanding the film as a process and the extent to which it works with human desires in order to generate desire within the act of spectatorship.

This type of psychoanalytic criticism, which is more common than the first, is derived from the works of French psychoanalyst Jacques Lacan.

5) *Semiology*

Semiological theory/approach/agenda/criticism comes from the work of Christian Metz (*Film Language*, 1974)

This type of film criticism focuses on how a film conveys meaning through signs and symbols, that is, as a system of significations: this system is based on the dichotomy inherent in all language systems, the dichotomy between the symbol and its referent—or, in semiological terms, the signifier and the signified.

As such, cinema is like a language; images like words.

For example, the sign is the minimal unit of signification in a film, not a shot; for a shot contains dozens of signs, forming an elaborate hierarchy of meanings: in one shot, there is an angle (a sign), patterns of light (a sign), color (a sign), etc.

Semiology is an attempt to develop film analysis on a scientific level; to with a text on a material basis only (the internal arrangement of the work).

6) *Structuralist*

Semiology is like the theoretical side of structuralism, which is a new approach (not a new discipline) to study linguistics, anthropology, psychology, rhetoric, and film.

Structuralists, who are also interested in signs, hold that a system of signification, such as film, must be studies within the context of the social, psychological systems that formed it and continue to form it.

Therefore, the approach to film, like semiotics, is language based and focused on how film communicates; but a film is a product of human culture and reflects its culture.

Structuralists are attracted to myths because myths were the first structures of a culture. For structuralists, therefore, society's mythic structures are pivotal in the formation of films.

Structuralist theory/approach/agenda/criticism is derived from the work of French anthropologist Claude Levi-Strauss who investigated "regional myths."

Structuralists look at particular examples of cultural/social "deep structures" found in a society's myths (stories, rules, mores handed down from generation to generation in a society—free of individual authorship); that is, material and imaginary organizations which help to organize daily life or, in other words, the way a society thinks and feels about itself.

These "deep structures" are codified/expressed in binary oppositions (that is, pairs of opposites) reflecting the dualism inherent in nature. (Therefore, myths resist the attempt to reduce them to a single meaning; for example, oppositions at the heart of Greek mythology are continually being reinterpreted).

Structuralists, then, determine the effect these "deep structures" have on surface structures such as language, and film; specifically, they list/describe many binary oppositions in a film and how they operate (traditional vs. modernization in Japanese cinema; individual vs. group in American cinema, etc.).

Structuralists use Freud, Marx, and their disciples Jacques Lacan, and Louis Althusser, and Roland Barthes to see how social/psychological factors influenced "deep structures" or are one part of them.

7) Star

Star theory/approach/agenda/criticism centers on the star, actor or celebrity and has two major thrusts.

The first is sociological (bordering on cultural materialist) and focuses on the star as social phenomenon, product of the film industry.

The second is semiotic and centers on the specific signification of a star in a variety of filmic discourses (the films themselves, the media, consumer commodities, etc.).

In each case, star criticism attempts to analyze the social significance of stars to film texts, culture, and ideology.

Star theory has been expanded recently to include the study of fan relationship to stars and the study of celebrities outside the film industry (TV performers, musicians, singers, sports figures, etc.).

8) Feminist

Feminist theory/approach/agenda/criticism takes two major forms.

Once concentrates on the subject matter of films and evaluates the kind of representations female characters are give. Some issues addressed are: whether or not the subject allows for a positive role for women; whether female characters are placed in positions of responsibility or dependency; etc.

This leads to a discussion of the ways in which women have been depicted and treated in films during the years; the ways women in society have been affected by sex roles presented in films; and qualities and concerns of films made by women.

The second is less concerned with individual films than with the effects of a film as a whole, and in particular the kind of spectator responses that are encouraged by cinematic structures. Some issues addressed are: who does the "looking" in a film since "looking" is central to the act of cinema spectatorship; if film persistently shows women being looked at by men rather than enabled to "look" themselves, then the spectator is asked to view woman as object rather than subject/person.

Feminist criticism is indebted to the work of French psychologist Jacques Lacan and his theory of the mirror stage of development.

The "mirror stage of development" refers to the point at which the infant first sees its image reflected in a mirror. According to Lacan, this produces an ambivalent feeling in the infant. The infant is attracted to the image because the image is an ideal image; the infant is repelled because the ideal can never be the real; therefore, the ideal is other than real.

The Hollywood studio system, a male-created and dominated industry, never seems to have gone beyond the mirror stage.

In film after film, woman is constituted as other, as object of male gaze, and as an exhibit or a spectacle in terms of anatomy (bosom, legs, mouth, butt) and fractured representation (close-ups and extreme close-ups).

This idealization of woman originated with the fear of castration: if "she" would not deny "him" his potency, "he" would idealize "her." Therefore, the universe remains phallocentric, dominated by symbols of male potency—the phallus (which according to Lacan is the signifier). The phallus represents male power and presence as opposed to the lack of a phallus on the part of women, signifying helplessness and absence.

9) *Queer*

Queer theory/approach/agenda/criticism attempts to move theories of spectatorship/reception/ consumption beyond theories of gender (as in feminism) and theories of sexuality (as in gay/lesbian/bisexual studies) because they are limited by notions of binary oppositions (i.e., male/female, straight/gay).

The presumption is that queerness is an inclusive (not an exclusive mode of perception), since it allows for multiple non-straight subject positions and the responses to culture (for example, gay men who take queer pleasure in a lesbian film).

In opposition to those who position queer readings of cultural texts as "marginal" or "subtextual" queer theory foregrounds the centrality of homosexuality to the production and consumption of a cultural text. "Queerness is," as Alexander Doty writes in *Making Things Perfectly Queer*, "incontrovertibly in the text and only heterosexist/homophobic cultural training prevents everyone from acknowledging its queerness."

10) *Historiography*

Historiography deals with theories of history (that is, the assumptions, rules, and methods of historical study).

Four types of film history and historiography theory/approach/agenda/criticism:

- first, aesthetic film history: film as art (history of masterpieces and great filmmakers);
- second, technological film history: film as a series of technological inventions (a concern with inventors; film technology and its function; and the effect aesthetically, commercially, and ideologically of this technology);
- third, economic film history: the financiers who sponsored and controlled filmmaking and their respective ideologies;
- and lastly, social history: movies as reflective of audience's mass sentiments during designated period.

11) *Neoformalist*

Neoformalist theory/approach/agenda/criticism is based on the ideas and doctrines of the Russian Formalists, whose major works were written between the mid-1910s and 1930. Neoformalists have also been influenced by the findings of cognitive psychology (a branch of psychology which studies how the brain processes information).

Neoformalist film critics begin with the assumption that we do not "read" art works in the way that we read, say, a street sign. Art works do not "communicate" in the normal sense of the work. As a result, neoformalist film critics do not see their role as "decoding" (i.e., interpreting) art works.

Neoformalists are not interested in the sociological and cultural significance of film. Rather, they focus on the formal properties of film and how these formal properties are harnessed by filmmakers to tell a story.

Neoformalists do not stop there, however. On the contrary, they argue that the spectator has as important a role as the filmmaker: he or she constructs the story in his or her own mind by making inferences based on the visual and aural "cues" provided by the film. Neoformalists attempt to understand how this process works: why the spectator makes the inferences he or she does.

Major works of neoformalist film criticism include David Bordwell's *Narration and the Fiction Film* (1985), David Bordwell, Janet Staiger, and Kristin Thompson's *The Classical Hollywood Cinema: Film Style and Mode of Production to 1960* (1985), and Kristin Thompson's *Breaking the Glass Armor: Neoformalist Film Analysis* (1988).

12) Political Interest Criticism (Race, Class, Gender)

Political interest criticism examines theories and practices relating to matters of race, class or gender in film, and recognizes film as an important form of cultural expression. The methodology of political interest criticism can come from a variety of theoretical discourses: Feminism, Marxism, Poststructuralism, or Cultural Materialism, to just name a few. It departs from these other methodologies in its heightened focus on race, class and gender as three key determinants on the production and consumption of film texts. Political interest criticism frequently examines film practices/film texts as both reflective and constitutive of broader historical, political, cultural and/or social dynamics. This type of criticism can be applied towards analyses of the aesthetic, social, political and/or national contexts of a film.

Credits